About OECD

The Organisation for Economic Co-operation and Development (OECD) groups 30 member countries sharing a commitment to democratic government and the market economy. With active relationships with some 70 other countries, NGOs and civil society, it has a global reach. Best known for its publications and its statistics, its work covers economic and social issues from macroeconomics, to trade, education, development and science and innovation. The opinions expressed and arguments employed in this publication are the sole responsibility of the authors and do not necessarily reflect those of the OECD or of the governments of its Member countries.

About the National Soil Tilth Laboratory

The National Soil Tilth Laboratory (NSTL) is one of USDA-Agricultural Research Service's network of research laboratories across the United States. NSTL is unique in its efforts to address the interaction between agricultural management practices and the resultant effect on environmental and soil quality. This interdisciplinary laboratory conducts research that builds on understanding the processes (laboratory and plot scale) up to watershed and regional scale assessment and application.

About the Soil and Water Conservation Society

The Soil and Water Conservation Society (SWCS) is a nonprofit scientific and educational organization that serves as an advocate for environmental quality professionals and for science-based conservation policy. SWCS seeks to advance the science and art of soil, water, and related natural resource conservation to achieve sustainability. Members practice and promote an ethic that recognizes the interdependence of people and their environment.

THE FARMER'S DECISION
Balancing economic agriculture production with environmental quality

Edited by:
Jerry L. Hatfield, Director of the National Soil Tilth Laboratory

Soil and Water Conservation Society
Ankeny, Iowa, USA

Published by the Soil and Water Conservation Society
945 SW Ankeny Road
Ankeny, Iowa 50023-9723

www.swcs.org

Printed in the United States of America

Library of Congress Cataloging-in-Publication Data
Hatfield, Jerry L., 1949-
THE FARMER'S DECISION
Balancing economic agriculture production with environmental quality.
p. cm.
Includes bibliographical references and index.
ISBN 0-9769432-1-2

Acknowledgement

Our deepest appreciation is expressed to OECD for their sponsorship of this workshop and providing the travel support for the attendees. I am grateful to all of the authors for sharing their ideas and concepts about how we can build a better understanding of our decisions that affect both the economic aspects of production and environmental quality. All of the authors and myself sincerely thank the Soil and Water Conservation Society for publishing these articles and for promoting this important topic area.

Contents

PART I. SHAPING FARMER'S DECISIONS

PART II. APPLICATION TO WATER AND NUTRIENT MANAGEMENT

PART III. DIFFERENT PERSPECTIVES

Figures

Tables

Improving the Balance Between Economic Agricultural Production and Environmental Quality Through Enhanced Decision Making

Decision making to achieve a balance between the economic goals of producers and environmental quality benefits is complex. Most of the time we consider that the balance is skewed to one side or the other and that there are winners and losers. From the production perspective, the loser is the economic return in exchange for environmental quality while from the environmental perspective, the loser is the environment at the expense of agricultural production and increased inputs. In reality, there are opportunities within agriculture for a win–win situation; however, to explore the endless possibilities that constitute acceptable solutions is extremely difficult.

Over the past few years there has been an increasing development of decision support tools that provide a framework that could be applied to agriculture. As I have worked with producers extensively over the past few years, it has become apparent that we could provide more information to the American producer that would help them evaluate different scenarios in their farming systems and evaluate potential alternatives through a combination of simulation tools and decision support systems. These are easy concepts to suggest, but more difficult to implement.

As an effort to expand our understanding of the potential of decision support tools for economic and environmental balance, a proposal was made to the Organisation for Economic Co-operation and Development (OECD) in two theme areas. The outcome yielded an international workshop that assembled an interna-

tional group of experts in decision support systems, simulation models, and agricultural production through industry, consultants, and producers. This group also addressed enhancing environmental quality in agricultural systems.

This group of esteemed scientists and colleagues assembled in Honolulu, Hawaii from November 9-12, 2004 to present their ideas, share their comments, and interact around the theme of understanding the current state of knowledge about decision support tools. The presentations are captured in the following chapters that better capture our understanding than I can portray in this foreword.

The topics range from our current understanding of decision support tools and why they have not had the impact once envisioned, to the use of geographic information systems as methods of displaying information in a visual context. There are applications of models, decision tools for nutrient and hydrologic management, and environmental impacts of nutrient excesses. The insights captured from the agribusiness and the producer/consultant perspective provides a framework for our assessment that begins to show the reality of the complexities in world agriculture.

Throughout these discussions there was a blend between field and watershed scale, and between observational studies and participatory research. There is no correct method of conducting research to achieve improved decision-making, nor is there a correct scale at which these studies and observations need to be collected and analyzed. One of the common themes across all of the topics was the complexity of the system and the need to develop a better understanding of how we quantify and interpret the reactions of physical, biological, and chemical processes that underlie agro-ecologically-based systems.

At the end of the workshop each participant was asked to provide a short summary of their experiences and these provided insights in what we had missed in our discussions, but also where the challenges remain in how we need to impact agriculture. There are a number of different aspects that need to be considered in trying to understand the dynamics of agricultural and ecological systems.

■ There are major changes in how we currently think about decisions, and make decisions, and we need to search for the commonality among different groups. These changing perceptions require a platform that is balanced and methods to resolve conflict if we are to truly achieve a balance between economic and environmental goals. Underlying these themes is the fact that we perceive humans to be selfish with little liklihood they'd change their own behavior, but very likely to suggest changes in everyone else's behavior. These programs and projects should serve as a springboard to involvement in policymaking, rather than removal from policy discussions.

■ Participatory research and programs require that everyone be engaged in the process, which makes the interdisciplinary approach an imperative; and imagination about potential solutions, a must. There are many facets to social learning and views about decisions, suggesting that participatory approaches may not lead to improved quality of decisions. Participatory research and programs will be strengthened by the incorporation of the hard sciences rather than discarding these process-driven components.

■ One of the major problems in discussing these issues (economic vs. environmental) is finding the common aspects of the problem so everyone can "see" the same problem. On a global scale, problems are very similar and common approaches could be used to address field or watershed scale problems throughout the world. In all of these problems it is critical to identify the target users of this information.

■ There are conflicting views about decision support systems because the element of social learning and engagement in the process of developing decision support tools, varies among researchers and research teams developing these tools. One of the underlying premises of a decision support tool is a model and often models are developed for their own purposes rather than more general usage across a number of application areas.

These synopses of the discussions provide an introduction into the chapters that follow. There is no correct approach nor is there a standard method for developing, applying, or evaluating decision support tools. We can enhance our ability to help the agricultural community form better linkages with the ecological community through increased discussions about the tradeoffs between economic return and environmental quality. The viewpoints expressed in the following chapters represent a desire by the writers to help science move forward with the goal of being able to impact the lives of fellow scientists, policymakers, planners, producers, and the consumers of food and fiber.

I express a heartfelt thanks to all of the participants and to OECD for their generous support and encouragement to conduct this workshop. The conclusions from the effort can be summarized in a very simple statement, "We have learned a lot and we have a lot to learn, but learn we must, if we are to continue to make this world a better place to live."

J.L. Hatfield
Editor

Overview of Various Global Environmental Issues

CHAPTER 1

J.M. Lynch

The original Organisation for Economic Co-operation and Development (OECD) Research Programme on Biological Resource Management for Sustainable Agricultural Systems (Balazs et al., 2000) was established to strengthen cooperative efforts among research scientists and institutions in the OECD member countries based on opportunities created by biotechnology to promote policy-driven research. For the past four years, there has been an emphasis on the socio-economic aspects. The OECD themes— 'Enhancing environmental quality in agricultural systems,' and 'Connecting scientific progress to sustainable and integrated agro-food systems'—are particularly pertinent to this workshop on improving the balance between economic agricultural production and environmental quality through enhanced decision-making.

In trying to present an overview of some of the global environmental issues, the concept of sustainability is inevitably the starting point. Thereafter, the focus will be on climate change, one of the biggest threats to the world, and on soil resilience, the basis on which agricultural and forestry production depends.

Sustainability. One of the major drivers to sustainability is the world population. Various estimates have been made, but generally speaking it is considered that the growth of these populations is currently

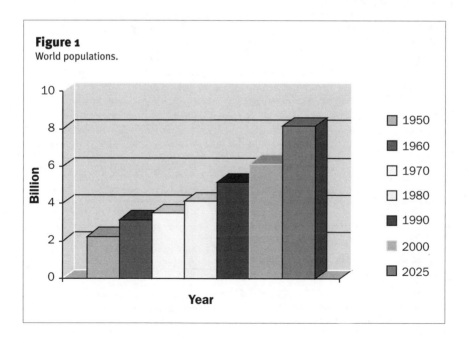

Figure 1
World populations.

Table 1. U.N. Conference on Environment and Development, Rio de Janeiro, Brazil 3-14 June 1992.

- Rio Declaration on the Environment and Development
- Framework Convention on Climate Change
- Convention on Biological Diversity
- Declaration on the principles relating to forests
- AGENDA 21

---

relatively linear (Figure 1). The first major international meeting that really addressed the issue was held in Rio de Janeiro in 1992 (Table 1). In this important meeting there were various agreements, which covered the environment in relation to development. The framework convention on climate change was decided, and in addition there was convention on biological diversity. There was another on the principles relating to forests and there was also Agenda 21, which particularly addressed the sustainability of urban, as well as rural communities (Table 1).

Definition of sustainability has always been somewhat difficult and probably the Bruntland Report is the most important first definition, which was "Sustainable development is development that meets the needs of the present without compromising the ability of future generations to meet their own needs." In relation to sustainable agriculture, definitions were made by Francis and Youngberg (1990). They indicated that definition could be (1) reduction in the use of non-renewable resources (coupled with the greater use of renewable resources) and (2) protection of the environment. A variety of strategic imperatives of sustainable development have been listed (Table 2). Essentially these imperatives link growth to population, risk, technology, and economics. It is important to have international agreement and focus, but each nation needs to analyze its own sustainable development. In Table 3 the recent publication of the UK statistics provides a measure of the progress being made (Department for Environment, Food and Rural Affairs, 2004). A variety of indicators can be used (Table 4). In the agriculture environment, these can be linked to biology, water use, nutrient balance, and socio-economics.

Climate change. There seems little doubt that climate change leading to global warming is a reality due in large part to the consequences of the high rate of carbon dioxide (CO_2) emissions. It is very disappointing in this context that the United States has not acceded to the UNCED Rio de Janeiro convention, or the later

---

Table 2. Strategic imperatives of sustainable development.

- Reviving growth
- Changing the quality of growth
- Meeting essential human needs
- Ensuring a sustainable level of population
- Conserving and enhancing the resource base
- Re-orientating technology and managing risks
- Merging environment and economics in decision making

agreements in Kyoto. Even so, we are seeing a stabilization or a small reduction in emissions. The Inter-governmental Panel of Climate Change (2001) outlined a variety of indications (Table 5).

It is clear that forestry has a particular role in carbon sequestration and therefore can reduce some of the consequences of carbon emissions. For example, one hectare of woodland grown to maturity and looked after forever, would absorb the carbon emissions of one hundred family cars driven for one year. Trees can also save up to 10 percent of energy consumption through moderation of the local climate. This becomes particularly important in warmer climates where extensive air conditioning is used. The contribution of forests is clear, but it is worrying that forest clearance not only leads to soil erosion, which will be discussed in the next section, but it also reduces an important carbon sink. Foreseeing such problems as forest clearance in Asia and Amazonia, as well as in some parts of Europe and North America, is a good target for the production of decision support tools.

Soil resilience. In terms of agriculture

Table 3. Some sustainable development indicators for the United Kingdom (Department for Environment Food and Rural Affairs, 2004).

- In 2003, 741,000 ha were organically farmed or in conversion. This compares with 276,000 ha in 1999 and just 55,000 ha in 1998.
- Farmland bird populations fell by 42 percent between 1970 and 2002, and woodland bird populations by 15 percent. From 1998 to 2002, farmland birds increased by 5 percent and woodland birds decreased by 3 percent.
- From 1974 to 1998, agricultural output rose by 23 percent and fertilizer use by 44 percent. Since then there has been a fall in agricultural output and fertilizer use.
- In 2003, 16 percent of mammals and birds and 16 percent of reptiles, amphibians and freshwater fish, and 33 percent of vascular plants were assessed as 'threatened."
- Approximately 12 percent of the United Kingdom is covered by forest and woodland, and the area has increased by c. 29 percent since 1980. Even though conifers are dominant and constant at c. 1,600,000 ha, broadleaves have increased by 44 percent since 1980 to c. 1,200.000 ha.

Table 4. Key sustainability indicators.

Biological indicators	*Water use indicators*
• Earthworm density	• Yield per mm rainfall
• Uncontrolled pests	• Soil structure index
• Pesticide resistance	• Depths to groundwater
• Residues in soil	• Soil salinity
• Biodiversity	• Soil acidity
Nutrient balance indicators	*Socio-economic indicators*
• Nutrient budget	• Market value of resource
• Organic matter	• Level of education/age mobility
• Protein levels in plants	• Off-farm income
• Fertilizer residues in soil	• Real interest rate/debt equity
	• Government policy

Table 5. Some implications of climate change (Intergovernmental Panel of Climate Change, 2001).

- Natural, technical, and social sciences can provide essential information and evidence needed for decisions on what constitutes "dangerous anthropogenic interference with the climate systems." At the same time, such decisions are value judgements determined through socio-political processes, taking into account considerations such as development, equity, and sustainability, as well as uncertainties and risk.

- The Earth's climate system has demonstrably changed on both global and regional scales since the pre-industrial era, with some of these changes attributable to human activities. Observed changes in regional climate have affected many physical and biological systems, and there are preliminary indications that social and economic systems have been affected.

- Carbon dioxide concentrations, globally average surface temperature, and se level are projected to increase under all IPCC emissions scenarios during the 21st Century. Projected climate change will have beneficial and adverse effects on both environmental and socio-economic systems, but the larger the changes and rate or change in climate, the more the adverse effects predominate. Adaptation has the potential to reduce adverse effects of climate change and can often produce immediate ancillary benefits, but will not prevent all damages.

- An increase in climate variability and some extreme events is projected. Green-house gas forcing in the 21st Century could set in motion large-scale high-impact, non-linear, and potentially abrupt changes in physical and biological systems over the coming decades to millennia, with a wide range of associated likelihoods.

- Inertia is a widespread inherent characteristic of the interacting climate, ecological, and socio-economic systems. Thus some impacts of anthropogenic climate change may be slow to become apparent, and some could be irreversible if climate change is not limited in both rate and magnitude before associated thresholds, whose positions may be poorly known, are crossed.

- Reducing greenhouse gas emissions can lessen the projected rate and magnitude of warming and sea level rise. Reducing emissions of greenhouse gases to stabilize their atmospheric concentrations would delay and reduce damages caused by climate change. Adaptation is a necessary strategy at all scales to complement climate change mitigation efforts. Together they can contribute to sustainable development objective.

- There are many opportunities including technological options to reduce emissions, but barriers to their deployment exist. Cost estimates by different models and studies vary for many reasons. Studies examined in the IPCC's Third Assessment Report suggest substantial opportunities for lowering mitigation costs. Technology development and diffusion are important components of cost-effective stabilization. Both the pathway to stabilization and the stabilization level itself are key determinants of mitigation costs.

- Local, regional, and global environmental issues are inextricably linked and affect sustainable development. Therefore, there are synergistic opportunities to develop more effective response options to these environmental issues that enhance benefits, reduce costs, and more sustainably meet human needs.

and forestry, soil is the primary factor in productivity. A variety of concepts have been used to place values on soil (Table 6). Of course, quality is important but degradation must be prevented and soil resilience is critical in terms of sustainability factors. In the OECD Workshop on the Ecological Foundations of Sustainable Agriculture (Greenland and Szabolcs, 1994) held in Budapest (Table 7), it was recommended that a global database be produced to prevent soil degradation.

Table 6. Concepts in valuing soil.

Soil quality is the capacity of the soil to produce healthy and nutritious crops, resist erosion, and reduce the impact of environmental stresses on plants.

Soil degradation is the antithesis of soil resistance and quality, and is the loss of the soil's capacity to produce crops, often as a result of soil erosion.

Soil resilience is the ability of the soil to recover after disturbance.

The characteristics of a healthy soil are indicated in Table 8. Soil has important consequences for all ecosystems (Figure 2). For example during soil erosion, extensive run-off of soil can enter the hydrosphere. Soil very much sits at the center of all ecosystems. However, there can be many problems, which are generated in terms of salinity, erosion, and structural decline (Figure 3). In an area which I have personally been familiar with, the Pacific Northwest of the United States, there is a particularly highly productive region for cereals, the Palouse. These soils were first used for agriculture at the time of settlement, at the beginning of the 20th Century. They are very fertile and deep and yet erosion on the sloping hillsides can run at a phenomenal rate and all types of erosion are seen (slip, gully, and rill) (Figure 4 to 6).

This leads to the Columbia River basin, which carries runoff from the region being quite heavy with mud during the winter rain season. Clearly this is a classic

---

Table 7. Workshop on the Ecological Foundations of Sustainable Agriculture, Budapest, 1992.

Develop global database of human-induced soil degradation and implement AGENDA 21 requiring:

1. Maintain and develop long-term monitoring programmes.

2. Identify key species, biotic assemblages and processes.

3. Determine quantitative indicators.

4. Identify appropriate management practices.

Figure 2

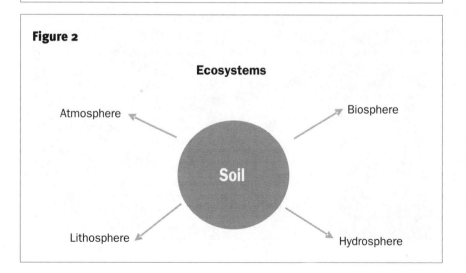

Ecosystems

Atmosphere

Biosphere

Soil

Lithosphere

Hydrosphere

Figure 3
Problems for soils.

Soil salinity
Excessive clearing of native vegetation
Excessive irrigation and inadequate drainage
Absence of deep rooted cross and pastures
Waterlogged soil
Surface soil dispersion
Salt intrusion from deep aquifers
Contribute to streamwater salinity

Soil erosion
Wind and water erosion
Water repellent soils
Excessive cultivation of fallowed land
Overgrazing
Lack of soil conservation structures
and inappropriate farm plans

Soil structural decline
High intensity of soil disturbance
Long cultivated fallows
Overgrazing and poor stock management
Loss of organic matter
Surface crusting
Subsoil compaction
Reduce water infiltration
Inappropriate fire management

Figure 4
Slip erosion, Washington State, United States.

illustration of non-sustainability of the soil resource. However, I have also seen comparable situations in South Australia, and surprisingly the very fertile wine growing regions of Tuscany in Italy. Clearly, soil productivity ultimately in terms of sustainability is a balance between the soil degradation process and the soil conservation practices (Figure 7). In order to attain this, we must all strive to the production of healthy soils (Table 8).

Concluding Remarks

It is essential that we use multidisciplinary approaches both nationally and internationally to recognize, define, and forecast environmental problems and solutions, which impact on sustainability. Radical approaches towards environmental sustainability are needed, although this could quite often return to some of the practices, which we have used in the past. For

example, we have gone extensively to monocultures of agriculture crops as well as producing forest monocultures. A mixed approach could generate a more optimum, as distinct from maximum, production systems (economically and environmentally) for our food and resources. Mixed farming was commonly practiced in the past, we should now even consider producing animals alongside trees. For example, I have seen at the Northmoor Trust in Oxfordshire, United Kingdom, chickens being produced in concert with woodland establishment and considerable economic benefits result. In the past there tended to be a practice of fertilizing for maximizing yield. Maximum production is unlikely to yield optimal production in relation to environmental sustainability. However, economics must be a driver to all production systems and one of the problems with traditional

Figure 5
Gully erosion, Washington State, United States.

Figure 6
Rill erosion, Washington State, United States.

Figure 7
Soil productivity.

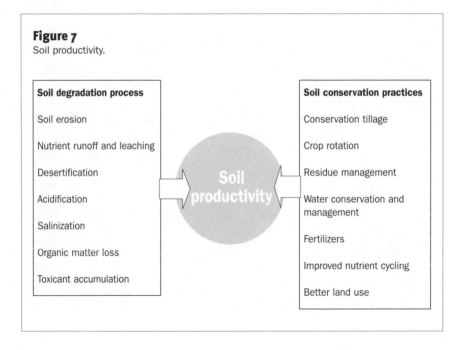

Soil degradation process	Soil conservation practices
Soil erosion	Conservation tillage
Nutrient runoff and leaching	Crop rotation
Desertification	Residue management
Acidification	Water conservation and management
Salinization	Fertilizers
Organic matter loss	Improved nutrient cycling
Toxicant accumulation	Better land use

Soil productivity

Table 8. Characteristics of a healthy soil.

- Good structure
- Good organic matter content
- Rich biota
- Good supply of nutrients for plant growth
- No chemical constraints (acidity, salinity)
- No toxicants

---

agriculture economics is to only consider the annual balance sheet. Clearly we must look at the long-term consequences of our action and generate an economic analysis, which reflects this viewpoint. The first step therefore, in decision support systems, must be to link decision support to sustainability. This is a massive challenge scientifically, but in my opinion an exciting and obtainable one.

References Cited

Balázs, E., E. Galante, J.M Lynch, J.S. Schepers, J-P Toutant, D. Werner, and P.A. Th.J. Werry (eds.) 2000. Biological Resource Management. Connecting Science and Policy. Springer, Berlin.

Department for Environment, Food and Rural Affairs. 2004. Sustainable development indicators in your pocket 2004. Defra Publications, London, England.

Francis, C.A. and G. Youngberg. 1990. Is agriculture sustainable: An overview. Pp. 1-23. *In:* Sustainable Agriculture in Temperate Zones. (eds.) C.A. Francis, C. Butler Flora, and L.D. King. John Wiley, New York, New York.

Greenland, D.J. and I. Szabolcs. 1994. Soil resilience and sustainable land use. CAB International, Wallingford, England.

Intergovernmental Panel on Climate Change (IPCC). 2001. Summary for Policymakers. IPCC Third Assessment Report, Wembley, United Kingdom.

New Thinking About Farmer Decision Makers

CHAPTER 2

R.L. McCown

"People (and not only managers) trust only their own understanding of their world as the basis for their actions."

de Geus (1994)

"It would appear then that as long as we conceptualize the issues of knowledge processes in terms of information transfer without giving sufficient attention to the creation and transformation of meaning at the point of intersection between different actors' life-worlds, [ ] we shall have missed the significance of knowledge itself.

Long and Long (1992)

In the late 1970s, agricultural scientists embarked on the exciting new adventure to make decision support systems for farmers. Two decades later, with my colleagues, Peter Carberry and Zvi Hochman, I set out to understand why farmers have not valued these products more. We began by visiting developers of some of the major decision support systems in the United States and Australia to hear their stories of development and delivery. This effort led to the publication by some of these key players of their experiences and learnings in a special issue of Agricultural Systems (Vol. 74, No. 1, 2002), entitled "Probing the Enigma of the Decision Support System for Farmers." Beyond our interest in documenting significant decision support system projects while key participants were still accessible, we felt that stimulation of critical reflection on the decision support system experience could be valuable to a research community that by and large interpreted any past decision support system 'failure' as a good

idea being 'ahead of its time'—ahead of farmers' readiness for this technology. Controversially, the special issue openly confronted the possibility that the decision support system for farming may be an idea 'whose future is past' (Ackoff, 1979; McCown, 2002b).

McCown (2002b) highlighted differences between objective knowledge embedded in a decision support system and the subjective knowledge which normally guides the actions of farmers in familiar situations—local, personal, and social environments. None of the fourteen decision support systems had become a routine tool that farmers used in their management year-in and year-out. But in some cases it was evident that computer models had provided significant value to farmers in other ways. The most important of these was as an aid to learning. It's not surprising that simulation might lead to learning, but what makes this significant to those interested in intervention to support better farm decision-making, is the nature of this learning and how it takes place. This learning is not often the result of 'knowledge transfer' from researchers to farm decision makers via computer software. It is rather the use of research products (including software) by intermediaries in situations of farming practice using processes that generate experiences in which farmers construct personal, subjective knowledge that is relevant to practical action.

Acceptance by our profession of this interpretation of decision support system history could have profound importance for the future of scientific intervention in farming practice using computers and telecommunication. But there is little indication that our profession is about to abandon the good-idea-ahead-of-its-time interpretation of our predicament. My aim in this essay is to provide evidence and argument that the success for decision support intervention that has been so elusive lies in using our scientific models to facilitate farmers in constructing new knowledge.

Facilitation of knowledge construction is a different intervention *paradigm* for information systems intervention to that of objective information/knowledge transfer, characteristic of the decision support system and expert system. As such, I am sobered by the observation by Kuhn (1962) of what "scientists never do when confronted by even severe and prolonged anomalies. Though they may begin to lose faith and then to consider alternatives, they do not renounce the paradigm that has led them into crisis." Recognition of this justifies the lack of any attempt in what follows to provide evidence of decision support system failure. On the other hand, I am somewhat encouraged in this undertaking by Kuhn's further observations that "The decision to reject one paradigm is always simultaneously the decision to accept another, and the judgment leading to that decision involves a comparison of both paradigms with nature and with each other." Hence, in advocating a new paradigm in this essay, my strategy includes analysis of the current paradigm as well.

This essay is also made challenging because so much of the evidence and argument is external to our familiar science domain, as are many of the concepts and terms. But this is problematic, I believe, not because the material is difficult to understand, but rather that considerable complexity results as elements are woven together. If this conjecture is true, my greatest risk is creating a picture that gets progressively confusing. I will attempt to avoid this by sketching a 'map' of the journey at a coarse scale before starting and at a finer scale for each section at the beginning of that section, and pausing, periodically, to consult the map to see where we are and where we are headed.

The first section traces the history of our traditional decision support system paradigm in a distant past in which scientific principles for management came to be viewed as superior to customary managerial expertise. Major developments in thinking are traced with the aid of a typology of 'systems' traditions and a simple model of behavior in which behavior is determined by 'factors' of environmental and personal structure. Much of the history of the decision support system can be seen as a periodic shift from preoccupation with one of these categories of structure to the other in response to failure to influence practical managers. The case is made that this failure was due to a normative theory of decision making in which intuitive judgment was seen as a problem to be overcome whenever possible by replacing it with formal analysis that provided a recommendation of what a rational manager ought to do in such a situation.

The second section deals with an alternative theory for understanding decision making in which purposeful managers make subjective sense of their situations and use their knowledge and agency to 'cause' meaningful and satisfactory actions. Intervention, in keeping such a view, assumes a *facilitative* role in which scientific models are used to support farmers' *sense-making* in conditions of uncertainty and ambiguity. This section explores both the characteristics of this paradigm and some logical reasons for scientists to embrace it. *Characteristics* are found in phenomenology, the philosophy of subjective experience in the life-world and in cognitive science, the study of subjective knowing and reasoning. *Justification* is found, surprisingly, in the philosophy of science of Karl Popper.

In the third section, answers to three questions about implications for decision support in this alternative paradigm are sought: (1) Under what conditions can the decision maker be expected to welcome support? (2) Just what is being supported? and (3) What does such decision support look like? Answers are synthesized from contributions from three fields of social theory (phenomenology; cognitive science, that is the science of subjective knowing and reasoning; and thirdly, the field of 'sensemaking', whose home is in social psychology). The successful practice of 'systems dynamics' modeling to facilitate learning contributes significantly to answering the third question.

A final section briefly explores the implications of a new respect for natural decision processes and of facilitative rather than normative intervention in farmers' management of natural resources.

Whether the manager of a farm is the owner of the family farm or is employed by the owner of the farm to manage it may be crucial to the use of a decision support system (McCown, 2002b). A similar distinction is whether the family farmer is his/her 'own boss' or is contract farming for a vertically—integrated agribusiness. The underlying issue here concerns the farmers degree of *discretion* and *agency*— his/her freedom to decide what to do and power to do it. History confirms the simple logic that when discretion and agency are low, farmers can more readily find it in their interests to use management aids that are advocated by those to whom they are accountable. The decision support system began as a little chunk of corporate bureaucracy in this sort of relationship (McCown, 2002a). Of far more interest is the decision support system adoption behavior of farmers with a *high* degree of agency. Since the family farm looks to remain the dominant structure in most forms of agricultural production for the foreseeable future, my focus in this paper is on the family farm with the considerable, although diminishing (Mooney, 1988), management agency normally found there.

Critical reflections on our traditional decision support paradigm

This section traces the evolution of ideas and tools that has shaped the decision support system intervention paradigm. Helpful 'maps' are provided from two sources. The first is from the systems movement, which Jackson (2000) differentiated into three traditions. The first two have influenced agricultural research and intervention at different times over the past half century in ways indicated in Figure 1.

In this section I will attempt to account for our agricultural decision support system tradition as a direct product of the 'problem solving' systems tradition, but significantly influenced by an earlier systems tradition *via* process modeling in agricultural science disciplines. A further 'map' is used to elucidate various changes in direction prior to and leading up to the decision support system. This is an abstract model of problem solving behavior, provided by Kurt Lewin, a social psychologist, who pioneered psychological research in the social world outside the laboratory. Lewin (1951) formalized 'the obvious' as $B = f(P, E)$, where B is individual behavior, P represents personal determining factors, and E, environmental factors. The history of decision research aimed at influencing management behavior can be seen as a sort of oscillation between emphasis on E and on P, driven by disappointment in the outcomes of the previous phase. It is significant that irrespective of the focus, *intervention* was normative, in that it aimed at providing superior substitutes for human mental processes.

Serious scientific study of 'work' behavior began with the 'time and motion' studies of customary manufacturing activity. In

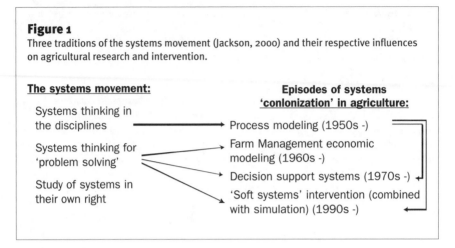

Figure 1

Three traditions of the systems movement (Jackson, 2000) and their respective influences on agricultural research and intervention.

North America, principles developed by Frederick Taylor concerning how labor activity can be analyzed and redesigned by experts for increased efficiency, were being "applied wholesale in U.S. industry" late in the 18th century (Anonymous, 2000). While originally centered on more efficient returns to manual work, 'Taylorism' spread to management. A new paradigm of management emerged, which competed with the traditional paradigm. In the traditional paradigm of management behavior, the "manager is a *craftsman*, a practitioner of an art of managing that cannot be reduced to explicit rules and theories" (Schon, 1983), but rather constitutes a unified *practical* rationality centered in P, in Lewin's model of behavior, B = f (P, W). In the modern paradigm, "the manager is a *technician* whose practice consists in applying to everyday problems...the principles and methods derived from management science"— a *technical/economic* rationality rooted in theory concerning the task environment (E) (Schon, 1983) and providing a basis for rational determination of behavior (B). These changes constituted displacement in workplace cultures of *customary* management practice, based on cumulative experience, by theoretical principles of

management in a 'typical' E. This rationalization of industrial culture was an important precursor to the emergence of systems thinking and practice. Management theory and principles for practical management coupled with high speed computing made possible simulation of the task environments and the solving of well structured problems in the systems fields of Operations Research and Management Science (OR/MS) following WWII (McCown, 2002a).

Although the agricultural decision support system is a product of the "problem solving" systems tradition (Figure 1), for many in the decision support system community their first 'systems' experience was "in the disciplines" of agricultural science. Systems thinking became prominent in agriculture in the 1960s in agronomy and animal husbandry and the physiology and of crops and farm animals. The unambiguous 'systems' signifier was the simulation model, and the interest of the modelers was predominantly theoretical. McCown (2002a) reports an interview with the pioneer of agricultural modeling, Prof. C.T. de Wit, in which he related his 'systems thinking' history. He traced the origins of the core technology of his renowned systems group at Wageningen to the university's recruitment of a professor in 1949 from OR/MS in the petroleum refining industry who had expertise in the simulation of distillation processes. De Wit's interest was unequivocally theoretical—to use physiological simulation models to explore the limits to crop production.

A second colonization of agriculture by "systems thinking" began in the 1960s as an attempt by agricultural economists in Farm Management Research, stimulated by achievements in OR/MS in industry, to enhance their tools for economic "problem solving" in farm management by replacing static 'production functions' with dynamic production models (Dent and Anderson, 1971). The essence of prevailing *normative* theory for Farm Management intervention is made especially clear by Hutton (1965).

> ...the model attempts to simulate the farmer's decision environment. The assumption is that the manager, without any formal analysis, is forced to use intuitive judgments in all his problem-solving activity. As a consequence his capacity to solve problems is low. Many defined problems are simply ignored. Also, the solutions he does obtain are relatively low quality since he is presumed to spread his analytical capacity, the scarce resource, over many pressing problems. Now, if formal analysis is introduced into such a situation, it has much the same effect as the introduction of a new production technique. Problems are more adequately solved and solutions are attempted over a larger number of problems. [ ] Our analytical models may be very roughly classified on a scale representing the extent to which they attempt to *substitute formal analysis for intuitive judgments*...(Hutton, 1965).

Such a *normative* approach features substitution for farmers' own assessment of the situation by theoretical analysis of the environment (E) and the provision of recommendations for action, i.e. decisions, that a farmer ought to follow, if he/she is rational. In the late 1970s, led by 'refugee' agricultural economists escaping a Farm Management enterprise in terminal decline, emphasis shifted from economic analysis to production technology-oriented 'systems analysis.'

The adoption of the decision support system idea in agricultural science can be seen as a third colonization of systems thinking from OR/MS during the 1970s (Figure 1). This decision support system concept was a response to the failure in business and industry of model-based normative approaches to be valued by real managers (McCown, 2002a). This crisis in OR/MS coincided with the emergence of two significant developments (Keen and Stabell, 1980). One of these was "a new science of management decision," based on novel theory in economics and cognitive psychology which emphasizes the dependence of decision behavior (B) on personal/psychological factors (P)—a shift away from optimization of B, based on E. A second development was interactive computing which provided an alternative to the OR/MS convention of experts with models advising managers. The idea was for managers to have access to models directly—models that are "simple, robust, easy to control, adaptive, as complete as possible, and easy to communicate with" (Little, 1970).

By the mid 1970s, a radically different paradigm of intervention was proposed for using models in management decision-making that combined these two developments. Looking back on the period, one of the key proponents, Peter Keen, reflected that:

> in 1976, Decision Support represented a radical concept of the use of information systems and analytical tools. [ ] It meshes human judgment and the power of com-

puter technology in ways that can improve the effectiveness of decision-makers, without intruding on their autonomy. There are better ways of applying the analytic methods of management science than to improve the normative approach of optimization science, which ignores the need to mesh decision-making process with the needs, habits and preferences of the decision maker, and to *respect rather than try to replace judgment* (Keen, 1987).

Comparison of the emphasized text with that emphasized in the quote above by Hutton indicates a 180 degree turn from normative intervention to by-pass intuitive judgment to 'facilitative' intervention that accepts preferences and judgment as integral to real human decision making, and the role of intervention is to support them.

But there is little indication of this shift to supporting a manager's judgment in the decision support system in agriculture, as illustrated in the description of SIRATAC, an early decision support system for cotton pest management.

This computer program processes data on numbers of insect pests and their predators, considers the stage of development of the cotton crop, calculates probable levels of pest survival and estimates what damage could result to the crop. The program then advises whether it is really necessary to spray for insect control Peacock (1980).

This is clearly a normative approach to decision making, especially so since the main aim was to achieve reduced levels of pesticides for environmental reasons, although this overlaid farmers' desire to reduce costs, other things being equal. The information generated is used to bypass a farmer's "intuitive judgment" rather than to support it.

I want to make two points. First, it is

enormously significant to the making sense of historical low levels of farmer adoption of the imported decision support system that agricultural innovators embraced the idea of personalized managerial computation from OR/MS *without* the accompanying learning of the failure of decades of *normative* intervention, i.e. advising what farmers *ought* to do. Yet, even today, to most of us agricultural scientists, Peacock's description of SIRATAC's approach seems eminently logical, which leads to the second point. SIRATAC's basic insect control logic proved to be sound, and at one point the system was used by some 30 percent of Australian cotton growers (Hearn and Bange, 2002). But in the end, routine usage was replaced by farmers' monitoring and judgments, but with standards of both raised by learning gained by using SIRATAC (Hearn and Bange, 2002). An unintended function of this decision support system, designed to guide routine pest management operations, was the aiding of learning about the environment and control measures to a point where the formal decision support system became superfluous. Yet, in our profession, realization of this unexpected, but successful, function of decision support systems did not bring about a new design strategy for software to aid farmer *learning*. But this history flags a possible future strategy with attractive potential.

The predisposition of scientists for normative intervention is reinforced by pointing out that although the agriculturalists pursued the normative approach in spite of its previous record of failure, the new approach, articulated above by Keen, was ignored not only by the agriculturalists, but, as it turned out, by most management scientists and interventionists in OR/MS as well. Keen later laments that the vision of the reformers for the decision support system in 1976 (quote above) proved to be mainly aspirational and was never widely accepted. Instead,

> ...the mission of decision support system attracted individuals from a wide range of backgrounds who saw it as a way of extending the practical application of tools, methods and objectives they believed in. While the definitional problem means that it has been hard to say what is *not* a decision support system, it has also not excluded any contribution or contributor who wanted to see theory turned into practice and technology into application Keen, 1987).

The commitment of scientists, both in and outside of agriculture, to the normative paradigm and our interpretation of past failure in ways that preserves the paradigm are eminently understandable. It is our profession's natural approach for agricultural science to serve agricultural practice. It has a pedigree that includes endorsement by the most influential philosopher of science in the last century, Karl Popper.

> A social science oriented towards objective understanding [of E], or 'situational logic,' can be developed independently of all subjective or psychological ideas [concerns with P]. Its method consists in analyzing the social situation of acting men sufficiently to explain the action [B] with the help of the situation [E], without any further help from psychology [P]. Objective understanding consists in realizing that the action was objectively appropriate to the situation. In other words, *the situation is analyzed far enough for the elements, which initially appeared to be psychological [P],...to be transformed into elements of the situation [E]* (Popper, 1976. Bracketed interjections and emphasis added).

There are good reasons, not

only for the belief that social science is less complicated than physics, but also for the belief that concrete social situations are in general less complicated than concrete physical situations. For in most social situations, if not in all, there is an element of *rationality*. Admittedly, human beings hardly ever act quite rationally (i.e. as they would if they could make the optimal use of all available information for the attainment of whatever ends they may have), but they act, nonetheless, more or less rationally; and this makes it possible to construct comparatively simple models of the actions and interactions, and to use these models as the approximations (Popper, 1964).

This philosophy featuring an objective 'situational logic' coupled with the presumption of rationality by the actor in the situation ('rationality principle') coincides with the dominant philosophy of economics that features economic rationality and optimization of economic behavior (Redman, 1991) and was the bedrock of operations research (OR) the early paradigm of management science.

The compelling case that the way forward was a shift from emphasis on E to P was provided by Herbert Simon, who won a Nobel Prize for establishing the legitimacy of the psychology of the decision maker (P) in theory about rational economic behavior (B). Simon distinguished two types of rationality.

> Behavior is *substantively* rational when it is appropriate to the achievement of given goals within the limits imposed by given conditions and constraints. Notice that, by this definition, the rationality of behavior depends upon the actor [P] in only a single respect—his goals. Given these goals, the rational behavior is determined

entirely by the characteristics of the environment in which it takes place [E]. Classical economic analysis [and Popper's situational analysis] rests on two fundamental assumptions [about P]. The first assumption is that the economic actor has a particular goal, for example, utility maximization or profit maximization. The second assumption is that the economic actor is substantively rational [i.e. has perfect knowledge about E.] Thus, the assumptions of utility or profit maximization, on the one hand, and the assumptions of substantive rationality, on the other, freed economic from any dependence upon psychology.

Behavior is *procedurally rational* when it is the outcome of appropriate deliberation [in P's mind]. Its procedural rationality depends upon the process that generated it. [The field of psychology] uses 'rationality' as synonymous with 'the peculiar thinking process called reasoning ' (Simon, 1979. Bracketed interjections and emphasis added).

Elsewhere, Simon elaborates how the two rationalities operate together in 'situational logic.' Situations have an outer environment [E] and an inner environment [P], and these interact. An economic actor's adjustment to her outer environment (her *substantive rationality*) is limited by her ability, through knowledge and analysis, to discover appropriate adaptive behavior in the situation (her *procedural rationality*) (Simon, 1996). This results in a 'bounded' substantive rationality that is simply part of the human condition. The implications for situational analysis were obvious:

It is illusory to describe a decision as 'situationally determined' [E-determined] when a part of the situation that determines it is the mind of the decision-maker [P] (Simon, 1996, Bracketed interjections and emphasis added.)

Simon's rationale for focus away from E to P was pivotal in the emergence of what became known as the 'behavioral' paradigm in economics and decision research. It also spawned the academic fields of cognitive science and artificial intelligence. In management science it provided the expert system and the theory for the decision support system innovation (Keen, 1987; McCown, 2001). Simon recognized the reality that managers could only have limited knowledge of E and that they had limited thinking power for analyzing information from E; this did not mean that managers were irrational, but they could only have 'bounded rationality.' Simon's strategy was to use computers, which, he argued, processed information in analogous fashion to brains, to provide 'intelligent machines' to augment managers' cognitive limitations.

Simon and his colleagues contributed immensely to better understanding of the structure of P as human cognition, but the new approaches to intervention in management decision making spawned by this understanding did little better than the old normative OR/MS. It has been 'back to the drawing boards' for intelligent machines and expert systems (Clancey, 1997). As it turned out, the decision support system to support human cognitive processes and the expert system as a proxy for human cognition suffered the same failure to achieve a market among real managers as did the decision support system for farmers, a decade later. In the most important respects, intervention to influence B conducted in the 'behavioral paradigm' was not radically different to that in which conditions in E were optimized. Both approaches treat P as an object rather than a free agent—an issue which is central the paradigm debate which is pivotal to this paper.

While Simon led a paradigm challenge,

a potentially more important challenge was to the behavioral approach by Simon's arch critic, the philosopher, Hubert Dreyfus. In 'What Computers Can't Do' (1972) and 'What Computers *Still* Can't Do' (1994), Dreyfus undertook the heroic challenge to replace the 'behavioral' paradigm with an alternative way of thinking about intelligent planning and action in the world of human affairs. This alternative philosophy, *phenomenology*, is concerned with how people, as (more or less) free agents, actually interpret the world around them, carry out activities in everyday life, including work, and learn from in action. Phenomenology is about behavior 'from the inside'—from the perspective of the person *producing* the behavior (as opposed to *observing* it). In 1972 Dreyfus lamented that:

> Such an alternative view has many hurdles to overcome. The greatest of these is that it cannot be presented as an alternative scientific explanation. We have seen that what counts as "a complete description" or an explanation is determined by the very tradition to which we are seeking an alternative. Thus Western thought has already committed itself to what would count as an explanation of human behavior. It must be a theory of practice, which treats man as a device, and object responding to the influence of other objects, according to universal laws or rules. [e.g. B = f (P, E)]

> But it is just this sort of theory, which after 2000 years of refinement, has become sufficiently problematic to be rejected by philosophers both in the Anglo-American tradition and on the Continent. It is just this theory which has run up against a stone wall in research in artificial intelligence. It is not some specific explanation, then that has failed, but the whole conceptual framework, which assumes that explanation of human behavior can and must take the Platonic form, successful in *physical* explanation [of E]; that situations can be treated like physical states; that the human world can be treated like the physical universe. If this whole approach has failed, then in proposing an alternative account we shall have to propose a different sort of explanation, a different sort of answer to the question "How does man produce intelligent behavior?..."

> There is a kind of answer to this question which is not committed before hand to finding the precise rule like relations between precisely defined objects. It takes the form of a phenomenological description of the behavior involved. It too can give us understanding if it is able to find the general characteristics of such behavior...(Dreyfus, 1994).

A phenomenological approach brings us back to the phenomenon of 'customary' management practice, discussed at the beginning of this section. This is management behavior grounded in the shared knowledge of a community of practice and in individual expertise developed through experience. This type of management behavior was what OR/MS, in the tradition of Frederick Taylor's work practice revolution, set out to replace with 'hard,' rationalistic, management principles. A *phenomenological* understanding of "intelligent behavior" referred to above by Dreyfus takes us outside the territory represented by Lewin's model of behavior-determining factors, B = f (P, E). It is the key to a reconceptualization of decision making, with customary practice as the starting point.

Recent conceptualization of the Nature of Decision Making

During the 1970s, the branch of the systems movement concerned with problem solving (Figure 1) experienced a paradigm revolution that left the field with two schools of thinking and methods—the traditional, 'hard,' school and a new 'soft' school, the differences articulated most authoritatively by Peter Checkland in 'Systems Thinking, Systems Practice' in 1981. Although soft systems didn't influence agriculture appreciably until the 1990s, it marked a significant turn from objective explanation of B in terms of attributes of P to treating behavior as action willed by P—a shift in behavioral science perspective from *causal factors* to *intentional actors*.

In keeping with this change in perspective, in this section, it is appropriate to find a replacement for Lewin's model of behavior, B = f (P, E), that provides a similarly abstract structure for actions and the variable mental states that lead to action via decision. In this, I rely heavily on two strands of the so-called 'cognitive revolution' in which behaviorism, with its exclusive focus on behavioral response (B) directly to environmental stimuli (E), was displaced by a psychology with emphasis on the mediation between environment and behavior by *subjective meanings* to the actor regarding the environment, the task, and the goal. People in situations interpret their situations and take meaningful action based on their desires and their beliefs and values shared in a culture. According to Bruner (1990), the cognitive revolution "was intended to bring the 'mind' back into the human sciences after a long cold winter of objectivism". He laments that the original focus on cultural 'meaning' was quickly displaced by a focus on the processing of information from the environment by minds and by computers simulating minds, i.e. the 'cognitive science' to which

Herbert Simon contributed so much, as we saw in the previous section.

The more recent 'revolution' discussed in this section concerns the bringing together information processing with cultural and personal meaning in an action-oriented approach to decision making. I attempt to capture the essence of this in a simple action model, drawing on both the *meaning-making* concepts found in some schools of social psychology (e.g. Blumer, 1969) and in cultural psychology (e.g. Bruner, 1990) and on the *information processing* framework that developed in cognitive science (e.g. de Mey, 1982). Although historically, these two fields of psychology have tended to see each other as antagonists, the offerings of both are essential to a theory of decision making that can ground a more effective approach to science-based decision support. After proposing an action-oriented model for decision making, I examine briefly the basic elements of the relatively new field of 'naturalistic decision making' to demonstrate correspondence with the action-oriented decision model. But I want to preface this by following the admonition of Dreyfus in the concluding quote of the previous section and look at the intelligent action (including decision making) as structured from the 'inside'—an alternative approach to objective structure provided by E and P earlier.

The structures of the life-world. In 'The Structures of the Life-World,' Schutz (1973) attempted to provide such 'general characteristics' of the nature of normal, everyday life as experienced. The *life-world* of a subject/actor/agent is the commonsense world of everyday life and the basis of each of our experienced realities as "wide-awake and normal adults." In this work (completed and published by Thomas Luckmann following the untimely death of Schutz), Schutz explicates the elementary structures of everyday life that provide the foundation of our experience, language, and action. This is the background reality of personal decision making and, arguably, the starting point for redesign of 'soft' decision support methodology.

The life-world, understood in its totality as the natural and social world, is the arena, as well as what sets the limits of my, and our reciprocal, action. In order to actualize our goals, we must master what is present in them and transform them. Accordingly, we act and operate not only *within* the life-world but also *upon* it. Our body movements gear into the life-world and transform its objects and their reciprocal relations. At the same time, these objects offer to our actions a resistance which we must either subdue or to which we must yield. The life-world is thus a reality which we modify through our acts and which, on the other hand, modifies our actions. We can say that our *natural attitude* of *daily life* is pervasively determined by a *pragmatic motive*.

Nevertheless, in the natural attitude the *world is already given to me* for my explication. I must understand my life-world to the degree necessary in order to be able to act in it and operate upon it. Likewise, thinking in the attitude of the life-world is also pragmatically motivated. Each step of my explication and understanding of the world is based at any given time on a stock of previous experience, my own immediate experiences as well as such experiences as are transmitted to me from my fellow-man and above all from my parents, teachers, and so on. All of these communicated and immediate experiences are included in a certain unity having the form of my stock of knowledge, which serves me as the *reference schema* for the actual step of my explication of the world. All of my experiences in the life-world are brought into relation to this schema, so that the objects and events in the life-world confront me from the outset in their typical character —*in general* as mountains and stones, trees and animals, more *specifically* as a ridge, as oaks, birds, fish, and so on [As an idealization], I trust that the world as it has been known to me up until now will continue further and that consequently the stock of knowledge obtained from my fellow-man informed by my own experiences will continue to preserve its fundamental validity. From this assumption follows the further and fundamental one: that I can repeat my past successful acts. So long as· the structure of the world can be taken to be constant, as long as my previous experiences valid, my ability to operate upon the world in this and that manner remains, in principle, preserved. Both idealizations and the assumptions of the constancy of the world's structure which are grounded on them—the validity of my previous experience and, on the other hand, my ability to operate upon the world—are essential aspects of thinking within the natural attitude (Schutz and Luckmann, 1973).

By Schutz' phenomenological account, we are 'situated' in our life-world in terms of both our physical and social environments. Although these constrain our actions, it is equally the case that our actions can 'transform' our environments to suit our purposes. Know-ledge acquired from our fellows and from our own past experience contributes to this latter 'mastering' of our situations. But as Polanyi (1958) argues, personal knowledge that 'subdues' and 'transforms' includes 'commitment' and 'passion.' These are all readily recognizable as part of 'pragmatic motive' in the 'natural attitude'. Regulation of knowledge and action by the 'pragmatic motive in our 'natural attitude' of everyday living means that we are inclined toward criteria for understanding and performance such as 'good enough' and 'just in time' and to repetition of behavior that has met these criteria in the past. Elsewhere, Schutz and Luckmann (1973) point out that regularization by 'conservative habits' and 'recipes' is normal and inevitable because these strategies are so often pragmatically successful. This behavior is *practical*.

Schutz sees everyday knowledge serving to provide 'typifications' and 'reference schema' that aid making sense of situations efficiently based on experience, ours and others. This conceptualization of knowledge as cognitive representations of objects and situations in the life-world that guide both perception of situations and interpretations relevant for action in particular situations is central to cognitive psychology and naturalistic decision making theory. I return to this important matter of mental representations later in this section.

More grounds for seeing decision making differently. As emphasized in Section 1, fundamental to a new theory of decision making is the shift in emphasis from decision events consisting of rational choice between alternative actions to mental assessment of situations, mental simulation of outcomes of possible actions, and resolution of the situation by committing oneself to action that promises to produce satisfactory outcomes. This 'naturalistic' decision making process tends progressively rule out alternatives rather than identify an optimum (Klein et al., 1995; Winograd and Flores, 1986). But equally fundamental, and deserving of its

emphasis in this and the following section, is recognition that intelligent actions are not always preceded by this process, i.e. by conscious decision. In normal *routine* activity, commitments are made, and action is taken without conscious deliberation. This is implicit in the third paragraph of the above quote from Schutz and Luckman. In the natural attitude of normal, routine life, there is a 'taking for granted' that the world and the validity of our experience will not change. This mode of automatic use of 'know how' in unproblematic situations is what Dreyfus and Dreyfus (1986) call 'intuition.' Recognition of this mode of behavior is most important for thinking about use of decision support systems: in a well functioning operation it is statistically the most prevalent mode. Most of the time there is no felt need for aids to decision making. It is only when a situation becomes *problematic* (Schutz and Luckman, 1973), i.e. is in a state of *irresolution* (Winograd and Flores, 1986), that deliberation becomes central and intervention becomes relevant. This issue of 'occasions for decision support' is discussed in the following section. The remainder of this section concerns the nature of deliberative decision process, as background for thinking about appropriate decision support intervention.

All of the above concernts *theory*. But a most convincing *practical* argument for an alternative approach to decision support is provided by Arie de Geus, a former senior executive of Shell Oil and sometime Fellow at the London School of Economics.

> I have not met a decision maker who is prepared to accept anybody else's model of his/her reality, if he knows that the purpose of the exercise is to make him, the decision maker, make decisions and engage in action for which he/she will ultimately be responsible. *People (and not only managers) trust only their own understanding of*

their world as the basis for their actions. "I'll make up my own mind" is a pretty universal principle for everyone embracing the responsibility of their life, whether private or business life (de Geus, 1994; p xiv. Emphasis added.)

If this is true for people who farm, what does it imply for our provision of decision support? If meaningful actions stem from subjective decisions based on the decision maker's beliefs about the world, i.e.

action ← decision = f (beliefs about the world),

any intervention other than the normative one of recommending the best action, must be directed at influencing a decision maker's beliefs.

Belief can be seen as linking the *real* and the *meaningful*. Much of what follows concerns the status of belief as a form of knowledge and processes of belief formulation in normal life and work, e.g. farming. This is related to differentiation of specific categories of belief in the above rudimentary action-oriented decision model, with the intention of creating conceptual 'entry points' for intervention to support subjective decisions, the subject of the following section.

I submit that farmers make decisions based on their subjective beliefs about the prospects of an action that are heavily weighted by their own experience concerning the task, and on their beliefs about 'what is the case' in an uncertain environment. This can be expressed as

action ← decision = f (g, b_E, b_T).

Decision concerning action is a function of the agent's goals (g), his/her beliefs about the environment (b_E), and his/her beliefs about the envisioned tasks (b_T). I think the eminent psychologist, Jerome Bruner, would call this an expression of 'folk psy-

chology.' My combining of beliefs and goals corresponds with Bruner's emphasis on the importance of processes involving information by which meaning is made by actors based on both personal *knowing* and *valuing*. He argues that all psychology must be grounded on naturalistic psychology— on everyday subjective and inter-subjective behavior in the life-world.

Folk psychology…is a culture's account of what makes human beings tick. It includes a theory of mind, one's own and others', a theory of motivation, and the rest. I shall call it ethnopsychology to make the term parallel to such expressions as ethnobotany, ethnopharmacology and those other native disciplines that are eventually displaced by scientific knowledge. But folk psychology, though it changes, does not get displaced by scientific paradigms. For it deals with the nature, causes, and consequences of those intentional states—beliefs, desires, intentions, commitments—that most scientific psychology dismisses in its effort to explain human action from a point of view that is outside human subjectivity…[e.g. B = f (P, E)] So folk psychology continues to dominate the transactions of everyday life. And though it changes, it resists being tamed into objectivity. For it is rooted in language and a shared conceptual structure that are steeped in intentional states—in beliefs, desires, and commitments. And because it is a reflection of culture, it partakes in the culture's way of valuing as well as its way of knowing (Bruner, 1990).

In naturalistic decision making, decision and action originate in the subjective, intentional mental states of beliefs, desires, intentions, and commitments. This provides a starting point for a replacement of

Lewin's function concerning causes of behavior. The underlying strategy for my action model is to achieve the simplest expression for decision making that 'causes' intentional action and that provides adequate 'hooks' for science-based intervention and that preserves the dimensions of knowing and valuing. My use of 'goals' is an attempt to capture the 'valuing' in Bruner's "desires, intentions, and commitments." From the standpoint of intervention, beliefs are key because under some conditions belief can be influenced by scientific knowledge, and there is obvious value in the differentiating these two domains of the agent's belief. Although, as indicated later, g, b_T, and b_E are not truly independent variables.

As we saw earlier, Karl Popper did his best to exclude psychological factors from analysis of behavior in situations. This was not, however, because he didn't recognize the importance of psychological determinants of behavior, but rather because he had a pragmatic motive about his goal to explicate an *objective* theory of knowledge that contributed to science achieving its aim of "increase in verisimilitude", i.e. resemblance of truth or reality (Popper, 1972). This unwavering focus tends to obscure his considerable insight into matters he claimed to have no interest, e.g. naturalistic decision making and action in the life-world. Popper fully acknowledges that our behavior is in part determined by subjective *dispositions to act* and our *expectations.*

> …we do have *expectations,* and we strongly *believe in certain regularities* (laws of nature, theories). This leads to the commonsense problem of induction. In the commonsense view it is simply taken for granted (without any problems being raised) that our belief in regularities is justified by those repeated observations which are responsible for its genesis (Popper, 1972)

Note the similarities to Schutz' descrip-

tion of our behavior in the natural attitude in the life-world. Elsewhere, Popper concurs with Schutz 'typifications' in perception: "…there is no observation which is not related to a set of typical situations— regularities…." Popper recognized the *practical* importance of beliefs. Although the theoretician enjoyed the luxury of pursuing open-ended knowledge and of unhurried deliberation, it was different for the "man of practical action. For a man of practical action has always to *choose* between some more or less definite alternatives, since *even inaction is a kind of action."* He sees no escape from the dilemma that while practice depends on beliefs acquired from repetitive experience, such inductive process is *logically* indefensible as a way of producing knowledge. But beliefs differ in type, and 'beliefs' that are unconscious dispositions to act in a certain way due to past repetitions of experiences are inferior to 'beliefs' in the form of personal 'theories,' even vaguely formulated.

> I do not think that such distinctions between different ' beliefs' are of any interest for my own objectivist theory of knowledge; but they ought to be interesting for anybody who takes the psychological problems of induction [i.e. learning from repeated experience] seriously—which I do not (Popper, 1972, p26).

Systems practitioners concerned about decision support that makes a difference in the activities of 'men of practical action' are not as comfortably quarantined from the real world as was Popper, the academic. Agricultural scientists who are serious about effective support for practical decisions and actions have good reasons for interest in farmers' beliefs and the processes that influence them. But the above examination of Popper's views shows that he would not disapprove of such a turn by scientists who pragmatically 'take this seriously'. He made clear that he was *not* a 'belief philosopher', but his views provide space for a phenomenological account of beliefs in the life-world of pragmatic motive and action.

Beliefs as mental models. "In order to believe something, it must first be present in the mind; some *mental representation* must be constructed that is a candidate for [ ] acceptance or non-acceptance" (Goldman, 1986; p227).

In both the phenomenology of Schutz and the science philosophy of Popper, the matching of the sensed world and stored mental representations is an important part of the processing of information about the world which constitutes the environment of a decision. The roles of subjective mental models in selective perception and interpretation in everyday life and work is constitutive of the *cognitive* view of intelligent behavior (de Mey, 1992).

> The central point of the cognitive view is that…information processing, whether perceptual (such as a perceiving an object) or symbolic (such as understanding a sentence) is mediated by a system of categories or concepts, which for the information processor constitutes a representation or a model of his world (de Mey, 1992).

We can take it for granted that farmers, like the rest of us, carry around cognitive structures that represent their worlds to themselves. The possible implications of this for agricultural scientists with intentions to support farmers' decisions are indicated by prior projects of interventionists in non-agricultural fields, e.g. management consulting:

> When we speak of capturing and expressing a manager's mental models we are essentially saying that we want to find out how the client thinks a situation works. Our models of how things work are what enable us to make sense of the world. They allow us to add structure to everyday events. They allow us to understand why something has happened and what its ramifications are. We have such models for almost every situation that we come across. When clients use phrases like, "That's not possible," "I don't think it works like that," or "No, he wouldn't have done that," they are appealing to their mental models of a system or person. Without mental models our lives would seem capricious, random, and meaningless. Models supply structure to a stream of events. The reason mental models are important is that they are what people use to make decisions. Thus to help a

Table 1. A framework of cognitive representations based on variation in scale of organization. Levels differ in the degree to which models "in the head" are augmented by information from the environment (from de Mey, 1982). 'Attitudes' are based on the phenomenology of Schutz and Luckman (1973).

Segmentation of *self* and *situation*	Mental representation	Level of organization	Attitude with pragmatic motive
Internal input: beliefs, desires	World model	World view	Natural
	Frame/Scheme, script	Context	Exploratory
	Mental model	Structural relationship	Theoretical
External input from env't: data, context	Typification	Object, event	Communicative

manager react to a problem, it is necessary to examine their mental model of how that problem works and, if necessary, help them to change it. This requires an array of tools and we will discuss these in more detail in the section below titled "Modeling as Learning Tools" (Lane, 1992).

In the following section I will pick up on Lane's 'modeling as learning tools,' but here I want to have a closer look at the notion of mental model. Although human cognition, our subjective knowing and reasoning, is commonly explained in terms of mental models, precise description of such structures is elusive in spite of decades of research (Johnson-Laird, 1987; Gentner and Stevens, 1983; Vennix, 1990). Frames of reference, mental models, mental maps, world views, world models, cognitive structures, scripts, paradigms are some of the terms that have been used for cognitive representations. In generalized language, these are beliefs and systems of beliefs about the environment (including goals), about ourselves, and about implications of both for action. But important structural differentiation can also be made.

De Mey (1992) distinguishes four levels of mental representation and associated levels of organization (Table 1). World models/worldviews enable actors to operate "automatically" in normal, routine situations where possibilities for actions are 'resolved' to one, or a few closely related alternatives. Information from the environment is minimal, enabling merely the selection of the appropriate world model. Although this 'mindlessness' sounds undesirable, this automatic selectivity is generally adaptively advantageous because in the routine situations that prevail in our lives, it frees sensory and cognitive resources for problematic matters, and because these situations are familiar and repetitious, the risk of error through inattention is low (de Mey, 1982).

When a situation becomes 'problematic' (Schutz and Luckman, 1973), or in a state of 'irresolution' (Winograd and Flores, 1986), the actor's attention is required in assessing the environment and deliberating on appropriate actions, i.e. decision-making. In the event of modest disruption, attention is at the specific context of action, requiring increased information from the environment, and the restorative attitude is 'exploratory'. More serious disruption may force attention to the level of structure of the environment, requiring even greater data from the environment, in a 'theoretical' attitude. These differences have important implications for intervention and are developed further in the following section.

Considerable research in cognitive science has been directed to better understanding of cognitive structures, whose assumed existence has proved so valuable in making sense of how humans perceive and interpret their situations and determine action. Although they remain vague entities, useful distinctions can be made between 'models' of situations that provide procedural guidance for action (world models, frames) and models of how the physical world works. Referring to the definition of 'frame' by Minsky (1975) as "a data-structure for representing a stereotyped situation," de Mey (1982) explicates the concept.

> Frames are large complex symbolic structures, which can be represented as a "network of nodes and relations." The "top level" nodes of a frame are fixed and stand for "things, which are always true about the supposed situation" e.g. in a room-frame: that a room has 'walls' or vertically supporting structures of some sort. At the lower levels, frames "have many *terminals* or 'slots' that must be filled by specific instances or data ['cues'].
> Frames represent units of knowl-

edge one brings to bear upon a situation. As structures, which have to be completed with data, they orient the information processing system toward specific aspects of that situation. A basic point of the frame theory is that frames are neither stored nor retrieved as empty or blank forms. The open slots, frame terminals, are filled in with 'weakly bound' default assignments, i.e. *typical* examples of the kind of concrete objects one *expects* to meet when the frame turns out to be applicable (emphasis added)(de Mey, 1982).

Failure to rigidly separate the environment and action is an important aspect of the cognitive paradigm at higher levels in Table 1. de Mey (1982) emphasizes that frames are as much about representing the 'self' as about representing the world. Frames contain "beliefs about what ought to be" (Starbuck and Milliken, 1988). They represent levels of aspiration conditioned by expectations of the attainable (Simon, 1996)

Such mental structures operationalize the *pragmatic motive* of Schutz and Luckman (1973).

A somewhat different type of cognitive model is that which represents physical structure or technical function, for which the term 'mental model' prevails. Norman (1983) observed that such a mental model reflects a person's beliefs about the physical system, acquired through observation, instruction, or inference. The technical model has dominated the field of mental model research because of easy availability of normative, theory-based conceptual models for comparison (Gentner and Stevens, 1983). But the 'pragmatic motive' in the life-world means that interest in function is generally confounded with 'action,' and mental models combine representations of 'how things work' with representations of 'how I proceed to get the outcome I want'. As part of decision process, these mental models are 'run' to predict the outcome of an action in a situation, i.e. the 'mental simulation' of Point 2 of Orasanu and Connelly (1995), later in this section (Norman, 1983; Lipshitz, 1995).

Elaborating the action–oriented decision model. Decision and actions are about the world, and any model of action must reflect this. But instead of the deterministic rela-

---

Figure 2

An action-oriented model of decision making when the situation is problematic. Deliberation centers on beliefs about the environment (b_E), beliefs about tasks (b_T) and goals (g).

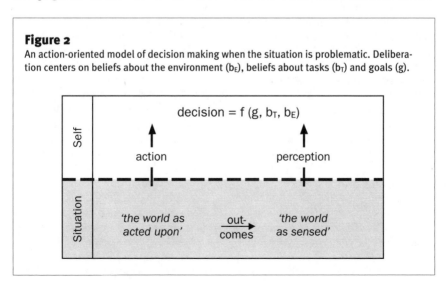

$$decision = f\,(g, b_T, b_E)$$

tion to behavior in Lewin's model, in this case it must be mediated by the mind of the actor, i.e. through goals, beliefs, mental models, etc. Simon (1996) describes a process by which this is accomplished.

The distinction between the world as sensed and the world as acted upon defines the basic condition for the survival of adaptive organisms. The organism must develop correlations [b_T] between goals [g] in the sensed world and actions in the world of process. When they are made conscious and verbalized, these correlations correspond to what we usually call means–ends analysis. Given a desired state of affairs [g] and an existing state of affairs [b_E], the task of an adaptive organism is to find the difference between these two states and then to find the correlating process [action] that will erase the difference. Most problem solving requires continual translation between the state and process descriptions of the same complex reality (Simon, 1996 interjections added).

This interaction of the organism, or from a subjective standpoint, the *self*, with the world, or *situation*, suggests an elaboration of my action-oriented model for decision-making, when situations are problematic, or unresolved (Figure 2).

(When the situation is not 'problematic,' i.e. routine, the world and outcomes are taken largely for granted and the decision expression is replaced by a 'world model' (Table 1) which enables action to follow perception 'automatically' without deliberation involving goals and beliefs.)

Perception is an active process in which what is sensed as a state of the world is influenced by what state is expected (an aspect of b_E) (de Mey, 1982; Weick, 1995). Interpretation of the situation is accomplished by reference to beliefs about tasks

and outcomes (b_T). Evaluation of sensed states are evaluated by reference to goals (g). Goals are both underspecified actions (de Mey, 1982) and are inseparable from beliefs about potential of the environment. As Shafer (1986) points out, "...the process of formulating and adopting goals creates a dependence of value on belief, simply because goals are more attractive when they are feasible" (quoted by Beach and Lipshitz, 1995). Through evaluation, problematic discrepancy between a goal and a state of the world as sensed can be alleviated by action to achieve the desired outcome or the discrepancy can be alleviated by downwards adjustment of the goal. But goal adjustment is not all one way. Through intervention that leads to a new learning about a task (change in b_T), farmers sometimes discover that they have been aiming too low (something that can easily go unrecognized in a variable environment) and lead them to formulate more ambitious goals (g) (Carberry, 2002).

Naturalistic decision-making. The implications of this theory pertaining to subjective decision and action can be seen in recent developments in decision research. Brehmer (1990) succinctly expresses the essence.

The study of decision-making in a dynamic, real-time context, relocates the study of decision making and makes it a part of the study of action, rather than the study of choice. The problem of decision making, as seen in this framework, is a matter of directing and maintaining the continuous flow of behavior towards some set of goals rather than as a set of discrete episodes involving choice dilemmas (Brehmer, 1990).

Since the mid-1980s a concerted research effort, largely funded by the U.S. Army and the National Aeronautics and Space Agency on decision making in natural, real world conditions has stimulated a new school of decision research labeled 'naturalistic decision making' (Klein et al., 1995). Five main features of this perspective are set out in Orasanu and Connelly (1995) and summarized below, in an altered order.

1. Reasoning about situations is aided by beliefs about the world and tasks to be undertaken. As frames and mental models, these greatly aid organizing problems, interpreting situations, and identifying information valuable for solution. A critical feature of the frame-driven approach is that people create causal models of the situation. They try to understand the significance of events and information by inferring causal relations.

2. In contrast to the traditional emphasis on rational selection among alternative actions, decision makers tend to conceptualize a 'best bet' solution that fits the situation and proceed to evaluate it, including using mental simulation.

3. Decision makers work toward 'satisfactory,' rather than optimal, solutions. From the naturalistic perspective this is viewed as being adaptively pragmatic when facing of ill-structured problems in uncertain, dynamic environments.

4. The major distinction between expert decision-makers and less expert decision-makers concerns their relative abilities in evaluating problematic situations rather than their reasoning processes and performance per se.

5. Reasoning and acting are interleaved. "Instead of analyzing all facets of a situation, making a decision, and then acting, it appears that in complex realistic situations people think a little, act a little, and then evaluate the outcomes and think and act some more." And in this decision cycle, actors learn.

Naturalistic decision making continues to be a very active research field, as evidenced by a recent issue of the Journal of Behavioral Decision Making dedicated to it (Yates, 2001), and promises to provide a valuable resource for those concerned with support for farmers' decisions.

Let's pause and assess where we are and how we got here. We have now seen that our decision support system heritage is firmly rooted in long-held normative theory about farm decision making: (1) farmers suffer the 'handicap' of having to make most decisions using their 'intuition,' based on customary practice and (2) supply of information that reflects economic rationality and/or scientific 'best practice' can replace intuition, with benefit. But in the aftermath of failure of this school of intervention to be accepted by managers, phenomenology puts farmers' customary practice in a new light, partly by reminding scientists that habitual behavior is inevitable and fundamentally adaptive— until a problem or opportunity arises. When either such an attention-focusing event occurs, a deliberative process, which utilizes the manager's beliefs about the task and the situation, interprets the situation and 'designs' appropriate action. Managers act in situations on the basis of their goals and beliefs, and they learn from experiences in their practical situations—theirs and those of others in their culture as communicated to them. We now can address the matter of what this radical change in perspective might mean for scientists with models in providing support for farmers' decisions.

Intervention to Support Farmers' Naturalistic Decision Processes

As software produced by scientists to influence the instrumental thinking of practitioners, the decision support system is both technical and social in nature (Keen, 1987; McCown, 2002a). Scientists' natural strategy for a decision support project is to invest in the technology and assume that rational farmers would welcome information products that are scientifically-sound, relevant to stereotypic practice and made readily accessible. This paradigm of intervention in decision-making has proved to be technically impressive, but socially naïve. In this section I am arguing that greater success in science-based decision support requires intervention with a different socio-technology, one that acknowledges the social reality that good farmers—progressive farmers—behaving normally in their life-worlds, will only *occasionally* behave as expected in the traditional decision support system paradigm, i.e. as eager consumers of science-based information and tools. The frequency of these occasions is too low to warrant continued production of decision support systems. The big question is whether a different type of intervention would be more appropriate and successful.

This alternative socio-technology, which I am advocating, of intervention to support a manager's subjective decision making processes raises three key questions: (1) Under what conditions can the decision maker be expected to welcome support? (2) Just what is being supported? and (3) What does such intervention look like? In search of answers to Question 1, I look to phenomenology and management science. To answer Question 2, I look to cognitive science (the science of subjective knowing and reasoning) and to the field of 'sense making', whose home is in social psychology. For Question 3, I rely heavily on experience in the field of 'system dynamics' as applied to business management.

What are occasions for effective support?
Once, in response to my question, "Why are decision support systems so little used by farmers?" a very savvy and computer literate farmer, familiar with local decision support system efforts, replied, "You need a doctor when you've got problems, not when you're traveling well enough." This response indirectly exposes what is arguably the most serious flaw in the decision support system paradigm, i.e. that the default rationale for expecting decision support system adoption is that superior

quality knowledge in, or generated from, a decision support system will be preferred over existing farmer's knowledge. I am not arguing that the presumed quality differences don't often exist, but rather that this ignores the crux of the matter— farmers' existing resources for making decisions in farming practice are only *occasionally* problematic. Most of the time, a farmer feels that he/she is "traveling well enough," and when this is the case, he/she can be expected to *"trust only their own understanding of their world* as *the basis for their actions."* These observations by managers of a farm and a multi-national oil company are congruent with the phenomenological theory of Alfred Schutz (Schutz and Luckmann, 1973).

Paraphrasing Schutz' first person account of the everyday experience, since the course of my life is a series of situations, in every moment of conscious life I find myself in a situation that requires a degree of control so that my actions will effectively achieve my goals, i.e. that I 'master the situation'. To a greater or lesser degree, a situation is imposed on me, in part this predetermination is that of the given, natural world; it is further determined, or limited, by social realities. But situations are never fully determined— they are 'open' to some degree, allowing some freedom for my personal decision, which leads to my action. But when the situation is 'familiar' and I am 'traveling well enough' in my activity, I am not actively, consciously, engaged in assessing and deciding. Rather I am mastering the 'taken for granted' situation using my stock of habitual knowledge quite automatically. As long as I believe that the situation is routine and unproblematic, it is good practice not to invest scarce resources, e.g. my time and attention, to gain more intimate knowledge of the situation or about alternative actions.

…I know that there are…"more precise" explanations for the events familiar to me and even that there are certain "people" who can transmit this knowledge to me: scientists…[etc]. Although I know that, I am really not interested in acquiring further knowledge about it. I'm sufficiently familiar "for my own purposes." The interest involved here is in the broadest sense a pragmatic one that determines the acquisition and interruption of knowledge. I would, or perhaps in principle be "interested" to know more about these things, but under the principle of "first things first" I have "no time," since I must "first" acquire knowledge more relevant for me. I want to keep a "place" open for more important or more urgent experience (Schutz and Luckmann, 1973).

But when the situation changes in a way that indicates that my habitual knowledge might not be adequate do deal with the new elements, the situation becomes 'problematic' and attention becomes focused. This new situation becomes the 'more important or more urgent experience.'

If such "new" elements entered into a situation, I must "deliberate." That is, I consciously try to correlate these elements with my stock of knowledge. Let us first assume that completely new elements are also explicated with the help of interpretation schemata and typifications, which are on hand, but not sufficiently for my plan-determined interest. My knowledge is not "clear" enough, "sure" enough, not sufficiently free of contradiction, for me to handle the current situation. I must thus further explicate the "open" elements of the situation until they have achieved the level of clarity, familiarity, and freedom from contradiction already given in the plan-determined interest. We will call such situations *problematic situations*. In contrast to routine situations, I must here either acquire new elements of knowledge or take old ones which are not sufficiently clarified for the present situation, and bring them to higher levels of clarity (Schutz and Luckmann, 1973).

In the first instance, my reference schemata ('types,' frames, mental models, etc.) shape my expectations of the situation and thereby largely determine what I perceive as relevant to mastery of the situation.

To the degree that I experience 'surprise,' these model-based pre-perceptions fail to match the reality I perceive in the specific situation. The situation is 'problematic' and I realize a need for learning, i.e. new, more applicable, mental structures.

If the current experience finally appears not "sufficiently typical" for determination and mastery of the situation, processes of explication are induced in which new typifications on other levels of determination are rendered familiar (Schutz and Luckmann, 1973).

But there is a very pragmatic limit to interest in acquiring new knowledge.

At this point we can focus this to answer Question 1, concerning realistic expectations for farmers' receptivity to decision support intervention. The indication from phenomenology is that the windows of opportunity for support offerings to be deemed relevant by farmers are limited to the experiencing of problems, and even there, there is a risk of missing the window in the other dimension by providing a level of detail of information in excess of that needed to deal with the problem. Because the conventional decision support system targets a stereotypic problem, it suffers an inability to respond to windows of receptivity. Both 'problem' and 'solution' are fixed at the time of computer programming. In the ideal intervention, what constitutes a 'problem' can be discussed and the level of intervention can be negotiated. Such flexible engagement is an important social characteristic of the alternative paradigm for the support that I am outlining.

Intervention to support what? I now turn to Question 2, "What is supported in this paradigm of intervention?" According to the phenomenological account of Schutz, the notion of 'support' only becomes relevant when the taken-for-granted routine activity becomes interrupted by a change in the situation—a change leading to the farmer perceiving the situation to be 'problematic'. Karl Weick (1995) argues that what are brought into play in these circumstances are not problem solving or decision-making processes, but *sensemaking* processes.

>...sense making begins with the basic question, is it still possible to take things for granted? [in the natural attitude in the life-world] And if the answer is no, if it has become impossible to continue with automatic information processing, then the question becomes, why is this so? And, what next? (Weick, 1995).

A problematic state concerning a taken-for-granted belief can be due to either *uncertainty,* the lack of information, or *ambiguity,* conflicting information or interpretations. The former is problematic because of *ignorance,* the latter because of *confusion* (Weick, 1995; Weick and Meader, 1993). A farmer's situation becomes problematic when a 'comfortable' belief becomes challenged or when attention is drawn to the high degree of uncertainty or ambiguity associated with beliefs that are the basis for everyday decision and action (Figure 2), especially if there is some new prospect for relieving uncertainty or ambiguity. It may concern beliefs about the state of the environment, about relevant environmental consequences, about the

action procedures or consequences, or about the appropriateness of the goal (Figure 2). In dryland farming systems in subtropical Australia, a farmer is normally hampered in decisions concerning crop selection and planting by a high degree of environmental *uncertainty.* This farmer experiences problematic *ambiguity* about decision and action when, after engaging in discussion of simulations of alternative rotations, his belief is confirmed that rotations featuring dryland cotton are by far the most profitable but also comes to believe, as the simulations indicate, that these rotations pose the greatest dryland salinity hazard because they are the most 'leaky,' i.e. they allow the greatest deep drainage because of the long bare fallows required to store soil water.

Sensemaking is an art of the possible. It is making do, coping, developing confidence when activity must continue in spite of uncertainty and ambiguity. According to Weick (1995), sensemaking processes can be driven by either tentative *beliefs* or tentative action.

>...even though sensemaking processes are elusive there seems to be at least four ways in which people impose frames on ongoing flows [of thinking and activity] and link frames with cues in the interest of meaning. Sensemaking can begin with beliefs and take the form of arguing and expecting. Or sensemaking can begin with actions and take the form of committing or manipulating (Weick, 1995).

One of the resources that is sometimes available is discussion with other people of one's beliefs about the situation or contemplated actions. When this takes the form of robust argument in which criticism serves to filter out weaknesses of a belief or replace a belief with a better one, more dependable understanding results.

>...when arguing is the dominant

form of sensemaking, weak definitions of the situation, embedded in tentative initial proposals, gradually become elaborated and strengthened as proposers confront critics. Sensemaking occurs as this "natural dialectic" begins to produce either a synthesis or a winner (Weick, 1995).

Another way a belief can serve as a driver for sensemaking is when it is embedded in expectations that guide interpretation of the situation and decision-making. In this coping process, expectations can be 'best guesses' or even 'wishful thinking;' either provides a starting point for meaning that can be reinforced by confirming action, generating what might be viewed as 'self-fulfilling prophesies.'

The point that people keep missing is that self-fulfilling prophecies are a fundamental act of sensemaking. Prophecies, hypotheses, anticipations—whatever one chooses to call them—are starting points. They are minimal structures around which input can form as the result of some kind of active prodding. That prodding is often belief driven, and the beliefs that drive it are often expectations. People do not have much to start with when their goal is to "get to know" [a situation]. This means that their expectations cannot help but be a force that shapes the world they try to size up (Weick, 1995).

...the evidence suggests that when perceivers are motivated by accuracy concerns, they do not produce self-fulfilling prophecies. But when they strive for stability and predictability, their interactions...will lead to behavioral confirmation of their beliefs and expectations (Weick, 1995).

Because beliefs and actions are so closely interrelated, sensemaking can start at any point at either end of Figure 2.

Structures of mutual causality mock the language of independent and dependent variables. They invite instead, description of those situations where beliefs can affect themselves through the mediation of action, and situations where actions can affect themselves through the mediations of beliefs (Weick, 1995).

Sensemaking processes that are driven by action rather than belief derive from the fact that organizations are above all, "activity systems that generate action." In spite of formalized descriptions of organizations (including farms) as rational systems for pursuing goals, Weick contends that "organizations are...loosely coupled systems in which action is underspecified, inadequately rationalized, and monitored only when deviations are extreme." This means that there is ample freedom for actions in times of uncertainty or ambiguity to originate out of personal *commitments* to act, e.g. to continue to do what a farmer does in this culture, but with a new degree of attention on cues in the environment and on feedback to beliefs from outcomes —attention not paid during unproblematic times (Figure 1). Weick's second action-originating strategy for making sense of a problematic situation is *manipulation* of the world in order to learn. Here action serves also as an experiment or probe that may start a process that leads to insight and new beliefs/mental models.

These 'sensemaking' processes are techniques for 'bootstrapping' decisions and action under conditions when uncertainty and/or ambiguity prevail. They provide a starting point for progression to a new, adapted, everyday management routine based on mental models of the situation that are products of these sensemaking processes.

Sensemaking, after all, is about the world. And what is being asserted about that world is found in the beliefs and categories implied by frames (Weick, 1995.)

Before turning to the third question concerning the nature of the alternative mode of intervention, it may be helpful to synthesize responses to the first two. The basic occasion for sensemaking support is most readily visualized as an unexpected change in the decision maker's environment—a surprise that destabilizes activity and creates uncertainty or ambiguity. But a need for making sense of the situation can also arise from a farmer's sense of new *possibility* beyond what had been assumed previously in goal setting (Weick, 1995). Although perception of an opportunity is more welcome than a threat, both bring the destabilizing, problematic effects of pressure to act, difficulty, and importance (Starbuck and Milliken, 1988). A third occasion for sensemaking, according to Weick (1995), and one especially important to interventionists, is initiated in response to a request for increased conscious attention, as when farmers are challenged by others to think about an issue or to answer questions about matters that are potentially problematic. Significantly, when a sense of the latent problematic can be channeled into a process of *inquiry,* the emphasis shifts from tactic to strategy, from deciding to *learning* that will influence future decisions.

What does sensemaking support look like? In a critique of the Group Decision Support System (GDSS), Weick and Meader (1993), acknowledge the potential value of simulation for support of groups whose deliberation and action are impaired by uncertainty and ambiguity, and which are in most need of support in sensemaking processes. There exists a considerable body of literature on the use of simulation models in the field of business management as instruments for enabling such learning by managers. The basic idea is the use of a comprehensive and competent model of a business to provide a virtual world in which a participating manager can engage in the realistic activities of assessing the environment, deliberating about meaning for the business which is represented in the simulator, making decisions, taking action, and evaluating the outcomes of his/her actions. These elaborate computer programs have been variously termed 'microworlds,' 'management games,' 'management flight simulators,' 'Computer-Based Learning Environments (CBLEs),' 'business simulators,' and 'learning laboratories' (Senge, 1990; Lane, 1995; Maier and Grobler, 2000).

Lane (1995) reviewed the 'second coming' of this phenomenon and noted that the first such product was created by the American Management Association in 1956 and was called 'Top Management Decision Simulation;' by 1966 they were used by the majority of U.S. business schools and the commercial market for simulations exceeded $US 100 million per year; by 1970, they were largely out of favor. They returned in the 1980s with personal computers. The major resurgence later in the '80s was due to activity in the field of 'systems dynamics,' a field pioneered in the 1960s by Jay Forrester. Led by groups in the Sloan School of Management, MIT, and the London School of Economics, numerous management simulators have been developed in conjunction with business corporations, e.g. People Express Airline Management Flight Simulator, B&B Enterprises Management Flight Simulator (Lane, 1995); Index Computer Company Microworld, Hanover Insurance's Claims Learning Laboratory (Senge, 1990); Mobile Phone Subscriber Microworld, Professional Services Microworld (Romme, 2002).

How does learning take place in a management simulator? The theory is that a participant learns from 'virtual' experience—experience that, while less authentic than firsthand experience, has peculiar advantages over many real life situations. Senge (1990) explains that "learning by

Figure 3

A real world action learning cycle (action, evaluation, reflection, decision) and a shunt in which simulated action substitutes for real evaluation. Bold terms are those of the action model, Figure 2.

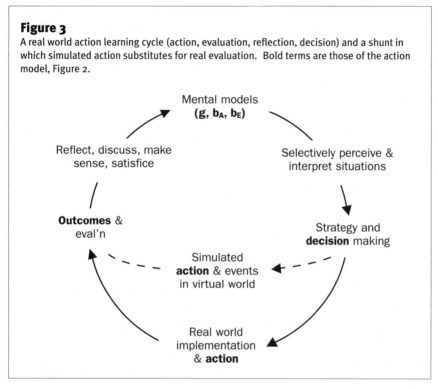

doing" only works so long as the feedback from our actions is rapid and unambiguous and this is often not the case. When we act in a complex system the consequences are often neither immediate nor unambiguous, but are removed from us in time or space. This leads to what he calls the dilemma of learning from experience: "we learn best from experience, but we never experience the consequences of our most important decisions." The rationale for management simulators is that 'virtual worlds' are created,

> ...learning environments where time can be slowed down or speeded up, complexity can be simplified, irreversible actions made reversible, and the risks of experimentation eliminated (Isaacs and Senge, 1992).

The processes in which learning takes place are represented in Figure 3, adapted from Isaacs and Senge (1992). In the real world, learning by experience takes place as actions are evaluated and mental models updated through processes of reflection, discussion, sensemaking, and satisfying. This new learning modifies subsequent perception and the interpretation of situations and the decisions and action that follow. Terms in bold text comprise the action model of Figure 2. When a management simulator is available, real world action, which can be slow, expensive, and risky, can be by-passed for purposes of learning, without changing the concepts in the cycle. Because of the reduced authenticity, I think this learning better qualifies as 'sensemaking,' i.e. as the generation of prototypes of new beliefs/mental models, which can be tested by action in the real world. This view seems to be supported researchers in virtual reality.

Virtual reality is not "real," but it

has a relationship to the real. By being betwixt and between, it becomes a play space for thinking about the real world. It is an exemplary evocative object. When a technology becomes an evocative object, old questions are raised in new contexts and there is an opportunity for fresh resolutions (Turkle, 1997).

The key feature of a simulator designed to aid management learning is its verisimilitude—its realistic mapping to the real world (Lane, 1995). Because of the complexity needed to achieve this, there is generally a need for a briefing session before the simulation and a debriefing session afterwards "which helps participants to reflect on their actions during the experience so as to derive the most learning from it" (Lane, 1995). One of the explanations for the demise of the 'first coming' of business simulations was poor facilitation, with the result that simulations were often run carelessly, merely for entertainment (Lane, 1995).

In principle, scientific support for agents' sensemaking entails facilitation of discovery learning of new concepts that lead to modifying beliefs/frames/mental models to varying degrees. Associated with this is 'paying attention' to new cues in the environment rather than acting on the taken-for-granted belief about the situation. The key tool for both such interventions is the computer simulation model.

Challenges. Although this intervention approach has an impressive track record, one of the harsh realities for management consultants has been that business managers are often reluctant to change their beliefs about the environment, their actions, or their goals—to change their mental models—in spite of management situations becoming problematic to a degree where change seems warranted to consultants. A great deal of attention has been given to methods for stimulating, in conditions suitable for inquiry and exploration, reflection that prompts learning rather than the defense of existing beliefs. A prominent business/organizational consulting approach, Action Science, is largely committed to this single activity (Argyris et al., 1986). Informed by the experience of action science, Isaacs and Senge (1992) interpret limitations they experience in using management simulators. Even with the advantages afforded by this approach …there are difficulties in the ways

Figure 4
Characteristics of management modes of Senge(1990) ──▶ Indicates direction of pragmatic preference.

Management modes	Characteristics
'Reactive' management	Manager in 'natural' attitude. Situation unproblematic. Manager not receptive to 'support.'
'Responsive' management	Manager in 'exploratory' attitude. Sensemaking ──▶ change of beliefs/mental models via 'experience.'
'Generative' management	Manager in 'theoretical' attitude. Learns system structure & function. Mental model change due to internalization of conceptual model.

human beings move from new understandings to new behavior. These difficulties are greatest when new understandings produce insights into the counter productivity of basic assumptions and values. Thus, even if computer-based learning environments can illuminate systemic factors, which confound learning, this will not guarantee that new policies will be recognized or implemented (Isaacs and Senge, 1992).

A common expression of this phenomenon is the selective use of simulation results by participants to reinforce their existing beliefs. These authors suggest adoption of action science methods for 'surfacing' tacit beliefs to enable their discussion as part of the encompassing facilitation methodology in which the management simulator sits.

In his best-selling management book *The Fifth Discipline* (Senge, 1990) distinguishes among three cognitive modes managers can use to interpret situations: *reactive* to events, *responsive* to behavior patterns, and *generative,* utilizing knowledge of systemic structure. The phenomenological account of Schutz identifies the first as characteristic of routine, unproblematic activity in the 'natural attitude' of everyday living and working. But management consultants in advanced capitalism tend to see this state as a liability in an environment that is fiercely competitive and rapidly changing. It is taken as 'the problem' and consultants intervene to move clients to more active cognitive levels. Senge (1990) strongly advocates the generative mode, which utilizes formal knowledge of the structure of E, because it is the "most powerful," but acknowledges that it is the least common.

In Figure 4, Senge's three management modes are used in constructing a framework to aid thinking about model-based intervention in farm management. This discussion is partly speculative and partly reflects experience over the past 12 years in the FARMSCAPE (Farmers', Advisers', Researchers' Monitoring, Simulation, Communication, And Performance Evaluation) project. FARMSCAPE is the only substantial case in agriculture of the use of a management simulator in a methodically constructed learning environment for farmers of which I am aware, and progress reports can be found in Carberry et al., (2002) and Hochman et al., (2000). (Analysis of the FARMSCAPE experience using the theory covered in the present essay is presently being finalized.)

A particular management mode refers to behavior pertaining to a specific problematic area or issue, rather than to a manager's approach to practice generally. I have assigned 'attitudes' to each management mode that characterizes behavior; 'natural' and 'scientific' were used by Schutz and Luckman (1973). The arrow emphasizes that managers move away from habitual practice in the familiar situation only as little as possible but as often and as far as is warranted by a problematic situation. Once the needed learning is achieved, it grounds a new habitual practice in an increasingly familiar situation allowing a return to a *reactive* management mode.

Figure 5 brings a number of typologies of activity in scientists' life-worlds together with Senge's typology of management cognitive modes. Oquist (1978) ordered the four types of research in the first column and is based on the logic that each type 'above' presumes the content of those 'below.' However, as discussed later, this is not the case regarding the relationship between action research and policy research. The first two types of systems thinking of Jackson (2000) (depicted earlier in Figure 1) align well with Oquist's research types, as do the sub-categories of 'problem solving. In the manager's life-world, as shown earlier by the phenomenological account of practice, there is no opportunity for intervention in the *reactive*

Figure 5

A synthesis of typologies of behaviors of scientists and managers that shows both congruence of concepts (horizontal alignment) and incongruence of pragmatic motives in their respective life-words (arrows in opposite directions, with direction indicating increasing pragmatism under 'normal' conditions and frequency in the science community)

Typology of research Oquist (1978)	Typology of systems thinking Jackson (2000)	Management intervention modes	Cognitive representation level	Implications for management	Management modes Senge (1990)
Action research			World model	· Farmer in 'natural attitude.' · Situation unproblematic · Farmer not receptive to 'support.'	'Reactive' management (in 'natural attitude')
	'Soft' systems	Model aided 'sensemaking' as virtual situated experience	Frame/scheme, script	Simulation enhanced 'experimentation', sensemaking, & change of beliefs via experience of 'virtual' history.	'Responsive' Management (in 'exploratory attitude')
Policy research	Systems thinking for 'problem solving'	Most decision support systems		Mainly normative recommendations for action	
	'Hard' systems	Model aided sense-making as insights to structure	Mental model	· Model-aided farmer learning about system structure & function. · Mental model change due to internalization of scientists' model.	'Generative' Management (in 'theoretical' attitude)
Nomothetic research	Systems thinking in the disciplines				
Descriptive research					

Manager's life-world

Scientist's life-world

mode of normal, everyday farm management, when the farmer is "traveling well enough," or at least feels like this is the case. Action can be taken without deliberation, under the overall control of a cognitive 'world model.'

Invitation to join in scientists and other farmers regarding potentially problematic, or unresolved, issues can prompt an 'exploratory attitude' in which a farmer takes interest in using the simulator to explore. As reported by Carberry (2002), some participants accrue 'virtual experience' which influences their subsequent management. During the inquiry, a few farmers find in the discussions a particular scientific concept to be a more useful mental model than one they held in the past, and can be considered to temporarily adopt a 'scientific attitude.' This better equips them for management that is more *generative* of solutions and innovations until a new unproblematic situation is created.

'Some decision support systems' appears in the column headed 'Management Intervention Modes.' It is often reported that farmers have ceased using a decision support system because they learn how to do what it enabled without continued use of the decision support system. Since such software is designed to be a tool in decision-making rather than to aid learning, any contribution to changing mental models is incidental. But these reports have led to the suggestion that this desirable result could be enhanced if the products were designed for this purpose.

The horizontal dashed line in mid-Figure 5 significantly indicates the demarcation of objectivist and subjectivist approaches—'hard' below and 'soft' above. Not surprisingly, the scientists' life-world 'territory' is dominated by 'the objective' and that of managers' by 'the subjective'. The central point of Figure 5 is that, based on theory, the prospects for successful scientific decision support for farmer's decision making are much lower than

those commonly entertained, or at least once entertained, in agricultural RD&E circles. The vertical arrows indicate direction of preferred mode of practice by managers and scientists respectively. Managers will move away from 'automatic,' reactive management to the degree that is required by the situation. They are much more prepared to explore action possibilities than to learn via new theory. Scientists on the other hand, generally prefer working in their discipline, but systems researchers are prepared to apply their knowledge and tools to Oquist's policy research (policy to guide *managers'* actions, rather than the government's). This has most often been in the form of design of best farming practice and decision support for stereotypic decisions, but, in general, farmers ignore this normative approach. Very few scientists have attempted to engage in action research, as per Figure 3, where the scientist's hard tools provide new possibilities for farmers' 'experiential' learning (e.g. Carberry, 2002). This indication that the preferences/interests of farmers and scientists lie in opposite directions will surprise few farmers or scientists, but it does provide an explanatory framework as a substitute for blame.

Explanation in terms of 'attitudes' of scientists who take their models into 'the wild' to engage farmers on relevant management matters is less well developed. Such activity will not be done in the 'natural attitude' until organizations formally reward it to a degree that makes it driven by scientists' pragmatic motive or it becomes successfully commercialized. Until then, participating scientists probably have an 'exploratory' attitude and, a few, a 'theoretical attitude.' It has become clear that scientists with both the intimate knowledge of the models needed for competent mimicking of farming and the skill in conducting compelling discussions are as yet rare. But it remains to be seen if large numbers will be needed and, if they are, if they can be produced cost-effectively.

The issues of ecological sustainability of farming and of off-farm ecological effects raise radically different and challenging decision making issues. Does this theory of decision-making and of intervention apply when the boundaries of farm decision making are shifted?

Implications for Intervention in Farmers' Decisions

One of the central unresolved (and perhaps irresolvable) issues in social science concerns the degree of the control of human behavior by constraining structures of the world, both natural and social on the one hand, and by the driver of human agency, free will on the other (Giddens, 1979). In this essay I have used Lewin's model of behavior, $B = f(P, E)$, to organize theories of structural determination. Various decision making and intervention theories have featured either constraints of the external environment, E, or of the internal environment, P. As an opposing model for agentive control of behavior, I have proposed an action-oriented model of decision-making (Figure 2).

Although I emphasized the limitations of the structural model's 'one eyed' view, I have waited until now to acknowledge that this 'action' model is equally one-eyed in that it ignores the very real, but partial, structural determinism that we all experience. But this omission seems justified in the context of the challenge of inventing effective intervention practice when acceptance of intervention is entirely voluntary. Creating a market for decision support in family farming depends on creating value where, as Arie de Geus says in an earlier quote, "People…embracing the responsibility of their life…trust only their own understanding of their world as the basis for their actions." But when system boundaries change to include not only decision and action being influenced by the external environment, but decision and action substantively *influencing* the

quality of the environment of others, the inadequacies of a purely agentive model of intervention stand out.

In terminating the review of 14 decision support systems, McCown (2002b) concluded that although the record of performance of the decision support system fell far short of expectations, there were reasons to expect a 'future' for some members of four categories of software for supporting farmers' decision making: (1) 'small,' technical calculators; (2) aids for recording conduct of environmental 'best practice'; (3) flexible simulators for system analysis by a consultant; and (4) flexible simulators in providing a learning environment for farmers. The second and fourth of these seem relevant to providing support for farmers on environmental matters, but in quite contrasting ways.

Support systems in the second category seem useful in the context of environmental regulations, which many farmers are facing or will face. Intervention with software that first supports 'best practice,' and then documents it, is support in the traditional knowledge transfer paradigm. In an example supplied by Hearn and Bange (2002), Australian cotton farmers are highly motivated to avoid negative political implications of environmentally damaging pesticide application. Documented adherence to best practice is enhanced by a prescriptive use of a 'hard' decision support system to determine a practice (B) and the keeping of similarly objective records of action actually taken.

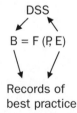

DSS

$$B = F(P, E)$$

Records of best practice

In a formal sense, farmers have not lost agency in this case because the conforming action is entirely voluntary. But the considerable influence on behavior of social pressures to conform and the risk of mandatory practices in the future amounts to an *effective* loss of agency.

Nevertheless, farming in advanced capitalism is predominantly a business, and for farmers acting in their life-worlds in the 'natural attitude,' their primary 'pragmatic motive' can be expected to be directed toward profit taking and wealth creation. However, to the degree that environmental issues become problematic in the farmer's life-world, attention can be expected to shift and new sensemaking take place. But the occasion for this new sensemaking is created by what makes the situation problematic. Candidates for this stimulus include visible negative effect on production, imposed legislative or social penalties, and interventions that raise consciousness of the potential to become problematic.

As is the case in most Western democracies, Australian governments are reluctant to impose environmental regulations on farmers. Although the threat to do so is a 'stick,' which is not all that well hidden, the preference is for voluntary changes. What might be the role for an action-oriented intervention to support farmers' sensemaking in these circumstances? Depending on the competence of the simulator, three classes of relevant interactions could be explored.

1. Time trends of detrimental effects of prevalent practices on politically sensitive aspects of the environment in relation to alternative practices, providing an opportunity for farmers to test their beliefs about their actions in relation to the environment.

2. The comparative profitabilities of production options within new boundaries of E 'imposed' by environmental political pressures.

3. The comparative profitabilities of production options when combined with provision of newly remunerated 'landscape services' such as clean water and, possibly, enriched biodiversity.

In 1 and 3, the simulator must be able to deal competently with effects of actions on the environment, whereas in 2, the requirements for the simulator remain those needed for simulating production in response to the environment.

Intervention of this nature is only embryonic. The FARMSCAPE team has only recently turned attention to production systems with the added dimension of environmental goals. A sobering early finding was that farmers who had demonstrated for some time a high degree of confidence in the simulator for exploring management possibilities in terms of production risk and profitability were quick to challenge the competence of the simulator when unwelcome outputs regarding the environment were produced. When the most profitable rotation produced the highest quantity of potentially hazardous deep drainage, the response tended to be, "This is only a model, and how do we know if it is telling the truth on drainage."

In summary, the environmental challenge to farming is, in many places stark, and farmers *need* for support in bringing about change in decisions and actions is often clear. However, in light of the history of the decision support system and the dramatic progress in naturalistic decision theory, any strategy based on technical extension of traditional decision support system technology seems extraordinarily heroic, if not doomed to failure. If decision support systems, which targeted farmers' primary concerns have been largely ignored by farmers, why would farmers use decision support systems that target environmental matters of, generally, only secondary importance to them? And when the situation is made problematic by environmental legislation, a decision support system may be seen to be an inefficient route to the achievement of compliance.

Use of the action-oriented intervention

paradigm has produced significant developments in effective intervention in farm *production* matters over the past decade. Although in FARMSCAPE we have done no more than pilot this new intervention paradigm in *environmental* matters, we expect that the results should be a source of encouragement to those who expect that model-based learning facilitation might be preferable to coercion as a way to influence farmers on environmental matters.

Concluding Remarks

The time has passed when decision support systems could be assumed to be the means by which results of research on matters of farm management would be 'communicated' to farmers. The evidence is overwhelming that, in the main, the decision support system for farmers is an inadequate idea. But to prevent the 'baby from being thrown out with the bath,' greater discrimination among products and approaches, as attempted in the four types of decision support of McCown (2002b), must be made. This essay has featured the dichotomy between products, which provide models applied to stereotypic problems and a mediated process in which scientists with flexible simulators facilitate farmer learning. I have attempted to show that there is a great body of convincing argument and some evidence that the mediated process more realistically accommodates the nature of farmers' cognitive behavior related to decision making. But the challenges to the cost-effective delivery of support in this mode create a dilemma. Mass delivery of a decision support system is highly feasible, but generally of low value. The mediated process is of generally of high value, but does not lend itself to mass delivery. Research on how to alleviate this bottleneck through training and accreditation of mediators and internet meetings is being conducted (Hargreaves et al., 2004; Carberry et al., 2002; McCown et al., 2002). Much work

remains to resolve this dilemma and opinions are divided as to which point of the dichotomy is the prudent starting point. I hope I have conveyed my belief that, although there are 'horses for courses,' the great relatively untried, opportunity lies in the new intervention paradigm I have advocated. While this paradigm is complementary to, rather than exclusive of, the traditional paradigm, 'making space' for it in our profession entails a battle for scientists' minds. I want to leave the 'last word' in this excursion to the anthropologist, Norman Long, who spent most of his career on the battlefield of ideas pertaining to intervention in farmers' life-worlds.

> It would appear then that as long as we conceptualize the issues of knowledge processes in terms of information transfer without giving sufficient attention to the creation and transformation of meaning at the point of intersection between different actors' life-worlds, and without analyzing the social interactions involved, we shall have missed the significance of knowledge itself. Therefore engineering the creation of the conditions under which a single knowledge system (involving mutually beneficial exchanges inflows of information between the different actors) could emerge—the main goal of knowledge management intervention—seems unattainable…(Long and Long, 1992).

Acknowledgements

My thanks to John Williams for encouragement and helpful advice on how to help readers keep their orientation in my extended and tortuous argumentation.

References Cited

Ackoff, R.L. 1979. The future of operational research is past. Journal of Operational Research 30:93-104.

Anonymous. 2000. History of the organization of work: Industrial psychology, Britannica© CD. 1994-1998. Encyclopædia Britannica, Inc.

Argyris, C., R. Putnam, and D.M. Smith. 1986. Action Science. Jossey-Bass, San Francisco, California.

Beach, L. and R. Lipshitz. 1995. Why classical decision theory is an inappropriate standard for evaluating and aiding most human decision-making. Pp. 21-35. *In:* Decision Making in Action: Models and Methods. G.A. Klein. J. Orasanu, R. Calderwood, and C.E. Zsambok (eds.) Aablex Publishing Corpor-ation, Norwood, New Jersey.

Blumer, H. 1969. Symbolic interactionism: Perspective and method. Prentice Hall, Englewood Cliffs, New Jersey.

Brehmer, B. 1990. Strategies in real-time decision-making. Pp. 262-279. *In: Insights in decision-making: A tribute to Hillel J. Einhorn.* R. Hogarth (ed.), University Chicago Press, Chicago, Illinois.

Bruner, J.S. 1990. Acts of meaning. Harvard University Press, Cambridge, Massachusetts.

Burrell, G. and G. Morgan. 1979. Sociological paradigms and organizational analysis. Heinemann, London, England.

Carberry, P., Z. Hochman, R. McCown, N. Dalgliesh, M. Foale, P. Poulton, J. Hargreaves, D. Hargreaves, S. Cawthray, N. Hillcoat, and M. Robertson. 2002. The FARMSCAPE approach to decision support: Farmers', advisers', researchers' monitoring, simulation, communi-cation, and performance evaluation. Agricultural Systems 74:141-178.

Checkland, P. 1981. Systems thinking, systems practice. John Wiley and Son, Hoboken, New Jersey.

Clancey, W. 1997. Situated cognition: On human knowledge and computer representations. Cambridge University Press, Cambridge, Massachusetts.

de Geus, A.P. 1994. Modeling to predict or to learn? Pp. xiii-xxii. *In:* Modeling for Learning Organizations. J.D.W. Morecroft and J.D. Sterman (eds.) Producti-vity Press, Portland, Oregon.

de Mey, M. 1982. The cognitive paradigm: An integrated understanding of scientific development. University of Chicago Press, Chicago, Illinois.

Dent, J. and J. Anderson. 1971. Systems analysis in agricultural management. John Wiley & Sons, Sydney, Australia.

Dreyfus, H. 1972. What computers can't do: A critique of arti-ficial reason. Harper and Row, New York, New York.

Dreyfus, H. 1994. What computers still can't do: A critique of artificial reason. The MIT Press, Cambridge, Masschusetts.

Dreyfus, H.L. and S.E. Dreyfus. 1986. Mind over machine: The power of human intuition and expertise in the era of the computer. Free Press, New York, New York.

Gentner, D. and A.L. Stevens. 1983. Mental models. L. Erlbaum Associates, Hillsdale, New Jersey.

Giddens, A. 1979. Central problems in social theory: Action, structure, and contradiction in social analysis. University of California Press, Berkeley, California.

Goldman, A.I. 1986. Epistemology and cognition, Harvard University Press, Cambridge, Massachusetts.

Hargreaves, D.M., S. Kethers, M. Brereton, R.L. McCown, Z. Hochman, and P.S. Carberry. 2004. FARMSCAPE online: Participatory design of Internet meetings with farmers. Vol II. Proceedings of the Participatory Design Conference 2004, Toronto, Canada.

Hearn, A. and M. Bange. 2002. SIRATAC and *CottonLOGIC*: Persevering with DSSs in the Australian cotton industry. Agricultural Systems 74:27-56.

Hochman, Z., J. Coutts, P. Carberry, and R. McCown. 2000. The FARMSCAPE experience: Simulations aid partici-pative learning in risky farming systems in Australia. Pp. 175-188. *In:* Cow up a tree: Learning and knowing processes for change in agriculture. Case Studies from industrialised countries. M. Cerf, D. Gibbon, B. Hubert, R. Ison, J. Jiggins, M.S. Paine, J. Proost, and N. Roling (eds.) INRA Editions, Versailles Cedex, France.

Hutton, R.F. 1965. Operations research techniques in farm management: Survey and appraisal. Journal of Farm Economics 47:1400-1414.

Issacs, W. and P. Senge. 1992. Overcoming limits to learning in computer-based learning environments. European Journal of Operational Research 59:183-196.

Jackson, M. 2000. Systems approaches to management. Kluwer Academic Publishers, New York, New York.

Johnson-Laird, P.N. 1987. Mental models. Harvard University Press, Cambridge, Massachusetts.

Keen, P. 1987. Decision support systems: The next decade. Decision Support Systems 3:253-265.

Keen, P. 1995. Decision support systems: The next decade. Decision support systems 3. Pp. 253-265. *In:* Companion to metaphysics. J. Kim and E. Sosa (eds.) Oxford, Basil Blackwell.

Keen, P. and C.B. Stabell. 1980. Series preface. *In:* Decision support systems: Current practice and continuing chal-lenges. S. Alter (ed.) Addison-Wesley Publishing, Reading, Massachusetts.

Kim, J. and E. Sosa. 1995. Husserl, Edmund. Companion to Metaphysics. Blackwell, Oxford, England.

Klein, G., J. Orasanu, and R.Z.C. Calderwood. 1995. Decision making in action: Models and methods. Ablex Publishing Corp, Norwood, New Jersey.

Kuhn, T. 1962. The structure of scientific revolutions. University of Chicago Press, Chicago, Illinois.

Lane, D. 1992. Modelling as learning: A consultancy method-ology for enhancing learning in management teams. European Journal of Operational Research 59:64-84.

Lane, D. 1995. On the resurgence of management simulations and games. Journal of the Operational Research 46:604-25.

Lave, J. and E. Wenger. 1991. Situated learning: Legitimate peripheral participation. Cambridge University Press, Cambridge, Massachusetts.

Lewin, K. 1951. Field theory in the social sciences. Harper and Row, New York, New York.

Lipschitz, R. 1995. Converging themes in the study of deci-sion making in realistic settings. Pp. 103-137. *In:* Decision making in action: Models and methods. G.A. Klein, J. Orasanu, R. Calderwood, and C.E. Zsambok (eds.) Aablex Publishing Corp, Norwood, New Jersey.

Little, J. 1970. Models and managers: The concept of a deci-sion calculus. Management Science. 16:B466-B485.

Long, N. and A. Long. 1992. Battlefields of knowledge: The interlocking of theory and practice in social research and development. Routledge, London.

Malcolm L. 1990. Fifty years of farm management in Australia: Survey and review. Review of Marketing and Agricultural Economics 58:24-55.

McCown, R.L. 2001. Learning to bridge the gap between scientific decision support and the practice of farming: Evolution in paradigms of model-based research and intervention from design to dialogue. Australian Journal of Agriculture Research 52:549-571.

McCown, R.L. 2002a. Locating agricultural decision support systems in the problematic history and socio-technical complexity of 'models for management'. Agricultural Systems 74:11-25.

McCown, R.L. 2002b. Changing systems for supporting farmers' decisions: Problems, paradigms, and prospects. Agricultural Systems 74:179-220.

McCown, R.L., B.A. Keating, P.S. Carberry, Z. Hochman, D. Hargreaves. 2002. The co-evolution of the Agricultural Production Systems Simulator (APSIM) and its use in Australian dryland cropping research and farm management intervention. Pp. 149-175. In: Agricultural systems models in field research and technology transfer. L.R. Ahuja, L. Ma, and T.A. Howell (eds.) Lewis Publishers, Boca Raton, Florida.

Maier, F.H. and A. Grobler. 2000. What are we talking about?—A taxonomy of computer simulations to support learning. Systems Dynamics Review 16:135-148.

Minsky, M. 1975. A framework for representing knowledge. In: The Psychology of Computer Vision. P. Winston (ed.) McGraw Hill, New York, New York.

Mooney, P. 1988. My own boss? Class, rationality, and the family farm. Westview, Boulder, Colorado.

Norman, D. 1983. Some observations on mental models. In: Mental models. D. Gentner and A.L. Stevens (eds.) Lawrence Erlbaum, Hillsdale, New Jersey.

Oquist, P. 1978. The epistemology of action research. Acta Sociologica 21:143-163.

Orasanu, J. and T. Connolly. 1995. The reinvention of decision-making. In: Decision making in action: Models and methods. G.A. Klein, J. Orasanu, R. Calderwood, and C.E. Zsambok (eds.) Ablex Publishing Corp, Norwood, New Jersey.

Peacock, W. 1980. SIRATAC: Management system for cotton. Agricultue Gazette Sydney, New South Wales, Department of Agriculture 91(4):7-10.

Polanyi, M. 1958. Personal knowledge: Towards a post-critical philosophy. University of Chicago Press, Chicago, Illinois.

Popper, K. 1964. The poverty of historicism. Harper Torch, New York, New York.

Popper, K. 1972. Objective knowledge: An evolutionary approach. Clarendon Press, Oxford, England.

Popper, K. 1976. The logic of the social sciences. In: The positivist dispute in German sociology. T.W. Adorno, H. Albert, R. Dahrendorf, J. Habemas, H. Pilot, and K.R. Popper (eds.) Heinemann, London, England.

Redman, D. 1991. Sir Karl Popper's philosophy of the social sciences: A disjointed whole. In: Economics and the Philosophy of Science. Oxford University Press, New York, New York.

Romme, A.G.L. 2002. Microworlds for management education and learning. http://www.unice.fr/sg/resources/articles/romme_2002_microworlds-management-ed-learning.pdf

Sawyer, R.K. 2002. Emergence in psychology: Lessons from the history of non-reductionist science. Human Development 45:2-28.

Schon, D. 1983. The reflective practioner: How professionals think in action. Basic Books, Philadelphia, Pennsylvania.

Schutz, A. and A. Luckman. 1973. The structures of the life-world (Vol. 1) (Studies in Phenomenology and Existential Philosophy). Northwestern University of Press, Evanston, Illinois.

Senge, P. 1990. The fifth discipline: The art and practice of the learning organization. Doubleday Currency, New York, New York.

Shafer, G. 1986. Savage revisited. Statistical Science 1:479

Simon, H. 1979. From substantive to procedural rationality. Pp. 65-86. In: Philosophy and economic theory. F. Hahn and M. Hollis (eds.) Oxford University Press, New York, New York.

Simon, H. 1996. The sciences of the artificial. 2nd ed., MIT Press, Cambridge, Massachusetts.

Starbuck, W. and F. Millikan. 1988. Executives' perceptual filters: What they notice and how they make sense. In: The executive effect: Concepts and methods for studying top managers. D.C. Habrick (ed.) JAI Press, Greenwich, Connecticut.

Turkle, S. 1997. Constructions and reconstructions of self in virtual reality: Playing in the MUDS. In: Culture of the Internet. S. Kiesler (ed.) Lawrence Erlbaum Associates, Mahwah, New Jersey. pp. 193.

Vennix, J. 1990. Mental models and computer models: Design and evaluation of a computer-based learning environment for policy-making. JAM Vennix, Beuningen, The Netherlands.

Weick, K. 1995. Sensemaking in organizations. Sage, Thousand Oaks, California.

Weick, K. and D. Meader. 1993 Sensemaking and group support systems. Pp. 230-252. In: Group support systems: New perspectives. L.M. Jessup and J.S. Valecich (eds.) Macmillan, New York, New York.

Winograd, T. and F. Flores. 1986. Understanding computers and cognition: A new foundation for design. Ablex Publishing Corporation, Norwood, New Jersey.

Yates, F.J. 2001. Forum on naturalistic decision-making. Journal of Behavioral Decision Making 14:329.

Zadoks, J. 1989. EPIPRE, A computer-based decision support system for pest and disease control in wheat: Its development and implementation in Europe. Pp. 3-29. In: Resistance and management. K.J. Leonard and W.E. Fry (eds.), Plant Disease Epidemiology Vol 2: Genetics. McGraw-Hill, New York, New York.

Getting Technical Information into Watershed Decision-Making

CHAPTER 3

W. Allen and M. Kilvington

Given the complexity and diverse social perspectives surrounding many watershed-scale resource management issues, the challenge facing science is how, where, and when can it best contribute to developing the understanding that will support more sustainable decision-making. This chapter introduces a collaborative learning approach to improve the use of information within environmental research initiatives. It illustrates this approach as a knowledge management cycle that helps different stakeholders access and integrate information more effectively, and ultimately changes how they see a situation and consequently go about managing it. It then looks at a similar cycle of science activities, but casts them into an interdisciplinary approach. Both cycles use examples drawn from resource management case studies in New Zealand. Focus is given to a key component of these cycles—that of improving learning, particularly in getting people to challenge their underlying assumptions. To achieve this it is suggested that interdisciplinary science teams need to broaden their membership to include specialists with integrative social skills.

Changing context for management

Over the past two decades, the challenges facing landowners and natural resource managers have multiplied. Where once rural agricultural and horticultural environments were viewed as single-sector-oriented productive landscapes, they now face the pressures of demands by new players who expect to be heard—for instance those interested in voicing their views on landscape, recreation, conservation, and/or tourism. Furthermore, a growing interest in developing policy to support sustainable development operates at a range of scales intersecting with decisions made at grass-roots, local, regional and national levels. While landowners may make the ultimate decisions "on-the-ground," others play an active role in creating the context (positive or negative) that guides sustainable development efforts. Only a decade ago, scientists working in most rural environments were at least confident in the knowledge they were dealing with what everyone knew was an agricultural system. Today, whether rural landscapes should be regarded as agricultural, tourism, recreation, conservation or even cultural systems—or some combination of all these—is increasingly problematic and contentious.

In response to these issues we are beginning to see the increased use of multi-stakeholder processes that facilitate the wide involvement of people in problem solving and decision making with respect to issues and plans that involve or impact on them. This multi-stakeholder approach anticipates that natural resource management is increasingly characterised by apparently conflicting social perspectives, and emphasises processes to provide those involved with a better understanding of other points of view. These approaches explicitly recognise that natural resource management in the age of sustainability is not characterised so much by problems for which an answer must be found, but rather by issues that need to be resolved and will inevitably require one or more of the parties to change their views (Bawden et al., 1984). However, in the main, the application of these more inclusive approaches within agricultural research and development still fail to grasp the nature of the rapidly evolving social forces that are driving rural systems today. There are few references in the agricultural research and development literature to participatory projects other than those that involve two main groups (farmers and scientists) dealing with agricultural management issues. Yet as communities and agriculture change, the juxtaposition of farming and other rural activities has become a battleground over water and related nutrient management issues, as well as other community impacts of changing land use (Abdalla and Kelsey, 1996).

Despite the important role which science can play within natural resource management, researchers need to be aware that ecological information is only one factor affecting the way in which decisions on natural resource management are made—and it is not always the most significant. Other factors include political judgement, legal or financial necessity, personal or group bias, and commercial or international pressures. While science has, in the past, derived much of its power from its independence, in contested areas this strength is also its weakness. To make a difference in real-world problems research teams must work closely with those who have the power to change practices on the ground, developing what Pretty (1988) calls "interdependent relationships" with key stakeholders involved in the problem situation. When information or knowledge-based systems are developed in conjunction with end-user groups, the technology is often more innovatively designed

around social, economic, or cultural values and needs, and may acquire a sense of ownership by groups such as community, agency, land manager or indigenous groups (Reynolds and Busby, 1996; Harmsworth, 1998). For this to happen science must be developed and integrated within the wider decision-making contexts of the organisations and groups involved in natural resource management.

In response to this there has been an increasing number of science programmes in the natural resource management area that are being developed through collaborative or social learning approaches in conjunction with different stakeholders. To be successful, the science in these programmes needs to be broadened from the conventional view of research, *i.e.* proceeding along a straight line, commencing with a hypothesis, seeking out facts that prove or disprove this, and finally pulling out conclusions, which may then be displayed in a model or published in a paper (Wadsworth, 1998). This broadened view of science (Figure 1) will include a number of questions, common to collaborative learning inquiries in other areas. These relate to the development of the hypotheses themselves, and the subsequent implementation of the resulting "new ideas"—to ensure that science is better placed to make a difference on-the-ground.

There are many scientists, and science programmes, that are adopting this wider view of research. Increasingly researchers and practitioners are sharing theories and methods that demystify science and follow collaborative problem solving and dispute-resolution principles such as inclusion, cultural sensitivity, developing shared definitions, and empowering end-users. However, because the collaborative learning component remains largely hidden in conventional research proposals and published conclusions, its application in design and practice can often be less rigorously reviewed than the design and practice of

Figure 1

Steps within the wider research process showing relationship between collaborative-learning-based and conventional research (Adapted from Wadsworth 1998).

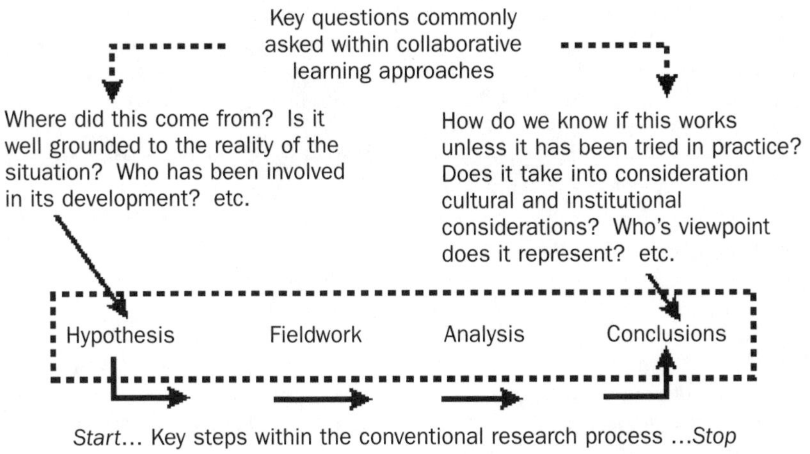

Key questions commonly asked within collaborative learning approaches

Where did this come from? Is it well grounded to the reality of the situation? Who has been involved in its development? etc.

How do we know if this works unless it has been tried in practice? Does it take into consideration cultural and institutional considerations? Who's viewpoint does it represent? etc.

Hypothesis   Fieldwork   Analysis   Conclusions

Start... Key steps within the conventional research process *...Stop*

other research steps. Accordingly, if the science community wishes to ensure the relevance and rigour of collaborative research initiatives within multi-stakeholder situations, then it needs also to overtly use review or evaluation approaches that ensure that programmes are examined within this broader context.

Collaborative (or social) learning, then, is one approach that makes its primary objective changing resource management practice by improving the use of information by different groups. It is best used when seeking to improve environmental management situations characterised by multiple social perspectives (Allen et al., 2001a). In general terms, collaborative learning refers to the capacity of a group to assess the results of their efforts, rethink how they go about their tasks, and use new ideas to change established practices (e.g. Huber, 1991). Underpinning the concept is the recognition that people learn through active adaptation of their existing knowledge in response to their experiences with other people and their environment.

In pursuit of a collaborative learning research program

Just gaining acceptance for this broader view of science within a traditionally structured research environment is no small feat. Moreover, implementation brings some additional challenges. Collaborative research requires the active participation of multiple-stakeholders already active in the problem context. The generation of information and active inquiry into its useful application can only take place through the living laboratory of the social system where resource management decisions are being made. However, effective collaboration is not always easy to arrange, especially in relation to environmental issues, which are often characterised by conflicting social perspectives.

One way of achieving this is to find a point where different groups of people (sectors and/or disciplines) agree on a common problem and work together to solve it. This might be by pooling different knowledge sources, sharing resources and skills, or each doing a different part of what needs to be done. However, a problem-solving system, in this sense, is more than just its resulting research components. Rather, it is a "social system" within which people learn by interaction to create new knowledge and broaden their perspective of the world (Ison, 1993).

Core to collaborative learning research programmes is the learning. Specifically, cyclical, reflective and inclusive processes of learning are needed to generate the connection between science and other information providers, and the appropriate decision makers in a watershed or region. Adaptive management, "learning-by-doing", and action research are all related cyclical-based learning approaches that offer methodological guidance to the management of contextual and problem-applied research programmes.

One promising initiative is in the area of adaptive management (AM) that is emerging through the integration of ecological and participatory research approaches (Lee, 1993; Gunderson et al., 1995; Bosch et al., 1996, Dovers and Mobbs, 1997; Christensen et al., 1996). Adaptive management in this sense refers 'to a structured process of "learning by doing" that involves much more than simply better ecological monitoring and response to unexpected management impacts' (Walters, 1997). Similarly, the process of learning by building on experience is a natural one for most people, and action research is gaining popularity as a framework for formalising and making this process more effective. As a number of reviewers point out, this learning consists of an iterative and cyclic approach with four major phases: plan, act, observe and reflect (Susman and Evered, 1978; Masters, 1995; Zuber-Skerritt, 1991). The underlying assumptions on which all these approaches rest is the existence of an experiential-based learning cycle (from Kolb et al., 1979) which suggests that people can learn and create knowledge: (a) on the basis of their con-

crete experience; (b) through observing and reflecting on that experience; (c) by forming abstract concepts and generalisations about what to do next; and (d) by testing the implications of these concepts in new situations, which will lead to new concrete experiences, and hence the beginning of a new cycle. This learning cycle is illustrated in Figure2.

Managing information and knowledge

The provision of timely and relevant information is obviously a key factor essential to improving learning. However, this is often difficult to achieve in natural resource management, where the wide range of stakeholders means that information is highly fragmented across groups. Access to such information can come from a range of sources. Science is a main contributor, but there is also a growing acknowledgement of the need to draw upon local and traditional knowledge systems. Formal monitoring of the results of management actions to confirm (or otherwise) their effectiveness is another key source of new information. However, to promote the sound use of information within a decision-making environment, a number of additional supporting social processes must also be provided. One approach is to view it as a learning cycle with some generic process steps required to support knowledge management. These steps are illustrated in Figure 2.

The skills required for managing this process will naturally vary according to the specifics of the initiative. For instance there is a substantial difference between pursuing a collaborative approach within an already well-functioning situation, and trying to initiate collaboration in a social environment characterised by existing conflict. In the latter case the need for effective facilitation and expert mediation of conflicts is definitely greater. This section of the chapter looks more closely at each of these steps in turn, paying particu-

Figure 2

Circles of learning. The inner circle illustrates an experiential learning or action research-based cycle (Kolb et al., 1979). The outer cycle shows similar steps in a knowledge management approach to collaborative science and stakeholder problem solving (from Allen et al., 2001a).

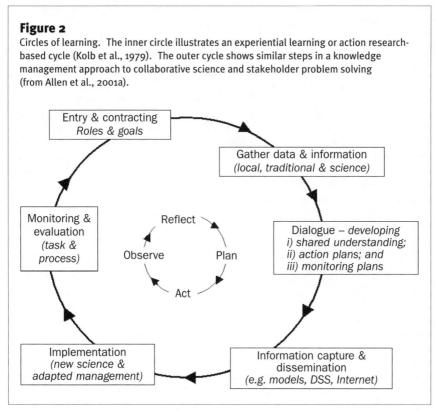

lar attention to issues of trust and relationships that may arise, and how these might be addressed.

Entry and contracting. This first phase includes identifying and involving relevant people, building relationships, and establishing the ground rules for working together. The aim in any successful participatory approach is to build relationships that make it easy for people to talk about their needs, share information, and work together. Stakeholders develop a common understanding of the perceived issue, and collectively decide on the project goals and the different roles that groups will undertake. Building this climate for change is the single most important step in initiating any collaborative approach.

Just as with personal relationships, previous experience is one of the most important influences on community attitudes to collaboration. People may be extremely reluctant to enter into a second participatory process if they have been involved in an unsuccessful one in the past— "we've already tried that and look what happened!" The emotional part of the conflict (which often forms a hidden barrier to uncovering the real issues) may have to be dealt with first.

Department of Conservation staff as part of their ongoing efforts to protect the black stilt (kaki), a rare New Zealand wading bird, provided a good example of how this challenge can be met. The agency was concerned that to gain better access to bird habitat on private land they had to increase private landholder involvement in recovery efforts. However, when landholders were canvassed to ascertain their support for a meeting to resolve these issues, it became apparent that they saw issues over the black stilt as symptoms of a wider problem of "lack of trust" between farming families and the Department of Conservation. In response, addressing the issue of access to the black stilt was postponed, and a series of workshops were held to improve relationships between local Department of Conservation staff and landholders (Allen et al., 1998). Common ground was reached during these workshops and a number of positive steps to improve working relationships were identified and implemented. Building trust in this way is one of the main reasons why successful participatory processes take time. Importantly, in this case, both parties regarded this exercise as being a first step in a much longer process.

Another major stumbling block in initiating collaborative approaches to environmental management is in identifying and gaining the active involvement of the right people within the process. This means time and resources must be allocated at the project level to achieve this, paying particular care to involve key stakeholders (e.g. farmers, local communities, women, industry) and groups with traditional or indigenous rights, who, in the past, have often been marginalised within the collective decision-making process. In New Zealand, the Treaty of Waitangi suggests that Māori are more than stakeholders. Rather they are in partnership with Government or local government.

However, gaining the involvement of key players is not always easy, and stakeholders may be unwilling to put time and resources into this initial phase of entry and contracting. In contrast to the black stilt project discussed above, the Whaingaroa Catchment Management Project (Kilvington, 1998) is an example of an attempt at establishing a collaborative environmental management initiative that was frustrated at the initial entry and contracting stage through a failure to address a fundamental conflict between key stakeholders. The intention of this project was to establish a working group of agency and community stakeholders to address issues such as erosion of the catchment and siltation of the harbour by generating a commonly agreed catchment management plan. Although the management rights of the indigenous community (tangata whenua) and their relationship with the local government environmental management agency were of primary concern to the tangata whenua, that issue was deemed a conflict outside the process of setting up a collaborative community and agency management group. This unresolved conflict resulted in a failure of participation of one of the key stakeholders to the detriment of the project as a whole.

Likewise, as Horn and Kilvington (2002) found, pest control operations can run into trouble when there is not enough time and effort invested in the early stages of a consultative process. Most institutions involved with pest control operations start consulting only after they have made a plan, so that the consultation process occurs only just before the implementation phase of an operation. The result is often a great deal of time spent dealing with conflict, which makes all concerned very uncomfortable. Greater investment at the early stages generates a great deal more benefit. The experiences of communicators involved in these processes shows us that if communities are involved in generating a plan rather than in just approving that plan, they will be more amenable to that plan being implemented both for the present project and for later projects. It takes a long time to generate a plan in this way but the time that it saves later in the process makes it worth the investment.

Other collaborative projects involving indigenous communities (Harmsworth, 2001) demonstrate the length of time required to build credible relationships and trust before entering into collaborative or participatory projects, and the need to build and maintain a solid platform for participation. Essential prerequisites when developing relationships with indigenous groups include respecting cultural protocols, following culturally appropriate steps, early identification of key players and viewpoints, and lengthy discussion of issues and work programmes through forums such as hui (participatory and culturally focused meetings).

This initial phase is also the stage at which ground rules for groups working together need to be established. This will minimise unnecessary "process" conflict caused by misunderstandings and lack of agreement on how the rules of dialogue and decision making are set. Intervention in conflict can occur at any stage, but is clearly much more likely to be effective when it is introduced early in a process of getting stakeholders to work together.

Gather data and information. Many groups possess information of a technical, cultural, or economic nature that is of great value for developing environmental solutions. However, the flow of this information between different levels and groups in society is often inadequate. For example, years of experimentation with different management strategies to achieve different goals have provided individual land managers with much knowledge about local land-use and environmental systems. Unfortunately, this knowledge is seldom available to the community on a collective basis. Similarly, much of the valuable knowledge accumulated by scientists is fragmented, held in different databases and, consequently, is not readily available, even to other scientists.

Often this information remains fragmented because we do not have the mechanisms to collect it. However, strong emotions associated with information also often create a barrier to its availability. Among science researchers much personal self-worth and commercial worth is linked to the information generated. Fear over misrepresentation affects researchers' willingness to offer their information for use in systems over which they have no future control. Many other stakeholders may have similar fears, with some justification, that their information might be used incorrectly, or against them, if released. In the broadest sense, information systems need to be designed to overcome such fears by building trust and confidence between information providers and users. In many cases, as the following examples show, this will need to be achieved through the development of clear guidelines or protocols for information use.

The implications for emerging research initiatives are well illustrated in the tussock grasslands of the South Island high country. Only a decade ago, research emphasis was directed towards improving the efficiency of an extensive pastoral system. Indeed, there are few references in the agricultural research and development literature internationally that refer to participatory approaches other than those that comment on farmers and scientists dealing with agricultural management issues (Allen, 1997). However, research funding today is increasingly directed towards addressing issues of sustainability, and hence meeting the needs of a range of different stakeholder groups concerned about the impact of natural resource management practices, who had for some time considered themselves in opposition to one another. When scientists in the Government-funded Tussock Grasslands Research Programme (Bosch, 1997) initially approached farmers about identifying proposed research sites to look at soil and vegetation trends, access was denied. Farmers were unsure about what use would be made of the subsequent research findings. However, because the project process was prepared to openly address this conflict, and bring in the appropriate skills, the situation was resolved. The subsequent conflict management exercise established information management protocols that enabled the research to proceed. These protocols protected the rights of landowners to be advised of research results prior to their being released to third parties, and provided for discussions by the different stakeholders involved of the implications of research results before publication (O.J.H. Bosch personal communication).

Conversely, in the Whaingaroa Catchment Management Project referred to previously, water quality data held by local landowners were withheld during the process of collecting and collating information on the catchment. The landowners were uncertain as to how this information might be interpreted by other members of the community. The use of conflict resolution skills and the development of clear, commonly agreed protocols for the use of this information would have allayed their concerns.

In participatory projects to develop information systems with indigenous groups (Harmsworth, 1998), the central focus of the research was how to build systems to record and store indigenous knowledge along with mainstream science knowledge, such as cultural heritage and natural resources, whilst protecting the confidentiality and sensitivity of information, maintaining cultural integrity, and acknowledging intellectual property rights. A number of useful models were produced which ranged from oral knowledge transfer to geographic information systems (GIS) and multi-media, where information was systematically organised and accorded degrees of protection to access using knowledge frameworks. These frameworks influenced the design of the information systems, and examples of GIS show that specific layers of confidential information can be protected and connected to other knowledge sources, such as people and organisations.

Dialogue: Making sense of information. Raw information needs to be understood and interpreted so that it becomes useful for addressing the issue under consideration. However, that information may have different meanings and hence values in different situations. Making sense of information has two principal components. First, all stakeholders must agree and clearly understand the intended use for the information. This may, for example, be to resolve a particular environmental problem or to attain a particular resource management goal.

The second component is the context within which the information was originally collected, which is a key to its strengths and weaknesses. This includes clarifying such issues as why the information was collected and by whom; what its source is (e.g. practical experience, observations, science research etc.); does the information relate to a specific situation or site and can it be extrapolated to other situations? Skilled facilitation is needed to ensure that all participants and stakeholders share a common understanding of these two components of new information.

Enormous gains can be made by promoting an understanding of what different stakeholders and other groups such as local land managers, or indigenous people, have to offer to the resolution of complex environmental problems. However, there is often an understandable reluctance on the part of agency and research staff to bring together factions where there is a risk, or perceived risk, of conflict. For example, staff in most, if not all, of the high country research initiatives that preceded the Tussock Grassland Programme have tended to work separately with Department of Conservation staff and local farming families, or solely with one or other group, largely to avoid having to deal with possible conflict. Yet, as these two groups collectively manage all the tussock grasslands in this area, and as one of the main land-use debates revolves around determining trade-offs and synergies between conservation and pastoralism, there is little doubt that both groups would have been better served by science had they been provided with more, well-facilitated opportunities to come together and discuss the implications of emerging research findings.

Similarly, stakeholder conflicts involving indigenous groups highlight the need for groups and researchers to have an in-depth cultural, political, and historical understanding before entering relationships, a commitment to focus on and resolve issues, and a desire to form partnerships. Generally when working with indigenous peoples it is essential to start discussions within a culturally safe and sometimes neutral environment, to identify potential conflicts early, and proceed sensitively with community dialogue processes and group interaction. A common New Zealand model, the "Treaty partnership model," is often used to illustrate the way indigenous peoples prefer to start dialogue in isolation of other stakeholder, government, or community groups until the timing for collaborative discussion is right. Indigenous groups often feel more comfortable discussing issues and research themes in their own environment first, such as on a marae (cultural and social meeting place) or a selected venue, before joining with other groups and researchers.

Once the right collaborative environment is established, the use, interpretation, and sharing of information and knowledge can then be discussed in the context of the issues being addressed. Collaborative working environments involving researchers, stakeholders, and tangata whenua are immensely valuable when in a context for addressing specific issues, because they provide forums which identify the present level of understanding, information availability, access, knowledge interpretation, new forms of knowledge, and information gaps and areas deficient in knowledge. The aggregation of shared knowledge between groups is pivotal to improved understanding of complex land-use and environmental systems, and greatly enhances the ability to make collective, informed, quality decisions relating to environmental, social, cultural, and economic issues.

An example of the ways in which trust can affect the ways in which information is used is provided by the information generated to support the widespread use of 1080 poison (sodium monofluoroacetate) for pest control operations in New Zealand. Agencies have tended to grapple with the science information about 1080 poison and develop plans without the input of other stakeholder groups. They then provide information to persuade the others that their plan is the right thing to do. The trouble is that where the information is provided primarily by one stakeholder to persuade others, the result has been blatant mistrust of that information, no matter how reliable and unbiased the provider believes it to be. Naturally, communities faced with the prospect of poison being dropped all over the local area are unhappy, and seek out information that might help them stop that happening. Interestingly in this situation, the pests are forgotten and the use of 1080 has become the central point of argument. This highlights a need to be clear about goals in the first place.

In comparison, sometimes agencies have gone into an area and reached agreement about killing pests (i.e. have been clear that their goal is to improve ecosystems by killing pests) and then asked the community to work with them to decide the best way to do it. In these situations the communities involved have been more open to the information that is provided and have been able to add their own perspectives into the plan. This means, for instance, that there are places where different techniques are used because people want some places to be safe for their dogs, or they want to protect their water supplies. The change in the process and the time of entry and contracting therefore can make a huge difference to the way in which information is used and the way in which groups trust each other's information.

When conflict erupts and is poorly handled it may be as damaging as conflict-avoidance. Bad experiences with former approaches may severely jeopardise the chances of building constructive future working relationships. This is often the case when working with indigenous groups, where bad experiences, previous conflict, and poorly developed initial approaches are very difficult to rectify. Managing successful community dialogue processes requires the creation and managing of safe environments for debate, including finding appropriate times, developing the right questions, and ensuring that the different scales and levels that stakeholders are operating on can be addressed. The worse the past experience a community has, the greater the time required to re-enter into some kind of collaborative working relationship.

Ongoing, and structured, community dialogue as described above provides those who participate in the process with immediate access to new ideas and perspectives, which may help them re-evaluate their current research, management, or policy strategies. There is still a need to capture, store, and provide this information for the benefit of those who did not have the opportunity to be directly involved. In this regard, the processes described above also provide the structured resources to support the development of a number of technologically based information components that are relevant to the needs of the wider community of potential users, and consequently more likely to gain their acceptance.

Information capture and dissemination. Using these collaborative approaches provides all those directly involved with a learning environment in which useful knowledge is developed through a participatory process. At the workshops, the participants clarify questions, sort information on the basis of its applicability to addressing these, and identify the starting points for all of the stakeholders and their consequent information needs. Essentially, this provides a way of understanding information relevant to the entire problem, and with this it is possible to develop an information management system so that the knowledge may benefit all those who have not had the opportunity to be directly involved.

The Internet is emerging as a useful platform for knowledge sharing, particularly for managing complex environmental information. A major strength of the Internet is that it allows people to create, annotate, link together and share information from a variety of media, including text, graphics, images, audio and video. Moreover, involving people in developing hypermedia-based systems, helps to promote collaborative learning and problem solving (Allen et al., 2001a). Not only are users of a system likely to have a greater commitment to one they have helped to develop, but also they are likely to have a greater understanding of any changes needed to make it work.

Implementation (new science and revised management). The idea, of course, is that by becoming involved in the process outlined above land managers and policy makers will get the support they need to develop new and improved strategies. Similarly, at any given time the information base can play an important role in helping land managers and scientists jointly to determine new research priorities. Because it acts as a framework to display existing knowledge, the information base helps identify knowledge gaps and prioritise new research initiatives. This is a continuing process, as evolving knowledge, technologies and value systems inevitably change our perceptions and provide new areas and issues for research (Stuth et al., 1991).

Monitoring and evaluation. Clearly, for such an information system to advance sustainable natural resource management successfully in the long term it needs to be continually refined and updated. It must also clearly define with end-users what the information needs are, and the form and context in which information and knowledge should be presented. Many of the issues already raised in this chapter will continually re-occur as the process continues. As new science emerges from the work of different groups and agencies, ways of ensuring its debate and dissemination will need to be renegotiated. As we seek to encourage the provision of new information from stakeholders (e.g. community-based monitoring systems), we will also have to provide the climate and assurances that such information will be used constructively to guide new ways forward— and not as a means of penalising the very people that are providing this information.

Participatory evaluation processes are particularly important in these kinds of long-term endeavours, not only to ensure that a project stays on track, but also to help reinforce to researchers and stakeholders alike that continued involvement is worthwhile (Allen, 1997; Kilvington, 1998). They are also essential for determining whether the project outcomes or the goals are being met and provide a dynamic mechanism for social, cultural and scientific interaction and evaluation. Tracking and acknowledging success can be combined with a number of other initiatives to avoid "burn-out" among the different participants and maintain enthusiasm and motivation.

Collaborative approaches should be flexible, and designed to grow. It may be appropriate to defer involvement of reluctant stakeholders in the beginning, and new stakeholders may be identified along the way. It is always important to consider the timing for bringing groups together and, as mentioned previously, it may be more culturally appropriate and progressive to work separately with some groups at the commencement of a project, with a view to building collaboration or participation as the project evolves. Overall the process must be able to change to accommodate this growth. Community involvement helps create ownership and a feeling of accomplishment in working together to solve a problem. This group dynamic will encourage others from the community and government agencies to participate and provide and manage the information required for making decisions about sustainable resource use.

Managing integrated and interdisciplinary initiatives

In trying to develop an approach to collaborative management, where science can make a valid contribution to enhanced understanding, it is impossible to go past the issue of interdisciplinarity. As multiple viewpoints impinge on complex environmental problems, so the usefulness of science knowledge generally requires the combination and integration of knowledge from various science disciplines (Van den Bessalaar and Heimericks, 2001). Multi-disciplinary approaches are more commonly attempted than interdisciplinary ones. These involve viewing the topic from a variety of disciplinary perspectives, but not examining the fundamental assumptions at the base of those perspectives, nor purposefully integrating knowledge from them into a novel interpretation. Interdisciplinary approaches include an explicit analysis of the underlying assumptions of each discipline, as the "facts" from any one area are critically evaluated in the light of the "facts" from the other disciplines (Randolph-Macon College n.d.).

Interdisciplinary research therefore requires different teams and skills to more conventional science. Minnis et al. (1994) point out that the core participants in a true collaboration "represent complementary domains of expertise." They plan, decide, and act jointly. They also think together, combining independent conceptual schemes to create original frameworks. They show commitment to sharing resources, power and talent, avoid the domination of single views, and vest authority for decisions in the group. The outcome of the collaborative endeavour reflects a blending of all contributions. This is no easy arrangement to set up or maintain and has significant implications for the manager of such an interdisciplinary-based initiative. Foremost the manager must carefully consider the composition of the team, the needs of the different members, and the unique management role required.

To draw together a team with diverse disciplinary backgrounds rests on developing a good collective sense of the whole at the same time as identifying the roles and contributions of the components. To function in a competitive research environment, interdisciplinary programmes must also address concerns of researchers trying to balance their need to progress within disciplines at the same time as investing in a collective enterprise. This will undoubtedly involve negotiations over intellectual property, authorship, and other cornerstones of science research careers. Furthermore to ensure that the integration and learning requisites for interdisciplinary and collaborative research take place, the programme needs to look beyond science research contributors in its team make up, and include skilled facilitators of multiparty learning processes.

Earlier we presented a cycle of steps (Figure 2) for developing knowledge through collaborative initiatives. In Figure 3 we reconsider these steps and present how different members of an interdisciplinary research team might manage them.

An interdisciplinary, collaborative learning research process clearly has too many roles to be filled by a generalist scientist. Each project or inquiry will be unique, but Figure 3 gives some sense of the range of skills that can be required. In this example, which is drawn from work carried out to help address the problem of an invasive weed in the South Island high country of New Zealand, members of the interdisciplinary initiative can be seen to comprise collaborative learning researchers, ecologists, researchers with skills in developing decision support systems, as well as farmers and conservation managers (Bosch et al., 1996; Allen et al., 2001b)

Because there are individuals from different disciplines, sectors, and even institutions involved in interdisciplinary projects, there are new challenges for those charged with nurturing and managing such initiatives. Perhaps one of the most visibly apparent challenges is that of building a common language. This needs to start with agreement of the problem or issue to be addressed. While this sounds easy, it is harder in practice. For example, while all parties may wish to restore a wetland in New Zealand, the ecologist in the group may wish to recreate a particular system that occurred say before colonisation. An indigenous Maori may wish to see the wetland restored in terms of cultural aspirations, which could include a focus on traditional uses such as weaving and food gathering.

Difficulties for learning-based approaches

The challenge for the interdisciplinary research leader lies in the fact that learning can be difficult, even at an individual level. Accepting new information that challenges the way we think and the things we do is, even with the best of wills, difficult to undertake, to accomplish, and to sustain (Michael, 1995). Finding out about problems also implies that we may have to act to correct them. What often stops us doing this is an anxiety, or the feeling, that if we allow ourselves to enter a learning or change process, if we admit to ourselves and others that something is wrong or not right, we will lose our effectiveness, our

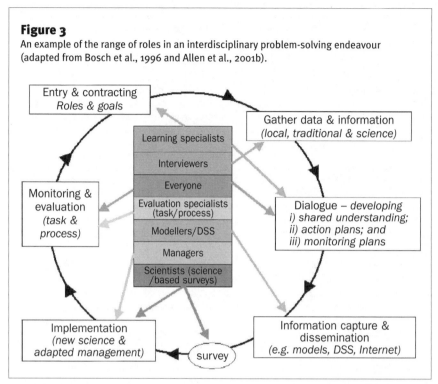

Figure 3

An example of the range of roles in an interdisciplinary problem-solving endeavour (adapted from Bosch et al., 1996 and Allen et al., 2001b).

esteem, and maybe even our identity. Most of us need to assume we are doing our best at all times, and it may prove a real loss of face to accept and even "embrace" errors. Adapting poorly or failing to realise our creative potential may be more desirable than risking failure and loss of esteem during the learning process (Allen and Kilvington, 1999).

Because of this, "learning, which mostly upsets beliefs and habits in individuals and organisations, is hardly likely to be embraced easily and enthusiastically, even though there is a growing, and sometimes powerful, recognition of the need for change" (Michael, 1995). Indeed, as Argyris et al. (1985) points out, individuals and organisations have a number of defensive reactions that resist change—or learning—by preventing open dialogue and the integration of new information that may challenge their existing world-views (values, assumptions, paradigms, etc.). These defenses include making some subjects "undiscussable", or an unawareness that their "espoused theory" —the world view and values people believe their behaviour is based on-is different to their "theory in use"—the worldviews and values implied by their behaviour (Argyris et al., 1985).

Accordingly, as these authors suggest, the first response to any inquiry into a mismatch between intention and outcome is likely to be the search for another strategy that will satisfy the "governing variables", the belief systems and values which the individual or organisation is trying to maintain. For example, if a land manager views his/her enterprise solely in terms of sheep production and notes that the vegetation condition of the land is deteriorating, the action strategy will likely be to try a different grazing regime. In such a case when new strategies are used to support the same governing variable (i.e. the land as a sheep production system) this is called single loop learning (Figure 4). A similar science example might arise in response to funder requirements for a scientist to be more participative. The response might be to find a "friendly" group of people to work with that are happy to acknowledge the scientist as the "unquestioned expert" —the governing variable.

However, another possibility is to change the governing variables themselves. For example, rather than try a new grazing strategy, the land manager may choose to initiate a more open form of enquiry. The associated action strategy might then be to look at how the enterprise could function as a tourism or forestry system for example. The scientist may choose to involve appropriate stakeholder groups in a more collaborative approach, changing the role of the scientist to one of a co-researcher and recognising that the role of "expert" is more a matter of perspective. These cases are called double-loop learning, and involve more fundamental shifts in people's belief systems and values. In this way they can often minimise the gap between espoused theory and theory-in-use.

Accordingly, Mezirow (1991; quoted in Bunning, 1995) draws attention to the need to address three elements through the reflective process: (a) content, the substantive issues involved; (b) process, how such issues were raised and addressed; and (c) premises, which are the values, assumptions, paradigms and whole framework of individual and collective mindsets, which inevitably influenced what was attended to and what was not, and other issues such as goals, process and interpretation.

Developing double-loop problem-solving approaches is thus a critical part of changing people's actions in respect to the environment. However, it also requires the action researcher to deal with the defenses of individuals and organisations—which is no small undertaking! In many cases this will mean having to address situations in which participants may feel embarrassed or threatened. However, as Grudens-Schuck (1998) points out, unless research and education programmes build specific processes

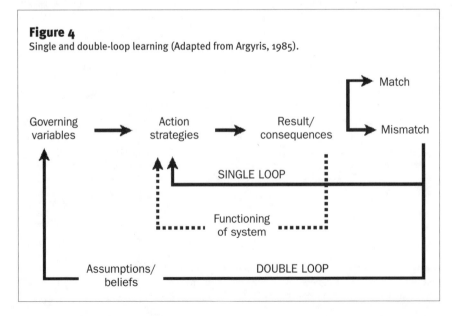

Figure 4
Single and double-loop learning (Adapted from Argyris, 1985).

for confronting people about unworkable theories and organisational defenses, the use of local knowledge and interpretations of events cannot be a sound foundation for collaborative learning and positive change.

Concluding comments

In the broadest sense, interdisciplinary research endeavours such as those described in this chapter are intended to improve efforts to share information by building trust and confidence between information providers and users. The aim is to help information providers and users work together to address important issues collaboratively. Under such a collaborative approach the guidelines and strategies developed by the stakeholders will draw on a larger base of information than that available to any one of the parties acting alone. Because these are developed against this richer information base, they are likely to result in more effective outcomes. The probability of commitment to, and adoption of, changed practices is also likely to be higher. Allotting appropriate time and skills to manage conflict and build relationships is an important component of planning projects if the aim is to help different stakeholders and indigenous groups share information and develop solutions to shared problems.

Finally, this chapter has identified some critical factors for ensuring the success of a collaborative learning approach to improve the use of technical information within natural resource management. They include:

■ Effective processes for building and maintaining trust.

■ The ability to communicate clearly and place problems and information in their wider context.

■ Time to develop a common context or language.

■ Cultural considerations and processes.

■ An appreciation that people do not learn easily and without effort.

■ The need to balance the development of technical information with social and cul-

tural processes to ensure that such information is effectively shared, understood, and used to change environmental practice on-the-ground.

To take up these challenges, interdisciplinary science approaches need to include personnel with complementary skills in the management of participation and conflict, and the integration of biophysical and social aspects of collaborative learning. As much attention will need to be paid to review and evaluate the processes by which such endeavours encourage learning, as is currently given to assuring that good technical research is being done.

Acknowledgements

This paper is based on Allen, W.J. and Kilvington, M.J. (1999). "Why Involving People Is Important: The Forgotten Part of Environ-mental Information System Management", Paper presented to 2nd International Conference on Multiple Objective Decision Support Systems for Land, Water and Environmental Management (MODSS '99) Brisbane, Australia, 1-6 August 1999. The authors thank Landcare Research for funding and support and all the individuals and groups we worked with during the case studies. We would particularly like to acknowledge the ideas, examples and comments from our colleagues, Garth Harmsworth and Chrys Horn, that have added to this paper. Work on this chapter has been supported by the OECD and the New Zealand FRST-funded research programmes: Restoring Indigenous Biodiversity in Human Landscapes (RIBHL) - Contract CO9X0205; and Integrated Water Resource Management in Complex Catch-ments (ICM-Motueka) - CO9X0214, and Building Capacity for Sustainable Development - Contract CO9X0310.

References Cited

Abdalla, C.W. and T.W. Kelsey. 1996. Breaking the impasse: Helping communities cope with change at the rural-urban interface. Journal of Soil and Water Conservation 51:462-466.

Allen, W.J. 1997. Towards improving the role of evaluation within natural resource management R&D programmes: The case for 'learning by doing.' Canadian Journal of Development Studies 16:625-638, Available online: http://nrm-changelinks.net/cjds.html

Allen, W.J. and M.J. Kilvington. 1999. Why involving people is important: The forgotten part of environmental information system management. Paper presented to 2nd International Conference on Multiple Objective Decision Support Systems for Land, Water, and Environmental Management (MODSS '99) Brisbane, Australia, 1-6 August 1999.

Allen, W., K. Brown, T. Gloag, J. Morris, K. Simpson, J. Thomas, and R. Young. 1998. Building partnerships for conservation in the Waitaki/Mackenzie Basins. Landcare Research Contract Report LC9899/033, Lincoln, New Zealand.

Allen, W., O. Bosch, M. Kilvington, J. Oliver, and M. Gilbert. 2001a. Benefits of collaborative learning for environmental management: Applying the Integrated Systems for Knowledge Management approach to support animal pest control. Environmental Management 27(2):215-223. Available on-line: http://nrm-changelinks.net/ahb_envmngmt.html

Allen, W., O. Bosch, M. Kilvington, D. Harley, and I. Brown. 2001b. Monitoring and adaptive management: Addressing social and organisational issues to improve information sharing. Natural Resources Forum 25(3):225-233. Available online: http://www.landcareresearch.co.nz/research/social/nrf_pap.asp

Argyris, C., R. Putnam, and D.M. Smith. 1985. Action Science. Jossey-Bass, San Francisco, California.

Bawden, R.J., R.D. Macadam, R.J. Packham, and I. Valentine. 1984. Systems thinking and practices in the education of agriculturalists. Agricultural Systems 13:205-225.

Bosch, O.J.H. 1997. Improved land management systems for Tussock grasslands. Unpublished research protocol, Contract C09803, between Foundation for Research, Science and Technology and Landcare Research, Lincoln, New Zealand.

Bosch, O.J.H., W.J. Allen, J.M. Williams, and A. Ensor. 1996. An integrated system for maximizing community knowledge: Integrating community-based monitoring into the adaptive management process in the New Zealand High Country. The Rangeland Journal 18:23-32. Available online: http://www.landcareresearch.co.nz/research/social/monadan.asp

Bunning, C. 1995. Professional development using action research. Action Learning, Action Research and Process Management Internet Conference, MCB University Press, Bradford, England. Available online: http://www.mcb.co.uk/services/conferen/nov95/ifal/paper1.htm

Christensen, N.L., A.M. Bartuska, J.H. Brown, S. Carpenter, C. D'Antonio, R. Francis, J.F. Franklin, J.A. MacMahon, R.F. Noss, D.J. Parsons, C.H. Peterson, M.G. Turner, and R.G. Woodmansee. 1996. The report of the Ecological Society of America on the scientific basis for ecosystem management. The Ecological Society of America, Washington, D.C.

Dovers, S.R. and C.D. Mobbs. 1997. An alluring prospect? Ecology, and the requirements of adaptive management. In: Frontiers in ecology: Building the links. Proceedings, Conference of the Ecological Society of Australia 1-3 October 1997, Charles Sturt University. Elsevier Science, Oxford, UK.

Grudens-Schuck, N. 1998. When farmers design curriculum: Participatory education for sustainable agriculture in Ontario, Canada. Unpublished thesis dissertation, Cornell University.

Gunderson, L., C.S. Holling, and S.S. Light. (eds.) Barriers and bridges to the renewal of ecosystems and institutions. Columbia University Press, New York, New York.

Harmsworth, G.R. 1998. Indigenous values and GIS: A method and a framework. Indigenous Knowledge and Development Monitor 6(3): 3-7.

Harmsworth, G.R. 2001. A collaborative research model for working with Iwi: Discussion paper. Landcare Research Contract Report LC 2001/119 prepared for the Foundation for Research, Science and Technology, Landcare Research, Lincoln, New Zealand.

Horn, C. and M. Kilvington. 2002. Māori and 1080. http://www.landcareresearch.co.nz/research/social/1080.asp

Huber, G.P. 1991. Organizational learning: The contributing processes and the literatures. Organization Science 2(1):88-115.

Ison, R.L. 1993. Changing community attitudes. The Rangeland Journal 15(1): 154-166.

Kilvington, M. 1998. The Whaingaroa Catchment Management Project: A multi-stakeholder approach to sustainable catchment management. New Zealand Ministry for the Environment Sustainable Management Fund Project No. 2973.

Kolb, D.A., I.M. Rubin, and J.M. McIntyre. 1979. Organisational psychology: An experiential approach (3rd edition). Prentice Hall, Englewood Cliffs, New Jersey.

Lee, K.N. 1993. Compass and gyroscope: Integrating science and politics for the environment. Island Press, Washington, D.C.

Masters, J. 1995. The history of action research. In: I. Hughes (ed.) Action Research Electronic Reader, The University of Sydney, online at http://www.behs.cchs.usyd.edu.au/arow/Reader/rmasters.htm

Michael, D.N. 1995. Barriers and bridges to learning in a turbulent human ecology. Pp. 461-485. In: Barriers and Bridges to the Renewal of Ecosystems and Institutions. L.H. Gunderson, C.S. Holling, and S.S. Light (eds.) Columbia University Press, New York, New York.

Minnis, M., V.P. John-Steiner, and R.J. Weber. 1994. Collaborations: Values, roles, and working methods. Research proposal submitted in August 1994 to the National Science Foundation.

Pretty, J. 1998. Participatory learning for integrated farming. Eng Long Foo and T. Della Senta (eds.), Proceedings of the Internet Conference on Integrated Biosystems. Available online: http://www.ias.unu.edu/proceedings/icibs/jules/paper.htm

Randolph-Macon College (n.d.) Collegiate Curriculum. Cross Area Requirement - Multidisciplinary or Interdisciplinary Course. Available online: http://www.rmc.edu/facstaff/nmultiDis.htm

Reynolds, J. and J. Busby. 1996. Guide to information management in the context of the convention on biological diversity. UNEP, Nairobi, Kenya.

Stuth, J.W., C.J. Scifres, W.T. Hamilton, and J.R. Connor. 1991. Management systems analysis as guidance for effective interdisciplinary grazingland research. Agricultural Systems 36:43-63.

Susman, G. and R. Evered. 1978. An assessment of the scientific merit of action research. Administrative Science Quarterly 23:582-603.

van den Bessalaar, P. and G. Heimericks. 2001. Disciplinary, interdisciplinary concepts and indicators. Pp.705-716. Paper in Proceedings 8th International Conference on Scientometrics and Informetrics, Sydney, Australia.

Wadsworth, Y. 1998. What is participatory action research? Action Research International. Paper 2. Available online: http://www.scu.edu.au/schools/gcm/ar/ari/p-ywadsworth98.html

Walters, C. 1997. Challenges in adaptive management of riparian and coastal ecosystems. Conservation Ecology 1(2):1 Available from http://www.ecologyandsociety.org/vol1/iss2/art1/

Zuber-Skerritt, O. 1991. Action research for change and development. Centre for the Advancement of Learning and Teaching, Griffith University, Queensland, Australia.

Weeding out Economic Impacts of Farm Decisions

CHAPTER 4

D.W. Archer

Decisions made at the farm level are heavily influenced, if not driven, by farm-level economic impacts. Producers make a myriad of decisions throughout the season, and even if they are not driven strictly by profit maximization goals, profit needs to at least be considered in order for the operation to remain economically viable. As a consequence, this paper will focus primarily on the relationships between management decisions and farm-level profit. What follows is a discussion of some of the factors that affect farm profitability, with the idea of providing insights into how management decisions may be influenced by economic considerations, and conversely, providing a broad overview of how enhanced decision making might affect farm profitability.

Basic production processes. The most direct economic impacts at the farm-level represent a summation of impacts occurring at the field or smaller scales relating the use of purchased inputs to crop outputs. This "crop response function approach" is one of the oldest and most widely used tools in agricultural economics (Heady and Pesek, 1954), and has seen renewed interest in the area of precision agriculture and variable rate applications (Bongiovanni and Lowenberg-DeBoer, 2001; Bullock et al., 2002; Mamo et al., 2003). An example of this approach is the relationship between nitrogen fertilizer applications and crop yield. If we know the functional relationship between the quantities of nitrogen fertilizer applied and crop yield, as well as nitrogen and crop price, it is quite easy to identify the

amount of fertilizer to apply in order to maximize net returns. However, in reality producers only have a general idea about the relationship between the quantity of fertilizer applied and crop yield. In addition, factors acting between the times the fertilizer is applied and when the crop is harvested result in uncertainty about yields and prices that will be realized. For example, yield is affected by nitrogen availability, weather, availability of other nutrients, pest pressures, etc. It is costly to gather more information about the relationship between the quantities of fertilizer applied and crop yield. Even with extensive information gathering, it is unlikely all of the uncertainty will be resolved. The important question is how much information is it worth collecting?

In many cases, the relationship between net return and applied nitrogen is relatively flat over a range of application rates, implying there is little economic benefit to gathering more information in order to fine tune rates. Figure 1 shows the gross margin for the nitrogen production function used by Mitchell (2003). The optimum nitrogen application rate in this example is 107 pounds per acre, resulting in a gross margin of $255.42 per acre. However, the nitrogen application rate can range anywhere from 61.5 to 162 pounds per acre, and gross margin will be within $5.00 per acre of the optimum. This has often been observed to be the case with other inputs (Hutton and Thorne, 1955; Anderson, 1975) and for other economic decisions including land use allocation decisions (Pannell, 2004). This "flat payoff function"

Figure 1
Gross margin response to applied nitrogen fertilizer in corn.

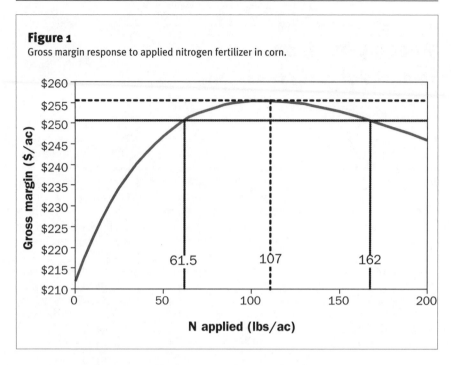

has some potentially positive implications in that producers have a wide margin for error in their production decisions which lends a degree of flexibility to their management options. This flexibility is a key issue in farm-level economics that will be discussed in more detail later. Focusing on a single input decision, this flat payoff function may lead one to conclude that there is potential to reduce input levels with little negative economic impact. For the nitrogen example, application rate could be reduced by over 40 percent with only a $5.00 per acre reduction in net return. In one of the examples provided by Pannell (2004), herbicide doses ranging from 60 percent of the optimum to 170 percent of the optimum would yield profits within 95 percent of the optimum. Even though the economic benefits to fine tuning rates may be small, it does not necessarily follow that environmental consequences would be small.

The nitrogen example shown in Figure

1 is admittedly a simple example in that it is based on a single location and single year response, so it does not include the risk and uncertainty (hereafter the terms risk and uncertainty will be used interchangeably, referring jointly to imperfect knowledge and uncertain consequences) faced by producers. Uncertainty can affect producer decisions in many ways, depending upon the source of the uncertainty. Motivated by the common idea that farmers apply "a little extra fertilizer just in case it is needed," Babcock (1992) showed that uncertainty regarding soil nitrate concentrations and potential yields could lead producers to increase nitrogen applications rates to maximize expected profits. In a simulation analysis of nitrogen application to corn in Iowa, Babcock showed that uncertainty could increase application rates by as much as 25 to 36 percent. This result is not generalizable to other production technologies. Pannell (1990; 1991) showed in many cases expected pesticide application

rates decline with increases in uncertainty.

At the whole-farm level, basic production processes include interactions among production activities. Crop rotation sequences can affect crop yields through effects on weed and disease pressures, nutrient cycling, and water use dynamics. Integration of crop and livestock production can affect profitability by reducing input costs and increasing productivity. As an example, Pannell (1999) discusses the importance of accounting for interactions in estimating the farm-level impacts of introducing lupins to a Western Australian farm. In the analysis, Pannell included the effects of lupins on fixing nitrogen, improving soil structure, reducing cereal disease levels, and use of lupin grain and residues as sheep feeds. He also included effects on efficiency of machinery use. Comparing the analysis to the case where no interactions were included showed that the economic benefits from lupins would be greatly underestimated without interactions.

Timeliness. As basic production processes are brought up to the farm scale, timeliness becomes important. Many farming activities must be carried out at specific times in order to be most effective. Crops need to be planted to make full use of the growing season, herbicide applications need to be timed to minimize yield loss due to weed competition, and crops should be harvested when they have reached maturity, but before yield loss or damage occurs. However, producers have limited equipment and labor to carry out these operations. Critical times may occur simultaneously at several locations around the farm making it impossible to reach all of the locations in a timely manner, or weather conditions may delay field operations. When these operations can not be completed at the appropriate time, there is generally a direct effect on crop productivity and therefore economic returns.

Producers make decisions to manage the economic effects of time constraints. They may select crop mixes or tillage practices to reduce the potential for conflicts to occur. They may purchase more or larger equipment and hire additional labor to increase their capacity to complete operations in a timely manner. These types of decisions can have significant farm-level economic effects. Because of the potential for significant farm-level economic effects, machinery selection has been the impetus behind the development of several software decision aids (Siemens et al., 1990; Ellinger, 2003) that include effects of timeliness. In addition, time constraints are an important part of comprehensive whole-farm optimization models (e.g. Doster, 2000; Pannell, 1996).

Flexibility. Flexibility in management options has long been conjectured to have significant economic impacts at the farm-level, but has received relatively little formal study. Schultz (1939) went so far as to say that individual farms are not necessary except in the face of change, writing:

> The criterion that measures entrepreneurial success is to be found in adjustments which may be looked upon as consisting of two interrelated parts: (a) correctly anticipating the type of adjustments that are needed; and (b) the best way or method for making the adjustment.

The idea is that producers have flexibility to make tactical adjustments in response to new information, and that these tactical adjustments can have significant farm-level economic impacts. It is this response to new information that distinguishes flexibility in decision making from timeliness issues.

Techniques and a theoretical basis for analyzing management flexibility have been available for quite some time (Rae, 1971; Antle, 1983b). However, application of these techniques has only become practical with advances in computer technology. Management flexibility was first studied for decisions involving a single enterprise or a single input (Mjelde et al., 1989;

Thornton, 1984; Harper et al., 1994; Mitchell, 2003). Studies evaluating whole-farm impacts of tactical adjustments are more recent and more limited (Kingwell et al., 1992; Kingwell et al., 1993; Kingwell, 1994; Etyang et al., 1998; Dorward, 1999; Ekman, 2000). In some cases the availability of tactical adjustments can have large farm-level economic effects. Kingwell et al. (1993), in a study of a representative Western Australia farm system, found the inclusion of tactical adjustments increased expected net return by 22 percent compared to the best inflexible strategy. In addition, the largest benefits of flexibility occurred in the most extreme seasons. This would indicate that producers who can make tactical adjustments, particularly in extreme conditions, may have a competitive advantage. However, Ekman (2000) showed only a three percent increase in expected net return using a flexible strategy compared to a fixed strategy for a representative Swedish farm. The differing impacts are likely due to the uncertainty effects considered in the alternative models. Kingwell et al. considered adjustments to seasonal weather observations that have direct and potentially large impacts on production, while Ekman considered adjustments to uncertain field-time availability which had generally indirect and marginal impacts on yields and were partially offset by reductions in cost. A challenge for both farm managers and economists is to recognize a *priori* when tactical adjustments are likely to have significant farm-level economic effects.

In some cases, timeliness and management flexibility may be the primary reasons producers use a specific technology. Bouzaher et al. (1992) modeled choices among herbicide strategies based on the time periods when specific herbicides could be applied and be effective. Herbicide strategies that allowed longer time periods for successful application at the lowest cost resulted in the highest expected net returns, and would be selected by profit maximizing producers. Similarly, Archer and Gesch (2003) evaluated the potential for a temperature-sensitive seed coating to be adopted by producers in the U.S. northern Corn Belt based on the added flexibility in planting time that the coating would provide. The analysis showed the new technology could increase whole-farm expected net returns by three to four percent with expected use on as much as 45 to 79 percent of the total crop acres. Note this benefit occurs for a technology *that has no direct effect on crop productivity.*

Several recent analyses have included the concept of "real options." The idea is that with some types of decisions, there is a value to waiting rather than taking immediate action. Real options can be used to assess the value of management flexibility. This approach has been used by Saphores (2000) to evaluate pest control decisions where "the farmer has to balance expected pest damages with the cost of applying the pesticide *plus the loss of flexibility* which comes from using one of its possibilities to reduce the density of the pest population by spraying the pesticide" (emphasis added). The approach has also been used in evaluating the decision to adopt new technologies. In analyzing the decision to invest in site-specific crop management, Khanna et al. (2000) showed that it may be more profitable for producers to delay adoption even though immediate adoption appears to be profitable. This situation occurs because payoffs are uncertain, investments in the technology are irreversible and costs of the technology are declining. In this analysis, adoption of site-specific crop management was shown to have environmental benefits due to reduced nitrogen runoff, so delaying adoption also delays environmental benefits. In a related study, Isik (2004) showed that uncertainty about the availability of cost-share subsidies for improved nutrient management (including site-specific technologies) can delay adoption when cost-share is not currently available but there is an expectation it may become available. The real options approach accounts for the possibility of producers delaying decisions into the future.

Information acquisition. Because tactical adjustments are made in response to new information, this has naturally lead economists to analyze the value of information. Hennessy and Babcock (1998) observed "there is wide spread belief that modern manufacturing emphasizes flexibility in accommodating new information," and "information technology is being used to enhance flexibility." The implicit recognition is that businesses not only utilize flexibility to make adjustments as information becomes available, but they make investments to increase flexibility by acquiring information. Information can be used to make management decisions as the season progresses (reducing temporal uncertainty) and/or information can be used to adjust management across the landscape (reducing spatial uncertainty).

Anderson et al. (1977) identified a method for estimating the value of information as the difference between the certainty equivalent value of the optimal strategy with the information and the certainty equivalent value of the optimal strategy without the information. (Note: certainty equivalent value is the amount of money that an individual would have to receive to be indifferent between a certain payoff and a given gamble. This is used to account for differences in individual risk preferences. For a risk-neutral producer, certainty equivalent is the same as expected profit.) Chavas and Pope (1984) outlined a theoretical model for the value of information in sequential decisions, where the decision maker can revise plans as new information becomes available. The model showed that the ability to revise

future plans tends to make the decision maker better off, indicating the value of flexibility in management. Antle (1983b) indicated the potential pitfalls of not including sequential decision making in economic analysis. The importance was confirmed by Mjelde et al. (1989) who showed a four to 10 percent increase in profits for a farm utilizing information to adjust nitrogen applications versus a farm that does not update applications based on weather conditions.

Applying the Anderson et al. approach, Pannell (1994) evaluated the value of information in weed-control decisions based on information about potential yields (via weather information) and weed densities. He showed that the expected value of information could reach as high as 15 percent of the expected gross margin. He also showed that expected herbicide applications should decline for a producer who adjusts herbicide applications based on weather observations and weed densities.

In evaluating the value of information, it is important to be clear about the assumptions being made about both the initial level of information producers have and the level of information that will be attained. In evaluating the value of information on late-spring soil nitrate levels, Babcock and Blackmer (1992) assumed producers initially know the probability distribution of soil nitrate levels, but not the actual values. They compared this to a state of "perfect information" where soil nitrate levels are known with certainty. Their analysis showed values of perfect information ranged from $6 to $22 per acre and expected total nitrogen applications were reduced by as much as 38 percent compared to the no soil test information case. Note, these values represent upper bounds on what producers would obtain if they either had better baseline information than assumed or if soil test information is imperfect.

Babcock and Blackmer's example

showed how, at least for nitrogen, information might serve as a substitute for purchased inputs. Uncertainty leads producers to apply higher nitrogen application rates, but information can allow producers to respond tactically, reducing uncertainty, and thereby reducing application rates. Unfortunately, this result is dependant on the underlying production relationship, so it is not necessarily generalizable.

Regarding spatial uncertainty, Hennessy and Babcock (1998) developed a theoretical model to evaluate how acquiring information about spatial variability affects both profitability and input use. For the case of perfect information, that is, moving from a condition of unknown variation across a field to known spatial variation across a field, Hennessy and Babcock showed that the value of information increases as variability increases. This supports the common finding that the economic performance of site-specific application technologies is positively related to spatial variation across a field (Forcella, 1992; Babcock and Pautsch, 1998; English et al., 2001). This also explains the observations of Olson and Elisabeth (2003) that adoption of precision agriculture technologies was positively related to soil variability for farms in southwestern Minnesota. Hennessy and Babcock could not identify a general relationship between information and input use without a more detailed understanding of the specific technology involved. However, in an applied analysis, Babcock and Pautsch (1998) found that soil test information could result in reducing fertilizer application rates by five to 32 percent. Even though Babcock and Pautsch showed positive economic values for perfect spatial information in variable rate nitrogen applications, it should be noted that the value of the information was relatively small, ranging from $1.53 to $7.43 per acre.

Of course, the assumption of perfect information is a limiting case. In reality, it is unlikely that all of the uncertainty will be resolved prior to making a decision. Mitchell (2003) extended the theoretical model of Hennessy and Babcock to include the possibility of imperfect information. He showed that the value of imperfect information about spatial variability is higher when it increases the efficiency of input use, and when the information is "good" in that it correlates well with the underlying stochastic factor and exhibits low variability. In an applied analysis, Mitchell showed that imperfect information could decrease nitrogen application rates by four to nine percent depending on the quality of the information. However, the economic value of the information was again relatively low, ranging from $1.07 to $1.38 per acre. In a similar analysis, Babcock et al. (1996) showed that nitrogen application rates might be reduced by 15 to 40 percent, with the value of the information ranging from $3 to $10 per acre.

This leads to the larger question of how producers strategically position themselves to take advantage of tactical opportunities. Investments in information acquisition are one tool producers can use. As Pannell et al. (2000) observed the key to maintaining an economically viable farm enterprise is getting the big decisions right, and that those who made incorrect major adjustments are the ones who are most likely to be under financial stress.

Financial considerations. Financial considerations often get overlooked in farm-level economic analyses. As Malcolm (2000) observed "financial feasibility is as important a criteria as economic returns" in farm management economic analysis. Several studies have looked at how farm investment and borrowing decisions are affected by year-to-year changes in production (Lowenberg-DeBoer, 1986; Featherstone et al., 1990; Atwood et al., 1996; Escalante and Barry, 2001; Atwood and Buschena, 2003); however, these generally lack detail in production practices. Consequently, interactions between production decisions and investment and borrowing decisions have not been analyzed in detail. However, it is these investment and borrowing decisions that are the "big decisions" Pannell et al. (2000) say are important for producers to get right. In order to get these decisions right, it is important to understand how they might constrain or be constrained by management options at a finer level. Escalante and Barry (2001) showed that the availability of share leasing arrangements might lead to a substantial increase in farm size due to effects on increasing cash flow. For a representative risk-neutral Illinois farm, they showed that both farm size and net farm income more than doubled with the availability of share leasing arrangements. However, because the model did not include other constraints related to production practices, it is unclear whether this response is realistic.

Whole-farm models often include financial constraints (Pannell, 1996; Dorward, 1999), but these don't include detail on the dynamics of year-to-year adjustments in investment and borrowing decisions that may be important for capturing the effects of financial considerations on farm-level decisions. Dorward (1999) showed an interaction between access to credit markets and benefits to on-farm tactical responses to risk, indicating that tactical responses may become less important when farms have access to effective credit markets. Understanding these types of interactions is important in understanding how financial considerations affect farm-level decisions.

Producer attributes. The preceding discussion neglects any consideration of differences among producers. Producers have individual tastes and preferences. They are part of a community and have social goals and environmental goals; and they have different mixes of skills, abilities,

and interests. While these attributes will not be discussed in detail here, it is important to illustrate some pertinent relationships to economic performance.

The most common tool for including individual preferences in economic analysis is the utility function. In most cases utility is used only to account for individual's aversion to risk. While there has been considerable research indicating that producers tend to be risk-averse, risk aversion is often included in economic analysis with little regard for whether it is economically important (Pannell et al., 2000; Just, 2003). In addition, considerable research has shown that behaviors often attributed to risk-averse preferences can be explained by appropriately capturing other aspects such as financial transaction costs (Atwood and Bushena, 2003) and production technologies (Antle, 1983a; Babcock and Shogren, 1995; Pannell et al., 2000). Pannell et al. (2000) argue, "Often, better representation of the biology, production alternatives, technology, taxation ramifications, resource endowments, weather-year and price conditions, and tactical opportunities will yield more valuable information about change at the farm-level than sophisticated inclusion of risk-aversion." For soil nitrate uncertainty, Babcock and Shogren (1995) showed that the direct effect of uncertainty on production accounted for 40 to 85 percent of the total premium producers would be willing to pay for risk reduction, with risk aversion accounting for the rest of the premium. This is not to deny that producers are risk-averse, but simply to point out that, depending on the situation, risk aversion may or may not play an important part in farm-level decisions compared to other factors.

Besides having different preferences, farmers have different mixes of skills and abilities. These differing levels of human capital affect both the sources of information farmers utilize and the usefulness of that information (Just et al., 2003). Griffin et al. (2004) identified human capital costs as one of the barriers to adoption of precision-agriculture technologies. They also observed that, although human capital costs appear to be a barrier to adoption, producers "seem to be skeptical of 'closed-loop' approaches that automate decision-making." It may be this skepticism of "closed-loop" approaches is an implicit recognition that these approaches do not contribute to building the human capital farmers rely on in making daily management decisions, and therefore are not as valuable to them.

Emerging technologies. What are the implications of the foregoing factors for farm-level economic impacts of emerging technologies? The "flat payoff function" phenomenon has been identified as a potential barrier to the adoption of precision-farming technologies (Pannell, 2004). Specifically looking at technologies in which inputs are varied based on site-specific conditions, commonly called variable rate technology, Pannell observed that flat payoff functions implies there are diminishing marginal returns to the benefits of more precise application of inputs. That does not necessarily mean that precision farming technology will not be adopted. As the hardware, data acquisition and processing costs decrease, even small payoffs should lead to increased adoption and this can have significant environmental effects. However, as noted earlier, Khanna et al. (2000) showed that declining costs can also serve as a barrier to adoption when producers decide it is better to wait for lower costs. There is some limited evidence to suggest that systems that manage multiple inputs are more profitable (Finck, 1998). However, unless precision farming technology results in substantial changes in input levels, the direct production function effects on profit are likely to be low.

There are some situations in which substantial changes in input use are known to occur. One is in "patch management" of perennial weeds, where herbicides are only applied to discrete patches where weeds have been identified. Indeed, Lowenberg-DeBoer (2003) identified this as the "no-brainer" in site-specific management. However, Pannell and Bennett (1999) indicate, even in this case, there are some complexities that can reduce the economic benefits. Specifically, Pannell and Bennett (1999) identified the importance of including the costs of weed competition where weeds occur at densities below the economic threshold for spraying or are missed in mapping, and therefore are not sprayed. Substantial changes in input use might occur in other situations as well. Babcock et al. (1996) showed that taking advantage of soil test information in variable rate nitrogen applications may require farmers to vary rates from 0 to 172 pounds per acre. Even if average rates do not change substantially, this can have significant economic and environmental effects.

Looking at the broader range of "precision-agriculture" technologies, are there opportunities for larger farm-level economic impacts? Lowenberg-DeBoer (2003) suggested that yield monitors may provide opportunities for whole-farm economic benefits through such things as diagnosis of crop problems, on-farm experimentation, improved logistics, land rental negotiations, legal documentation, environmental management, and crop insurance claims. Global positioning system (GPS) guidance is a technology that has multiple potential economic impacts. A direct impact is in the reduction of overlaps and skips, and potentially an increase in speed of field operations. Analysis for a representative 1800 acre Indiana farm (Watson and Lowenberg-DeBoer, 2002) indicated that lightbar guidance technology would be profitable based on these field efficiency improvements alone. Watson and Lowenberg-DeBoer (2002) also indicated that GPS guidance may allow farmers to expand farm size with the same set of equipment, which made all types of GPS guidance profitable for the representative Indiana farm. Other uses for GPS guidance include farming practices that require driving accuracy and the ability to return to the same place for subsequent operations. This includes controlled traffic and strip tillage farming systems. In a simple farm budgeting analysis, Watson and Lowenberg-DeBoer (2002) showed a $44,000 increase in annual whole-farm net returns for an 1800 acre Indiana farm using GPS auto guidance to switch to a controlled traffic system.

Remote sensing is a precision agriculture technology for which the farm-level economic impacts are not yet clear. Used as a tool for adjusting input rates, the economic impacts are again limited by the flat payoff function problem. This is confirmed by Tenkorang and Lowenberg-DeBoer (2004) in a preliminary review of studies which include estimated economic impacts. Even in the absence of image processing and analysis costs, returns to remote sensing were typically low. Possible exceptions were for high-valued crops such as sugar beets and cotton. However, because remote sensing is technology that can help resolve both temporal and spatial uncertainty, its potential value in information acquisition and making tactical adjustments should not be overlooked.

Bullock and Bullock (2000) argued that agronomic information has become more valuable with the advent of precision agriculture technology. In their discussion, they are careful to separate the value of precision agriculture technology from the value of the information needed to make use of the technology. For example, they separated the value of variable rate applications from the value of site-specific production functions needed to determine appropriate application rates. They argued that precision agriculture technology and information are complements, so the availability of one increases the value of the other. Continuing the example, variable rate technology is not particularly useful without site-specific production function information, and conversely, site-specific production function information is not as useful without the technology for varying site-specific application rates.

Information and the flexibility to adapt as information becomes available are important drivers of farm-level economic performance. This means producers need to be able to utilize information to make the appropriate adjustments, and perhaps more importantly, they need to be able to analyze the potential impacts of the "big decisions" that really constrain how they can react to changing conditions. These two types of management decisions will be discussed separately.

First, regarding the ability to utilize information to make appropriate adjustments, as Pannell (1996) noted, producers do a pretty good job with their day-to-day management decisions. However, that is not to say that improvements cannot be made, particularly as farms increase in size, and as technologies for collecting more and more detailed raw data proliferate. Technologies that help with recordkeeping and processing data into useable information become more important. These include the use of single-issue decision aids that either provide a specific recommendation or provide information that producers can use in making adjustments (Freebairn et al., 2004; Archer et al., 2001; Archer et al., 2002). In order to be adopted, these decision aids must be quick and easy to use and must use readily available inputs. In some cases, decision aids have now been incorporated into web-delivered information services that automate input retrieval, eliminating the need for user data entry (e.g. Growth Stage Consulting; North Dakota State University). As precision agriculture technology improves, automated procedures for converting site-specific data into readily useable information or even application prescriptions are becoming available (Fridgen et al., 2004). These technologies offer the potential to provide incremental improvements in economic returns, but it is important to recognize that these improvements can be overshadowed by one "big" mistake.

Regarding the ability to analyze the potential impacts of big decisions, budgeting techniques remain standard tools that have stood the test of time (Malcolm, 1990). A survey in 1996 of U.S. Great Plains' producers, showed that of those using computers, 89 percent reported using word processing software at least once a year followed by accounting/recordkeeping software (85 percent), tax software (74 percent), spreadsheets (73 percent), production records (57 percent), financial planning (56 percent), and production decision aids (25 percent) (Ascough et al., 1999). This indicates that a fair number of producers are already using spreadsheets and financial planning software, which have applications in farm-level management. Financial recordkeeping software is a core component of farm business education programs in the United States, and financial planning software has been used successfully in conjunction with extension consultation to assist producers in evaluating dairy management alternatives (Robb et al., 2001).

Malcolm (2000) indicated that there is a reasonable chance farmers will adopt spreadsheet farm budgeting tools in the future. Stochastic budgeting, which is an extension of traditional budgeting techniques that allows the inclusion of uncertain variables, has seen considerable recent use in economic analysis (Lien, 2003; Archer et al., 2003). Recent introduction of commercial spreadsheet add-ins for stochastic budgeting will make stochastic budgeting tools available to producers. However, it is likely that this will increase the chances of misuse as with standard budgeting techniques (Ferris and Malcolm, 1999).

In addition to budgeting tools, whole-farm simulation modeling has long held promises for helping farmers improve strategic decision making. However, the sheer amount of data and skills needed to build, maintain, and run these models have limited their use by individual farmers. Recent applications of simulation modeling in a participatory setting have shown promise (Attonaty et al., 1999; Meinke et al., 2001; Keating and McCown, 2001; Carberry et al., 2002). This approach relies critically on the interface between what has been called the "hard" scientific systems approach and the "soft" social systems approach. As Keating and McCown (2001) observed, it is this interface that presents the greatest challenges and opportunities for successful farming systems analysis.

Concluding Remarks

The objective of this paper was to provide a broad overview of the mechanisms by which farm management decisions affect economic returns. Economic impacts of farm-level decisions can range from very simple impacts affecting a small part of a single enterprise to very complex impacts affecting every part of the farm operation. Impacts are inextricably tied to resource endowments (including natural and financial resources), production technologies and personal skills, abilities, and goals. As such, impacts are difficult to generalize. This also represents a challenge in providing tools and information that producers can use to improve decision-making. Recent research has shown that the use of information in making management decisions and flexibility in adapting to changing conditions can have substantial farm-level economic impacts. However, there is a need for better understanding about how farms can position themselves strategically to best respond to changing conditions.

References Cited

Anderson, J.R. 1975. One more or less cheer for optimality. Journal of the Australian Institute of Agricultural Science 41:195-197.

Anderson, J.R., J.L. Dillon, and J.B. Hardaker. 1977. Agricultural decision analysis. Iowa State University Press, Ames, Iowa.

Antle, J.M. 1983a. Incorporating risk in production analysis. American Journal of Agricultural Economics 65:1099-1106.

Antle, J.M. 1983b. Sequential decision-making in production models. American Journal of Agricultural Economics 65:282-290.

Archer, D., J. Eklund, M. Walsh, and F. Forcella. 2002. WEEDEM: A user-friendly software package for predicting annual ryegrass and wild radish emergence. Pp. 252- 253. *In:* WEEDS: Threats Now & Forever? H. Jacob, J. Spafford, J. Dodd, and J.H. Moore (eds.). 13th Australian Weeds Conference Papers and Proceedings, Perth, Washington, September 8-13, 2002.

Archer, D.W., F. Forcella, J.J. Eklund, and J. Gunsolus. 2001. WeedCast Version 2.0. http://www.morris. ars.usda.gov

Archer, D.W. and R.W. Gesch. 2003. Value of temperature-activated polymer-coated seed in the Northern Corn Belt. Journal of Agricultural and Applied Economics 35:625-637.

Archer, D.W., J.L. Pikul, Jr., and W.E. Riedell. 2003. Analyzing risk and risk management in cropping systems. Pp. 155-164. *In:* Proceedings of the Dynamic Cropping Systems: Principles, Processes, and Challenges. J.D. Hanson, and J.M. Krupinsky (eds.). Bismarck, North Dakota.

Ascough II, J.C., D.L. Hoag, W.M. Frasier, and G.S. McMaster. 1999. Computer use in agriculture: An analysis of Great Plains producers. Computers and Electronics in Agriculture 23(3):189-204.

Atwood, J.A. and D.E. Buschena. 2003. Evaluating the magnitudes of financial transaction costs on risk behavior. Agricultural Systems 75(2-3):235-249.

Atwood, J.A., M.J. Watts, and A. Baquet. 1996. An examination of the effects of price supports and federal crop insurance upon the economic growth, capital structure, and financial survival of wheat growers in the Northern High Plains. American Journal of Agricultural Economics 78(1):212-224.

Attonaty, J-M., M-H. Chatelin, and F. Garcia. 1999. Interactive simulation modeling in farm decision-making. Computers and Electronics in Agriculture 22(2/3):157-170.

Babcock, B.A. 1992. The effects of uncertainty on optimal nitrogen applications. Review of Agricultural Economics 14(2):271-280.

Babcock, B.A. and A.M. Blackmer. 1992. The value of temporal input nonuniformities. Journal of Agricultural and Resource Economics 17(2):335-347.

Babcock, B.A., A.L. Carriquiry, and H.S. Stern. 1996. Evaluation of soil test information in agricultural decision-making. Applied Statistics 45:447-461.

Babcock, B.A. and G.R. Pautsch. 1998. Moving from uniform to variable fertilizer rates on Iowa corn: Effects on rates and returns. Journal of Agricultural and Resource Economics 23(2):385-400.

Babcock, B.A. and J.F. Shogren. 1995. The cost of agricultural production risk. Agricultural Economics 12(2):141-150.

Bongiovanni, R. and J. Lowenberg-DeBoer. 2001. Precision agriculture: Economics of nitrogen management in corn using site-specific crop response estimates from a spatial regression model. Selected paper, American Agricultural Economics Association Annual Meeting. August 6, 2001. Chicago, Illinois.

Bouzaher, A., D. Archer, R. Cabe, A. Carriquiry, and J.J. Shogren. 1992. Effects of environmental policy on trade-offs in agri-chemical management. Journal of Environmental Management 36(1):69-80.

Bullock, D.S. and D.G. Bullock. 2000. From agronomic research to farm management guidelines: A primer on the economics of information and precision technology. Precision Agriculture 2(1):71-101.

Bullock, D.S., J. Lowenberg-DeBoer, and S.M. Swinton. 2002. Adding value to spatially managed inputs by understanding site-specific yield response. Agricultural Economics 27(3):233-245.

Carberry, P.S., Z. Hochman, R.L. McCown, N.P. Dalgliesh, M.A. Foale, P.L. Poulton, J.N.G. Hargreaves, D.M.G. Hargreaves, S. Cawthray, and N. Hillcoat. 2002. The FARMSCAPE approach to decision support: farmers', advisers', researchers' monitoring, simulation, communication and perfor-mance evaluation. Agricultural Systems 74(1):141-177.

Chavas, J. and R.D. Pope. 1984. Information: Its measurement and valuation. American Journal of Agricultural Economics 66(5):705-710.

Dorward, A. 1999. Modeling embedded risk in peasant agriculture: Methodological insights from northern Malawi. Agricultural Economics 21:191-203.

Doster, D.H. 2000. Summary of B-20 contents and uses. Department of Agricultural Economics, Purdue University, West Lafayette, Indiana.

Ekman, S. 2000. Tillage system selection: A mathematical programming model incorporating weather variability. Journal of Agricultural Engineering Research 77(3):267-276.

Ellinger, P.N. 2003. FAST Tools Machinery Economics spreadsheet. Department of Agricultural and Consumer Economics. University of Illinois Urbana-Champaign, Illinois. http://www.farmdoc. uiuc.edu/fasttools/index.html

English, B.C., S.B. Mahajanashetti, and R.K. Roberts. 2001. Assessing spatial break-even variability in fields with two or more management zones. Journal of Agricultural and Applied Economics 33(3):551-565.

Escalante, C.L. and P. Barry. 2001. Risk balancing in an integrated farm risk management plan. Journal of Agricultural and Applied Economics 33(3):413-429.

Etyang, M.N., P.V. Preckel, J.K. Binkley, and D.H. Doster. 1998. Field time constraints for farm planning models. Agricultural Systems 58:25-37.

Featherstone, A.M., P.V. Preckel, and T.G. Baker. 1990. Modeling farm financial decisions in a dynamic and stochastic environment. Agricultural Finance Review 50:80-99.

Ferris, A. and L.R. Malcolm. 1999. Sense and nonsense in dairy farm management. Agribusiness Perspectives. Paper 31. Agribusiness Association of Australia, Kent Town, South Australia.

Finck, C. 1998. Precision can pay its way. Farm Journal Mid-January: 10-13.

Forcella, F. 1992. Value of managing within-field variability. Proceeding of the First Workshop on Soil-Specific Crop Management: A Workshop on Research and Development Issues. American Society of Agronomy, Crop Science Society of America, Soil Science Society of America. Madison, Wisconsin.

Freebairn, D.M., J.B. Robinson, and S.F. Glanville. 2004. Software tools for learning and decision support. Agricultural Productions Systems Research Unit, Department of Natural Resources. Toowoomba, Queensland. http://www.apsru.gov.au/apsru/wfs/pdffiles/ModsimFreebairnGlanvilleRobinson.pdf

Fridgen, J.J., N.R. Kitchen, K.A. Sudduth, S.T. Drummond, W.J. Wiebold, and C.W. Fraisse. 2004. Management zone analyst (MZA): Software for sub-field management zone delineation. Agronomy Journal 96(1):100-108.

Griffin, T.W., J. Lowenberg-DeBoer, D.M. Lambert, J. Peone, T. Payne, and S.G. Daberkow. 2004. Adoption, profitability, and making better use of precision farming data. Staff Paper No. 04-06. Site-Specific Management Center, Purdue, University. West Lafayette, Indiana. http://www.purdue.edu/ssmc

Growth Stage Consulting Inc. CMS Crop. Management.System(tm). http://www.growthstage.com/

Harper, J.K., J.W. Mjelde, M.E. Rister, M.O. Way, and B.M. Drees. 1994. Developing flexible economic thresholds for pest management using dynamic programming. Journal of Agricultural and Applied Economics 26(1):134-147.

Heady, E.O. and J. Pesek. 1954. A fertilizer production surface. Journal of Farm Economics 36(3):466-482.

Hennessy, D.A. and B.A. Babcock. 1998. Information, flexibility, and value added. Information Economics and Policy 10(4):431-449.

Hutton, R.F. and D.W. Thorne. 1955. Review notes on the Heady-Pesek fertilizer production surface. Journal of Farm Economics 37(1):117-119

Isik, M. 2004. Incentives for technology adoption under environmental policy uncertainty: Implications for green payment programs. Environmental and Resource Economics 27(3):247-263.

Just, R.E. 2003. Risk research in agricultural economics: Opportunities and challenges for the next 25 years. Agricultural Systems 75(2-3):123-159.

Just, D.R., S. Wolf, and D. Zilberman. 2003. Principles of risk management service relations in agriculture. Agricultural Systems 75(2-3):199-213.

Keating, B.A. and R.L. McCown. 2001. Advances in farming systems analysis and intervention. Agricultural Systems 70(2-3):555-579.

Khanna, M., M. Isik, and A. Winter-Nelson. 2000. Investment in site-specific crop management under uncertainty: Implications for nitrogen pollution control and environmental policy. Agricultural Economics 24(1):9-21.

Kingwell, R. 1994. Effects of tactical responses and risk aversion on farm wheat supply. Review of Marketing and Agricultural Economics 62(1):29-42.

Kingwell, R.S., D.A. Morrison, and A.D. Bathgate. 1992. The effect of climatic risk on dryland farm management. Agricultural Systems 39(2):153-175.

Kingwell, R.S., D.J. Pannell, and S.D. Robinson. 1993. Tactical responses to seasonal conditions in whole-farm planning in Western Australia. Agricultural Economics 8:211-226.

Lien, G. 2003. Assisting whole-farm decision-making through stochastic budgeting. Agricultural Systems 76(2):399-413.

Lowenberg-DeBoer, J. 1986. The microeconomic roots of the farm crisis. Praeger Publishers, New York, New York. 185 pp.

Lowenberg-DeBoer, J. 2003. Precision farming or convenience agriculture. Proceedings of the 11th Australian Agronomy Conference. Geelong, Victoria.

Malcolm, B. 2000. Farm management economic analysis: A few disciplines, a few perspectives, a few figurings, a few futures. Paper presented at Annual Conference of Australian Agricultural and Resource Economics Society. Sydney, Australia.

Malcolm, L.R. 1990 Fifty years of farm management in Australia. Review of Marketing and Agricultural Economics 58(1):24-55.

Mamo, M., G.L. Malzer, D.J. Mulla, D.R. Huggins, and J. Strock. 2003. Spatial and temporal variation in economically optimum nitrogen rate for corn. Agronomy Journal 95(4):958-964.

Meinke, H., W.E. Baethgen, P.S. Carberry, M. Donatelli, G.L. Hammer, R. Selvaraju, and C.O. Stockle. 2001. Increasing profits and reducing risks in crop production using participatory systems simulation approaches. Agricultural Systems 70(2-3):493-513.

Mitchell, P.D. 2003. Value of imperfect information in agricultural production. Agricultural Systems 75:277-294.

Mjelde, J.W., B.L. Dixon, and S.T. Sonka. 1989. Estimating the value of sequential updating solutions for intrayear crop management. Western Journal of Agricultural Economics 14(1):1-8.

North Dakota State University. NDAWN Center North Dakota Agricultural Weather Network. http://ndawn.ndsu.nodak.edu/

Olson, K. and P. Elisabeth. 2003. An economic assessment of the whole-farm impact of precision agriculture. Paper presented at the American Agricultural Economics Association Annual Meeting. Montreal, Canada.

Pannell, D.J. 1990. Responses to risk in weed control decisions under expected profit maximization. Journal of Agricultural Economics 41:391-403.

Pannell, D.J. 1991. Pests and pesticides, risk and risk aversion. Agricultural Economics 5(4):361-383.

Pannell, D.J. 1994. The value of information in herbicide decision making for weed control in Australian wheat crops. Journal of Agricultural and Resource Economics 19(2):366-381.

Pannell, D.J. 1996 Lessons from a decade of whole-farm modeling in Western Australia. Review of Agricultural Economics 18:373-383.

Pannell, D.J. 1999. On the estimation of on-farm benefits of agricultural research. Agricultural Systems 61(2):123-134.

Pannell, D.J. 2004. Flat-earth economics: The far-reaching consequences of flat payoff functions in economic decision making. Contributed paper presented at the 48th Annual Conference of the Australian Agricultural and Resource Economics Society. Melbourne, Victoria.

Pannell, D.J. and A.L. Bennett. 1999. The economics of monitoring crops at the micro level: Precision weed management. Pp. 138-148. *In:* Precision Weed Management in Crops and Pastures. R.W. Medd and J.E. Pratley (eds.) CRC for Weed Management Systems, Adelaide, Australia.

Pannell, D.J., B. Malcolm, and R.S. Kingwell. 2000. Are we risking too much? Perspectives on risk in farm modeling. Agricultural Economics 23(1):69-78.

Rae, A.N. 1971. Stochastic programming, utility, and sequential decision problems in farm management. American Journal of Agricultural Economics 53:448-460.

Robb, G.W., R. Betz, B. Dartt, and S. Nott. 2001. Dairy farmers' use of Financial Long-Range Planning (FINLRB) to aid in decision-making. Staff Paper 2001-21. Department of Agricultural Economics. Michigan State University, East Lansing, Michigan.

Saphores, J-D. M. 2000. The economic threshold with a stochastic pest population: A real options approach. American Journal of Agricultural Economics 82(3):541-555.

Schultz, T.W. 1939. Theory of the firm and farm management research. Journal of Farm Economics 21(3):570-586.

Siemens, J., K. Hamburg, and T. Tyrrell. 1990. A farm machinery selection and management program. Journal of Production Agriculture 3(2):212-219.

Tenkorang, F. and J. Lowenberg-DeBoer. 2004. Observations on the economics of remote sensing in agriculture. Site-Specific Management Center. Purdue, University. West Lafayette, Indiana. http://www.purdue.edu/ssmc

Thornton, P.K. 1984. Treatment of risk in a crop protection information system. Journal of Agricultural Economics 36:201-209.

Watson, M. and J. Lowenberg-DeBoer. 2002. Who will benefit from GPS auto guidance in the Corn Belt? Site-Specific Management Center. Purdue, University. West Lafayette, Indiana http://www.purdue.edu/ssmc

Applying Models to Decision Support Tools

CHAPTER 5

G.J. Kovacs

Model development and the application of models to improve our understanding of the physical, biological, and chemical processes within an agricultural system has been the goal of research programs throughout the world. The experiences of this author to evaluate the advantages and shortcomings of crop models have enriched the ability to understand how models could play a critical role in the application to improved decision-making. The goal is to make models useful for other researchers, students, and for those whose life physically connected to the fields. The most exciting exercise remains to better understand creation and to learn how we can best fit into nature without ruining it. It all depends on our decisions. *Is a decision support system a scientific discipline or a branch of extension?* Creating decision's support tools is a new chapter in modern sciences. The goal of a decision support system is to apply all the available knowledge to solve real problems within a segment of the world. Some may consider this extension of knowledge, rather than science to create knowledge and understand processes. The goal is the same, the difference comes from the fact that the decision support system utilizes much more knowledge than a human individual can consume, evaluate, and utilize. It does not mean that decision support system tools are currently at a level that local experts could not recommend better advice to the farmers or any other decision makers than a given decision support system. Decision support tools have to develop more before we can state that the security of a decision support system locally, will outperform the wisdom of an experienced local farmer. However, while the farmer's wisdom is limited by his location, facilities, inheritance, age, etc., the decision support systems are based on widely or even globally accumulated and incorporated knowledge bases. The amount of information and the structure of stored knowledge and the need of a theory how to apply the accumulated knowledge in decision-making at different levels make it imperative that decision support system be treated as a branch of science rather than a technical problem (Wierzbicki et al., 2000; Kropff et al., 2001).

What decision pressures make agriculture interested in a decision support system? Experience was satisfactory for making good decisions at traditional farming. Significant changes have placed farmers in a more complicated situation. They have to be aware of the fast changing ecological and economical conditions. The open economy and globalization sharpened the competition. Multi-choice new technologies, growing environmental hazards, and food quality restrictions increase the pressure to make an informed decision from a larger information based that require a tool to oversee the advantages, hazards, and risks of all the options. Farmers, extension specialists and government decision makers need a decision support system that is capable of tracking the important variables of the entire agricultural system (Matthews and Stephens, 2002).

Profit and environmental safety are the

two categories from a multitude of goals that can be included in the array of decisions. If we want to develop decision support tools by application of models, we need to know the goals that the models should satisfy. Profit is a priority interest of farmers; obviously, system models should not stop at production amounts but express the results in market terms. Environmental safety is more detached from the decision processes. If the farmer is a long time owner of the land and a resident on the farm, he has more desire and motivation to protect environment quality. Another factor is the legal pressure. Beside crop production and market processes modelers should consider relevant environmental legislation concerning food quality and ground water quality that may force that these issues to be equivalent factors to profit. Furthermore, in case of a sound legal system the fines and benefits can turn some of the environmental quality factors into profit factors. Still there is a moral portion of factors that effects decisions but they are not as strong as the pressure of the yearly survival. Therefore, system models should be able to project the expected profit and the long-term consequences of several optional technologies in the soil, water and atmosphere.

Sustainable development is one of the driving forces of decision support system development. With the increasing intensity of agricultural production, there is growing interest in assessing the sustainability of these systems. Maintaining system function (by maintaining capital stocks) for future generations, and the distribution of resource use over long time frames suggest that the prediction problem should be characterized as a long-term goal. Sustainability is a prediction problem on policies and conditions as a result it is a decision problem. (Belcher et al., 2004)

Analyzing agricultural systems and their alternative management options experi-

mentally in real time is generally not feasible because of the length of time and amount of resources required. For instance, to sample the effects of climatic variability and associated management responses adequately may require decades of experimentation, particularly in areas with large climate variability. Alter-natively, well-tested simulation approaches offer a time and cost-efficient alternative to experimentation on the physical system and results obtained in hours or days rather than years or decades (Meinke, 2001).

The role of model application among decision support system tools

In order to put the model application into perspective, we need to determine other tools that could be applied in decision support.

Categories of decision support system solutions. An understandable typology helps to reduce the confusion for farmers and decision makers investigating and discussing decision support systems. Taxonomy also helps users and developers communicate their experiences with decision support systems.

Alter's (1980) taxonomy is based on the degree to which decision support system output can directly determine the decision. These generic operations range from extremely data-oriented to extremely model-oriented. Decision support systems may involve retrieving a single item of information, providing a mechanism for *ad hoc* data analysis, providing pre-specified aggregations of data in the form of reports. Decision support systems may also include estimating the consequences of proposed decisions and proposing decisions. Alter categorized the decision support system in terms of the generic operations they perform, independent of type of problem, functional area or decision perspective. His seven types based on agricultural examples include:

■ **File drawer systems** that provide access to databases. Farm-level examples include real-time monitoring of tools and materials for field treatments, monitoring of crop development and health. Simple query and reporting tools are included.

■ **Data analysis systems** that support the manipulation of data by computerized tools tailored to a specific task and setting or by more general tools and operators. Examples may include budget analysis and variance monitoring, and analysis of management opportunities.

■ **Analysis information systems** provide access to a series of decision-oriented databases and small models. Examples include sales forecasting based on a marketing database, competitor analyses, product planning and analysis. Online analytical processing systems fall into this category.

■ **Accounting and financial models** calculate the consequences of possible actions. Examples include estimating profitability of a new product, analysis of operational plans using a goal-seeking capability, break-even analysis, and generating estimates of income statements and balance sheets. These types of models should be used with "What if?" or sensitivity analysis.

■ **Representational models** estimate the consequences of actions based on simulation models that include relationships those are causal as well as accounting definitions. Examples may include crop models, risk analysis models and equipment and production simulations.

■ **Optimization models** provide guidelines for action by generating an optimal solution consistent with a series of constraints. Examples include scheduling systems, resource allocation, and material usage optimization.

■ **Suggestion models** perform the logical processing leading to a specific suggested decision for a fairly structured or well-understood task. Examples include cultivation, fertilization, irrigation treatments, insurance calculation, and an optimal bond-bidding model.

Power (2000) talks about five main categories of a decision support system as Data-Driven, Model-Driven, Knowledge-Driven, Document-Driven and Communications-Driven decision support system.

■ **Data-Driven** systems place their emphasis on access to and management of large databases of structured data, mainly time-series data. They have query and retrieval tools and are able to manipulate data to perform specific tasks. Examples of Data-Driven decision support system are as follows: file drawer and management reporting systems, data warehousing and analysis systems, executive information systems (EIS), geographic information systems (GIS), business intelligence systems (BIS). Online analytical processing (OLAP) offers the highest level of functionality and decision support linked to analysis of large collections of historical data (Dhar and Stein, 1997).

■ **Model-Driven** systems emphasize access to and manipulation of a model. Simple statistical and analytical tools provide the most elementary level of functionality. Some online analytical processing systems allow complex analysis of data and may be classified as hybrid decision support systems providing modeling, data retrieval, and data summarization. Model-Driven decision support systems use data and parameters provided by decision-makers to aid them in analyzing a situation, but they are not usually data intensive.

■ **Knowledge-Driven or Expert System systems** recommend actions to the decision makers. The terminology for this category of decision support system is still developing. Appropriate alternative is the "Suggestion decision support system" (Alter, 1980) or "Expert Systems." These decision support systems are computerized systems with specialized problem-solving expertise. Experts, who understand the problems within a particular domain, give their opinions to the "editors" who formulize the knowledge of the domain, and "skill" at solving some of these problems. An associated concept is 'data mining.' It refers to a class of analytical applications that search for hidden patterns in a database. Data mining tools can be used to create mixed (Data-Driven and Knowledge-Driven) decision support systems.

▪ **Document-Driven** system is a new type of decision support system to help decision makers retrieve and manage unstructured documents and websites. A range of storage and processing technologies is integrated in a Document-Driven decision support system. Enormous amount document databases are available on the Web including hypertext documents, sounds, images, video materials, scientific papers, course notes, laboratory procedures, product specifications, catalogs, minutes of meetings, and important correspondence. A search engine is a powerful decision-aiding tool associated with a Document-Driven decision support system (Fedorowicz, 1993).

▪ **Communications-Driven** and **Group** systems include communication, collaboration and decision support technologies that do not fit within those decision support system types identified by Alter. Group decision support systems (GDSS) remind us to the medical consultation when a hospital patient has a life threatening situation. A broader category of Communications-Driven decision support system or groupware can now be identified. A group decision support system is a hybrid decision support system that emphasizes the use of both communication and decision models. A group decision support system is an interactive computer-based system intended to facilitate the solution of problems by decision-makers working together as a group. Groupware supports electronic communication, scheduling, document sharing, and other group productivity and decision support enhancing activities. We have a number of technologies and capabilities in this category in the framework—group decision support system decision rooms, two-way interactive video, white boards, bulletin boards and email.

The decisions have an element of risk and consequently responsibility. This is why in complex problems the final decisions are by humans, and tools are used as support for these decisions. In simpler and less risky situations, decisions can be automated. In tactical decisions at a farm, e.g., irrigation scheduling, can be made from the simulated moisture content of soil at different parts of the field. However, in case of an investment, the decision has to be made by the farmer and decision support systems can be only a support.

These decision support system alternatives can be ranked according to ratio of implicit/explicit expressions. One end is an individual opinion telling the solution of a problem without any reasoning, the other end is a closed mathematical formula describing all the factors and results with the details of the operation of the system. The last one is mechanistic simulation model. As the formulization is increasing and the knowledge content of the algorithms is growing, fewer but more exact data and parameters are necessary for a good simulations of systems.

An experienced specialist at their location and circumstance can use simple data to support the decisions using their intelligence. An individual expert can give excellent advice locally based on knowledge and experiences but it remains local, subjective, and may lack sufficient alternatives. Collective experience is the next level of resources. Personal communication and published documents provide different forms and levels of support.

When a set of problems is pre-solved for several scenarios using opinions of several experts structured in a user-friendly manner it is called an "expert system." This extends the validity, objectiveness, and marketability of an individual expert opinion. Recommendations gained from expert systems are not necessarily based on the knowledge of the processes but rather an intuitive judgment from collective experience. Human brain has enormous capacity to make intelligent prognosis within the limits of the domain of experiences. When scientists are involved in the construction of an expert system, analytical knowledge, and practical experience are building blocks. However, expert systems remain partially subjective and the validity is local.

Huge number of relationships are expressed in statistical functions most of which are assumed to have valid causal relationships. When knowledge is structured into algorithms of processes and systems in time, we call it simulation model.

Assessment of the role of modeling in agricultural decision support systems. Model based decision support system use algorithms to mimic processes and systems and to optimize solutions. These models can be simple statistical and empirical functions or sophisticated models full of differential equations. Users of model-driven decision support systems need to provide input parameters, input data and initial values of many variables. Modeling is knowledge intensive procedure, relatively smaller quantity of input data are needed but models are quite sensitive to the quality of the input parameters and data.

Data based decision support system are based on case studies, e.g., quantify the environmental risk from nonpoint source pollution to ground water. Vulnerability maps of aquifers do not allow a dynamic evaluation of interactions resulting from management intervention and depict a static view of the agricultural system. In order to evaluate the possible consequences of different agricultural management practices on the environment, it is essential to develop dynamic tools that aid in quantifying the effect of management options on critical variables.

Probabilistic quantification is an essential qualification of simulation models. Cropping systems can be characterized by well-tested models in their complex plant/soil/environment interactions. These cannot be obtained from field experimentation or farm observation. (Thornley and Johnson, 1990). Long-term sustainability of management practices may be assessed by the combination of cropping system ls and hydrological models (Carberry et al., 2000). This approach is necessary because experimental data collected in diverse environmental conditions have resulted in different conclusions with respect to the potential risk of contamination of groundwater (Rossi Pisa, 1995; Grignani et al., 1994; Sequi et al., 1995). Reliable simulation approaches propose a possible solution to overcome debates on these issues.

What is new in today's science in relation to modeling? We are in an era of synthesis in many fields of sciences. During the past centuries, researchers accumulated tremendous amounts of analytical data and many processes of nature and economy have been well described, but the operation of whole systems far from understood. The scientific explanation of the agricultural system has largely been given and relationships of environmental factors and individual processes expressed in mathematical formulas. However, it is not known well enough how agricultural systems work, e.g. what mechanisms control a complex ecological and economical interactions. In order to help decision-making we need to understand complex systems and determine what happens to the system's outputs when different treatments are applied. The recognition of these needs mobilized many research teams in the world to build simulation models that include available analytical knowledge into operational systems.

What kind of model can be applied to a decision support system? Statistical models can serve a decision support system very well in case the models were created from databases of the location where the decision support system is used. These models usually include statistical relationships of crop yields and the local weather conditions, and fertilizer or irrigation treatments, sequencing, etc. The expected values, limits and rules may work very well for estimation but they will not be applicable to another soil type or different crop or abnormal weather. To create more general rules we need to follow the cause and effect relationships, model the processes in time, and utilize a wide range of conditions. However, this leads us to a different type of modeling, called simulation.

Simulation models are developed from scientific quantification of causal relationships of the main processes of a system and integration of these processes to mimic the real system's behavior. Simulation models consist of algorithms of processes and interactions among processes of the system in time. Simulation models—together with the databases that serve the algorithms with input parameters and environmental data— are capsules of working knowledge from all available disciplines in relation to the studied system. Simulation is a descriptive tool for prediction. Simulation becomes necessary when the system is too complex to be handled by optimization models. Simulation describes and predicts the characteristics of system under different circumstances. Once these characteristics are set, alternative actions can be assessed. Simulation experiments can be conducted many times to obtain estimates of the overall effect of certain actions on the system.

Why simulation model is the way of future? A simulation model based correct algorithms and driven true parameters and data is able to supply scientific prognosis of the behavior of a system independent of the location on the Earth. Current simulation models are constructed as modules, so the user can select from several scientific theories for a given process depending on the goals

and the available input data. Simulation modeling may be the best scientific approach to support decisions but it will take time until it will be commercially competitive with the advice of local experts and the locally produced statistical models.

Simulation models are used in a wide range of sciences, industry and sales management as predictors of change, aids for decisions, and demonstration of the functions of complex systems. There are several reasons for their popularity: simulation theory is relatively easy to understand since it works with elementary relationships and interdependencies. Their practicality, on the other hand, is clear: simulation allows the decision maker to ask "what-if" questions; simulation models can be focused on real world problems at simple or very complex systems. Users can experiment with different variables to determine which are important and with multiple alternatives to determine which is best. A large number of scenarios can be produced to gain a long-term perspective of various policies within a short time. User-friendly interfaces and help programs make it possible to use these models without a deep understanding of the system. Simulation can include a wide variety of performance measures like visual aids. Graphic display of the results, animation of the simulation outputs made simulation to be one of the most successful developments in computer-human interaction and problem solving.

Present contribution of simulation modeling to decision support systems

In decision support, one part is as important as the other part since all work together to support the decision makers. Development of decision-making processes depends on the balanced improvement of each segments of the support system. There are several areas where system simulation models successfully serve decision support systems. Highly specialized regional decisions, e.g., cotton farming at a region or an irrigated desert region, are well supported (Remy, 1994; Keating and McCown, 2001; Kropff et al., 2001; Matthews and Stephens, 2002). Successful simulation examples can be found, as well, at areas where otherwise inconceivable and unmanageable global issues are examined, like the effects of global warming on crop production (Baethgen and Magrin, 2000; Richter and Semenov, 2004.) System simulation models can be used in solutions of theoretical problems, like how can we respond in an unexpected rise or decrease of the ground water level or what kind of genetic changes would produce the greatest benefit.

On the average farm, the pure scientific "mechanistic" models today may be less effective than the local extension service or consultant due to the unmet input requirements of a system simulation models. The solution at the presently applied system simulation models is the mixed routines where simplified process simulation is linked with empirical elements. This makes the models run, after regional parameterization, relatively well with minimum data sets but extremely region specific.

In strategic decisions. Strategic (preplant) decisions can be made for one or for several years. Fertilization, selection of cultivar, planting date, plant density, and basic plant protection are decisions for the single growing season. (Kovács et al., 1998; Rajkai et al., 2004) There are strategies when fertilizers are applied to meet the nutrient requirements for multiple cropping seasons. Long time strategy decision is an investment for an irrigation system or equipments for precision farming, etc. These decisions could be supported by simulation studies. Farmers can run the models—directly or by the help of an extension agent—to obtain scenarios with respect to profitability, economic and environmental risks. Remy (1994) showed that farmers used GLICIM before they plant soybean

(*Glycine max* (L.) Merr.) to compare estimates of simulated yields from different cultivars on farm fields by using a range of plant populations, fertilizers, irrigation schedules, etc. GUICS decision support shell helps them to interact with the model and handle the inputs and outputs.

There are examples where model-driven decision support systems serve a special group, like cabbage growers in the island of Maui, to decide whether a given tract of land is suitable and feasible to grow that crop. In order to support local farmers at a "point-and-click" manner with this information, the model needs to get input data from a geographic information system (GIS)(Tsuji et al., 2002).

Sustainability can be assessed by crop models linked together in a rotation or a continuous sequence of crops and the results can be analyzed in graphical and tabular fashion. Some simulation systems make it possible to study the accumulation, downward and upward movement of the pollutants in the soil even as deep as 10 to 15 meters from the surface. The 4M Model predicts the nitrate concentration of the water within the soil profile and under the water table (Fodor et al., 2002).

Economic analysis is vital component of decision support packages allowing users to assess profitability of different technologies counting the prices of the applied materials and energy as well as the income from the agricultural products.

GIS linked with biophysical and economic compartments of the decision support system tool provides a spatial tool for evaluating different systems. Upendra Singh and his team developed an information and decision support tool including DSSAT models and the economic model called DREAM (Wood et al., 2001) and a GIS database. One use of the information and decision support tool long term has been to compare sequential cropping simulations at different technology levels with the analysis of the biophysical sustainability of a system coupled with the generation of relevant and structured economic information to support decision-makers implementing agricultural policy, assigning priorities, and allocating limited resources over a large area (Singh et al., 2002).

An example of use of simulation in decision support for technology transfer at a larger geographical area is the deep point-placement of urea supergranules in India. (Singh and Thornton, 1992; Mohanty et al., 1999). These studies showed the appropriate niches for urea supergranules deep point-placement in contradiction to other areas where the economic and ecological conditions did not support the benefits of this technology. The motivation for this research was to test the suitability of a new technology to specific areas by modeling large and heterogeneous land areas, like India or Bangladesh before recommendations are passed to farmers.

Simulation studies showed (Singh et al., 2002) that the poor maize (*Zea mays* L.) yield in Koukombo, Togo could be increased by two to four times if better suited planting date, higher fertilizer treatments, and appropriate genotypes would be applied. Under rainfed conditions the simulated yield was 7 to 8 tons ha^{-1} but only 1.5 to 3.2 tons ha^{-1} when local average fertilizer amounts (N=20 kg ha^{-1}, P_2O_5=15 kg ha^{-1}) were used in the simulations. The simulated yields were equal to the observed local average farm yield. It was shown that yields could be improved through additional fertilizer and better selection of genotypes coupled with optimal planting dates without the need for a large investment into irrigation systems.

Expected climate change and their effects on agriculture cannot be forecast without simulation. Government agencies require model aided decision support tools for long term planning of adaptation to consequences of global climate changes. Several examples of the results from agricultural

simulation studies throughout the world have been documented (Kovács, 1998).

Many theoretical questions of climate changes are worthy of study, but some of them have significant relevance for the present, not only for the future. There is a special worldwide interest in the impacts of ENSO (El Niño/Southern Oscillation) on agricultural production throughout the world. Not only descriptive results can be gained from the climate change simulation studies, but also there are conclusions usable to control the agricultural effects of changes. For example, Baethgen (1998) suggested that in Uruguay the yield losses, experienced in La Nina years, could be reduced, if short-season maize hybrids are sown two months later than in other years. Several studies dealt with ENSO-based climate forecast and its consequences in agriculture for Argentina (Baethgen and Magrin, 2000; Magrin et al., 1999; Baethgen, 1998; Podesta et al., 1998).

The role of simulation models in handling complex systems is well documented by the Information and Decision Support Systems. The Information and Decision Support System was developed by the International Fertilizer Development Center for the agricultural sector, in collaboration with national agricultural research centers in Latin America. Their aim was to unify the advantages of modern information tools, large and complex databases, and crop modeling. The Information and Decision Support System includes simulation models (for crop growth, for the dynamics of soil organic matter, nutrients and soil erosion), climatic maps, regional statistics, prices, remotely sensed vegetation and weather data, climate forecasts. All of these are within a shell, a decision support system specifically designed for agrotechnology transfer containing tools like GIS and an automated land use evaluation system (Baethgen and Magrin, 2000). Without system simulation, it would not be possible to process the vast amount of information needed to describe these complex soil-plant-atmospheric-oceanographic systems and be able to create applicable forecasts of agricultural production.

Practical applications of modeling is presented in the Information and Decision Support System (Baethgen, 1988a). It links maps and databases through GIS, which allows spatial analyses at the regional and at the farmer level. Areas of application include:

■ forecast crop and pasture production,

■ issue drought and flood alert reports,

■ conduct impact studies of inter-annual and long-term climatic variability,

■ perform economical and environmental impact studies including risk assessment.

■ land use feasibility classes for different agricultural production systems, and

■ drought and flood alerts, and famine early warning systems (FEWS).

The following quotation from (International Research Institute for Climate Prediction, 2003) demonstrates how significant role modeling plays in developing decision support tools. (Hansen et al., 2004)

"Decision strategies require information at varying scales and for a variety of environmental variables that are influenced by climate. Focusing on the seasonal time-scale, the information may be developed through both environmental monitoring and/or information rooted in seasonal climate predictions. How to extract the required information from the predictable component of seasonal climate is a key research topic. Extracting the information from General Circulation Model seasonal prediction output can be undertaken using statistical transformations or using dynamical downscaling methods. Methodologi-cal advances are emerging through testing in different locations, either as part of regional projects, or inde-pendently when there is opportunity to advance this research question. Developing methodologies to predict crop yield establishes necessary advances for exploring decisions in the agriculture sector. For example, Figure 1 gives an example of predictability of district wheat yield evaluated for Queensland.

The result suggests that, in this example, this methodology of transforming seasonal predictions adds substantial information to yield predictions that are based on monitored climate information alone.

The figure shows that some predicta-bility is possible from monitoring pre-season climate conditions, but that predictability is substantially enhanced by including information from General Circulation Model seasonal predictions. Coupling the seasonal climate forecast to crop models permits exploration of both crop yield predictability and its quantitative incorporation into decision strategies."

In tactical decisions. Tactical (postplant) decisions made within the growing season about irrigation scheduling, yield prediction, top dressing by nitrogen or micronutrients, plant protection, and harvest timing, etc. are directed toward enhancing crop yield. As an example, Remy (1994) reported the results from tactical decisions using model-driven decision support systems from Mississippi State University. Soybean growers in the area attributed a significant yield increase (29 percent) and four times greater irrigation use efficiency to the use of simulation aided decision support system (GLYIM/GUICS). Irrigation was more efficient since the moisture content of the soil was estimated for each day of the season for the whole profile, and farmers began to irrigate before the soil was too dry. Soil water conductivity never dropped too low, so the time and the

Figure 1

Correlation between best estimate prediction and observed October Queensland wheat yields (all results cross-validated). Left panel: Yields predicted by applying a model output statistics methodology to transform large-scale GCM output fields (simulations with ECHAM4.5) to the predicted wheat yield data. Right panel: Yields predicted using monitored climatological information prior to May.

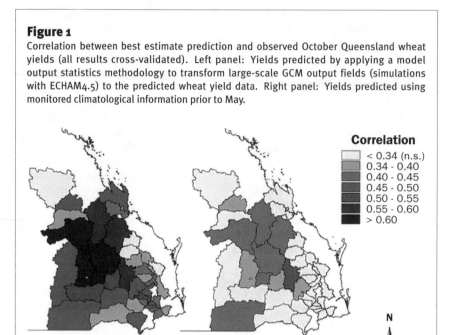

amount of irrigation were smaller. In case of a dryer soil, it would take much longer time to rewet the soil profile.

Yield forecast within season can be made with better precision as the harvest is closer. Runs of models—that have this capability—can be stopped at the actual date. Then selected estimated variables can be corrected according to actual measurements or observations. Short-term forecasts and longer-term scenarios for the season can also be considered. Usually several options are run for the remainder of the season, counting possible interventions, as well. Data for resetting the model during the season can come from field observations (soil and plant sampling, weighing or laboratory analysis, or other instrumental readings) or it can be remote sensing (LAI for growth or temperature for stress).

Timlin et al. (2002) mention a "side benefit" of process oriented decision systems: "Many growers, after viewing simulation results during the growing season, would go to their fields often to check their crop growth stage and compare to GLYCIM's predictions of phenology. As a result, they would be more aware of details of their fields and crops, and the crops' responses to the environment."

Precision (or site specific) agriculture[+] can be considered a product of strategic thinking but this is a detailed tactical technology when the farmer pays attention the spatial variability within the crop fields and treats the different spots rationally. The question is what treatments are feasible and environmentally sound if the same spot behaves different ways in different weather conditions concerning to both production and pollution?

Kersebaum et al. (2002) stated "Agricultural system models provide a tool to transfer the spatial heterogeneity of time-stable soil and terrain attributes, which have to be estimated once for a field, into a temporal dynamic of the relevant state variables of the soil-crop nitrogen dynamics." They used a simple system model called HERMES (Kersebaum and Richter, 1991) for field level fertilizer recommendation for cereals and estimated nitrate leaching on a regional scale (Kersebaum and Beblik, 2001).

In risk assessment. Risk analysis deals with uncertainties of the outcomes of the simulation. Since both the biophysical and the economic environment of agricultural systems are exposed to major changes, we need to work with input scenarios and probabilities. Several system simulation models in agriculture (like DSSAT, APSIM, 4M, etc.) are built into shells that are equipped with risk analysis procedures to allow selection of strategies under conditions of uncertainty and to provide due recognition to farmers' attitudes to risk and mean outcome (Thornton and Wilkens, 1998; Keating and Meinke, 1998). Meinke et al. (2001) used participatory system simulation approaches to increase profits and reduce risks in crop production.

Frequently we need to differentiate what causes a change, e.g., a stress on the vegetation, loss of yield etc., but in a multi component system it is nearly an impossible task. Modeling can create a probable solution that may need to be tested by experiments (Máthé-Gáspár et al., 2003; Kovács, 1997).

Richter and Semenov (2004) carried out simulation assessment of drought-related risk in England and Wales. The impact of changing weather patterns on wheat production was simulated with the mechanistic model Sirius, (Jamieson et al., 1998) which simulates grain yields from biomass accumulation until anthesis and during grain filling. Simulations of potential and water-limited yields were compared in three regions: the West and East Midlands and East Anglia, representing nearly 50 percent of the total wheat area. In large parts of England (East Midlands, East Anglia), the overall drought impact on potential yield was predicted to differ little between baseline and future scenarios. There, the overall risk of yield losses greater than 25 percent is likely to remain at a probability of 0.10. In spite of a predicted increase of drought in the future, compensating effects of rising CO_2 are likely to be stronger than the effect of water shortage in England and Wales. The uncertainty of estimated wheat yields did not increase when considering the coefficient variation and the probability of below average yields. However, dry years may cause substantial reductions in grain yield on droughty soils more frequently. Breeding and selecting varieties as well as other management practices to maintain the GLAI longer may further increase future yields by 1 t ha^{-1}. The average wheat yields are likely to increase by 1.2 to 2 t ha^{-1} (15 to 23 percent) by the 2050's because of a CO_2-related increase in radiation use efficiency. Grain yields are likely to be less variable but the probability of the annual coefficient of variation exceeding 15 percent remains the same.

A Hungarian study will be used as an example to demonstrate several advantages and shortcomings of current simulation modeling in agriculture. Nitrate pollution of groundwater was a major risk during the 1980's in Hungary (Németh, 1996b;c; and d). Voluntarism controlled crop production therefore unlimited amount of nitrogen fertilizer was used (often rates of 300 kg N ha^{-1} yr^{-1}) to reach the plan of the ruling party's decision. When scientists wanted to know the amount pollution and the risk of further pollution, they found a unique region for leaching studies in Hungary. Three main ecological characteristics made it suitable for the study: well-drained soil parent material, modest rainfall, and deep level of groundwater (13 m). Practically all the extra nitrogen that exceeded the amount of plant N-uptake was found deeper in the soil profile (Németh, 1993; Németh et al., 1988; Kádár et al., 1989). The area is the western edge of the Great Hungarian Lowland, between the river Danube and the lake Balaton in the county called Fejér. It is typical loess plateau of the Carpathian Basin. The depth of the loess reaches 30 to 40 meters. Loess is built up from coarse loam texture, the structure comes from the approximately. Ten percent of $CaCO_3$ content. It is well aerated having good water holding capacity and high water conductivity. The soil is calcaric chernozjem with 1 meter humic horizon and characterized by high fertility. Main crops are corn and winter wheat. The yield-limiting factor is water, average yearly precipitation is 550 mm and the yearly ambient temperature is 10.5°C.

On the experimental field of Research Institute for Soil Science and Agricultural Chemistry (RISSAC) of the Hungarian Academy of Sciences there is a long term NPK fertilizer experiment started in 1967 (Németh, 1994; 1995). CERES model was parametrized and used for prediction for the first 20 years of the experiment (Kovács et al., 1995; Nagy et al., 1994; Kovács et al., 1997; Kovács, 1997).

This time, the 4M simulation and decision support system package was used to simulate the cropping system between 1989 and 1998. The 4M Model was based on CERES and CROPGRO models to develop a package for the present requirements and opportunities of our country and region (Fodor et al., 2002). The development of 4M (both concerning content and user friendliness) is continuous.

The crop rotation in the experiment was wheat-corn-corn-wheat, at the first year in examination (1989) wheat was harvested since it was first year of the rotation. After the model was parameterized, predicted yields were compared

with measured yields for the 10 years in Figure 2a and 2b where the 150 and 250 $kg \cdot ha^{-1} \cdot yr^{-1}$ treatments are shown. Yearly simulated yields are compared with the measured yields of the field experiment and the average yield of entire Fejér County (Figure 3). Yields of the county can be accurately simulated using the set of inputs from the experiment (50 $kg \cdot ha^{-1} \cdot yr^{-1}$ fertilizer rate was close to the actual N rate in the 1990's.) This approach provides an opportunity to use the estimates at the county level.

Figure 4 shows the simulated nitrate-N leaching versus measured leaching. In this study we considered leaching all the nitrate moved past from the rooting zone below 150 cm from the surface. Though the soil was sampled till a depth of 300 cm, it was still not deep enough to catch the whole amount of leached nitrate. Only the distribution of the accumulation until 300 cm can be compared (Figure 4). The N rate of 50 $kg \cdot ha^{-1} \cdot yr^{-1}$ had practically the same nitrate concentrations as the control treatment and is not shown on the figure. Evaluating the nitrate-N distribution in the profile, simulation obviously had a bit slower N-transport than the observed data would suggest.

The following simulation and data comparisons demonstrate the usefulness of simulation in cases when direct measurements are not available but some important characteristics of the system are known (Figures 5, 6, and 7). Simulation is a good tool to estimate the risk of nitrate leaching, to forecast the time when the pollution reaches the depth of the water table even if measured data are not satisfactory for conclusion. On the figures, the simulation shows how nitrate-N accumulation most probably changed over the 10-year period of the experiment. (We used the measured values for 1988 as initial values for the runs till a depth of 300 cm, the rest was simulated.) It was observed that the front of nitrate accumulation (where the curve

Figure 2

Figure 2a. Measured and simulated yields in N=150 kg·ha^{-1}·yr^{-1} treatment, 1980 to 1989, Nagyhörcsök, Hungary. Figure 2b. Measured and simulated yields in N=250 kg·ha^{-1}·yr^{-1} treatment, 1980 to 1989, Nagyhörcsök, Hungary.

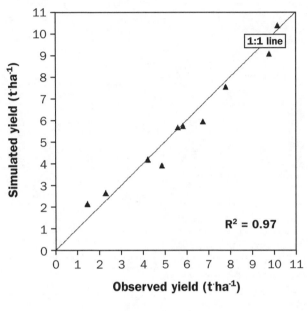

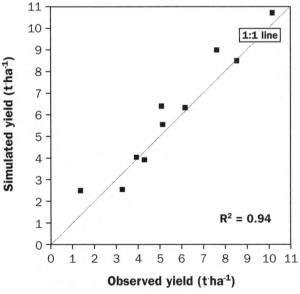

Figure 3
Measured and simulated yields in the experiment and in Fejér County.

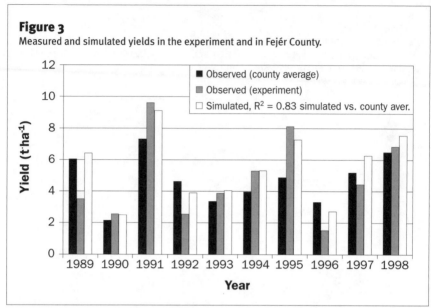

of a treatment reaches the curve of the control plot) is moving downwards and the distribution is becoming wider, and the peeks are less steep. The rate (as much the fronts were moving downward) was 3 to 4 m over the 10 years. The total leached-N amount was 8, 11, 18, 35, 65 kg·ha^{-1}yr^{-1} for the 0, 50 100, 150, 200 and 250 kg·ha^{-1}yr^{-1}

Figure 4
Measured and simulated NO$_3$-N accumulation after 30 years of treatments in 3-meter soil profile.

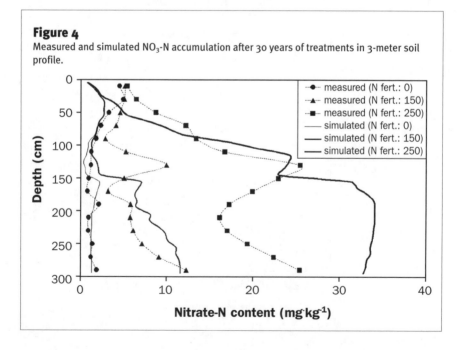

Figure 5

Distribution of NO₃-N accumulation in the soil profile in the 20th year of the experiment (measured till a depth of 300 cm and estimated further, 1988, Nagyhörcsök, Hungary).

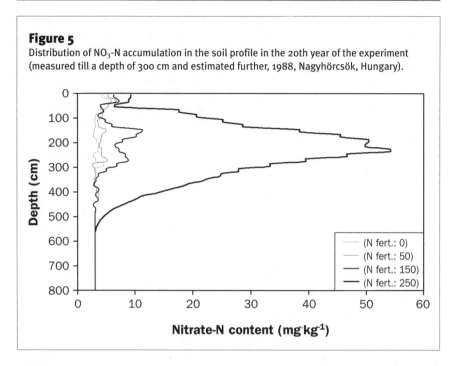

treatments respectively (Figure 8). Distribution of leaching events and amounts were not even during these 10 years. Simulation was an excellent tool to estimate the leaching events over time. There were years when no leaching occurred, from late 1993 till early 1998. In contrast, following the dry and low yielding years, above normal rainfall years showed tremendous amount of nitrate was leached (e.g. the winter of 1993). We can learn from this study to be cautious with nitrogen fertilizer applications following poor production.

At the experimental location the water table is 13 m from the surface. Counting the capillary zone we simulated the N-transport passing the depth of 11 m. The simulated nitrogen contamination at 11-m depth was 5 kg in 1998, 130 kg in 2004 and 780 kg in 2010. (Note that initial input nitrate level for this run was set to zero under 7 m depth in 1988.)

Dual criteria optimization is necessary to help decisions about nitrogen fertiliza-

tion strategy. Most of the times profit and environmental protection, are considered as opposing criteria. In the Hungarian study there was not antagonism between profit and environmental quality. On Figure 9, the modified cumulative probability function was used (Tsuji et al., 1994) to find the nitrogen rate for the highest profit. Using these criteria the 50 and 100 kg·ha⁻¹yr⁻¹ treatments were the best for the bi-crop rotation. From the "1- cumulative probability" function one can read the probability of the profit that is at least as much as the actual readings from the graph. (In DSSAT the cumulative probability function shows the opposite, where probability of the profit is read from the graph.) On Figure 10, the Mean-Gini value shows the best option (50 kg·ha⁻¹yr⁻¹) but it can also be seen that practically there is no difference in profit level within a wide range (50 to 130) of nitrogen rates. It is obvious that the N-dose 130 kg·ha⁻¹ causes twice as much nitrate-N leaching

(240 kg·ha⁻¹ in 10 years) than the 50 kg·ha⁻¹ N rate (Figure 8). It helps to support a clear-cut decision on the optimal N rates.

There is a further question whether the shift of the ratio of the split N fertilizer application from the customary (50 percent fall and 50 percent spring) to a less risky (25 percent fall and 75 percent spring) would decrease the amount of leaching (Nagy, 1995). The simulated difference, from 4M, in leaching is less than expected, on the average only 1 to 2 kg·ha⁻¹yr⁻¹ at the optimum dose, and at 250 kg·ha⁻¹ yearly N application the difference is still less than 4 kg·ha⁻¹yr⁻¹ (Figure 11).

As a part of this risk assessment we made an estimate of nitrate leaching and denitrification for the counties of Hungary (Figure 12 and 13). The reason for using administrative counties instead of natural units was the availability of average yield data. The model was parameterized using the yearly average yields of the main crop of the counties. The loss of N was

expressed over decades. The difference among years is so great that it would be misleading to express it in the scale of years. In the western part of Hungary leaching is the major risk factor while in the eastern part it is denitrification. It is related to the lighter (loess) structure of the soil in the west side and more clayey soils in the eastern counties.

Most scholars at agricultural universities come to the realization that the scientific knowledge has to be somehow coordinated and encapsulated in a better way than in books of the libraries. The following example shows how a team of agricultural economists reached this conclusion. In a risk assessment economic study Sumelius et al. (2002) concluded that Croatian farmers exceed profit-maximizing levels of N-fertilizer use in maize cultivation if the N-content of manure is taken into account. The system of adding N fertilizer with large manure rates significantly increased the NO₃-N-levels in the

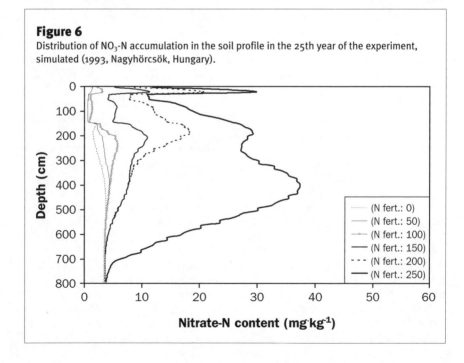

Figure 6

Distribution of NO_3-N accumulation in the soil profile in the 25th year of the experiment, simulated (1993, Nagyhörcsök, Hungary).

Figure 7

Distribution of NO$_3$-N accumulation in the soil profile in the 30th year of the experiment, simulated (1998, Nagyhörcsök, Hungary).

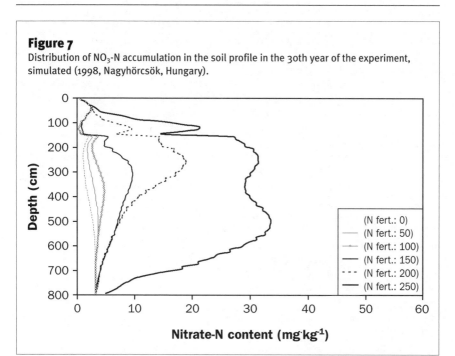

Figure 8

Simulated NO$_3$-N leaching in 10 years (over 150 cm depth) (1989 to 1998, Nagyhörcsök, Hungary).

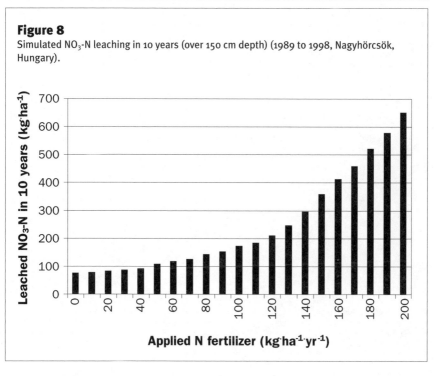

groundwater. They estimated the marginal abatement cost (MAC) at farm level of reducing NO_3-N leaching through economic instruments like a tax on optimal N-rates, a product tax and an N-fertilizer quota. They found the profit maximizing levels of fertilization in maize production to be 172 kg $N\cdot ha^{-1}$. NO_3-N levels in waters at this level were estimated to 14.03 mg NO_3-N l^{-1} or 62.11 mg $NO_3 l^{-1}$. This exceeds the critical level stipulated by the nitrate directive (11.3 NO_3-Nl^{-1} or 50 mg $NO_3 l^{-1}$). The average N applied by farmers as artificial fertilizers, 160.56 kg N/ha, were close to this level. If the N included in the manure is taken into account total N-fertilizers rates were higher, 206 to 230 kg N/ha. The corresponding NO_3-Nl^{-1} level in groundwater was 18.46 mg NO_3-Nl^{-1} – 21.69 mg NO_3-Nl^{-1} (81.71 mg NO_3/l – 96.02 mg NO3/l) or about two times higher than the critical level mentioned in the Nitrate Directive. The possible yield level obtained in experimental conditions at profit maximizing N-intensity level is 8,904 kg maize/ha.

One way to try to influence the nitrate leaching is through applying economic instruments. A 100 percent N-tax or a 50 percent product tax would reduce profit maximizing N-rates to around 74 kg N/ha (i.e. a reduction of 98 kg/ha) and nitrate levels from 14.03 mg NO_3-Nl^{-1} to 3.38 mg NO_3-Nl^{-1} approximately from 62.11 mg NO_3/l 14.95 mg NO_3-/l). This is a reduction of 10.65 mg NO_3-N/l or 47.16 mg NO_3-/l (76 percent leaching reduction). It was found that a quota corresponding to that reduction level of NO_3-Nl^{-1} has the lowest farm level marginal abatement cost, 4.08 €/mg NO_3-Nl^{-1} or 0.92 €/mg NO_3/l. The fertilizer tax had the second lowest MAC (16.16 €/mg NO_3-Nl^{-1}) and the product tax the highest MAC (41.25 €/mg NO_3-Nl^{-1}).

Another way to reduce the risk of ground water pollution is to introduce a code of good agricultural practices

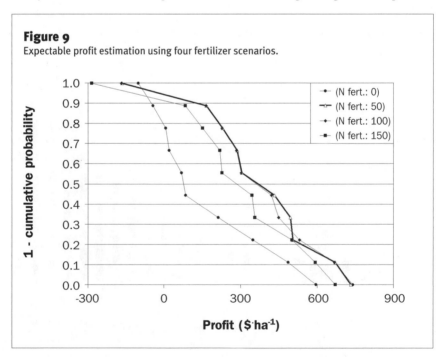

Figure 9

Expectable profit estimation using four fertilizer scenarios.

1 - cumulative probability

Profit ($\cdot ha^{-1}$)

- (N fert.: 0)
- (N fert.: 50)
- (N fert.: 100)
- (N fert.: 150)

Figure 10

The economic optimum of nitrogen (N)-fertilizer treatments.

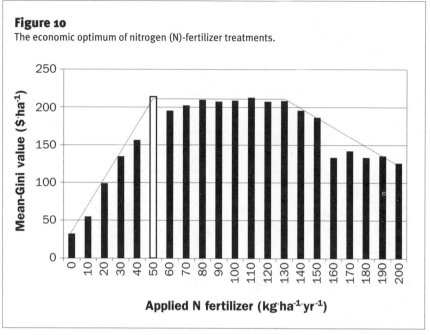

(Sumelius et al., 2002). This would include reduced tillage, crop rotation, choice of proper varieties for maize and wheat, observation of nutrient content in manure and proper plant protection. They concluded that, "there is a need of creating a computer model, based on contemporary scientific and professional practice and methodology to determine the impact of agricultural production on surface and ground waters." The model should also produce a favorable allocation of production for utilization of the area due to soil sustainability principles and of keeping the population in the rural area.

In policymaking. A case study demonstrates that a dynamic modeling approach has much to offer for policy-related decisions. It has the potential to significantly contribute to a more informed government behavior in legislation in the field of agricultural production and systems management within the context of natural resource management. In a case study, (Meinke et al., 2001) diverse cropping systems in two areas in northern Italy were evaluated using the simulation model CropSyst (Stockle and Nelson, 1994). They assessed the possible amount of nitrate leaching for three existing cropping systems of northern Italy to quantify the reduction of nitrate leaching when fertilization rates were determined based on the expected crop uptake from target yields rather than traditional application rates. The study quantified the variability of leaching as a function of the amount of potentially leach able nitrogen in the cropping system. In contrast to local expectations and general assumptions made by policymakers, simulation results suggested that leaching is not an inevitable consequence of cropping in these regions. Even in cases of elevated levels of nitrogen application and under unfavorable soil–climatic situations, nitrogen leaching does not necessarily follow. Hence, current fertilizer recommendations might result in loss of yield potential without further enhancing sustainability or reducing off-site effects of

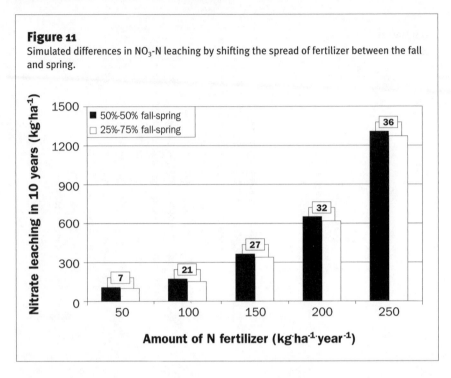

Figure 11
Simulated differences in NO_3-N leaching by shifting the spread of fertilizer between the fall and spring.

cropping. Further, the choice of rotation and the amount of nitrogen applied can have substantial impacts on nitrate leaching. Meinke et al. (2001) found similar simulation results from wheat (*Triticum aestivum* L.) crops in Western Australia. Such analyses may convince policymakers to evaluate and compare the impact of policy options and producers to assess the effect and impact of legislative compliance.

There is evidence that simulation modeling influenced decision making in Australia. For instance, the determination of appropriate drought policies and the evaluation and declaration of state of emergency in relation to drought are issues that require objective information regarding the impact of climate variability on agricultural production. Simulation models are decision support tools to evaluate management responses that result in a better drought preparation at the farm, region or state. Studies showed that it is important

to differentiate between climatologically, production, and economic droughts in the assessment. Since the seasonal climate forecasting developed fast in the past decade, the models can be supplied with the necessary weather scenarios, this has resulted in a much higher level of drought preparation in Australia, and consequently farmers can better tolerate the negative drought impacts (Meinke et al., 2001).

Belcher et al. (2004) introduced a policy oriented simulation model, called SAM (sustainable agroecosystem model). The spatial scale of SAM is an ecodistrict, which makes it an unusual model. An ecodistrict is defined by landform, vegetation and soils that are relatively homogeneous in these characteristics as compared to the surrounding landscape. Farms within an ecodistrict are considered to be relatively homogeneous in terms of their economic characteristics. The purpose of SAM is to evaluate regional agroecosystem sustainability from a systems perspective by using regional economic, soil and climate characteristics in a simulation model framework. SAM dynamically integrates an economic model that simulates land use decisions, based on a constrained short-term profit maximization criterion, and a soils and crop growth model that simulates crop yield, soil quality and soil function. Model output was used to evaluate sustainability by monitoring changes in indicators reflecting the economic (profitability, risk) and soils (soil organic matter, crop yield, carbon loss) system. A detailed description of the model is available in Belcher and Boehm (2002).

Belcher et al., (2004) targeted four agroecosystems in an area of southwestern Saskatchewan, Canada. The four annual crop rotations are: (1) wheat-fallow (WF); (2) wheat-wheat-fallow (WWF); (3) wheat-canola-pea (WCP); and (4) wheat-fallow-pea (WFP). Policy initiatives with agroecosystem sustainability objectives have taken into account, for example, in response to climate change and proposed policies that tax the embodied carbon content of production inputs. Such policies would discourage rotations, which are more input intensive. However, the higher rates of organic matter decomposition and smaller soil organic matter carbon stocks associated with these rotations may result in greater emission of CO_2 from cropland soil. As a result, the carbon tax may actually result in increases of CO_2 emissions where wheat-fallow-pea is a viable production option. Further, these changes in soil organic matter carbon stocks will influence crop yield and yield variability on annual cropland. Changes in yield patterns may, in turn, influence future land use decisions. These land use decisions are higher order consequence of the initial carbon   tax policy and are difficult to quantify without an integrated framework like SAM. There-fore, the SAM model could inform

policy appropriate for the specific economic and environmental conditions of targeted agroecosystems and reflect the secondary and tertiary effects caused by policy incentives.

Another example demonstrates the necessity of a decision support system like SAM, when a decision in a complicated system can cause an unexpected, and sometimes antagonistic, result compared to the original intent. In a study described by Belcher et al. (2004) a policy increased the economic viability that increased the opportunity cost of other land use such as hay and native land. Therefore, this policy, while potentially increasing the economic sustainability of the agroecosystem, decreased the habitat area thereby decreasing a component of the environmental sustainability of the system.

The most troublesome limitations of simulation today

There are some major disadvantages of simulation. Constructing a simulation model is frequently a slow and costly process. Sometimes the problems are already solved before the simulation model is finished (Tsuji et al., 2002). Simulation is a tool and not a discipline. The prerequisite of a simulation model is to have all the necessary knowledge in correct mathematical formula and all the input parameters and data available. Unfortunately non of these are true in practice. So, many times a modeling action is similar to an art, and need much insights about the system in order to fill the gaps of knowledge and data.

Process simulation. Knowledge gaps are the most difficult modeling problems. There are several processes in crop models in which common sense knowledge is not quantified due to lack of suitable methodology (root growth, partitioning of assimilates in plants, the role of soil structure in fertility of plants, etc.) consequently they are not expressed in mathematical formulas for modeling. Every simulation model has some more or less arbitrary solutions for these knowledge gaps. An example is mineralization of nitrogen in unfertilized soils. In case of higher nitrogen rates the yield prediction of crop models (CERES, 4M, etc.) is more or less satisfactory (Figure 2a and 2b) as shown from the Hungarian case study. But with less fertilizer less accurate estimation was made (Figure 14a and 14b). Another extreme example is nitrogen mineralization in soils with high organic carbon (Kovács et al., 1996). These multi-factorial processes are modeled using more empiricism than established causal relationships with exact mathematical expressions. This is why local adaptations are often needed.

Experience with CERES model showed that it required a deep rooting depth input in order to simulate comparable biomass and yield as measured in the field experiment, even if there was no evidence of root penetration as deep as 2 m in the cornfield. Many times the simulated corn did not survive water stress while the experimental field produced a significant grain yield. In the Hungarian study, we found that nitrate was moving much faster and deeper then the CERES model predicted. More water was necessary to drain through the soil for these amounts of nitrate. Through a series of evaluations we determined that rainfall was correct and then we evaluated the evapotranspiration amounts. The radiation input to the model was tested since it was derived from sunshine hours. We concluded that the measure for change in radiation was unrealistically large. After having been tested the soil characteristics the only way was to modify the function that defined transpiration in relation to LAI. As a result we gained not only more water for nitrate leaching but the yield response was improved for all the 10 years. This kind of trials can't be considered as elegant solutions and require more research, but it demonstrates we are far from a complete understanding of the processes of the system. These simulation trials generate questions and hypotheses in key problem areas for systems research.

System simulation. System simulation

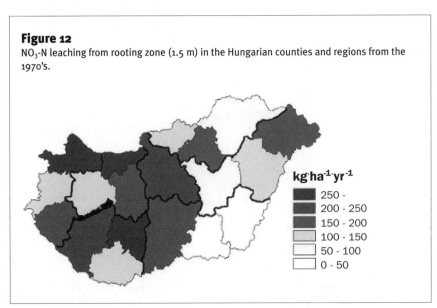

Figure 12
NO$_3$-N leaching from rooting zone (1.5 m) in the Hungarian counties and regions from the 1970's.

kg·ha^{-1}·yr^{-1}

- 250 -
- 200 - 250
- 150 - 200
- 100 - 150
- 50 - 100
- 0 - 50

models would be the ultimate answer for decision support systems if they were perfect. However, these models are far from perfect since simulation is a simplification of the real system and may never work exactly like the real one. When modelers select the important processes from the insignificant ones, certainly put subjective elements into the selection. An optimal or best solution cannot be guaranteed. Since system simulation models include many statistical, empirical relationships and some rough estimates, the forecast can be applied regionally. Some integral parts of the reality are either missing from the simulation models or unbalanced simplifications are introduced in the systems models, e.g., cropping models, frequently have none or only rough compartments to model plant health issues and the cures of a crop stand or they cannot estimate the effect of soil cultivation.

Many of the unsolved problems come out of the contradiction of point models versus spatial characteristics of the modeled system. Most crop models simulate the behavior of an individual plant rather than the crop stand. In field conditions, there are many differences within the field

due to soil heterogeneity, uneven surface morphology, water, run-off and run-on, erosion, sedimentation, uneven plant stands after emergence, weeds, pests, etc. Most models cannot deal with all of these potential interactions.

Keating and McCown (2001) described the heart of the problem with system's simulation as follows. "The vision has existed since the 1970s that management models would become indispensable tools in farm management. Such models would be capable of customization to mimic the reality of individual farms (e.g. the 'skeleton model' concept of Blackie and Dent, 1974) and that optimization would be a powerful tool to identify 'best' practices and decisions (e.g.Van Keulen and deVries, 1993). We have seen great enthusiasm for 'packaging' 'ideal' information and recommendations derived from models or implicit in imbedded models as Decision Support and Expert Systems as a way of reaching real farmers but far too little critical evaluation of use or usefulness of such tools. Clearly the visions of the 1970's have not been reached and after 30 years of effort, there is a need for greater question-

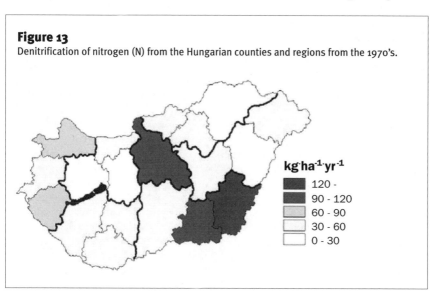

Figure 13
Denitrification of nitrogen (N) from the Hungarian counties and regions from the 1970's.

kg·ha⁻¹·yr⁻¹

120 -
90 - 120
60 - 90
30 - 60
0 - 30

ing of the basic principles underlying our attempts to connect a hard systems view of Production Systems (encapsulated in simulation models) with the human dimension of Management Systems."

Weaknesses in precision (or site specific) agriculture come from the lack of knowledge. Variability can be easily observed by remote sensing and GPS supplied yield monitors on combines. Application of differential treatments within a field are possible by controllers on farm machinery. These are available on the world market. The main problem is that science (agricultural chemistry, crop production, water management, micro-economy, etc.) are not prepared with how to treat these different spots in order to eliminate the disadvantageous effects and whether the treatments are economical. We need to know the different reactions of the yields on all areas under diverse circumstances.

For example, a depression at a portion of a field can yield more at a dry year since more water is stored in the soil of the depression then in the surrounding area. On the contrary, at a wet year the plants can suffer by the lack of aeration or by diseases induced by wet soils. Similarly, there is a by fold effect on the transport of the water-soluble nitrate toward the depression. The extra nitrogen supply of plants can be beneficial in wet conditions, but it can cause a salt effect and yield decrease in dry conditions. The risk of nitrate pollution or the loss by denitrification is increased from increasing nitrate-N concentration in depressions.

Similar problems can occur when a spot is less fertile because of other reasons like salt effects or erosion, etc. The decision should determine whether more or less nitrogen should be applied to those areas. There is reason to add more nitrogen in order to even the yield on the field, and there is reason to add less to avoid a non-remunerative treatment and/or to decrease the chance of nitrate leaching.

Kersebaum et al. (2002) concluded in their site-specific nitrogen fertilizer study "To benefit from potential of precision farming technologies in terms of increasing nitrogen fertilization efficiency, it is important to consider spatial variability of the most relevant influences of a specific site. This requires more detailed and accurate spatial information and a better knowledge of the interactions between site conditions and yield formation." He expressed concern that the resolution of traditional soil maps is insufficient and grid sampling with analysis is too expensive for practical purposes.

Parameterization. Weak parameters deteriorate all the huge work of model building, calibration, data collection. Models for system simulation are based on cause and effect relationships of nature and the economy. Because of the complexity of both nature and economy several coefficients, exponents are required to the models as input parameters. These parameters are often defined through a high investment in data collection and analysis. In addition, these parameters vary for each soil series or genetic material. Therefore, one of the main tasks is to collect right input parameters to run the models successfully.

Parameter estimation is a continuous work for model users. Most input parameters are unknown, the model user has to either define or estimate. Modelers circulate parameter data that gained by trial and error. For example, breeders should know the crop genetic parameters e.g. heat requirements for phenological stages, sensitivity to sunshine duration, maximum grain number, maximum grain growth rate, etc. Unfortunately, these attributes are unknown to crop breeders since the determination is costly and farmers do not require them. The users then try to determine those parameters but it is mostly impossible because of the lack of time and resources. These coefficients are generated

Figure 14

Figure 14a. Prediction capability of 4M at zero nitrogen (N) treatments in 10 years (1989 to 1998) Nagyhörcsök, Hungary. Figure 14b. Prediction capability of 4M at 50 kg·ha⁻¹·yr⁻¹ N treatments in 10 years (1989 to 1998) Nagyhörcsök, Hungary.

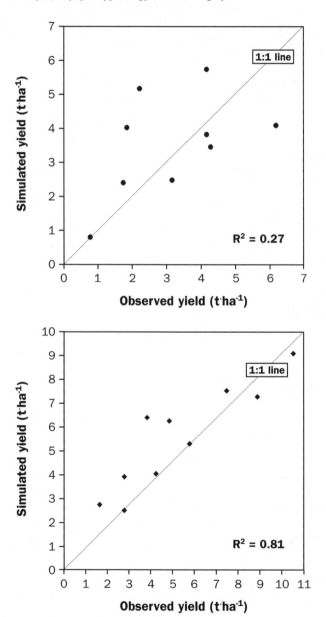

through rough estimation and 'optimization' based on limited experiments. Soil parameters are not much better and measurements are sometimes less reliable than estimation, especially if spatial heterogeneity is considered there are routines to estimate drained upper limit and lower limit from particle size distribution. The products of those published routines may be very different.

Supply of input data. Shortage of input data causes most of the failure of modeling projects. Singh et al. (2002) reported about Sub-Saharan Africa where a number of persons and organizations tried to help agriculture by modeling projects. Several of these projects were discontinued during the phase of data collection. Available weather, soil data and projects plans were overly optimistic about the time and money required for data collection. Incompatibility of methodologies, poor laboratory equipments, unreliable analyses, plot variability caused by presence of trees, less than perfect weeding, insects, and diseases were factors that limited the data reliability.

Reliability of input data was studied by Ritchie over the world. (Perry et al., 1982). Ritchie found the measurements of global radiation were biased even in U.S. meteorological observation stations. Some data were physically impossible and others had discontinuity by some technical measuring problems. He and his Hungarian colleagues published papers on the consequences of these biases (Kovács et al., 1995; Fodor and Kovács, 2003; Fodor et al., 2003) and proposed methods to screen and replace faulty data. (Fodor et al., 2000). In many places of the world historical data for global radiation is calculated from sunshine hours. The algorithms can result inaccurate in inaccurate radiation estimates for different reasons. Sensitivity of CERES- Maize is high to the miscalculation of solar radiation. In a parallel field and simulation experiment Kovács et al. (1995) used two different algorithms to calculate radiation. One worked right but the other algorithm systematically overestimated the values of daily radiation. Higher solar radiation lowered the yield of maize by increasing transpiration and drought (Figure 15).

Fodor and Kovács (2003) tested the sensitivity of CERES model and 4M Model to the inaccuracy of the measured meteorological data. The general level of biases of the measurements were considered as ± 2 percent, ± 0.2 °C, ± 3 percent for global radiation, temperature, precipitation, respectively. The base input dataset was modified by these errors and all the 27 combinations were used for the test runs. The simulation was more sensitive to errors of input values in case of the yield output than the biomass output. The uncertainty of the model results was 6.0 percent (± 0.9 percent at α = 0.05) considering the yield, and 3.2 percent (± 0.3 percent at α = 0.05) considering the biomass. The inaccuracy was significantly larger in low yielding years than in high yielding years.

Table 1 shows the results in changes of yields in 20-year averages. Four out of 27 combinations caused more than 10 percent differences in 20-year average yields. These combinations were mirrors of each other as extremes. They reflect the known fact that water is the yield-limiting factor under the Hungarian climate. The decrease of precipitation and the increase of evaporation both lead to yield loss. Obviously any raise of radiation energy leads to increased evapotranspiration. These results call the attention of the modelers in the area to be extremely careful with radiation data (Fodor et al., 2003).

Locked up data sets. Without input data, there is no modeling. If someone wants to use simulation models to solve real world problems, they need input (weather, soil, crop, technology, market) data representative of the target area. This is the most sensitive part of modeling. In the United States, all the results of research and observations paid from the taxpayer's money is considered public properties. Consequently, they are available to everyone. In most other countries, the national weather services sell the observed results at a high price, consequently most decision makers and researchers are not able to use them. As market economy grows, the situation becomes worse. File cabinets are full with measured data sets at universities, research institutions and the data goes to waste when the owner retires or dies. A paradigm shift is needed. An old colleague noted, "I measured for 40 years why would someone else get a fruit of it. The modelers should make experiments and measurements and they can play with them."

Development of decision support tools by modeling

Convincing scientific partners for collabo- *ration.* One of the major tasks of modelers is to reach the point when breeders will determine and publish the major crop characteristics. It would serve their interests since simulation would help breeders in many breeding issues. We need to step forward in standardization of soil tests and analyses internationally. A number of estimation techniques should be established or made more universal and robust.

Knowledge gaps are revealed when modelers try to assemble the whole system from parts. The research policy makers should be convinced to support research areas where the knowledge is limited. For example, a priority area would be root studies, control system of partitioning of assimilates, water and solute transport in the soil-plant continuum, etc. Many parts of the system are understood well enough or at least there is no balance among the knowledge about the different compo-

Figure 15
Observed and modeled yields summed through 20 years of experiment, and sensitivity for input solar radiation. (The case "modeled with higher radiation" caused by faulty calculation from sunshine hours.)(After Kovács et al., 1995).

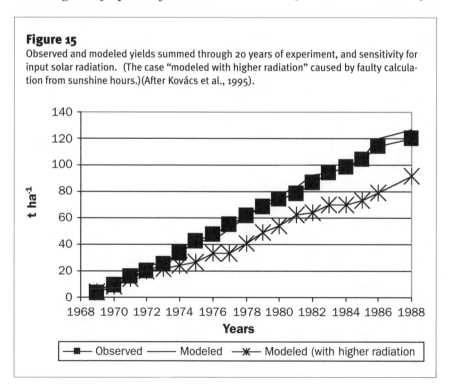

Table 1. Influence of biases of input combinations on estimated yields as an average of 20 years.

Combination nr.	Change of global radiation (%)	Change of temperature (˚C)	Change of precipitation (%)	Changes of yield kg·ha⁻¹	Standard deviation of changes of yield
18	-2	+0.2	+3	638	540
12	-2	0	+3	445	340
9	0	+0.2	+3	409	442
15	-2	-0.2	+3	401	555
16	-2	+0.2	0	387	511
3	0	0	+3	315	239
10	-2	0	0	210	262
6	0	-0.2	+3	191	469
27	+2	+0.2	+3	156	512
21	+2	0	+3	118	262
17	-2	+0.2	-3	100	444
7	0	+0.2	0	80	447
13	-2	-0.2	0	68	423
1	0	0	0	0	0
11	-2	0	-3	-79	171
24	+2	-0.2	+3	-84	350
4	0	-0.2	0	-116	286
25	+2	+0.2	0	-141	486
19	+2	0	0	-160	222
8	0	+0.2	-3	-194	433
14	-2	-0.2	-3	-208	431
2	0	0	-3	-262	165
22	+2	-0.2	0	-341	371
5	0	-0.2	-3	-354	351
26	+2	+0.2	-3	-391	514
20	+2	0	-3	-491	293
23	+2	-0.2	-3	-588	344

nents of the system. Many times modelers have to start analytical experimentation since there are no data in the scientific literature for key elements of the system. Frequently there is no way to run the model without those "white spots on the map" (missing functions, parameters or input data) and at the same time it would take years of experimentation and much money to gain adequate results to fill the knowledge gaps. These are the times when modelers have to use estimates and many uncertainties are built into the models. One significant result of simulation modeling is the revelation of important topics that need further research work for the basics understanding how the systems work at the real world.

International bodies recognized the usefulness of simulation techniques for decision support. The World Meteorological Organization and Global Programs (IGBP,

IHDP and WCRP) co-sponsored International START Secretariat (Global Change System for Analysis, Research and Training) initiated the CLIMAG (Climate Variability and Agriculture) project. CLIMAG wants to mobilize the growing ability to predict forthcoming climate variations to improve cropping systems management and decision making and decrease risks associated with the changes, increase production at local, national and international scales (Meinke et al., 2001).

Developing communication among farmers, extension, state decision-makers NGOs, and researchers. The development of cropping systems simulation capabilities all over the world combined with easy access to powerful computing has resulted in an abundance of agricultural models and therefore, model applications. However, the scientific credibility of such applications and their relevance to farming practice is questioned.

The ultimate role of simulation will be achieved when decision makers, experimental scientists and modelers build more trust and recognition of the need for each other for the best answers to real world problems. The farmers and government decision makers should openly express what kinds of decisions require support.

Simulation models can be extremely useful where there is trust and communication between decision makers in the governments, farmers, extension service personnel, experimentalists, and modelers. A good example is found in Australia where the whole society is a winner of the good communication among the partners.

Tsuji et al. (2002) published negative experiences from their own homeland while IBSNAT project was successful in many countries of the world. He reported about a model-driven decision support project that aimed to help replace sugarcane when that industry lost 21 plantations out of 23 within a period of a decade in Hawaii. The model was able to mimic the development and production of Taro crop as the main candidate to replace sugarcane but the at the end Tsuji noted: "We are not aware if decision makers at the government level or at the farm level used any of the outputs or recommendations from the research project." The other example from the same publication describes the history of the cabbage model within CROPGRO family. The model aimed to help cabbage growers to find suitable locations at the island of Maui since a sect killed most of the cabbage crops at the original locations because of the built up resistance of the sect to the insecticide. Prior to conclusion of the modeling project "a new pesticide and new more resistant cabbage variety made the simulated outcomes meaningless to the grower or to the extension agent" (Tsuji et al., 2002).

Meinke et al. (2001) are convinced that well-defined on-farm financial and environmental benefits can be obtained from the use of models. These examples highlight the importance of 'relevance' and hence the importance of true partnerships among all stakeholders (farmer, scientists, advisers) for the successful development and adoption of simulation approaches. They found three key points essential for successful model applications: (1) issues to be addressed must be neither trivial nor obvious; (2) a modeling approach must reduce complexity rather than proliferate choices in order to aid the decision-making process; (3) the cropping systems must be sufficiently flexible to allow management interventions based on insights gained from models. There are different conditions for the successful application modeling at different parts of the world. Depending on the climatic variability, farm field areas, high or low input agriculture, and technological development. They showed examples from different continents where the conditions differ from one another.

Often, researchers make statements about applications for decision making without a clue as to what is necessary to make it work. Pay-offs can only be expected when a truly integrated systems approach is employed that includes decision makers as partners and guarantees that they have ownership of this process. Only the truly participatory approach ensures that the issues addressed are relevant to the decision-maker (Meinke et al., 2001).

Argyris et al. (1985) suggested the 'action research' principles be relevant, to make more effective links between our science and farm management practice. Keating and McCown (2001.) wrote this "The fact that learning is two way makes it a more modest endeavor than the notion which permeates decision support system developments that science is 'providing the answers for management'...While important challenges and opportunities exist in model development, the biggest challenge facing the practitioners of farming systems modeling over the next 10 years, is not to build more accurate or more comprehensive models, but to discover new ways of achieving relevance to real world decision making and management practice."

Decision support system development makes it imperative to build cooperation with the farmers. One way to get closer collaboration with farmers is to approach the advisers and agribusiness partners. Another way for quality interactions is to join to pilot farmer groups. Among the pilot farmers group in Australia the demand for simulations has increased rapidly to the point where APSRU and associated public sector extension personnel cannot meet the demand. Because of the demand, special simulation- decision support system training and accreditation was made available to agribusiness companies (Meinke et al., 2001).

An alternative was the 'Whopper Cropper' software product made for less educated users to access crop yield simulations. It is a database of pre-run APSIM simulations with an easy-to-use graphical interface facilitating time series, probability and diagnostic analyses. It is a discussion support system designed in response to a demand from extension professionals for easy access to cropping systems modeling and seasonal climate forecasting (Hammer et al., 2001).

In South America, especially in Uruguay and Argentina, there is wide acceptance of the simulation based decision support systems. The reason is similar to one in Australia, there is a good communication between agricultural modelers and the general public. Short workshops are conducted where climate scientists, agricultural researchers, technical representatives of all the major farmer associations and government agricultural planners meet on a regular basis. Since climate change is relevant factor in agriculture, similar to Australia, there is a real sense of mutual interest of the partners from the scientific and the farming communities. The seasonal forecast has been developing rapidly that made the agricultural practitioners trust modelers. The meetings are published in the newspapers and on the TV to inform the public about the seasonal weather forecast and the expected effects on agriculture.

In Europe, many case studies have demonstrated the potential usefulness of model application to decisions at state level; however, there is little evidence to date that policy formulation is based or even influenced by dynamic, quantitative approaches. The reason for the difference between Australia and South America and Europe is related to the objective alarm situation in the Southern hemisphere and the relatively successful seasonal weather forecast. When there is a real emergency situation and people feel the need for one another there is greater sense of need in communicating with one another, there is more acceptance of the knowledge of the scientists even if they can not make very good forecast but a hope to become better. In Europe the change of weather pattern is not seen as drastically, yet. The climatic behavior is also less predictable then the El Niño and La Niña at the southern hemisphere.

Developing system simulation modeling. The best we can do to develop decision support system today is to develop the tool kits of system simulation models. If we want better decision support, we need better system simulation models more correct algorithms with much better input parameters and input databases.

We should consider system simulation models as tools of future in decision support systems. At present, we need to use them together with other alternatives as local expert opinions, statistical models and expert systems. As system simulation models develop, the roles of other decision resource alternatives will decrease.

The precision and reliability of a system simulation models usually depends on the input parameters and input data rather than on the algorithms. Common interest of modelers and users is on the collection of reliable input parameters and data. An inclusive development will occur when different decision support system tools are incorporated into one package. Frequently a decision support system includes a simulation frame but contains several empirical elements and the user can run a help to estimate different input parameters supported by expert systems. As the knowledge grows about the mechanisms of the processes and less empirical and subjective estimations will remain in system models since the biologically, chemically, physically, economically and mathematically correct algorithms will take place within the system models.

The operation of systems has to be observed with greater care. What signals the system to react differently? Strange phenomena within the system should not be neglected. For example, an observation of field growth analysis about times when the above ground part of maize and wheat plants did not grow for one or two weeks at all or even lost biomass. These events

always occurred after a heavy rainy period at dry summer and followed by a fast loss of soil nitrate and then soil water. The questions partially still have not been solved (Kovács, 1982; Kovács, 2003).

In order to develop decision support system the modules of simulation models and the decision support system has to be easily replaceable. The teams of users as well a developer have to manage changes mentally and technically. Flexibility is a part of the system but often the decision support system developer has to be flexible when a new result in science makes it necessary to change the structure, and the user also has to learn to use a new interface.

There are too many groups of modelers working independently and duplicating each other. There are groups where modelers can work together in workshops and try to standardize methods. The problem is not really with modeling but the lack of knowledge and local information. Until the functions are not universal, in the interim period, the regional developments can be advantageous. In this period of time and development we may focus on regional problems and solutions. The knowledge gaps of mechanistic modeling are filled by more empirical, experimental functions, that are not suitable everywhere on the globe. As the scientific knowledge is growing, gradually the empirical (non-causal) functions will be replaced by mechanistic descriptions of the processes. These are true for both the biophysical and the economic development.

There is a healthy competition between simulation modeling based on causal relationships and processes as the blocks of a higher hierarchy called system and expert systems. Plant et al. (1998) described the relationship between the numerical models (that we call system simulation models) as one that simulate the behavior of the crop and its environment, while the so called qualitative simulation models that may be considered to simulate experts' reasoning about the behavior of the crop. They developed "QTIP Cotton" to simulate primarily expert knowledge about cause and effect in cotton growth and development, and only secondarily the growth and development process. Therefore, construction of the model explicitly becomes a process of knowledge acquisition. The model becomes a dynamic database of expert knowledge about cause and effect in cotton plant growth. This knowledge is the same as that communicated in extension bulletins to farmers and crop management consultants. Therefore, a major source of knowledge built into the model is from extension publications, and many of the citations in the next section refer to these documents."

Simulation modeling and expert systems both have strengths and weaknesses and both try to utilize something from the other. Many times when there is not enough formalized knowledge to produce a mechanistic process model, the experiences of one or several experts are used to substitute the process. It is a kind of shortcut that might work better then a descriptive function without good parameters.

When someone wants to answer a very practical set of questions it might be better to construct an expert system rather than invest much resources into a system simulation model.

There are the so-called 'second-generation' expert systems. They attempt to incorporate some of the strengths of both simulation models and diagnostic expert systems (Kuipers, 1984). These new expert systems are closer to the more fundamental cause and effect models than to the first-generation expert systems. Domain knowledge is represented similar to simulation models, but in qualitative rather than quantitative form. For this reason, second-generation systems are qualitative simulation models.

Independent from the phraseology there is a mixture of the expression of knowledge even in the model based decision support systems. This is mostly not because of choice, but rather a lack of precise knowledge. There are two forces that seem to fight each other in decision support and in science as a whole. One is the problem solving necessity, applying knowledge, and the other is the human desire for exact cognition of nature and human society. Time to time we see the season of basic research or the applied research. Decision making will always be supported more by the applied research people, but the human mind will never be satisfied with less then causal reasoning. This way the tendency will move toward more and more mechanistic system models but they will never be good enough to be able to neglect the expert's opinions.

Concluding Comments

Development of agricultural decision tools will be guided by the scientific and technological advances as resources and by the challenges of the real world problems in agriculture and the human environment. The debate between the practical and the theoretical side will never end. Only cataclysms can bring the extremes together, when all efforts are required for survival. There are some examples for this kind of developments. One relevant example is the ENSO phenomena. The most theoretical global circulation modelers and the Uruguay-Argentine farmers associations can work together. This is a rare opportunity when scientist and farmers learn from one another.

Australian decision support system people emphasize the collaboration of the farming and the scientific communities in order to find the solutions for the real problems. They were able to operate simulation research on a market basis. The focus on the practical problems helps modelers not wasting time on 'useless' topics. Nevertheless, in the long run, the so-called basic research should also contribute more and we can't avoid to face the gaps in our understanding the world around us. Finally, process modeling and mechanistic systems simulation will be the ultimate solution for most problems. The only reason that keeps us, humans back from this kind of modeling the lack of knowledge. It is very expensive to learn more. We all want to short-cut problem solving with fast methods. Until the sciences can't answer many questions on the process level as well as the systems operation level, several other decision aids will flourish: databases, statistical local models, personal expert recommendation, experts systems, communication aids.

Simulation modeling challenges the rest of the scientific community to move the emphasis of the research on the parts and topics that are really important for understanding the operation of the systems around us and serve with data and parameters. Europeans tend to be more theoretic than practical. Modelers can't play as important role in society as their Australian and American colleagues. Lately there is some merging tendency. In the EU projects the practical view has gained space, at least on the surface level.

The technologies and software associated with decision support systems continues to change rapidly and development tools are overlapping for some applications. In general, agricultural managers need to recognize that the overall technological and social context of decision support system and business management is changing fast. Those who take advantage of the technological advances and globalization will introduce the newest decision support system tools as soon as they are available on the Internet. They will have expectations from decision support systems; they will be customers of computerized decision support. The Web technologies will facilitate improved decision support system tools connected with local GIS information centers. From that time on, nobody will be able to be competitive without system simulation aided decision support systems.

References Cited

Alter, S.L. 1980. Decision support systems: Current practice and continuing challenge. Addison-Wesley, Reading, Massachusetts.

Argyris, C., R. Putnam, and D.M. Smith. 1985. Action Science. Jossey-Bass, San Francisco, California.

Baethgen, W.E. and G.O. Magrin. 2000. Applying climate forecasts in the agricultural sector of South America. Pp. 38-44. *In:* Proceedings of the International Forum on Climate Prediction. Agriculture and Development, April 2000, International Research Institute for Climate Prediction (IRI), Palisades, New York.

Baethgen, W.E. 1998a. Applying scientific results in the agricultural sector: Information and decision support systems. Proceedings of the Inter-American Institute for Global Change Research (IAI) Science Forum: Global Change in the Americas, Arlington, Virginia. June 1998.

Baethgen, W.E. 1998b. El Niño and La Niña impacts in Southeastern South America: Review on the causes and consequences of cold events. M. Glantz (ed.) Proceedings of the A la Niña Summit. National Center for Atmospheric Research, Boulder, Colorado.

Belcher, K.W., M.M. Boehm, and M.E. Fulton. 2004. Agroecosystem sustainability: A system simulation model approach. Agricultural Systems 79(2):225-241.

Belcher, K.W. and M.Boehm. 2002. Evaluating agroecosystem sustainability using an integrated model. *In:* Managing for Healthy Ecosystems. D.J. Rapport, B.L. Lasley, D.E. Rolston, N.O. Nielsen, C.O. Qualset, and A.B. Damania (eds.) CRC Press, Boca Raton, Florida.

Blackie, M.J. and J.B. Dent. 1974. The concept and application of skeleton models in farm business analysis and planning. Journal of Agricultural Economics 25:165-175.

Carberry, P., G.L. Hammer, H. Meinke, and M. Bange. 2000. The potential value of seasonal climate forecasting in managing cropping systems. Pp.167-181. *In:* Applications of Seasonal Climate Forecasting in Agriculture and Natural Ecosystems: The Australian Experience. G.L. Hammer, N. Nicholls, and C. Mitchell (eds.) Kluwer Academic Publishers, Dordrecht, The Netherlands.

Dhar, V. and R. Stein. 1997. Intelligent decision support methods: The science of knowledge. Prentice-Hall, Upper Saddle River, New Jersey.

Fedorowicz, J. 1993. A technology infrastructure for document-based decision support systems. Pp. 125-136. *In:* Decision support systems: Putting theory into practice (Third Edition). R. Sprague and H.J. Watson (eds.) Prentice-Hall, Upper Saddle River, New Jersey.

Fodor, N. and G.J. Kovács. 2003. Sensitivity of crop models to the inaccuracy of meteorological observations. Physics and Chemistry of the Earth. Poster. European Geophysical Society- American Geo-physical Union - European Union of Geosciences, Nice, France, April 6-8. Elsevier Science, Amsterdam, The Netherlands.

Fodor, N., G.J. Kovács, and J.T. Ritchie. 2000. A new solar radiation generator for Hungary. Poster. Agronomy Society of America-Crop Science Society of America-Soil Science Society of America, annual meetings. November 5-9, 2000, Minneapolis, Minnesota, Abstract 23 pp.

Fodor, N., G.J. Kovács, and K.Pokovai. 2003. Reliability of estimated global radiation for crop model input. Idöjárás 107(3-4):273-281.

Fodor, N., G. Máthéné-Gáspár, K. Pokovai, and G.J. Kovács. 2002. 4M - software package for modeling cropping systems. European Journal of Agriculture 18(3-4):389-393.

Grignani, C., A. Reyneri, and A. Cavallero. 1994. Effect of three different soils on nitrogen utilization and leaching with maize and lucerne. Pp. 806-807. In: Proceedings of the Third European Society of Agronomy (ESA) Congress, ESA, Abano-Padova, Italy.

Hammer, G.L., J.W. Hansen, J.G. Phillips, J.W. Mjelde, H. Hill, A. Love, and A. Potgieter. 2001. Advances in application of climate prediction in agriculture. Agricultural Systems 70(2-3):515-553.

Hansen, J.W., A. Potgieter, and M. Tippett. 2004. In press. Using a general circulation model to forecast regional wheat yields in Northeast Australia. Agricultural and Forest Meteorology. 127(1-2): 89-90

Hansen, J.W., J.W. Jones, G.O. Magrin, S.G. Meira, E.R. Guevara, M.I. Travasso, R.A. Díaz, M. Marino, R. Hordij, C. Harwell, and G. Podestá. 1996. ENSO effects on yields and economic returns of wheat, corn and soybean in Argentina. Proceedings of CONGREMET VII-CLIMET VII. (Pp. 89-90).

International Research Institute for Climate Prediction (IRI). 2002. http://iri.columbia.edu/climate/ENSO/societal/example/Baethgen.html

International Research Institute for Climate Prediction (IRI). 2003. http://iri.columbia.edu/des/intro.html

Jamieson, P.D., M.A. Semenov, I.R. Brooking and G.S. Francis. 1998. Sirius: A mechanistic model of wheat response to environmental variation. European Journal of Agronomy 8:161-179.

Kádár, I., T. Németh, and G.J. Kovács. 1989. Nitrogen efficiency and nitrate leaching on a calcareous chernozjem soil. Pp. 155-158. In: Protection of water quality from harmful emissions, with special regard to nitrate. E. Welte and I. Szabolcs (eds.) Goltze-Druck, Goettingen. 5th International Symposium of CIEC, Sept. 1-4, 1987 Balatonfüred, Hungary.

Keating, B.A. and H. Mainke. 1998. Assessing exceptional drought with a cropping system simulator: A case study for grain production in northeast Australia. Agricultural Systems 57:315-332.

Keating, B.A. and R.L. McCown. 2001. Advances in farming systems analysis and intervention. Agricultural Systems 70:555-579.

Kersebaum, C.K. and J. Richter. 1991. Modeling nitrogen dynamics in soil-plant system with a simple model for advisory purposes. Fertilizer Research 27:273-281.

Kersebaum, K.C. and A.J. Beblik. 2001. Performance of nitrogen dynamics model applied to evaluate agricultural management practices. Pp. 551-571. In: Modeling Carbon and Nitrogen Dynamics for Soil Management. M. Shaffer, L. Ma, and S. Hansen (eds.) CRC Press, Boca Raton, Florida.

Kersebaum, K.C., K. Lorenz, H.I. Reuter, and O. Wendroth. 2002. Modeling crop growth and nitrogen dynamics for advisory purposes regarding spatial variability. Pp. 229-252. In: Agricultural System Models in Field Research and Technology Transfer. L.R. Ahuja, L. Ma, and T.A. Howell (eds.) Lewis Publishers, Boca Raton-London-New York-Washington, D.C.

Kovács, G.J. 1997. Study of nitrate leaching in a long-term experiment: Combination of field and simulation experiments. Agrokémia és talajtan 46(1-4):135-143.

Kovács, G.J. 1998. Estimation of the effect of global warming on yields and environment of arable crops in Hungary. Agrokémia és Talajtan 47(1-4):133-144.

Kovács, G.J. 2003. Modeling of adaptation processes of crops to water and nitrogen stress. Physics and chemistry of the earth. Elsevier Science, Amsterdam, The Netherlands (in print) Poster. European Geophysical Society- American Geophysical Union - European Union of Geosciences, Nice, France, April 6-8.

Kovács, G.J., J.T. Ritchie, and T. Németh. 1998. CERES models in multiple objective decision-making process. Pp. 281-290. In: Proceedings of the First International Conference on Multiple Objective Decision Support System (MODSS), for Land, Water, and Environmental Management: Concepts, Approaches and Applications: MÁLAMA' ÁINA 1995. Honolulu. El-Swaify and D.S. Yakowitz (ed.) Lewis Publishers, Boca Raton, Boston, London, New York, Washington, D.C.

Kovács, G.J., T. Németh, L. Radimszky, and T. Szili-Kovács. 1996. Modeling of nitrogen transformation in the soil. Pp. 419-424. In: Progress in Nitrogen Cycling Studies. O. van Cleemput et al. (eds.) Kluwer Academic Publishers, The Netherlands.

Kovács, G.J., G. Zsigrai, and L. Blaskó. 1997. Modeling of soil-plant-environment relationships. Pp. 137-150. In: Soil Plant-Environment Relationships. J. Nagy (ed.) Debreceni Agrártudományi Egyetem. Debrecen.

Kovács, G.J. 1982. Ecophysiological relationship between water- and nutrition dynamism in maize. Növénytermelés 31(4):355-365.

Kovács, G.J., T. Németh, and J.T. Ritchie. 1995. Testing simulation models for assessment of crop production and nitrate leaching in Hungary. Agricultural Systems 49(4):385-397.

Kropff, M.J., J.W. Jones, and G. van Laar. 2001. Advances in systems approaches for agricultural development, Agricultural Systems 70(2-3):353-354.

Kuipers, B. 1984. Commonsense reasoning about causality: Deriving behavior from structure. Artificial Intelligence 24:169-203

Máthé-Gáspár, G., N. Fodor, K. Pokovai, and G.J. Kovács. 2003. Crop modeling as a tool to separate the influences of the soil and weather on crop yields. Physics and Chemistry of the Earth. Elsevier Science, Amsterdam, The Netherlands (in print). Poster. EAE03-A-12201 for the European Geophysical Society- American Geophysical Union - European Union of Geosciences, Nice, France, April 6-8, (Session AS10)

Matthews, R.B. and W. Stephens (eds.). 2002. Crop-soil simulation models: Applications in developing countries. Cranfield University, U.K. 304 pp. ISBN: 0851995632

Meinke, H., W.E. Baethgen, P.S. Carberry, M. Donatelli, G.L. Hammer, R. Selvaraju, and C.O. Stockle. 2001. Increasing profits and reducing risks in crop production using participatory systems simulation approaches. Agricultural Systems 70:493-513.

Mohanty, S.K., U. Singh, V. Balasubramanian, and K.P. Jha. 1999. Nitrogen deep placement technologies for productivity, profitability, and environmental quality of rainfed lowland rice system. Nutrient Cycling in Agroecosystems 53:43-57.

Nagy, J., L. Huzsvai, K. Petö, and G.J. Kovács. 1994. Validation of crop models based on field experiments for environmental education. Pp. 409-419. *In:* Modeling the fate of agrochemicals and fertilizers in the environment. C. Giupponi, A. Marani, and F. Morari (eds.) Proceedings of the International Workshop of European Space Agency held in Venice, Italy. March 3-5, 1994.

Nagy, J. 1995. Evaluation of fertilization effect on the yield of maize (*Zea mays* L.) in different years. Növénytermelés 4:493-506.

Németh, T. 1993. Effect of N fertilization on the nitrate-N content of soil profiles in long-term experiment. Agrokémia és Talajtan 42:115-120.

Németh, T. 1994. Nitrate-N accumulation in the soil profiles of long-term fertilizer experiments. Agrokémia és Talajtan 43:231-238.

Németh, T. 1995. Nitrogen in Hungarian soils: Nitrogen management relation to groundwater protection. Journal of Cont. Hidrocarbons 20:185-208.

Németh, T. 1996a. Organic matter and nitrogen turnover of soils. (Hungarian) RISSAC. Alfprint.

Németh, T. 1996b. Nitrogen balances in long-term field experiments. Fertilizer Research 43:13-19.

Németh, T. 1996c. Nitrogen balance studies in a long-term crop rotation field experiments. Pp. 343-346. *In:* Progress in Nitrogen Cycling Studies. O. Van Cleemput et al. (eds.) Kluwer Academic Publishers, The Netherlands.

Németh, T. 1996d. Long-term N-fertilization calibration experiments: Environmental aspects. Pp. 371-377. *In:* Nitrogen Economy in Tropical Soils. N. Ahmad (ed.) Developments in Plant and Soil Sciences. Kluwer Academic Publishers, The Netherlands.

Németh, T., G.J. Kovács, and I. Kádár. 1988. A NO₃,SO₄ and 'water soluble salts' accumulation in soil profile of a long-term fertilization experiment. Agrokémia és Talajtan 36-37:109-126.

Perry, C.R., J.L. Rogers, and J.T. Ritchie. 1982. A comparison of measured and estimated meteorological data for use in crop growth modeling. AgRISTARS Publication No. YM-J2-04359.

Plant, R.E., T.A. Kerby, L.J. Zelinski and D.S. Munk. 1998. A qualitative simulation model for cotton growth and development. Computers and Electronics in Agriculture 20(2):165-183.

Podestá, G.P., C.D. Messina, M.O. Grondona and G.O. Magrin. 1998. Associations between grain crop yields in central-eastern Argentina and El Niño-Southern Oscillation. Journal of Applied Meteorology 38:1488-1498.

Power, D.J. 2000. Decision support systems hyperbook. DSSResources.COM, HTML version, Cedar Falls, Iowa. at URL http://dssresources.com/subscriber/password/dssbookhypertext.

Rajkai, K., G. Szász, and L. Huzsvai. 2004. Agroökológiai modellek. Debrecen University. ISBN 963 472 856 1 Debrecen.

Remy, K. 1994. GLYCIM soybean model proves its worth. Research Highlights, MAFES Publication No. 57. Mississippi State University, Mississippi State, Mississippi.

Rossi Pisa, P., 1995. Azoto perduto per lisciviazione. Pp. 125-138. *In:* Guida alla lettura ed interpretazione del Codice di Buona Pratica Agricola per la protezione delle acque dai nitrati. Quaderno No. 2. A.A.M. Del Re, E. Capri, S.P. Evans, P. Natali, and M. Trevisan (eds.) Collana del progetto Finalizzato PANDA, Edagricole, Bologna, Italy.

Sequi, P., A. Benedetti, and R. Francaviglia. 1995. Stato dell'arte sul problema 'Nitrati' in Italia. Pp. 29-40. *In:* Guida alla lettura ed interpretazione del Codice di Buona Pratica Agricola per la protezione delle acque dai nitrati. Quaderno No. 2. A. Benedetti and R. Sequi (eds.) Collana del progetto Finalizzato PANDA, Edagricole, Bologna, Italy.

Singh, U. and P.K. Thornton. 1992. Using crop models for sustainability and environmental quality assessment. Outlook Agriculture 21:209-218.

Singh, U., P.W. Wilkens, W.E. Baethgen, and T.S. Bontges. 2002. Decision support tools for improved resource management and agricultural sustainability. Pp. 91-117. *In:* Agricultural System Models in Field Reearch and Technology Transfer. L.R. Ahuja, L. Ma, T.A. Howell (eds.) Lewis Publishers, Boca Raton-London-New York-Washington, D.C.

Stöckle, C.O. and R. Nelson. 1994. The CropSyst user's manual. Biological Systems Engineering Depart-ment, Washington State University, Pullman, Washington.

Sumelius, J., Z. Grgic, M. Mesic, and R. Franic. 2002. Farm level cost of reducing nitrate leaching by economic instruments in Croatian farming systems. Central and Eastern European Sustainable Agriculture, Discussion Paper No. 11. ISSN 1616-9166.

Thornley, J.H.M. and I.R. Jonhson 1990. Plant and crop modeling: A mathematical approach to plant and crop physiology. Claredon Press, Oxford, Great Britain.

Thornton, P.K. and P.W. Wilkens. 1998. Risk assessment and food security. Pp. 339-345. In: Understanding Options for Agricultural production. G.Z. Tsuji, G. Hogenboom, and P.K. Thornton (eds.) Kluwer Academic Publishers, Dordrecht, The Netherlands.

Timlin, D.J., Y. Pachepsky, F.D. Wishler, and W.R. Reddy. 2002. Experience with on-farm applications of GLYCIM/GUICS. Pp. 55-69. In: Agricultural System Models in Field Research and Technology Transfer. L.R. Ahuja, L. Ma, and T.A. Howell (eds.) Lewis Publishers, Boca Raton-London-New York-Washington, D.C.

Tsuji, G.Y., A. du Toit, A. Jintrawet, J.W. Jones, W.T. Bowen, R.M. Ogoshi, and G. Uehara. 2002. Benefits of models in research and decision support: The IBSNAT experience. In Agricultural System Models in Field Research and Technology Transfer. L.R. Ahuja, L. Ma, T.A. Howell, Eds, Lewis Publishers, Boca Raton-London-New York-Washington, D.C. 71-89

Tsuji, G.Y., G. Uehara, and S. Balas. 1994. DSSAT version 3. IBSNAT Project, University of Hawaii, Honolulu, Hawaii.

Van Keulen, H. and F.W.T. Penning de Vries. 1993. Farming under uncertainty: Terminology and tech-niques. International Crop Science 1:139-143.

Wierzbicki, A., M. Makowski, and J. Wessels (eds.). 2000. Model-based decision support methodology with environmental applications. Kluwer Academic Publishers, Dordrecht. Series: Mathematical Modeling and Applications 492 pp. ISBN: 0-7923-6327-2.

Wood, S., L. You, and W. Baitx. 2001. DREAM user man-ual. International Food Policy Research Institute, Washington, D.C.

Responding to agricultural impacts with policy

CHAPTER 6

O. Oenema

This book deals with improving the balance between agricultural production and environmental quality through enhanced decision-making. Nutrient elements play a crucial role in both agricultural production and the environmental quality associated with this production, and seeking the proper balance between these two through improved nutrient management has been on research and policy agendas for quite a long time already. However, the issue of nutrient losses associated with agricultural production is extremely diverse, complex and stubborn, and the progress in improving the balance between agricultural production and environmental quality in practice through improved nutrient management is as yet relatively small.

This chapter discusses the increase in nutrient losses following the intensification of the agricultural production in Europe during the 20th Century and the subsequent response of governmental policies to decrease these losses. Following brief descriptions of the nutrient case in general and of the basic characteristics of European agriculture, the treatise focuses on the driving forces for the intensification of agricultural production, the environmental pressures ensuing from the intensification of agriculture and increased nutrient use, the current environmental state with regards to nutrient concentrations and its ecological impact, and the subsequent policy responses. This so-called DPSIR approach (Driving forces—Pressure—State—Impact Response) is commonly applied in environmental assessment studies.

Introducing the nutrients case

There are at least 13 nutrient elements known to be essential for plants and 18 for animals (Marschner, 1995; Whitehead, 2000). The quantity of a nutrient element required by plants and animals depends on its metabolic functions and varies widely from element to element (up to a factor 10^6). Depending on local soil fertility, specific crop requirement and management, various nutrients are in short supply for sustaining maximum plant growth. This is especially the case in situations where nutrients are removed regularly with harvested crops, without adequate nutrient replenishment. Here, growth rate and nutrient concentration will increase when the supply or availability of an essential nutrient increases, although with diminishing returns. At the so-called critical concentration of a particular nutrient, growth rate is at its (near) maximum. When the supply of the nutrient is increased further, there is a further increase in concentration (luxury consumption), but not in growth rate. Eventually, the nutrient concentration may reach toxic levels, which than results in a decline in yield and quality.

Current emphasis in nutrient research and in nutrient management in practice is often on nitrogen (N) and phosphorus (P). These nutrients are the main crop-yield-limiting nutrients, and also have the largest environmental impacts. However, the efficiency of N and P utilization in crop and animal production also depends on the availability of other nutrients and neglecting these can be counterproductive. Soil and weather conditions, pests and diseases, and crop management also influence agricultural production and nutrient utilization, and hence nutrient losses.

The beneficial effect of adding nutrient elements to soils for agricultural productivity has been known for more than two millennia, but critical concentrations and optimum, luxury and toxic concentrations ranges in soils and plants have been established only during the last century. The increased understanding of the functions of nutrients in plant and animal metabolism, along with the development of bioavailability concepts in soil chemistry have led to the development of fertilizer recommendations for a wide range of crops. The discovery of ammonia synthesis and the subsequent large-scale production of N fertilizers in the early half of the 20th Century, together with improved crop and animal breeds and its management have given the final incentives to the huge increases in crop and animal production during the last century. At present, approximately 50 percent of the global food production depends on fertilizer derived nutrients, and this percentage will likely increase further during the next decades (Smil, 2000; 2001).

Despite the relatively good knowledge that existed during the first half of the 20th Century about the effects of nutrients from manure and fertilizers, the consequences for the wider environment of the mobility of nutrients in soil water and atmosphere were not understood until surprisingly recently (SNV, 1994). The effects of nutrients on freshwater ecosystems were known in the 1920s, but began to have full impact only in the 1960's when municipal sewage discharges had changed many lakes. The effects of nutrient losses from agriculture became fully recognized from the 1970's onwards, and the notion that marine eutrophication was the result of increased nutrient inputs became accepted from the 1980's onwards. The

fact that soil and vegetation were affected by atmospheric N from agricultural sources was not recognized until the second half of the 1980's. Governmental policies and measures to regulate the use of N and P in agriculture were implemented from the second half of the 1980's onwards, in response to increasing public awareness of the damaging environmental effects of nutrient losses from agriculture (Oenema, 2004).

In retrospect, it is perhaps easy to say that not always the proper decisions have been made in the past. Agriculture is now under large pressure to reform. Especially intensive agricultural production has been implicated for the industrialization of production detached from the natural environment, for its deleterious effects on the wider environment. Significant systems improvements and efficiency gains in agriculture are needed worldwide in the next decades, to be able to feed the increasing global population and at the same time, circumvent large-scale deterioration of natural ecosystems and deterioration of ecosystem services through agricultural activities (Smil, 2000; Tilman et al., 2001; 2002).

Agriculture in the European Union

European agriculture is extremely diverse, ranging from highly intensive and specialized commercial holdings in especially Western Europe to subsistence farming using mainly traditional practices in parts of central and southern Europe. Impacts of agriculture on the environment therefore greatly vary in scale and intensity. Most countries in Europe are now members of the European Union (EU). At the foundation of the EU in 1957 (at that time European Economic Community), there were six member states. In the course of time, various countries have entered the EU. Following the accession of ten central European countries in 2004, there are now 25 member states (EU-25). As statistical information about the ten new member states is still scarce, the discussion is limited here to the EU-15.

The EU-15 covers 3.2 million km^2 and currently has 380 million inhabitants (Table 1). The utilized agricultural area is 1.29 million km^2, i.e. 40 percent of the total surface area. The five largest countries—France, Spain, Germany, United Kingdom, and Italy—together possess 79 percent of all agricultural land in the EU-15. In 1997, there were nearly seven million farms in the EU-15. Farms in the UK were the largest (average size 69 ha), and those in Greece the smallest (average size 4.3 ha). Farm structure in EU-15 is different from that in U.S. and CC-10 (Table 1). In 1998, 4.7 percent of the working population found employment in agriculture, ranging from 1.7 percent in the UK to 18 percent in Greece. The mean contribution of primary agriculture to the gross domestic production was 1.5 percent, ranging from 0.8 percent in Germany to 5.8 percent in Greece.

Cereals (wheat, barley, corn, and rye) are grown on 28 percent of the utilized agricultural area. Permanent pasture and green fodder crops, used for animal farming, cover 37 and 3.6 percent of the area, respectively. The remaining 31 percent of the utilized agricultural area is used for oil seeds (4.6 percent), olive trees (3.3 percent), vineyards (2.6 percent), sugar beet (1.6 percent), potatoes (1 percent), and various other small crops. Switzerland (71 percent), Ireland (69 percent), UK (64 percent), and The Netherlands (64 percent) have the largest relative area of pasture and fodder crops used for (grazing) animals. Sweden and Finland have the largest forest area.

Driving forces for changing in agriculture

In the 19th Century, prevailing traditional farming practices changed into modern farming practices, following the rapid changes in technology, availability of energy, and changes in the European society. The agrarian societies with more than 50 percent of the population working in agriculture in early 19th Century were transformed into industrialized urban societies. Currently, only five percent of the population is working in agriculture in EU-15 and 13 percent in the new member states (Table 1).

In general, changes in agriculture are a response to external and/or internal 'events' that provide the incentive for structural change. Major events or 'driving forces' for changes in European agriculture were:

1. Changes in population pressure and prosperity of the society, resulting in changing quests for food;
2. Changes in natural conditions (climate, diseases, wars);
3. Changes in international markets and market prices;
4. Innovations and new technology;
5. Changes in education, standards, values and judgments; and
6. Governmental policies and measures.

Most driving forces were external events, to which the agricultural community responded. Education and changes in standards and values within the agricultural community can be considered as an important internal driving force for change. In general, the more serious the 'event' and the more attractive the alternative, the greater the response of the agricultural community. The response also depends on the education level and the adjustability and fragility of the agricultural system.

We distinguish 11 possible responses of 'individual' farmers and two responses of farmers 'collectively' (Oenema et al., in prep.). The 11 possible responses made by farmers individually are:

1. Land reclamation, i.e. reclaiming common grounds, draining peat land and salt marshes;
2. Specialization, i.e. benefiting from the efficiency of specialization;
3. Intensification, i.e. producing more per

Table 1. Basic agricultural data of member states of the European Union (EU-15). At the bottom, selective basic information of the 10 new member states and the United States have been included.

Country	Population million	Employment in Ag., (%)	Agricultural area		Cereals (%)	Grassland (%)	Livestock number (millions)			Livestock number		Farm size (ha)
			% of total	M ha			Cattle	Dairy	Pigs	ha	holding	
Austria	8	7	41	3	25	53	2.1	0.7	3.4	0.82	19	16
Belgium + L*)	11	2	46	2	22	47	3.1	0.6	7.7	3.14	84	21
Denmark	5	4	63	3	56	14	1.9	0.6	11.6	1.59	96	43
Finland	5	7	7	2	52	5	1.1	0.4	1.5	0.59	26	24
France	59	4	52	28	30	35	20.2	4.4	15.9	0.88	48	42
Germany	82	3	48	17	41	30	14.9	4.8	26.1	1.10	48	32
Greece	11	18	27	4	37	57	0.6	0.2	1	0.66	5	4
Ireland	4	11	61	4	7	69	6.6	1.2	1.8	1.60	48	29
Italy	58	6	49	15	24	28	7.2	2.1	8.4	0.72	15	6
Netherlands	16	4	56	2	11	53	4.2	1.7	14	3.85	104	19
Portugal	10	14	41	4	17	26	1.4	0.4	2.4	0.61	7	9
Spain	40	8	51	26	23	35	6.3	1.2	22.4	0.44	27	21
Sweden	9	3	7	3	41	15	1.7	0.4	2.1	0.68	37	35
United Kingdom	60	2	66	16	22	64	11.2	2.5	7	1.02	94	69
EU-15	378	5	40	128	28	37	82.7	21.1	125	0.90	33	18
New members	75	13	51	38								4
United States	285	2	40	381								177

L*) Luxembourg

unit surface area through non-factor inputs;

4. Extension and enlargement, i.e. benefiting from the economics of scale;
5. Mechanization and automation, i.e. investing in technology to decrease labor input and increase labor efficiency;
6. Improving management, i.e. increase resource use efficiency;
7. Diversification, i.e. taking a subsidiary branch with added value or less risk;
8. Switching (partly) to non-agricultural income sources, to increase income and spread risk;
9. Extensification, i.e. decreasing non-factor inputs and labor and capital inputs;
10. Scaling down and shrink farming activities; and
11. Buckle down and retreat from farming.

The first six to seven responses increase agricultural production, while the last four to five responses decrease agricultural production. The choice for one or the other option depends on the farmer, the local agricultural conditions, and the economic situation outside agriculture. Hence, responses of individual farmers to the these driving forces can be different, depending on local environmental, social and economic conditions, and personal style.

Collective responses of farmers were (i) organized into interest, lobby and pressure groups, and (ii) organized of co-operatives for facilitating finance, supplies, processing, and marketing in the whole production chain. The individual and collective responses are not independent; collective responses often facilitate individual responses and vice versa.

With two World Wars, a serious economic crisis and regular food shortages in mind, there were strong feelings and incentives in European countries after World War II to stimulate the economy and to boost industrial and agricultural productivity. The establishment of the European Economic Community in 1957 ensued from these general feelings. At that time, Western Europe was a net importer of food, and understandably, the Common Agricultural Policy of the EU was strongly focused on stimulating agricultural production and stabilizing markets. The original objectives of the Common Agricultural Policy were: (i) to increase agricultural productivity; (ii) to ensure a fair standard of living for the agricultural community; (iii) to stabilize markets; (iv) to ensure stability of supplies; and (v) to ensure that supplies reach the consumers at reasonable prices. This policy has been successful in achieving its objectives, as production strongly increased, facilitated also by cheap fossil energy and modern technology (green revolution). The Common Agricultural Policy has given a strong impetus to intensification and rationalization of agricultural production. Within a couple of decades, Common Agricultural Policy indeed changed the EU from a net importer to a net exporter of food. Initially, these food surpluses were regarded as pleasant, but because of the price support, the surpluses became a financial burden.

The incentives provided by the Common Agricultural Policy were not without economic costs; the expenditures for supporting Common Agricultural Policy have risen steadily from about 12 billion euro in 1980 to 25 billion in 1990 and to more than 40 billion in 2000. This support is about 40 percent of the total expenditures of the European Commission, but less than two percent of the total governmental expenditures of the EU-15, and less than 1.27 percent (maximum level) of the gross domestic production. For the next six years (2003 to 2008), expenditures to support Common Agricultural Policy have been fixed at a maximum of 43 billion euro. Following the reform of the Common Agricultural Policy in 1992, there has been a shift from price support to income support. Following the next reform according to Agenda 2000 (European Commission, 1999) and more recent reforms (Mid Term Review in June 2003), there have been further shifts from price support to income support and a further shift from supporting agricultural production to the (maintenance) of rural areas (European Commission, 2003). The support for animal agriculture (meat and milk) ranged between five and 10 billion during the last 20 years; currently it is about 25 percent of the total expenditures for the Common Agricultural Policy.

Pressures on the environment

The extent of agricultural practices varies significantly across Europe, notably by farm and crop type. The continuing search for increased production efficiency, lower costs and increased scale of production results in pressures on the environment, landscapes and biodiversity, particularly in the most intensively farmed areas. At the same time, agriculture is essential to the maintenance of many cultural landscapes. This dual role is relevant throughout Europe, with farming systems of high nature value found mostly in areas with low input and more traditional agriculture (EEA, 2003). Much of the biodiversity is found on or adjacent to farmland, and agricultural habitats support the largest number of bird species of any broad habitat category in Europe, including the greatest number of threatened species (Heath and Tucker, 1994). However, species dependent on farmland are threatened by changes in management practices and a decline in habitat diversity.

Livestock density, fertilizer use, and surpluses of N and P are important environmental pressure indicators. Livestock density is a strong indicator for the emissions of ammonia into the atmosphere and subsequent deposition of atmospheric N to the biosphere. Livestock density is also an indicator for the amount of N and P in animal manure applied to agricultural land and the emission of methane (CH_4) from especially ruminant animals into the atmos-

phere. Fertilizer N use together with the amount of N in animal manure and cropping systems a strong indicator for the N surplus, the emission of nitrous oxide into the atmosphere and for the contamination of soils with metals like cadmium, copper, and zinc. The N surplus is an appropriate tool to identify the potential leaching of N to groundwater and surface waters. Fertilizer P use together with the amount of P in animal manure and cropping systems a strong indicator for the mean P surplus, and the P surplus is an appropriate tool to identify the built-up of soil P, which in turn determines the potential risk for P leaching to groundwater and surface waters, depending on hydrological pathways.

Mean livestock density in EU-15 is 0.9 livestock units per ha (Figure 1). Highest density is in The Netherlands and lowest in the Mediterranean and Nordic countries. In the 20th Century, the number of animals has risen steadily, until the 1990's. Especially the number of swine and poultry has increased greatly in the second half of the 20th Century. The halt in the increasing number of animals at the end of the 20th Century reflects the influence of governmental policies (milk quota, less price support, environmental regulations) and changing market conditions. Number of animals in EU-15 remained stable in the 1990's, while the number of animals in central and eastern European countries was halved, following the political changes in the early 1990's. Currently, EU-15 ranks fifth in the number of cattle (83 million, of which 21 million are dairy cows) in the world, after India (about 220 million), Brazil (175 million), China (110 million) and the United States (90 million). The average number of dairy cows per farm in 1999 was 24, ranging from a mean of five in Portugal to 44 in The Netherlands, 51 in Denmark to 69 in the UK. Total number of swine is 125 million. EU-15 ranks first in number of swine in the world, followed by China (80 million) and the United

States (59 million). Largest swine producers in EU-15 are Germany, Spain, Netherlands, France, and Denmark. The average number of swine per farm was 106, ranging from 18 in Portugal to 605 in Denmark, 723 in The Netherlands, and 859 in Ireland.

Fertilizer use slowly but steadily increased in the first half of the 20th Century. Following World War II, fertilizer use increased strongly until it dropped again between the 1970;s and 1990's. The pattern of increase and decrease was different for N, P, and K and also different for western, central, and Eastern Europe (Table 2). In the 20th Century, fertilizer inputs of N have risen steadily until somewhere between the 1980's and 1990's, and that of fertilizer P until somewhere between the 1950's and 1980's. Fertilizer P use has decreased by more than 50 percent between 1970 and 2000. Countries

with the steepest increase in fertilizer use reached the highest levels and showed the earliest onset of decreasing fertilizer use. The decrease in fertilizer use simply reflects the built-up of soil fertility (especially soil P), the increasing amounts of manure N and P due to the increasing number of livestock, and the effects of governmental policies and measures. A special case is the dramatic drop in fertilizer use in central and eastern European countries following the political changes in the early 1990's; decreased market opportunities for agricultural products and declining profitability of agriculture due to decreased state support and the widespread reorganization of farming led a fertilizer use of 10 to 25 percent of the pre-1990 level.

The average amounts of N applied to agricultural land in 1997 via animal manure and fertilizers ranged from 47 and 37 kg·ha^{-1} in Austria to 100 and 124 kg·ha^{-1}

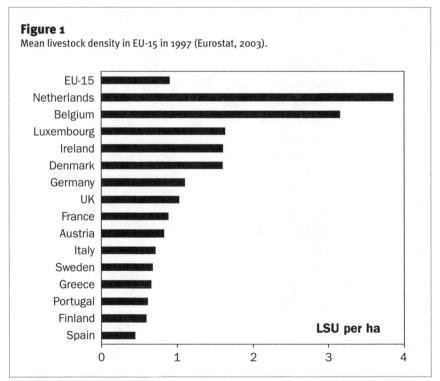

Figure 1
Mean livestock density in EU-15 in 1997 (Eurostat, 2003).

Table 2. Consumption of fertilizer N, P₂O₅ and K₂O in Western Europe, Central Europe, and Eastern Europe & Central Asia (former Soviet Union) in the period 1960 to 2000, in billion kg (Tg), after IFA, 2004.

Year	Western Europe			Central Europe			Former Soviet Union		
	N	P_2O_5	K_2O	N	P_2O_5	K_2O	N	P_2O_5	K_2O
1960	3.4	3.9	3.7	0.8	0.6	0.7	0.8	1.1	0.8
1970	7.1	5.9	5.4	2.7	1.9	2	4.6	3.1	2.6
1975	7.9	5.4	5.2	3.4	2.6	3.2	7.3	4.7	5.2
1980	10.2	5.9	5.6	4.2	2.8	2.7	8.3	5.6	4.9
1985	11.1	5.3	5.7	4.6	2.8	2.7	11	7.6	6.8
1990	10.4	4.5	5.1	3.4	1.5	1.5	8.6	7.8	5.2
1995	9.8	3.6	4.3	2.0	0.7	0.6	2.6	0.8	0.9
2000	9.3	3.1	3.6	2.4	0.6	0.6	2.6	0.6	0.7

in Denmark and to 307 and 186 kg ha⁻¹ in The Netherlands, respectively. Similarly, the average amounts of P applied to agricultural land in 1997 via animal manure and fertilizers ranged from 24 and 7 kg ha⁻¹ in Austria to 43 and 8 kg ha⁻¹ in Denmark to 104 and 13 kg ha⁻¹ in The Netherlands, respectively. The Average N surplus in the

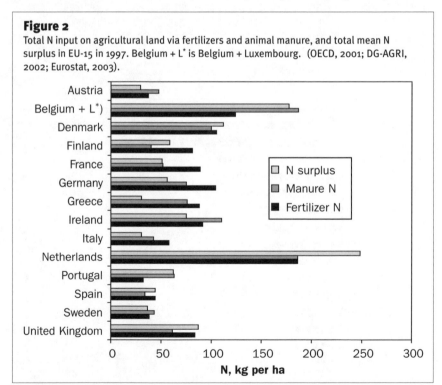

Figure 2
Total N input on agricultural land via fertilizers and animal manure, and total mean N surplus in EU-15 in 1997. Belgium + L* is Belgium + Luxembourg. (OECD, 2001; DG-AGRI, 2002; Eurostat, 2003).

L*) Luxembourg

EU-15 was 57 kg ha^{-1} in 1997, ranging from 30 kg ha^{-1} in Greece to 112 kg ha^{-1} in Denmark and 249 kg ha^{-1} in The Netherlands. There is strong correlation between livestock density, N fertilizer input and N surplus per ha; countries with the highest livestock density also have the highest N fertilizer input and highest N surplus on the soil surface balance (Figure 2). Correlation coefficients for linear relationship between fertilizer N, manure N, and N surplus in the EU-15 range between 0.8 and 0.9. Major determinants of N surplus at farm level are structural characteristics and farm management. Nitrogen surpluses vary widely among farms because of differences in farm structure, crop rotation, livestock composition, and management practices. Lowest N surpluses are found on cereal farms and highest N surpluses on confined animal feeding operations (Table 3). However, confined animal feeding operations have a small share in the utilized agricultural area and therefore have a share of only seven percent in the total N surplus in the EU. There is also a large variation between farms within a type of farming system. Variations in N surplus are much larger within confined animal feeding operations than within cereal farms or arable farms. Dairy farms take an intermediate position (Brouwer and Hellegers, 1997).

The N budget for Europe is shown in Table 4. The three principal driving forces of the acceleration of the European N cycle are fertilizer production, import of N in products (mainly animal feed products), and fossil fuel combustion by industry and traffic. Total fertilizer production was 14 Tg (billion kg) in 2000, of which 2.2 Tg was exported. Combustion processes in industry and traffic add another 3.3 Tg and biological N_2 fixation 2.2 Tg. Deposition of NH_3 and NO_X (7.3 Tg) roughly equaled the emission of NH_3 and NO_X (7.8 Tg). A relatively large source of N is the N in imported products (animal feed, food, and forestry products). The N import exceeds the N export in products (note that the export includes the export of 2.2 Tg N fertilizer). The major sink of N is suggested to be denitrification, i.e., the microbial transformation of nitrate and nitrite into di-nitrogen (N_2). The emissions of NH_3 and NO_X in Europe are a factor three higher than the world average (Van Egmond et al., 2002). Table 5 shows that European N fertilizer use is about 14 percent of the total world use. In the next decades, N fertilizer use is expected to rise further again, once agriculture in the former Soviet Union has recuperated.

There is less detailed information about P surpluses than N surpluses in European agriculture. Soil P status of most agricultural soils was rather low at the end of the 19th Century. In the 20th Century, soils

Table 3. Mean nitrogen surpluses by farming type in the EU in 1990/1991 (after Brouwer and Hellegers, 1997).

Farming type	Nitrogen surplus, Kg per ha	Share of utilized agricultural area, (%)	Share of N surplus in EU, in (%)
Cereal farms	32	14	6
Common arable farms	57	27	21
Dairy farms	114	18	29
Beef farms	47	21	14
Animal feeding operations	688	1	7
Mixed farms	85	19	23

Table 4. Nitrogen budget for Europe (excluding the area of the former Soviet Union) in 2000. (Van Egmond et al., 2002).

Inputs of N, in Tg		Outputs of N in, Tg	
N fertilizer production	14.0	Denitrification	13.8
Combustion of fossil fuels	3.3	Riverine transport to sea	4.0
Biological N fixation	2.2	Sewage and industry discharges	2.6
Deposition of NH_3 and NO_x	7.3	Emission of NH_3 and NO_x	7.8
Imported products	7.6	Exported products	6.3
Total	34.5	Total	34.5

have been enriched with on average 2000 to 5000 kg of P_2O_5 ha^{-1}, because the input of P via fertilizers and animal manure exceeded the output via crop removal. Countries with the largest livestock density and hence animal manure production have the largest surplus of P. In the mid 1990's, Austria, Germany, and Sweden had a P_2O_5 surplus of less than 25 kg ha^{-1}yr^{-1}, while Denmark, Finland, France, Greece, Ireland, and Norway had a surplus of 25 to 50 kg ha^{-1} and The Netherlands had more than 50 kg ha^{-1} (Steen, 1997). Increasing trends of soil-test P levels have been observed in many countries. Despite the decrease in fertilizer P consumption from the 1970's onwards, it continues to increase because of the increasing amounts of P from animal manure and because of the continuing P surplus (Tunney et al., 1997). Importantly, the risk of P losses from agricultural soils via run-off and leaching greatly increase with an increase in soil-test P levels (Sharply et al., 2000).

State of the environment

Agriculture is a main source of nitrate in groundwater, of N and P in surface waters and of ammonia and nitrous oxide in the atmosphere. Estimates suggest that the contribution of agriculture to the emissions of ammonia is about 90 percent and that of nitrous oxide in the range of 30 to 60 percent. The contribution of agriculture to the loading of surface waters with N ranges between EU member states from 30 to 80 percent and that of P between 20 and 45 percent (OECD, 2001). For the Rhine River, the fourth largest river basin in Europe (after Volga, Danube, and Wisla) with a total surface area of 185,000 km^2, agriculture contributes 40 and 32 percent of the total loading of N and P, respectively (Van der Veeren, 2002). Other main sources of N and P in surface waters are industry, sewage treatment plants, and untreated sewage discharges from households.

Depending on soil type and land use, a substantial portion of European ground-

Table 5. Projections of nitrogen (N) fertilizer use in the world in 2000 to 2050 by continent. (Wood et al., 2004).

Region	2000	2007/2008	2020	2050
Europe	11.6	11	14 - 17	15 - 21
Africa	2.5	3	3 - 5	4 - 9
Asia	45.9	55	52 - 66	59 - 94
America	17.2	19	21 - 23	23 - 31
Oceania	1.2	2	1 - 2	2 - 3
World	81	92	96 - 117	106 - 171

water bodies is affected by nitrate from mainly agricultural sources. Inventories indicate that the standard of 50 mg per litre (as NO_3) is exceeded at various sampling sites (Van Egmond et al., 2002). A long-held concern is that nitrate-rich drinking water and food is harmful to human health. This concern has been the incentive for many governmental policies regulating the use of N in agriculture (see also below). However, drinking water usually provides only a minor portion (0 to 25 percent of the body's external intake of nitrate, while vegetables account for 60 to 80 percent of the intake (L'hirondel and L'hirondel, 2002). Excessive nitrate intake has been linked to various forms of cancer, as nitrite can restrict the hemoglobins ability to transport oxygen in the human body (Follett and Follett, 2001). However, recent findings challenge the suggested deleterious effects of nitrate on human health and suggest that nitrate may also have beneficial effects on human health (Addiscott and Benjamin, 2004).

Levels of P have generally been decreasing in rivers and lakes in EU-15 during the 1990's. This decrease reflects the general improvement of the sewage treatment and the ban of P in detergents. In contrast, the loss of P from agriculture to surface waters has not changed much. Because of the strong decrease in the loading of P from sewage treatment plants, households and industry, and the persistent loss of P from agriculture, the relative contribution of agriculture to surface water loading has steadily increased in the 1990's. Levels of P in rivers and lakes are much lower in Northern Europe compared to Western Europe, which reflects differences in population density and agricultural intensity. The proportion of lakes with less than 25 µg P l^{-1} has increased and the proportion with high concentrations (more than 50 µg P l^{-1}) had decreased, suggesting that eutrophication in European lakes is decreasing. Natural concentrations are approximately

five to 50 µg P l^{-1}, while waters containing concentrations above 150 to 500 µg P l^{-1} are considered as being bad quality as significant effects of eutrophication can be expected (EEA, 2003).

Levels of N in surface waters have remained relatively unchanged during the 1990's. In many catchments, the main source of N is leaching and runoff from agricultural land. For The Netherlands, it has been estimated that approximately 12 percent of the N surplus in agriculture is discharged into surface waters and another 10 percent into groundwater. These percentages are relatively low, because the greater part of the N surplus disappears via denitrification, which is a dominant N loss pathway in wet and flat soils. In well-drained and sloping soils, leaching and runoff are relatively more important and here a greater proportion ends up in surface waters and groundwater.

Mean nitrate concentrations in European rivers is about three mg per litre, with a tendency of lower concentrations in large rivers and higher concentrations in small rivers. Concentrations are highest in the densely populated delta of Western Europe and lowest in Northern Europe. Ammonia concentrations have steadily decreased in the 1990's from a mean of about 0.25 mg per litre in 1990 to a mean of about 0.15 mg per litre in 1998, reflecting an improvement in sewage treatment (EEA, 2003). Concentrations of nitrate below 0.3 to 1 mg l^{-1} are considered to be natural or background levels for most European rivers. The corresponding figure for ammonium is 0.015 mg N l^{-1}. Concentrations of nitrate above 5.6 to 7.5 mg N l^{-1} are considered to be of poor quality. Concentrations of ammonia exceeding 9 mg N l^{-1} are expected to have significant toxic effects on aquatic life.

There is a direct relationship between riverine and direct discharges of N and P into coastal sea waters and the concentrations of nutrients in coastal seas and estuaries. Discharges of P to the North Sea from urban wastewater and industry have been significantly decreased between 1985 and 2000, while decreases from agriculture have been less. Agriculture is now the major source of N and P discharges into the North Sea. For the Baltic Sea, agriculture is the main source of N and urban waste water the main source of P. Comprehensive data for the Mediterranean is lacking, but all coastal cities discharge their (treated or untreated) sewage into the sea, indicating that the nutrient input from this source may be high. In the 1990's, concentrations of P in coastal waters in winter tend to decrease in response to decreasing P discharges. However, concentrations of nitrate in coastal water in winter have remained at about similar levels.

Background concentrations of N and P generally decrease from rivers to estuaries to coastal seas and open seas. However, background concentrations are quite different for the European seas. The Mediterranean Sea and Black Sea are naturally oligotrophic and background nutrient levels would be expected to be lower than in the North Sea and Baltic Sea. Background nitrate N concentration (in mg per litre) is 0.1 to 1.0 for rivers, 0.1 for the North Sea, 0.01 for the Mediterranean Sea, and 0.001 for the Black Sea. Background P concentration (in $\mu g\, l^{-1}$) is ten for rivers, 40 for the North Sea, and one for the Mediterranean Sea and the Black Sea.

Ecological impacts

Worldwide, biodiversity is deteriorating at an unprecedented rate. As almost half of the land area of EU-25 is farm land, agriculture has shaped much of Europe's landscapes and biodiversity and the abundance of characteristic species has been decreased on average to about 45 percent of its level some 150 years ago. This means that many characteristic species have become much less abundant and widespread, as a result of the intensification of land use (RIVM, 2004b). However, 15 to 25 percent of the European countryside qualifies as farm land with a high nature value, mainly semi-natural grasslands which are biodiversity hot spots. There are still large areas of low-intensity agricultural land with high nature value, especially in the southern and eastern parts, but the high level of biodiversity is vulnerable here. Evidently, loss of biodiversity will remain a key issue in the decades to come. The challenge is to give explicit value to the common but as yet non-marketable benefits of the preservation of biodiversity, nature, and valuable landscapes. Typical though, only a small proportion of consumers are willing to pay a higher price for products and services that reflect environmental, natural, or social values. Thus, the common values of nature, biodiversity, and landscapes have to be protected through proper policies and measures, in line with agri-environmental regulations and the EU's Common Agricultural Policy reform (RIVM, 2004b).

Long-term N enrichment of European terrestrial ecosystems via atmospheric deposition has gradually increased the availability of N in several vegetation types, resulting in increasing occurrence of more nitrophylic plants at the cost of characteristic species adapted to N poor conditions. This is clearest under oligotrophic and mesotrophic soil conditions. Soil acidification through increased atmospheric deposition of N and sulfur is especially important in weakly buffered soil systems with acid-tolerant species increasing at the expense of plants typically growing on intermediate soil pH (Van Egmond et al., 2002). Some 36 percent of the EU-25 territory is covered with forest and they are a key feature in European nature although they have a long history of human exploitation. Currently, about 20 percent of all trees are rated as damaged by defoliation through air pollutants, despite decreasing levels of air pollutants. In part, forests suffer from too high ammonia concentrations in the atmosphere and from a high level of N deposition. Currently, some 55 percent of terrestrial ecosystems in EU-25 receive N loads above the critical values (RIVM, 2004b). In response, EU member states agreed upon national emission ceilings which require a decrease in the emissions of ammonia and N oxides between 1990 and 2010 of up to 60 percent. However, model calculations indicate that critical loads for N deposition will still be exceeded in large areas, suggesting that biodiversity is still at risk in these areas.

Increased losses of N and P from agriculture to surface waters contribute to eutrophication and associated adverse effects, including low oxygen and hypoxic/anoxic conditions caused by the bacterial degradation of dead phytoplankton. About 40 percent of rivers and lakes in the EU-15 show signs of eutrophication. Bottom-dwelling animals and fish die if oxygen concentrations fall below 2 mg O_2 l^{-1}. Eutrophication also leads to the disappearance of bottom vegetation and to the occurrence of harmful algal blooms. There are clear differences in the geographical distribution of concentrations of chlorophyll-like pigments, as observed from satellite imagery. Chlorophyll-a concentration is highest in estuaries and close to river mouth and big cities, and lowest in open marine waters. High concentrations are found in summer in the Baltic Sea, in the North Sea along the coast and estuaries, ibid in the English Channel and along the coast of France and Portugal, some shorelines of the Mediterranean Sea and the Black Sea (EEA, 2003).

The bathing quality of the surface water is also negatively affected by eutrophication. Results indicate that the bathing quality of coastal waters and inland waters have steadily increased during the 1990's following improved sewage water treatments.

Policy responses

Environmental side effects of the intensification of agricultural production became apparent since the 1970's. The overproduction of butter, beef, and cereals was at the costs of the environmental sustainability. The surpluses became financial and environmental burdens. This led to a series of reforms of the initial Common Agricultural Policy, to stimulate less intensive production methods with environmental benefits. Milk quotas established in 1984 provided a mechanism for a stepwise decrease of dairy cow numbers. Lower quotas and increased milk yield per cow resulted in a 40 percent decrease in the number of dairy cows over the last 20 years. Environmental side-effects of the intensification of the agricultural production were not addressed initially, partly because of the lack of recognition, and partly because the European Commission did not have the necessary legal means to deal effectively with environmental problems in the EU-15, until 1986 (De Clercq et al., 2001). Nowadays, all farmers in EU are confronted with an increasing number of regulations and burden of administration, which limit the degree of freedom in farming, especially in intensive animal production (De Walle and Sevenster, 1998). Implementation of environmental policies and measures implies in part that the environmental cost of agricultural production is internalized in the decision making and economic costs of farming. Farmers will have to change farming practices and may have to invest in for example manure storage facilities, manure applicators and manure disposal. Some of these changes are economically beneficial, especially for arable farmers and many dairy farmers, but not for specialized livestock farmers

From the early 1990's onwards, EU environmental policies and measures have increasingly affected agricultural production and started to overrule national environmental policies and measures.

Currently, there are two types of environmental legislation in the EU, namely regulations and directives. Regulations are binding and directly applicable in all member states. Regulations must be complied with fully by those addressed (individuals, member states, institutions). Directives are also binding, but the objectives of the directives can be achieved in different ways by member states (choice of form and methods to apply). With the reform of the Common Agricultural Policy, there is a clear trend of integrating environmental targets in agricultural policy.

Currently, agriculture and especially the use of animal manure and fertilizers are affected by three categories of EU policies and measures (De Clercq et al., 2001): (1) Agenda 2000 and the reform of Common Agricultural Policy; (2) Water Framework Directive; and (3) Air quality Directive. These are further discussed below.

Agenda 2000. Agenda 2000 is an action program launched in 1999 by the EU to increase competitiveness, to enhance standards of food safety and quality, and to ensure a fair standard of living for the agricultural community (European Commission, 1999). It addresses the reform of the Common Agricultural Policy and the structural policy, including the uncoupling of production and income support. Within Agenda 2000, there are two regulations that affect N and P use. First, Regulation No. 1259/99 establishes common rules for direct payments to farmers in return to agri–environmental commitments. Secondly, Regulation 1257/99 supports sustainable rural development to restore and enhance competitiveness. The focus of Agenda 2000 is on (1) less-favored areas and areas with environmental restrictions, and (2) on agricultural production methods designed to protect the environment and to maintain the countryside. Hence, farmers who apply good farming practices, decrease livestock density, upkeep the landscape, and/or conserve areas with high nature value, can be granted a compensatory allowance.

Water Framework Directive. The Water Framework Directive is the most substantial piece of EU water legislation. It requires all inland and coastal waters to reach good ecological status by 2015. It will do this by establishing a river basin district structure within which demanding environmental objectives will be set, including ecological targets for surface waters. It addresses all compounds that affect the ecological status of surface waters, including N and P from agriculture. The Water Framework Directive establishes also a framework for the Integrated Program on Water Quality Management. It includes: (a) water quality standards; (b) emission limits; and (c) legislations and measures. It encompasses a large number of other directives. So far, most important for agriculture is the Nitrate Directive (91/676/EC), which has been agreed upon by all member states in 1991 and which must have been implemented by 2003. In the next decade, the demanding environmental objectives for P in surface waters in the Water Framework Directive itself will have an even greater impact on agriculture that the Nitrate Directive currently has.

The main objective of the Nitrate Directive is "to decrease water pollution caused or induced by nitrates from agricultural sources and prevent further such pollution". For this, all member states have to take various measures (i.e., designate vulnerable zones and establish action and monitoring programs and a code of good agricultural practices for these zones). Nitrate vulnerable zones must be designated on the basis of monitoring results which indicate that the groundwater and surface waters in these zones are or could be affected by nitrate pollution from agriculture. So far, Austria, Denmark, Finland, Germany, Luxembourg, and The Netherlands have designated the whole territory as nitrate vulnerable zone, while other member states have designated only a part of the country as nitrate vulnerable zone. The difference in designation between member states is only partly related to the actual pollution with nitrate. Some member states designated the whole territory to keep uniform measures, to avoid unfair competition between different groups of farmers, and to raise environmental awareness among all farmers (De Clercq et al., 2001).

The action program must contain mandatory measures relating to: (i) periods when application of animal manure and fertilizers is prohibited; (ii) capacity of and facilities for storage of animal manure; and (iii) limits to the amounts of animal manure and fertilizers applied to land. These measures must ensure that for each farm in vulnerable areas the amount of N applied via animal manure, including that deposited by grazing animals, shall not exceed 170 $kg\,ha^{-1}yr^{-1}$. Member states are obliged to monitor the nitrate concentrations of groundwater and surface waters to assess the impact of the measures, and to report the results to the European Commission. So far, there is a wide variation between member states in the interpretation and implementation of action programs and codes of good agricultural practices (De Clercq et al., 2001).

The limit of 170 $kg\,ha^{-1}yr^{-1}$ of N from animal manure on a farm basis has been questioned, as this limit strongly limits livestock density per farm, and there is no scientific justification for one uniform limit for all agricultural land. A note in the annex of the Nitrate Directives may provide a way out; member states may derogate from this limit and may apply more N via animal manure when justified on the basis of scientifically and practically sound data and arguments. A few countries are in the process of applying for derogation. Points of discussion are the height (250, 230, 210 $kg\,ha^{-1}yr^{-1}$ of N), and the criteria (e.g., surface area, land use,

drainage, duration) for derogation.

EU Air Quality Directive. The EU Air Quality Directive (1999/30/EC) sets limits to the emission of ammonia and N oxides (and other gases, mainly from industrial sources and traffic) into the atmosphere, so as to abate acidification, eutrophication, and ground-level ozone. The directive sets targets for emission reduction to be reached in 2010 relative to the reference year 1990. The emission reduction targets for ammonia range between 0 and 43 percent for individual member states. Mitigation measures for agriculture focus on the use of urea and ammonium-based fertilizers, manure application, manure storage, animal housing, and an advisory code of good agricultural practice. The strict emission reduction targets necessitate livestock farmers in some member states to use low-protein animal feed and low-emission techniques for the storage, handling, and application of animal manures.

Concluding remarks

Agriculture exerts various effects on the wider environment. Until recently, these effects were considered to be beneficial, or were simply ignored. This general perception changed from the 1970s onwards, when the effects became much larger, following the large-scale intensification of agricultural production and better understood through the advancement of science. Current perception is that especially intensive agriculture has various negative effects on the environment. Awareness of the side-effects of intensive agricultural production marks a major change in the relationship between agriculture and society (Mannion and Bowlby, 1992). Traditionally, agriculture was a major source of natural values and a key mediator of natural morality. The imposition of regulatory controls has in part stigmatized farmers as environmental criminals, especially in countries with high livestock density. Environmental pollution by agriculture has become a politicized problem (Lowe and Ward, 1997).

Eutrophication of the environment through N and P from agriculture is chiefly a product of the Industrial Revolution. It is the price that society has to pay for increasing agricultural production, rapid population growth, and urbanization (Mannion and Bowlby, 1992). It has created economic repercussions and has become an important political issue, because it affects vital resources as biodiversity, forests, nature areas, and surface waters. These are most clear in areas with intensive animal production as in The Netherlands (Oenema, 2004; Oenema and Berentsen, 2004; RIVM, 2004b).

Brouwer et al. (2000) compared the environmental and health-related concerns related to agriculture in the EU, Untied States, Canada, Australia, and New Zealand, and explored the influence of these concerns on the relative competitiveness of agriculture in the world market. Nutrient enrichment of the environment, pesticides residues in food and the environment, ammonia, and odor emissions, decrease of biodiversity and genetically modified organisms (GMO's) were the top five issues out of a list of 18 concerns. These top five issues were of greater concern in EU than in the other countries, except perhaps for pesticides. Though the concern was different between countries, standards in the control of the environment and human health were rather similar. However, there were real differences in the approach to solving the problems, with voluntary approaches in the Untied States and Canada and a mix of regulatory and voluntary approaches in the EU. On average, the cost of environmental compliance in agriculture were estimated to be not high (three to four percent of the gross revenue), although there are large differences between countries. Comparison is complicated because there is a lack of data on the relative cost of sectors and international comparison of costs is problematic because of differences in production practices and because of aspects like exchanges rates. Brouwer et al. (2002) conclude that compliance with environmental regulations in crop production is as yet no driving force for determining the location of production, but that compliance costs in animal production have significantly increased over the last years and that this may have an effect on the location of animal production in the near future.

The loss of N from agriculture has been the subject of a large amount of research, especially in Europe and North America (Goulding, 2004). The focus and scale of this research has gradually shifted as the scale and intensity of the N loss problem increased and in response to the implementation of governmental policies and measures. For example, the relative large number of research papers on nitrate leaching in Europe (Goulding, 2004) may be related to the implementation of the EU Nitrate Directive in 1991. Galloway and Cowling (2002) make an integral analysis of the cause-effect relationship between the creation of reactive N and a sequence of environmental effects, using the so-called N cascade. The N cascade illustrates the movement of human-produced reactive N as it cycles through various environmental reservoirs in the atmosphere, terrestrial ecosystems, and aquatic ecosystems before it returns to the atmosphere as non-reactive N_2 following denitrification. When it cascades through the environment, it creates a whole bunch on beneficial and detrimental effects, which are not all understood equally well. Evidently, N losses from agriculture have local, regional, continental, and global dimensions, depending on the N species and the size and scale of the losses.

Forecasts suggest that further intensification of agricultural production using current technologies may even have dramatic effects on the wider environment during the next decades (Tilman et al., 2001). Fertilizer N consumption will increase by 20 to 40 percent during the next decades (Wood et al., 2004), and forecasts by FAO suggest increases in animal numbers in the range of 30 to 50 percent, with largest increases for poultry (Bruinsma, 2003). Increases will be relatively large in the developing countries while a (further) decrease is anticipated in some affluent countries, in response to globalization of markets and to societal concerns about animal welfare and environmental burdens of intensively managed confined animal production systems. The expected trend towards more (intensive) animal production systems may have important environmental and social implications. Animal production systems have a relatively large share in the emissions of ammonia (NH_3), nitrous oxide (N_2O) and methane (CH_4) into the atmosphere. Locally and regionally, animal production systems also contribute to eutrophication of groundwater and surface waters with N and P (Oenema and Tamminga, 2005). Intensive animal production systems have also been implicated for the use of various feed additives (e.g., antibiotics, micronutrients), high water and energy uses, and unnatural housing systems (Smil, 2002). Evidently, significant system improvements and efficiency gains in agriculture are needed worldwide in the next decades, to be able to feed the increasing global population and at the same time circumvent large-scale deterioration of natural ecosystems and ecosystem services through agricultural activities (Tilman et al., 2001; 2002).

Currently, use efficiency of applied nutrients in agriculture is low because of large N losses by leaching, runoff, ammonia volatilization, or denitrification and because of a mismatch between supply and demand (Mosier et al., 2004). Prospects for increased nutrients use efficiency lie with improvement nutrient management

and improved management of crop, animal, soil, and residues (Dobermann and Cassman, 2004; Sharply et al., 2000). Matching nutrient supply to nutrient demand has been a challenge ever since mineral nutrition of plants was established as a scientific discipline in the 19th Century and even more, following the acceptance from the 1960's that excess nutrients can have detrimental effects on the wider environment. This challenge has provided the impetus for a large body of agricultural research, and from the 1980's onward also for series of governmental policies and measures to regulate N and P in agriculture, especially in Europe. Progress though has been modest. More than 10 years after the approval, there is a serious delay in the implementation of the Nitrates Directive in almost all member states of the EU (European Commission, 2002; Pfimlin, 2004).

As regards environmental policy, governments have only two main instruments, namely stimulation and regulation (Baumol and Oates, 1988). Stimulation means that desired behavior is rewarded and undesired behavior is discouraged. Desired behavior may be stimulated through extension, education, research, and financial incentives such as subsidies and levies. Regulation as the alternative instrument forbids undesired behavior and penalizes transgressors. Regulations can efficiently solve site-specific problems restricted to certain spots. The choice between the two types of instrument usually depends on the trade-off between transaction and implementation costs on the one hand and the precision and effectiveness of the instruments on the other hand (Romstad et al., 1997). This choice is not easy, as there are many complexities involved, as illustrated by the manure policy of the Netherlands (RIVM, 2004b; Oenema and Berentsen, 2004). The Nitrates Directive is based on regulations, while the mineral accounting system introduced in The Netherlands in 1998 is an economic instrument based on levies.

Whatever the instrument, implementation of environmental policies in agriculture confronts farmers with changes for which their experience provides little guidance. During the last decades, European farmers are confronted with an increasing number of environmental policies that in terms of their own experience are rapid, substantial and novel. Farmers need time to adopt new techniques and management styles to adjust to improved farming practices. They have to learn and they have to be convinced of the need for change, otherwise they remain reluctant to change and ignorant of improved practices. In general, many of the tools offered to farmers to improve the management of the farm have not been very effective (McCown, 2002). Yet, some progress has been made, and these cases show that targeted policies, farm and site-specific information and direct guidance provides the best basis for improving nutrient management (Dobermann and Cassman, 2004; RIVM, 2004b).

References Cited

Addiscott, T.M. and N Benjamin. 2004. Nitrate and human health. Soil Use and Management 20:98-104.

Baumol, W.J., and W.E. Oates. 1988. The theory of environmental policy. Cambridge University Press, Cambridge. UK

Brouwer, F.M. and P Hellegers. 1997. Nitrogen flows at farm level across European Union agriculture. Pp. 11-26 In: Controlling Mineral Emissions in European Agriculture. Economics, Policies, and the Environment. E. Romstad, J. Simonsen and A. Vatn (eds.) CAB International, Wallington, UK

Brouwer, F.M., D. Baldock, C. Carpentier, J. Dwyer, D. Ervin, G. Fox, A. Meister, and R. Stringer. 2000. Comparison of environmental and health-related standards influencing the relative competitiveness of EU agriculture vis-à-vis main competitors in the world market. Report 5.00.07. Agricultural Economics Research Institute LEI, The Hague, 154 pp.

Bruinsma, J.E. 2003. World agriculture: Towards 2015/2030. An FAO perspective. Earthscan Publications Ltd, London.

De Clercq, P., A.C. Gertsis, G. Hofman, S.C. Jarvis, J.J. Neeteson, and F. Sinabell, (eds). 2001. Nutrient management legislation in European countries. Wageningen Press, The Netherlands.

De Walle, F.B., and J. Sevenster. 1998. Agriculture and the environment. Minerals, manure, and measures. Kluver Academic Publishing, Dortrecht, The Netherlands.

DG-AGRI. 2002. European agriculture entering the 21th Century. European Commission, Directorate General for Agriculture, Brussels, Belgium. Also on http://europa.eu.int/comm/dg06/agrista/index_en.htm

Dobermann, A. and K.G. Cassman. 2004. Environmental dimensions of fertilizer nitrogen: What can be done to increase nitrogen use efficiency and ensure global food security. Pp. 261-278. In: A.R. Mosier, J.K. Syers, and J.R. Freney (eds.) Agriculture and the Nitrogen Cycle. SCOPE 65. Island Press, Washington, D.C.

European Commission. 1999. Agenda 2000. Volume 1. For a stronger and wider EU. Luxembourg Office for Official Publications of the European Communities, No. CB-CO-97-380-EN-C. http://www.europa.eu.int/comm./agenda2000.

European Commission. 2002. The implementation of Council Directive 91/676/EEC concerning the protection of waters against pollution caused by nitrates from agricultural sources. Report COM 2002, 407, Brussels, Belgium.

European Commission. 2003. Proposal for Reform of Common Agricultural Policy. COM 2003, 23 definite, Brussels, Belgium (22.01.2003).

Eurostat. 2003. Agriculture in the European Union-Statistical and economic information http://europa. eu.int/comm/dg06/agrista/index_en.htm.

EEA, 2003. Europe's environment: The third assessment, environmental assessment. Report No. 10, EEA, Copenhagen, Denmark.

Follett, J.R. and J.F. Follett. 2001 Utilization and metabolism of nitrate by humans. Pp 65-92. In: R.F. Follett and J.L. Hatfield (eds.) Nitrogen in the Environ-ment: Sources, Problems, and Management. Elsevier, Amsterdam.

Galloway, J.N. and E.B. Cowling. 2002. Reactive nitrogen and the world: 200 years of change. Ambio 31: 64-71.

Goulding, K.T. 2004. Pathways and losses of fertilizer nitrogen at different scales. Pp. 209-219. In: A.R. Mosier, J.K. Syers and J.R. Freney (eds.) Agriculture and the Nitrogen Cycle. SCOPE 65. Island Press, Washington, D.C.

Heath, M. and G. Tucker. 1994. Birds in Europe: Their conservation status. Birdlife International, Cambridge, UK.

L'hirondel, J. and J.L. L'hirondel. 2002. Nitrate and man: Toxic, harmless or beneficial? CABI Publishing, Wallingford, UK.

Lowe, P., and N. Ward. 1997. The moral authority of regulation: The case of agricultural pollution. Pp. 59-72. In: Controlling Mineral Emissions in European Agriculture. Economics, Policies and the Environment. E. Romstad, J. Simonsen and A. Vatn (eds.). CAB International, Wallington, UK.

Mannion, A.M. and S.R. Bowlby. 1992. Environmental issues in the 1990s. John Wiley & Sons, Chichester, UK, 349 pp.

Marschner, H. 1995. Mineral nutrition of higher plants, 2nd edition, Academic Press. London, 889 pp.

McCown, R.L. 2002. Changing systems for supporting farmers' decisions: Problems, paradigms, and prospects. Agricultural Systems 74:179-220.

Mosier, A.R., J.K. Syers and J.R. Freney (eds.). 2004. Agriculture and the Nitrogen Cycle. SCOPE 65. Island Press, Washington, D.C.

Organisation for Economic Co-operation and Development (OECD).2001. Environmental indicators for agriculture, methods, and results. Volume 3. OECD, Paris, France.

Oenema, O. 2004. Governmental policies and measures regulating nitrogen and phosphorus from animal manure in European Agriculture. Journal of Animal Sciences 82:196-206.

Oenema, O. and P.B.M. Berentsen. 2004. Manure policy and MINAS: Regulating nitrogen and phosphorus surpluses in agriculture of The Netherlands. OECD report COM/ENV/EPOC/CTPA/CFA(2004)67. OECD Headquarters, Paris, France, 45 pp.

Oenema, O. and S. Tamminga. 2005. Nitrogen management in animal production systems. Science in China (in press).

Oenema, O., G.J. Monteny, J. Verloop, B. van Hove and P.B.M. Berentsen (in prep.) Transitions in agriculture of the Netherlands 1850-2030.

Pfimlin, A. 2004. Implementation of the Nitrates Directive in 2002 to 2003 in eight European member states and twelve dairy regions. Report Institute de l'Elevage, Paris, 76 pp.

RIVM. 2004a. Minerals better adjusted: Fact-finding study of the effectiveness of the Manure Act. RIVM, Bilthoven, The Netherlands (in Dutch).

RIVM. 2004b. Outstanding environmental issues: A review of the EU's environmental agenda. RIVM, Bilthoven, The Netherlands.

Romstad, E., J. Simonsen, and A. Vatn. 1997. Controlling mineral emissions in European agriculture. Economics, policies and the environment. CAB International, Wallington, UK.

Sharpley, A.N., B.H. Foy, and P.J.A. Withers. 2000. Practical and innovative measures for the control of agricultural phosphorus losses to water: An overview. Journal Environmental Quality 29:1-9.

Smil, V. 2000. Feeding the world: A challenge for the 21st Century. MIT Press, Cambridge, Massachusetts.

Smil, V. 2001. Enriching the earth. Fritz Haber, Carl Bosch and the transition of world food production. MIT Press, Cambridge, Massachusetts.

Smil, V. 2002. Eating meat: Evolution, patterns, and consequences. Population and Development Review 28:599-639.

SNV, 1994. Eutrophication of soil, fresh water and the sea. The environment in Sweden: Status and trends. Swedish Environmentla Protection Agency. Report 4244, Solna, Sweden, 208 pp.

Steen, I. 1997. A European fertilizer industry view on phosphorus retention and loss from agricultural soils. Pp. 311-328. *In:* H. Tunney, O.T. Carton, P.C. Brookes and A.E. Johnston (eds.) Phosphorus Loss from Soil to Water. CABI Publishing, Wallingford, UK.

Tilman, D., J. Fargione, B. Wolff, C. D'Antonio, A. Dobson, R.W. Howarth, D. Schindler, W.H. Schlesinger, D. Simberloff, and D. Swackhamer. 2001. Forecasting agriculturally driven global environmental change. Science 292:281-284.

Tilman, D., K.G. Cassman, P.A. Matson, R. Naylor and S. Polasky. 2002. Agricultural sustainability and intensive production practices. Nature 418:671-677.

Tunney, H., A. Breeuwsma, P.J.A. Withers, and P.A.I. Ehlert. 1997. Phosphorus fertilizer strategies: Present and future. Pp. 177-203. *In:* H. Tunney, O.T. Carton, P.C. Brookes, and A.E. Johnston (eds.) Phosphorus Loss from Soil to Water. CABI Publishing, Wallingford, UK.

Van Egmond, K., T. Bresser, and L. Bouwman, 2002. The European nitrogen case. Ambio 31:72-78.

Van der Veeren, R.J.H.M. 2002. Economic analyses of nutrient abatement policies in the Rhine Basin. PhD thesis Free University of Amsterdam. 272 pp.

Whitehead, D.C. 2000. Nutrient elements in grassland. Soil plant animal relationships. CABI Publishing, Wallingford, UK. 369 pp.

Wood, S., J. Heneao, and M. Rosegrant. 2004. The role of nitrogen in sustaining food production and estimating nitrogen fertilizer needs to meet the food demand. Pp. 245-259. *In:* A.R. Mosier, J.K. Syers, and J.R. Freney (eds.) Agriculture and the Nitrogen Cycle. SCOPE 65. Island Press, Washington, D.C.

Motivating Farmers to Manage Nutrients Efficiently

CHAPTER 7

C.J.M. Ondersteijn, A.G.J.M. Oude Lansink, G.W.J. Giesen, and R.B.M. Huirne

Pollution of groundwater bodies by agricultural nutrients has led to strict European regulations with regard to nitrogen (N) (specified in the Nitrate Directive (91/676/EEC)). The Nitrate Directive essentially limits the usage of N from manure for fertilization purposes. Since Dutch agriculture is highly intensive in terms of cattle units per unit of land, this Directive has a serious impact on the viability of individual farms if it were to be implemented directly. Dutch policymakers decided to deviate from the general standard for manure application and introduced a nutrient bookkeeping system in 1998, also called Mineral Accounting System (MINAS). MINAS allows farmers to individually address the nutrient problem on their farm, and fines those who do not manage to comply with the nutrient surplus standards (Brandt and Smit, 1998; Ondersteijn et al., 2002). The system is output oriented, meaning that farmers are fined according to their final nutrient surplus, irrespective of the way they arrive at it. In this way, the Dutch government aims at internalizing the negative externalities (bads) associated with inefficient nutrient use. The incentive for change in nutrient management in The Netherlands was most substantial in 2003, when the Mineral Accounting System reached the final introduction phase[i] (Ondersteijn et al., 2002). To meet these standards, Dutch farmers had to improve their nutrient management considerably. To gain insight into the possibilities of nutrient management improvement, the Dutch government and farm organizations joined forces and initiated a three-year nation-wide project, in which participating farmers received support to enhance nutrient management on their farms. The goal of the project was to investigate how nutrient management can be improved effectively through changes in nutrient management, and gather and diffuse knowledge about nutrient management on commercial farms.

If farmers want to meet the environmental policy measures, they have to improve nutrient performance. To do so, it is essential to learn from successful colleagues who can act as benchmarks, rather than focusing on average performance. Since the goal of (environmental) performance research is to improve this performance, a frontier approach, in which farm performance is measured relative to the best practice frontier, provides important insights. The estimated efficiency measures reveal the possibilities for improvement far better than for instance regression coefficients, which focus on average rather than best performance. Besides the position of farms with respect to the best practice farms, it is also useful to check whether or not possibilities for improvements over time exist. Either improving nutrient efficiency, i.e. moving towards the frontier, or changing the technology with which nutrients are used, i.e. a shift of the frontier itself, contribute to improvements in environmental performance over time. Nutrient efficiency has been studied by Fernandez et al. (2002); Reinhard (1999); and Piot Lepetit and

Vermersch (1998). These studies focus on how to measure efficiency in the presence of detrimental outputs and do not analyze changes due to technological and efficiency change in environmental performance. This paper develops the concept of subvector productivity change (productivity change in one dimension) in order to provide insight into the possibilities for improvement of nutrient performance, through efficiency change and technical change over time.

Using the data of specialized dairy farms participating in the project, this paper studies the feasibility for Dutch dairy farmers to improve nutrient performance through technical and efficiency change. First, data envelopment analysis is used to estimate technical and nutrient efficiency. Second, overall productivity and nutrient productivity changes and the underlying technological and efficiency changes are calculated. This is done using the concept of Malmquist Total Factor Productivity and the development of a Malmquist Subvector Productivity Index. Finally, the data envelopment analysis efficiency measures of the technical and efficiency change are explained using farm structure and farm management characteristics in Tobit regression analyses.

Method

Technical and nutrient efficiency. Farrell (1957) specified an operational definition of efficiency that complies with the theoretical definition of Pareto efficient production (a producer is technically efficient if an input reduction requires an increase in another input or a decrease in at least one output). The Farrell input-oriented measure of technical efficiency is defined as one minus the maximum equiproportionate reduction in all inputs that still allows continued production of given outputs. A score of unity indicates full efficiency, whereas a score less than one suggests that a reduction in inputs is possible

without sacrificing output.

Efficiency measurement in agriculture is complicated by the fact that agricultural processes have a stochastic element due to instance weather. The choice of stochastic frontier analysis seems obvious (Coelli, 1995; and Coelli et al., 1999). The problem with stochastic frontier analysis, however, is that it assumes a functional form for production technology, which can confound the efficiency results (Reinhard, 1999). It also expects the researchers to choose a distributional form for the inefficiency effect, which is rather arbitrary. Finally, parametric approaches also assume that the estimated production frontier applies to each observation, thus enforcing some average technology on all decision-making units. Non-parametric programming approaches, currently known as data envelopment analysis, have more flexibility in that they avoid a parametric specification of average technology and the distribution of efficiency, and can easily incorporate multiple outputs (Coelli et al., 1999; Charnes et al., 1994). It optimizes the efficiency measure for each observation rather than estimating an average benchmark. On the other hand, any statistical noise due to for instance weather fluctuations will be attributed to the inefficiency measure. Given this shortcoming, data envelopment analysis is used in this study because of its flexibility. Furthermore, dairy farming in The Netherlands is for the main part under the control of the farmer because the main activity (dairy farming) is done indoors, and the fact that the data available for this study are of high quality (little measurement error)[ii].

Data envelopment analysis computes Farrell-efficiency for a farm relative to the best practice farms in the sample using linear programming. In an input oriented data envelopment analysis model the objective is to produce the observed outputs with as little inputs as possible. This is a reasonable assumption in European milk production, which is limited by a quota for every individual farm. In a homogenous market with input and output prices equal for all producers and more or less constant over short time periods, the only way to maximize profit is thus input minimization. Therefore, in this study, an input orientation is used.

The production of milk on Dutch dairy farms generates negative externalities in the form of nutrient surpluses. These nutrient surpluses are not harmful if they can be contained but if they start leaching into groundwater, or emitting ammonia in the air, the environment can be at risk. To prevent and avoid these risks, these 'bads', i.e. nutrient surpluses, associated with the production of milk are not freely disposable. If the nutrient surpluses exceed the standards, farmers will be taxed. In order to avoid taxation, farms could for instance dispose of manure or change to a more extensive farming system, all leading to costs. These cost involved with disposing of bads cannot be ignored if we want to get a true measure of technical efficiency (Pittman, 1983; Färe et al., 1989). Tyteca (1997) and Ball et al. (2000) realized that the incorporation of bads into the production process provided the opportunity to measure environmental performance, and changes in performance under environmental constraints (Tyteca, 1997; Ball et al., 2000). Bads can be modeled as a weakly disposable output in a distance function approach (Ball et al., 1994; Chung et al., 1997), or as a weakly disposable input to be minimized (Hailu and Veeman, 2001; Reinhard et al., 1999; Shaik and Helmers, 1999). Since the nutrient surpluses can be seen as net inputs rather than outputs resulting from the production process, they are modeled as weakly disposable inputs in this study.

Programming problem (1) is used to calculate the Farrell input-oriented overall technical efficiency under variable returns to scale conditions, incorporating nutrient surpluses as weakly disposable inputs:

$$F(y, x \mid V,W) = Min\ \theta$$

$$\text{Subject to:} \quad y_i \leq Y\lambda \qquad (1)$$
$$\theta x_i \geq X^s \lambda$$
$$\theta w_i \geq X^w \lambda$$
$$N'\lambda = 1$$
$$\lambda \geq 0$$

In which θ represents overall technical Farrell-efficiency ($\theta \in [0,1]$) for the i-th firm under the assumption of weak disposability of the nitrogen (N) and phosphate surplus, Y is the observed vector of outputs, X^s is the observed vector of conventional (strongly disposable) inputs and X^w is the observed vector of the environmentally detrimental (weakly disposable) inputs (N and phosphate surplus). The intensity variables or firm weights are represented by an $N \times 1$ vector λ, where N is the number of farms in the sample. The intuitive interpretation of the problem is to takesthe i-th firm and then seek to radially minimize the input vector, made up out of X and W, while still remaining within the feasible input set (Färe et al., 1994a; Coelli et al., 1999). The first and second constraints reflect strong disposability of outputs and conventional inputs respectively. The equality in the third constraint imposes weak disposability of the nutrient surpluses. The fourth constraint allows for a technology characterized by variable returns to scale (VRS), which envelopes the data most tightly, compared to constant returns to scale and non-increasing returns to scale. Figure 1 gives a graphic explanation of the concept of input-orientated technical efficiency, using two inputs, x_1 and x_2. A, B, and P^t, represent farms that use a different combination of x_1 and x_2 in time-period t. Data envelopment analysis creates a piecewise linear isoquant t from the observations, representing the most efficient technologies used by the farms in the sample in time period t (in this case

Figure 1
Input-oriented technical efficiency and Malmquist Total Factor Productivity Growth.

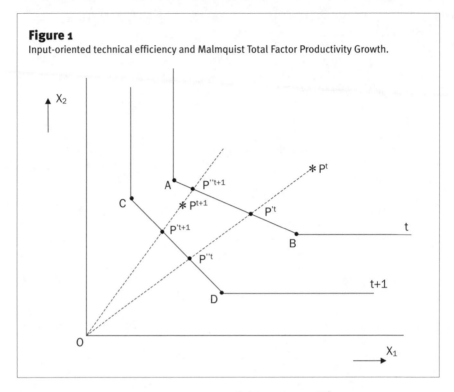

farm A and B). Technical efficiency for farm P^t can be calculated as the radial measure OP^t/OP^t.

Using the concept of non-radial efficiency (Färe et al., 1994a), an efficiency estimate for surpluses of both nutrients simultaneously can be calculated providing an indication of nutrient performance of the farm. Nutrient efficiency is defined as the ratio of minimum feasible to observed nutrient surpluses, conditional on levels of outputs and conventional inputs (Reinhard et al., 2000). In other words, nutrient surpluses of one particular farm in the sample are compared to the lowest nutrient surpluses observed in the same sample, corrected for the ratio of other inputs and outputs used. This is described in linear programming problem (2):

$$SF\ (y, x, w\ |\ V,W) = Min\ y \tag{2}$$

Subject to: $\quad y_i \leq Y\lambda$
$\qquad\qquad\quad x_i \geq X^s\ \lambda$
$\qquad\qquad\quad yw_i = X^w\ \lambda$
$\qquad\qquad\quad N'\lambda = 1$
$\qquad\qquad\quad \lambda \geq 0$

Nutrient Farrell-efficiency for the i-th firm is represented by λ. The other variables are analogous to the previous linear programming problem. The interpretation is this problem is that it takes the i-th firm and then contracts only the inputs of interest (in this case both the N and phosphate surplus, represented by X^w). Figure 2 explains the way nutrient efficiency, a non-radial measure of efficiency, is derived. Again, A, B, and P^t, represent farms that use a different combination of x_1 and x_2 in time-period t. Suppose x_1 represents the nutrient surpluses. Farm P^t can reduce the nutrient surpluses on the farm by S^tP^t. Nutrient efficiency can then be calculated as O^tS^t/O^tP^t.

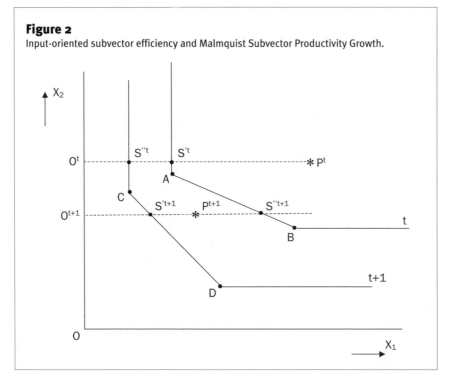

Figure 2
Input-oriented subvector efficiency and Malmquist Subvector Productivity Growth.

Separate production sets and efficiencies are calculated for each year of the panel, as done by Reinhard et al. (2000).

Total and nutrient productivity growth. The availability of panel data has the advantage that changes in performance, which over time can be studied. In studying the concept of performance changes, the concept of total factor productivity is used, which is defined as an index of output divided by an index of total input usage. A change in productivity, or total factor productivity growth, is then equal to the change in total factor productivity between periods t and t + 1. Total factor productivity growth is defined as the net change in output due to efficiency change and technical change (Färe and Grosskopf, 1996). The former equals the change in the distance between an observation and the frontier, and the latter equals a shift in the production frontier itself (Grosskopf,

1993; Coelli et al., 1999). These are calculated using the geometric mean version of total factor productivity growth, introduced by Färe et al. (1994b). The Malmquist Index is based on distance functions (D), which are inversely related to technical Farrell-efficiency measures. Calculating input-oriented Malmquist indexes requires constant returns to scale technology (C) and strong disposability of inputs (S) in order to assure feasible solutions to the programming problem. The Malmquist Input-Based Total Factor Productivity Index is defined as (Färe et al., 1994b):

$$(3)$$

$$M_i(y^{t+1}, x^{t+1}, y^t, x^t \mid C, S) =$$

$$\left[\frac{D_i^t(y^{t+1}, x^{t+1} \mid C, S)}{D_i^t(y^t, x^t \mid C, S)} \times \frac{D_i^{t+1}(y^{t+1}, x^{t+1} \mid C, S)}{D_i^{t+1}(y^t, x^t \mid C, S)} \right]^{\frac{1}{2}}$$

or, in terms of Farrell-efficiency measures:

(4)

$$
\frac{F_i^{t+1}(y^{t+1},x^{t+1}|C,S)}{F_i^t(y^t,x^t|C,S)} \times
$$

$$
\left[\frac{F_i^t(y^{t+1},x^{t+1}|C,S)}{F_i^{t+1}(y^{t+1},x^{t+1}|C,S)} \times \frac{F_i^t(y^t,x^t|C,S)}{F_i^{t+1}(y^t,x^t|C,S)} \right]^{\frac{1}{2}}
$$

Figure 1 explains the concept of Malmquist total factor productivity growth. It shows two isoquants, t and t + 1, and two data points, P^t and P^{t+1}, for time period t and time period t + 1. The Malmquist total factor productivity growth is equal to

$$
\frac{OP'^{t+1}/OP^{t+1}}{OP'^t/OP^t} \times
$$

$$
\left[\frac{OP''^{t+1}/OP^{t+1}}{OP'^{t+1}/OP^{t+1}} \times \frac{OP'^t/OP^t}{OP''^t/OP^t} \right]^{\frac{1}{2}}
$$

In the present study, the changes in nutrient performance are of importance because farmers need to adjust their nutrient management in order to meet the standards of 2003. A measure similar to total factor productivity growth but focused on nutrients, would provide insight into this matter. Analogue to total factor productivity growth, a measure of growth of a subvector (in this case nutrient surpluses) of inputs can be established and decomposed in a measure of subvector efficiency change and change in subvector technology.

(5)

$$
SM_i(y^{t+1},x^{t+1},w^{t+1},y^t,x^t,w^t|C,S)=
$$

$$
\left[\frac{S_i^t(y^{t+1},x^{t+1},w^{t+1}|C,S)}{S_i^t(y^t,x^t,w^t|C,S)} \times \frac{S_i^{t+1}(y^{t+1},x^{t+1},w^{t+1}|C,S)}{S_i^{t+1}(y^t,x^t,w^t|C,S)} \right]^{\frac{1}{2}}
$$

or, expressed in Farrell-efficiency measures,

(6)

$$
\frac{SF_i^{t+1}(y^{t+1},x^{t+1},w^{t+1}|C,S)}{SF_i^t(y^t,x^t,w^t|C,S)} \times
$$

$$
\left[\frac{SF_i^t(y^{t+1},x^{t+1},w^{t+1}|C,S)}{SF_i^{t+1}(y^{t+1},x^{t+1},w^{t+1}|C,S)} \times \frac{SF_i^t(y^t,x^t,w^t|C,S)}{SF_i^{t+1}(y^t,x^t,w^t|C,S)} \right]^{\frac{1}{2}}
$$

The concept of subvector productivity change is graphically explained in Figure 2. Suppose x$_1$ represents the input of interest. P^t represents a farm in period t and P^{t+1} is the same farm a period later. As is the case with subvector efficiency, subvector productivity change is a nonradial measure, consisting of a non-radial shift of the frontier, and a non-radial change in efficiency:

$$
\frac{O^{t+1}S'^{t+1}/OP^{t+1}}{O^tS'^t/OP^t} \times
$$

$$
\left[\frac{O^{t+1}S''^{t+1}/OP^{t+1}}{O^{t+1}S'^{t+1}/OP^{t+1}} \times \frac{O^tS'^t/OP^t}{O^tS''^t/OP^t} \right]^{\frac{1}{2}}
$$

The Malmquist subvector productivity index represents the changes that occurred in part of the production process. In the case at hand, the subvector productivity index gives an indication of the changes in nutrient efficiency (shift of efficiency in one dimension) and the changes in the technology with which nutrients are used (shift of the frontier in one dimension). The product of these two measures gives an indication of the change in the productivity with which nutrients are used.

Data Description

Data of 114 specialized dairy farms were collected over a period of three years (1997 to 1999) as part of a large government supported project called Farm Data in Practice (FDP, Project Praktijkcijfers in Dutch). The goal of the project was to gain empirical insight into nutrient management on 'real-life' farms and to support and improve nutrient management practices. Since mineral surpluses on most dairy farms were still far below the threshold levels of taxable surpluses in this period, the effects reported in this paper will be a reflection of active nutrient management rather than economic incentives (e.g. surplus taxes). Farms were selected to give an accurate representation of specialized dairy farms in The Netherlands. Farms are classified as a specialized dairy farm if at least 95 percent of all Dutch Size Units (DSUs) can be attributed to dairy production (the DSU is an economic size unit, based on standard gross margins). Both financial and nutrient accounting data were collected as well as data on farm structure and management characteristics. Screening and cleaning of data was done twice, once by the project organization and once by the authors.

A problem that may arise in data envelopment analysis efficiency measurement is that of dimensionality, i.e. efficiency ratings are dependent on the number of firms and the number of defined outputs and inputs. Tauer and Hanchar (1995) used Monte Carlo simulation to compare random input and output data for different numbers of firms with empirical studies and showed that defining ten or more inputs will result in almost all firms being efficient. Parsimony of inputs and outputs is therefore desirable. On the other hand, compromising on completeness of all resources used and outputs produced is dangerous, since observed inefficiency may then represent misspecification of the production model. Aggregation of similar inputs and outputs is therefore necessary but one should be cautious not to incorporate aggregation bias into the model.

Aggregation is usually achieved by linearly summing up separate inputs using prices as relative weights. The technical efficiency measure then approximates economic efficiency, comprising both technical and allocative efficiency, thus creating an aggregation bias (Thomas and Tauer, 1994). Therefore only those inputs that are measured in the same physical units are aggregated. In total eight inputs and two outputs are used, of which descriptive statistics are shown in Table 1 for the total sample (three years).

The outputs distinguished are total milk production corrected for fat and protein content, and the value of cattle output, expressed in 1997 €. They represent the major outputs for the highly specialized farms. The inputs used are cultivated land in hectares (ha), total stock, aggregated in livestock units (LU), total labor used (both unpaid and paid) in full time equivalents (FTE), total N from chemical fertilizer in kg, and total phosphate from chemical fertilizer in kg. Net feed purchases contain both concentrates and roughage, aggregated using Net Energy for Lactation in Megajoules (MJ NEL), and corrected for sales and stock changes[iii]. Environmentally detrimental inputs are the N and phosphate surpluses, calculated as the difference between the production and use of nutrients[iv]. Incorporation of both fertilizer and surpluses does not hamper the calculation of the efficiency measures. Fertilizer may be a component of the nutrient surplus but the surplus is a result of the total production process and therefore the result of many other factors, i.e. purchases and sales of cattle and feed. Furthermore, fertilizer is a strongly disposable input, whereas nutrient surpluses are considered weakly disposable because of the costs involved with ridding of them. All other inputs are considered strongly disposable as well. Even though land may be seen as a factor that is hard to acquire, disposing of it easy, which is the relevant characteristic

Table 1. Descriptive statistics of inputs, outputs, farm structure, and management characteristics.

	Mean	Standard deviation
Input		
Cultivated land (ha)	41.65	11.93
Livestock (LU[a])	92.43	28.83
Labor (FTE[b])	1.76	0.54
Nitrogen fertilizer (kg N)	11013	5304
Phosphate fertilizer (kg P_2O_5)	1677	1307
Net feed purchases (MJ NEL[c])	1233679	699915
Nitrogen surplus (kg N)	11163	4467
Phosphate surplus (kg P_2O_5)	2152	1238
Output		
Milk production (kg FPCM[d])	590437	201928
Cattle output (1997 €)	21196	8568
Farm structure		
Farm size (DSU[e])	161.2	50.8
Farm intensity (quota (4.25% fat)/ha)	13867	3490
FPCM/cow	8340	744
% Grassland	85.9	12.8
Farm management		
Female young stock LU/10 cows	2.8	0.6
Ratio of organic and chemical fertilizer for extra N supply	-0.05	0.20
Concentrates used in MJ NEL/100 kg FPCM	197.7	30.6
Grazing intensity (LU grazing days/ha)	126	42

[a]LU = Livestock units
[b]FTE = Full time equivalent
[c]MJ NEL = MegaJoules net energy for lactation
[d]FPCM = Fat and protein corrected milk production
[e]DSU = Dutch Size Unit

in an input-oriented data envelopment analysis model. Specialized dairy farming in the Netherlands relies mainly on family labor. Adjustment costs of acquiring or disposing of hired labor is therefore of minor importance. Furthermore, tension on the labor market in The Netherlands and recent experiences with Classical Swine Fever (1997) and Foot and Mouth Disease (2001) showed that farmers who are temporarily without farm work can easily find replacing employment. Labor is therefore also modeled as strongly disposable. Both the N and phosphate surplus are assumed to be weakly disposable, since there is a cost involved in disposing of it.

The advantage of a highly homogenous group of farms like the present one, and low aggregation level of inputs and outputs is that variance found can be more correctly attributed to management characteristics, rather than to noise in the data. While the inputs and outputs described above determine the location of the production frontier, the variables described below (farm structure and farm management in Table 1) explain the distance to the frontier in a so-called two-stage approach (Coelli et al., 1999)[v]. The first stage determines the efficiency and productivity with data envelopment analysis, the second stage tries to explain the differences in efficiency and productivity between farms. Efficiency measures are bound by a lower and upper limit (0 to 100), and productivity by a lower limit of 0, and therefore a Tobit model (Tobin, 1958), which allows for limited distributions, is appropriate (Greene, 1997). Four farm structure characteristics are considered. Size is of importance because farmers may be able to make use of economies of scale. On the other hand, the size of the dairy operation may be limiting the optimization of the dairy production process because of labor restrictions. Size is represented by the total of DSUs on the farm. Intensity of the dairy enterprise, expressed in milk quota per ha, greatly affects nutrient surpluses because of the high amounts of inputs relative to land. For a highly intensive farming system to meet the environmental regulations, the quality of management, and therefore efficiency, has to be high (Aarts et al., 1999a). The production potential of the dairy stock, expressed in kg of fat and protein corrected milk (FPCM) per cow, reflects the efficiency with which the dairy herd is able to convert feed into milk. Highly productive cows are more energy and protein efficient (Veerkamp et al., 1993). High milk production per cow means that less cows and therefore less input is needed on a farm to produce the same amount of outputs as a farm with low productive cows (Steverink et al., 1994). Land use on dairy farms in The Netherlands consists mainly of grass and maize. Grass is the more nutrient efficient crop (Willems et al., 2000) but leads to a large amount of protein in the dairy ration. Also, when grass is used to graze cattle, this efficiency advantage is lost, due to grazing losses. Land use is therefore represented by the percentage of grassland.

Farm management is represented by four variables. Heifer management (the number of livestock units (LU) of young stock per ten cows) is important because selection of good quality replacement heifers ensures the maintenance of a high quality and highly productive dairy herd. A large number of heifers on the farm does, however press heavily on the nutrient balance (Mourits et al., 2000). A reduction might therefore improve efficiency. Fertilizing is another important aspect of management. Dairy farms use manure produced by the dairy herd and supply the farm with additional N from either organic manure of chemical fertilizer, the latter being easier to utilize (Aarts et al., 1999a). Fertilizing management is therefore represented by the ratio between net use of organic and of chemical fertilizer to supply the farm with extra N. In theory, this ratio can range from negative to positive infinity. For this sample, all observations lie between -1 and +1. Feeding management (MJ NEL of concentrates used per 100 kg of FPCM) concerns forage production and ration formulation, which results in the amount of concentrates needed. Concentrate supply according to the individual needs of the animals will improve concentrate utilization and will therefore reduce concentrate inputs (Aarts et al., 1992). Finally, grazing tactics are of importance because grazing is an inefficient form of manure nutrient use (Aarts et al., 1992). Restricting grazing time is assumed to increase nutrient efficiency and reduce nutrient surpluses (Aarts et al., 1999a). Grazing management is expressed in the total number of days that cattle are grazed corrected for the grazing system used. Years 1997, 1998, and 1999, and soil type were included as dummy variables (40.4 percent sandy soils, 44.7 percent clay soils, and 14.9 percent peat soils). Note that soil type, size, intensity, and land use reflect regional differences. Other regional effects were not expected. The farm structure and farm management variables are selected for the second stage of the analysis because they are dependent on preferences, motivation, and management skills of the farmer, and thus influence efficiency and productivity.

Results and Discussion

Technical and nutrient efficiency. Technical and nutrient efficiency measures were calculated according to models 1 and 2. Both average technical and nutrient efficiencies over three years and for every individual year are presented in Table 2. It appears that a large proportion of the farms in the sample were technically efficient, especially within years (73.7 percent). Because of this and the small spread in efficiency, average efficiencies were also high. The mean efficiency score of farms that were not fully efficient was calculated separately. Over the whole period, 52 percent of all farms were 100 percent efficient, and the average efficiency score of the non-efficient farms was high (95.25 percent).

Nutrient efficiencies, incorporating both N and phosphate efficiency, were considerably lower (Table 2). The nutrient efficiencies for the separate years were approximately 80 percent. The number of fully efficient farms differed slightly among years, with 1998 having the highest number (61 percent) of fully efficient farms. The mean nutrient efficiency for the non-efficient farms increased over time, indicating that the non-efficient farms had made improvements. The three year average was 80 percent, meaning that a simultaneous reduction of 20 percent was possible for the N and phosphate surplus. Only 29 percent of the farms in the sample were fully efficient over the three-year period, and the farms which were not, can lower their surpluses by about 28 percent if they were to produce on the frontier. Technical and nutrient efficiency were highly correlated ($\rho = 0.58$, P<0.01), indicating that technical and nutrient efficiency could be achieved simultaneously. This result is in agreement with an earlier study by Reinhard et al. (1999).

One of the causes of a deviation from the efficient frontier can be scale inefficiency. Considering their input mix, farms can produce at either too small or too large scales. This inefficiency can be defined as the ratio between CRS efficiency and VRS efficiency (Färe et al., 1994a). A comparison of different returns to scale

Table 2. Input reducing technical efficiency, and nutrient efficiency scores.

	1997	1998	1999	1997-1999
Technical efficiency				
Mean all farms	98.02	97.70	97.41	97.71
% of fully efficient farms	73.7	73.7	73.7	51.8[a]
Mean non-efficient farms	92.47	91.27	90.17	95.25
Nutrient efficiency				
Mean all farms	78.04	81.96	80.49	80.16
% of fully efficient farms	55.3	61.4	56.1	28.9[a]
Mean non-efficient farms	50.90	53.25	55.52	72.08

[a] **Farms may be fully efficient in individual years, but not necessarily in the whole period.**

technologies shows that, for the three year average, 20.2 percent of all farms were producing at an optimal scale (mean TE = 99.22, mean NE = 89.90). Of the other farms, 64.9 percent were producing at increasing returns to scale (mean TE = 97.48, mean NE = 79.49), indicating that increasing the use of all inputs simultaneously would be beneficial for technical and nutrient efficiency, whereas 14.9 percent were producing at decreasing returns to scale (mean TE = 96.67, mean NE = 69.90), meaning that a reduction in input use would, *ceteris paribus,* improve efficiency. Apparently, the scale-efficient farms also perform best with regard to nutrients. The farms producing at decreasing returns to scale farms perform considerably worse (20 percent less efficient) than the scale-efficient farms.

Based on earlier Monte Carlo simulation studies mentioned in section 3 (Tauer and Hanchar, 1995), it may be expected that approximately 30 to 50 percent of farms is fully efficient. In the present study, this percentage is as high as 74 percent for the separate years and 52 percent overall, indicating that the dairy farms in the sample are highly efficient. The average technical and nutrient efficiencies that were found in this study were also high compared with other studies (Weersink et al., 1990; Reinhard, 1999). The facts that the results were obtained from a highly homogenous group of specialized farms, having at least 95 percent of all their enterprises in dairy farming, and inputs were only aggregated in physical units and corrected for quality differences, may explain the high efficiencies found.

To explain differences in efficiencies between farms a Tobit model is estimated using data of the three consecutive years with dummies for the time effect, for both technical and nutrient efficiencies. The maximum likelihood estimates of the Tobit analysis are shown in Table 3. The size of the farm affected technical efficiencies

negatively, i.e. larger farms tend to be less efficient. This can be due to a loss of control and overview of an enterprise that is largevi. Another possible reason is that the pressure to be efficient with the use of inputs is smaller, since the sheer bulk of the operation provides the farmer with enough income to meet his financial objectives. The farm structure characteristics that positively influenced technical efficiencies are intensity in terms of quota per ha, and production capacity in terms of milk production per cow. In an intensive farming system the degree of control on input-output relationships is generally higher, which explains the positive effect. The positive effect of a high production capacity (FPCM per cow) can be explained by the fact that highly productive cows use less input (e.g. feed) per unit of output. The percentage of grassland had a negative effect on technical efficiencies. Generally, maize production yields more energy in terms of feed than does grassland production (Aarts, 2000). A high percentage of grassland will therefore lead to relatively more feed purchases. Grazing is the only management characteristic that had an effect on technical efficiencies. Grazing is accompanied by 'grazing losses' that occur because of low utilization of nutrients excreted by the cows while grazing, causing efficiency to decrease. The McKelvey-Zavoina R^2 (R^2_{mz}) (Veall and Zimmermann, 1994) for the technical efficiencies regression was 25.8[vii].

Nutrient efficiency had slightly different determinants. The size of the farm was negatively related to nutrient efficiencies, whereas intensity showed a positively relationship with nutrient efficiencies. Farm size, and the related lack of control and absence of the need for technical efficiency, may also be the reason that larger farms show lower nutrient efficiencies. The lack of fine tuning of the production process causes a loss in nutrient input use which results in higher nutrient surpluses per unit of output than are technically necessary. Farm intensity had a positive effect on nutrient efficiencies. The need to make more feed purchases enables an intensive farm to better gear to feeding needs of the dairy cattle. Furthermore, intensive farming systems often dispose of their manure, thus lowering nutrient surpluses on the farm. High production capacity (FPCM) per cow also positively influenced nutrient efficiencies. High milk production per cow generally means more nutrients leaving the farm through milk, not ending up in manure. Land use, in terms of the percentage of grassland of the total acreage was negatively related to nutrient efficiencies. This is due to the fact that, considering the high fertilization levels of grassland, silage maize proves to be a more efficient production process than grassland produc-

tion (Aarts, 2000). Furthermore, due to the high percentage of grassland, the feeding ration will be high in N. This will not be fully used by the cattle and will be excreted in manure, which is a less efficient fertilizer, especially during the grazing period. Among the management characteristics, the ratio of organic and chemical fertilizer for extra N supply affected nutrient efficiencies negatively. For a ratio between 0 and 1, this means that the more the extra N stems from organic fertilizer instead of chemical fertilizer, the lower the nutrient efficiency. When the ratio lies between 0 and -1, organic fertilizer is disposed of and replaced by chemical fertilizer (input of inorganic fertilizer exceeds manure disposal in this range, resulting in a net supply). This has a positive (double negative) effect on nutrient efficiencies.

Table 3. Maximum likelihood estimates of the Tobit regression for technical and nutrient efficiency.

Variable	Technical efficiency Parameter	t-ratio	Nutrient efficiency Parameter	t-ratio
Constant	1.009	6.072**	1.545	2.904**
Dummy 1998	-0.023	-1.054	-0.016	-0.221
Dummy 1999	-0.032	-1.457	-0.019	-0.265
Dummy sandy soils	0.000	0.008	-0.095	-0.964
Dummy clay soils	0.036	1.440	0.056	0.643
Size (DSU[a])	-0.055	-2.620**	-0.253	-3.757**
Quota (4.25% fat)/ha	0.118	2.908**	0.326	2.536**
FPCM[a]/cow	0.031	2.175**	0.086	1.838*
% Grassland	-0.191	-2.168**	-0.801	-2.843**
Female young stock LU[a]/10 cows	-0.015	-0.796	-0.053	-0.860
Ratio of organic and chemical fertilizer for extra N supply	-0.000	-0.219	-0.508	-5.414**
Concentrates MJ NEL[a]/100 kg FPCM	0.029	0.159	-0.735	-1.223
Grazing (LU grazing days/ha)	-0.051	-2.219**	-0.155	-2.108**
μ^b	0.118	11.575**	0.446	14.797**
McKelvey-Zavoina R^2	25.8%		24.0%	

*$P < 0.10$

**$P < 0.05$

[a] See Table 1

[b] std. error of the model

Table 4. Average changes in (nutrient) technology, (nutrient) efficiency and (nutrient) productivity growth, and average total change per year over the period 1997 to 1999.

	1997-1998	1998-1999	1997-1999
Technological change	1.026	0.992	1.009
Technical efficiency change	0.998	0.998	0.998
Total factor productivity change	1.029	1.001	1.015
Nutrient technological change	1.840	0.783	1.312
Nutrient efficiency change	1.092	1.452	1.272
Nutrient productivity change	1.981	1.515	1.602

Grazing tactics influenced nutrient efficiencies negatively as well. Farms that tended to graze their cows for a long period of time showed lower nutrient efficiencies. Even though soil type is often considered an important determinant of nutrient performance, the Tobit regression did not show any statistical evidence of this. Also, the dummy for the year showed no significant effect indicating that the average efficiency level did not differ between years. The R^2_{mz} for nutrient efficiencies is 24.0 percent

Total and nutrient productivity. The overall total factor productivity index and subvector productivity index for nutrients are shown in Table 4. Table 4 shows that a total factor productivity growth of 1.5 percent per year was achieved as well as a subvector productivity index growth of as much as 60 percent. total factor productivity growth was mainly achieved through technological change, which compensated for a slight decrease in technical efficiency. Subvector productivity index growth was achieved by a change in nutrient technology, as well as a change in nutrient efficiency. The focus of change was different for each year of the sample, however. The first year, farmers focused mainly on changing the technology with which nutrients are used, whereas the second year efficiency became the focal point of management. The total factor productivity index and subvector productivity index are signifi-

cantly positively correlated ($\square$ = 0.48, P = 0.01). This shows that not only high technical and nutrient performance can go together, but technical productivity growth and nutrient productivity growth can be achieved simultaneously.

The large improvements found here for nutrient productivity can be explained by the incentive given by the project organization for active, rather than passive nutrient management. Furthermore, farms have received advice and support on their management practices, and were monitored for three years. Note that improvements in technology and efficiency do not necessarily mean a reduction of nutrient surpluses. If farms improve their nutrient performance either through a technology change or an efficiency change, but at the same time intensify production, the net result may be just a small decrease or even an increase of surpluses. (Aarts et al., 1999b; Ondersteijn et al., 2001). In this study this appeared to be the case. Farm intensity increased on average with approximately 600 kg of milk quota (4.25 percent fat) per ha over the whole period. The average N surplus showed a slight increase of 4 kg of N per ha, compared to 1997, the average phosphate surplus increased with 9 kg of P_2O_5 per ha.

Tobit analyses were executed to explain changes in technical and nutrient efficiency and changes in general and nutrient technology (Table 5). A change in technical

Table 5. Maximum likelihood estimates of the Tobit regression for technical efficiency and technology change, and nutrient efficiency and nutrient technology change.

Variable	Technical efficiency change		Technology change		Nutrient efficiency change		Nutrient technology change	
	Parameter	t-ratio	Parameter	t-ratio	Parameter	t-ratio	Parameter	t-ratio
Constant	0.774	5.883**	0.594	2.833**	0.700	0.712	0.729	0.455
Dummy 1998	0.002	0.105	0.035	1.527	-0.357	-3.318**	1.088	6.198**
Dummy sandy soils	-0.000	-0.001	0.058	1.400	0.047	0.243	-0.183	-0.576
Dummy clay soils	-0.020	-0.844	-0.005	-0.143	-0.088	-0.504	-0.134	-0.470
Size (DSU[a])	-0.002	-0.134	0.005	0.200	-0.019	-0.160	0.028	0.147
Quota (4.25% fat)/ha	-0.027	-1.051	-0.019	-0.468	-0.468	-2.411**	-0.096	-0.302
FPCM[a]/cow	0.026	2.241**	0.028	1.530	0.125	1.434	0.070	0.494
% Grassland	-0.017	-0.254	0.114	1.061	-0.316	-0.623	0.073	0.088
Female young stock LU[a]/10 cows	0.014	0.879	-0.028	-1.109	0.111	0.934	-0.127	-0.650
Ratio of organic and chemical fertilizer for extra N supply	-0.0003	-4.015**	-0.0002	-1.477	-0.002	-3.948**	-0.001	-1.090
Concentrates MJ NEL[a]/100 kg FPCM	0.144	0.907	0.538	2.123**	0.893	0.750	0.915	0.472
Grazing (LU grazing days/ha)	-0.010	-0.529	-0.015	-0.506	0.870	0.637	-0.260	-1.165
μ[b]	0.106	21.354**	0.169	21.354**	0.795	21.354**	1.296	21.354**
McKelvey-Zavoina R^2	41.2%	58.6%	90.5%	15.6%				

* P < 0.10

** P < 0.05

[a] See Table 1

[b] std. error of the model

efficiency was positively related to the high production capacity per cow. Farms who manage a highly productive herd generally have better management skills. These skills have been put to use to increase the overall technical efficiency of the farm, not just of the dairy herd. The ratio of organic versus chemical fertilizer for additional N-supply is negatively associated with technological efficiency changesbecause of the difficulty of fully utilizing nutrients from organic compared to inorganic fertilizers. Tech-nological change is positively related to the amount of concentrates used per unit of milk. The amount of concentrates used may lead to use of automated concentrate feeding, which increases milk production per cow due to accurate performance-related concentrate provision (Van Asseldonk et al., 1999). These farmers may also receive more advice from their concentrate supplier to improve their dairy production process. R^2_{mz} of 41.2 and 58.6 percent were calculated for technical efficiency change and technology change respectively.

Nutrient efficiency and nutrient technology change differs between years. The efficiency change was much smaller in 1998, whereas the technology change was much larger in the first year, which was also shown in Table 4. This is very likely due to the focus of the project support, which was on nutrient technology change the first year rather than on efficiency improvement. Farm intensity has a negative impact on nutrient efficiency change. The more intensive farming systems already showed high nutrient efficiencies, indicating that not much room for improvement is left. These farms should shift their production frontier in order to improve performance but there is no significant relationship between intensity and nutrient technology change. As with technical efficiency change, the ratio of organic versus chemical fertilizer is negatively related to the change in efficiency. Fully utilizing the nutrients in manure is a problem. The R^2_{mz} for nutrient efficiency

change is as high as 90.5 percent, while the R^2_{mz} nutrient technology change is 15.6 percent. Nutrient efficiency changes are better explained by characteristics of the farm than changes in technology. Tobit analyses for the total factor productivity index as well as the subvector productivity index are the product of the two components of the respective indices. The same variables are significant in similar directions.

Concluding Remarks

The relative technical efficiencies found in this study showed that the farms in the sample are highly technically efficient producers. Nutrient efficiencies on the other hand, showed that there is still significant room for improvement of the latter. It must be noted that the measures calculated here are relative to the best management practices of the sample. Introduction of farms in the sample that are able to produce the same amount of output with less input will cause calculated efficiencies of the current sample to drop. A positive relationship between technical efficiency and nutrient efficiency indicated that better environmental performance does not have to be achieved at the expense of worsened technical results. Furthermore, full efficiency does not mean that there is no improvement possible. First of all, subvector efficiencies showed that an individual input could still be reduced, even for technically efficient farms. Second, farms that produce on the frontier can improve nutrient management by improving technology and therefore shift the frontier towards better input/output ratios.

The results from the Tobit analyses indicate that frictions may exist between current agricultural and environmental policy and farmers' interests. These frictions arise due to the different requirements government bodies put on dairy farmers. Intensive farming systems, in terms of quota per hectare, show higher efficiencies, both on a technical and nutrient level. The result is relatively low nutrient surplus per kilogram of produced milk. However, due to their intensity, they tend to have higher absolute levels of nutrient surpluses per hectare, even though they shift a large part of fodder production to less intensive farms by buying their excess fodder. Improving nutrient efficiency by increasing intensity will therefore lead at the same time to higher nutrient surpluses per ha, which are the base for taxation in the Dutch nutrient bookkeeping system, the Mineral Accounting System (MINAS). This point was empirically analyzed further in Ondersteijn et al. (2001). Another point of friction is grazing. Grazing cattle is considered to be part of the Dutch landscape by consumers and policymakers. However, this study shows that the longer the grazing period, the less efficient farms are in terms of both technical and nutrient efficiency. Currently, policymakers are considering mandatory grazing. The results in this study show that this collides with nutrient policy and will therefore complicate matters further for Dutch dairy farmers.

Both total factor productivity and subvector productivity growth were attained by the farmers in the sample. Especially nutrient productivity increased enormously, indicating that large improvements in environmental performance can be achieved in a short time period when farmers actively try to increase their efficiency. The farmers in the sample were participants in a project specifically focusing on nutrient management. The changes in productivity found here may therefore be high, compared to other Dutch farms, who did not receive the same kind of support. These large improvements will therefore likely not be sustained, but will level off when the maximum nutrient productivity is being approached. However, the important observation to make here is that, with some effort, it is possible to considerably improve nutrient performance and thus produce in a more environmentally sound way. The positive relationship between total factor productivity growth and nutrient productivity growth indicates that this does not have to mean a decrease in technological progress. The main conclusion from the Tobit analyses was that the intensity of the farm is a limiting factor in nutrient productivity growth. These are the farms which will have the most trouble meeting the environmental standards in 2003 since their intensity leads to higher nutrient surpluses per ha, even though their nutrient efficiency shows a lower surplus per unit of output. If they want to maintain the current level of intensity, innovation is required to improve productivity.

The goals farmers try to optimize are different for each one of them and do not only pertain to economic goals (Gasson, 1973; Huirne et al., 1997). Deviation of the efficient frontier can therefore be a (deliberate) result of the pursuit of alternative objectives (Reinhard, 1999). Also, differences in changes in technological and efficiency may arise from other than technical or economical causes. Depending on alternative objectives and their preferences and motivations, farmers adopt different strategies to meet their goals and this includes strategies to meet nutrient regulations.

The flexibility of MINAS gives farmers the opportunity to meet the environmental targets in a way that suits them and their farm best will disappear. The Mineral Accounting System, as a way to meet the Nitrate Directive, was overruled by the European Court in October 2003. The Court of Justice of the European Communities decided that MINAS was insufficient to meet the targets of the Nitrate Directive and should implement at least maximum application standards for N. Previous to this decision, the Dutch government implemented animal production rights, manure transfer agreements, and regulations for the use of manure, but this was considered insufficient by the Court. This decision led to a discussion about the sensibility of the Mineral Accounting System and the question as to whether to modify the system or to introduce a new system. The last option was chosen, not only because of the decision of the Court but also because the Mineral Accounting System had become a complex system and did not fit all farm types as well as it did dairy farming. From 2006 on, new regulations will be put in place, based on application standards for fertilizers (manure application, total N application, and total phosphate application). This switch from an output-oriented system to an input oriented system will reduce the farmer's opportunities for 'made-to-measure' activities to reduce the environmental burden of the farm. Furthermore, input restrictions do not guarantee Good Agricultural Practice and it could therefore be questioned whether this policy switch will have the desired results.

Footnotes

[i]The final standards are set to 180 kg ha^{-1} of nitrogen (N) for land covered with grass and 100 kg for arable land. An excess of 20 kg of phosphate (P_2O_5) is allowed per hectare regardless of cropping type. Farmers will be taxed € 2.30 for every kg of N that exceeds the standard, and € 9.00 for every kg P_2O_5.

[ii]For further information on the benefits of data envelopment analysis over stochastic frontier analysis or other parametric approaches see for instance Jaforullah and Whiteman (1999), Färe et al. (1996), and Cloutier and Rowley (1993).

[iii]Data on machinery and equipment were considered to be of insufficient quality to be used in the analysis, and data on work by contractors do not accurately represent the level of mechanisation. Omission of these inputs in the data envelopment analysis model may result in a small negative bias of the technical efficiency scores.

[iv]Production is calculated by correcting the output of nutrients in animal products, plant products and organic manure for changes in stock of animal and plant products. Use of nutrients was calculated by correcting the inputs in feed, fertiliser (both organic and inorganic) and start material corrected for stock changes.

[v]A recent report by L. Simar and P.W. Wilson (2003) points at possible problems related to this method due to serial correlations. Nonetheless, since this paper has not (yet) been peer reviewed we follow the currently prevailing approach.

[vi]The negative impact of farm size as reflected by Dutch Size Units on technical efficiency seems to contradict our result that most farms operate in the range of increasing returns to scale. The explanation for this result is that Dutch Size Units are a measure that is inferred from land use and the number of livestock on the farm (with weights depending on the contribution to the gross margin). In the DEA model, size is a reflection of the quantities of all inputs distinguished (with equal weights).

[vii]R^2_{mz} is a Pseudo-R^2, and is the best predictor of what OLS-R^2 would be under uncensored data (Veall and Zimmermann, 1994).

Acknowledgements

The authors wish to thank the Farm Data in Practice Project for the use of the data and A.C.G. Beldman and C.H.G. Daatselaar from the Economic and Agricultural Research Institute in The Hague for their contribution to this paper.

References Cited

Aarts, H.F.M., E.E. Biewinga, and H.Van Keulen. 1992. Dairy farming systems based on efficient nutrient management. Journal of Agricultural Science 40(3):285-299.

Aarts, H.F.M., B. Habekotte, G.J. Hilhorst, G.J. Koskamp, F.C. Van der Schans, and C.K. De Vries. 1999a. Efficient resource management in dairy farming on sandy soil. Journal of Agricultural Science 47(2):153-167.

Aarts, H.F.M., B. Habekotte, and H.Van Keulen. 1999b. Limits to the intensity of milk production in sandy areas in The Netherlands. Journal of Agricultural Science 47:263-277.

Aarts, H.F.M. 2000. Resource management in a 'De Marke' dairy farming system. Wageningen PhD thesis, Wageningen Agricultural University.

Ball, V.E., C.A.K. Lovell, R.F. Nehring, and A. Somwaru. 1994. Incorporating undesirable outputs into models of production: An application to U.S. agriculture. Cahiers d'Economie et Sociologie Rurales 31:59-73.

Ball, V.E., C.A.K. Lovell, H. Luu, and R.F. Nehring. 2000. Incorporating environmental impacts in the measurement of agricultural productivity growth. Paper presented at the International Conference on Sustainable Energy: New challenges for agriculture and implications for land use. Wageningen, The Netherlands.

Brandt, H.M.P.v.d. and H.P. Smit. 1998. Mineral accounting: The way to combat eutrophication and to achieve the drinking water objective. Environmental Pollution 102(1):705-709.

Charnes, A., W.W. Cooper, A.Y. Lewin, and L.M. Seiford. 1994. Data envelopment analysis: Theory, methodology, and application. Kluwer Academic Publishers. Dordrecht, The Netherlands.

Chung, Y.H., R. Fare, and S. Grosskopf. 1997. Productivity and undesirable outputs: A directional distance function approach. Journal of Environmental Management 51:229-240.

Cloutier, L.M. and R. Rowley. 1993. Relative technical efficiency: Data envelopment analysis and Quebec's dairy farms. Canadian Journal of Agricultural Economics 41(2):169-176.

Coelli, T.J. 1995. Recent developments in frontier modeling and efficiency measurement. Australian Journal of Agricultural Economics 39(3):219-245.

Coelli, T.J., D.S.P. Rao, and G.E. Battese. 1999. An introduction to efficiency and productivity analysis. Kluwer Academic Publishers, Dordrecht, The Netherlands.

Färe, R., S. Grosskopf, C.A.K. Lovell, and C. Pasurka. 1989. Multilateral productivity comparisons when some outputs are undesirable: A nonparametric approach. review of economics and statistics. WHAT JOURNAL?? 71(1):90-98.

Färe, R., S. Grosskopf, C.A.K. Lovell. 1994a. Production frontiers. Cambridge University Press, Cambridge, Massachusetts.

Färe, R., S. Grosskopf, M. Norris, and Z. Zhang. 1994b. Productivity growth, technical progress, and efficiency changes in industrialized countries. American Economic Review 84:66-83.

Färe, R. and S. Grosskopf. 1996. Intertemporal production frontiers. Kluwer Academic Publishers, Boston, Masschusetts.

Färe, R., S. Grosskopf, and D. Tyteca. 1996. An activity analysis model of the environmental performance of firms: Application to fossil-fuel-fired electric utilities. Ecological Economics 18(2):161-175.

Farrell, M.J. 1957. The measurement of productive efficiency. Journal of the Royal Statistical Society 120(3):253-281.

Fernandez, C., G. Koop, and M.J.F. Steel. 2002. Multiple-output production with undesirable outputs: An application to nitrogen surplus in agriculture. Journal of the American Statistical Association 97(458):432-442.

Gasson, R. 1973. Goals and values of farmers. Journal of Agricultural Economics 24(3):521-537.

Greene, W.H. 1997. Econometric analysis. Prentice-Hall International, Upper Saddle River, Connecticut.

Grosskopf, S. 1993. Efficiency and productivity. Pp. 160-194. In: H.O. Fried, C.A.K. Lovell, and S.S. Schmidt (eds.). The measurement of productive efficiency: Techniques and applications. Oxford University Press, Oxford, STATE.

Hailu, A. and T.S. Veeman. 2001. Non-parametric productivity analysis with undesirable outputs: An application to the Canadian pulp and paper industry. American Journal of Agricultural Economics 83(3):605-616.

Huirne, R.B.M., S.B. Harsh, A.A. Dijkhuizen. 1997. Critical success factors and information needs on dairy farms: The farmer's opinion. Livestock Production Science 48:229-238

Jaforullah, M. and J. Whiteman. 1999. Scale efficiency in the New Zealand dairy industry: A non-parametric approach. Australian Journal of Agricultural and Resource Economics 43(4):523-541.

Mourits, M.C.M., P.B.M. Berentsen, R.B.M. Huirne, and A.A. Dijkhuizen. 2000. Environmental impact of heifer management decisions on Dutch dairy farms. Netherlands Journal of Agricultural Science 48(2):151-164.

Ondersteijn, C.J.M., A.C.G. Beldman, C.H.G. Daatselaar, G.W.J. Giesen, and R.B.M. Huirne. 2002. The Dutch Mineral Accounting System and the European Nitrate Directive: Implications for N and P management and farm performance. Agriculture Ecosystems and Environment 92(2/3):283-296.

Ondersteijn, C.J.M., A.J.G.M. Oude Lansink, G.W.J. Giesen, R.B.M. Huirne. 2001. Improving nutrient efficiency as a strategy to reduce nutrient surpluses. Pp. 866-872. In: Optimizing Nitrogen Management in Food and Energy Production and Environmental Protection: Proceedings of the 2nd International Nitrogen Conference on Science and Policy. TheScientificWorld 1.

Piot Lepetit, I. and D. Vermersch. 1998. Pricing organic nitrogen under the weak disposability assumption: An application to the French pig sector. Journal of Agricultural Economics 49(1):85-99.

Pittman, R.W. 1983. Multilateral productivity comparisons with undesirable outputs. The Economic Journal 93:883-891.

Reinhard, S. 1999. Econometric analysis of economic and environmental efficiency of Dutch dairy farms. Wageningen PhD thesis, Wageningen Agricultural University.

Reinhard, S., C.A.K. Lovell, and G.J. Thijssen. 1999. Econometric estimation of technical and environmental efficiency: An application to Dutch dairy farms. American Journal of Agricultural Economics 81(1):44-60.

Reinhard, S., C.A.K. Lovell, and G.J. Thijssen. 2000. Environmental efficiency with multiple environmentally detrimental variables: Estimated with SFA and DEA. European Journal of Operational Research 121:287-303.

Shaik, S. and G. Helmers. 1999. Shadow price of environmental bads: Weak vs. strong disposability. Annual meeting of the American Agricultural Economics Association, Nashville, Tennessee.

Simar, L. and P.W. Wilson. 2003. Estimation and inference in two-stage, semi-parametric models of production processes. Technical Report 0310, IAP Statistics Network, http://www.stat.ucl.ac.be/IAP.

Steverink, M.H.A., A.F. Groen, P.B.M. Berentsen. 1994. The influence of restricting nitrogen losses of dairy farms on dairy cattle breeding goals. Journal of Agricultural Science 42(1):21-27.

Tauer, L.W. and J. Hanchar. 1995. Non-parametric technical efficiency with K firms, N inputs, and M outputs: A simulation. Agricultural and Resource Economics Review 24(2):185-189.

Thomas, A.C. and L.W. Tauer. 1994. Linear input aggregation bias in non-parametric technical efficiency measurement. Canadian Journal of Agricultural Economics 42(1):77-86.

Tobin, J. 1958. Estimation of relationships for limited dependent variables. Econometrica 26:24-36.

Tyteca, D. 1997. Linear programming models for the measurement of environmental performance of firms: Concepts and empirical results. Journal of Productivity Analysis 8(2):183-197.

Van Asseldonk, M.A.P.M., A.W. Jalvingh, R.B.M. Huirne, and A.A. Dijkhuizen. 1999. Potential economic benefits from changes in management via information technology applications on Dutch dairy farms: A simulation study. Livestock Production Science 60(1):33-44.

Veall, M.R. and K.F. Zimmermann. 1994. Goodness of fit measures in the Tobit model. Oxford Bulletin of Economics and Statistics 56(4):485-499.

Veerkamp, R.F., G.C. Emmans, J.D. Oldham, and G. Simm. 1993. Energy and protein utilization of cows of high and low genetic merit for milk solids production on a high and low input diet. Proceedings of the 4th Zodiac Symposium: Biological basis of sustainable animal production.

Weersink, A., C.G. Turvey, and A. Godah. 1990. Decomposition of technical efficiency for Ontario dairy farms. Canadian Journal of Agricultural Economics 38:439-456.

Willems, W.J., T.V. Vellinga, O. Oenema, J.J. Schroder, H.G. Meer, B. van der Fraters, and H.F.M. Aarts. 2000. Onderbouwing van het Nederlandse derogatieverzoek in het kader van de Europese Nitraatrichtlijn. Bilthoven, RIVM-Report 102 (In Dutch).

Decision Support for Improved Nutrient Management

CHAPTER 8

J.F. Angus and R.L. Williams

The average efficiency of nutrient use on farms is notoriously low. Improved nutrient efficiency offers a means to increase farm profit and reduce nutrient loss to the natural environment. Research and extension about nutrients and fertilizers has long been provided to farmers by public extension agencies and agribusiness. Despite many decades of research and extension, nutrient efficiency remains far below potential and many nutrient-related environmental problems continue to worsen: soil acidification, stream and groundwater pollution, ocean hypoxia, and release of the greenhouse gas nitrous oxide (N_2O).

Decision support systems have been offered to farmers and advisers to assist in improving fertilizer use efficiency. They are used less widely to specifically address nutrient loss to the natural environment. The potential improvement offered by a decision support system is that it can apply to a particular field in a particular year. In principle improved nutrient efficiency on farm should lead to less nutrient loss. Decision support for environmental aspects of nutrient use may include not only formal decision support systems, but also normal extension advice, regulations and economic signals provided by government such as price and production subsidies.

Our objective in this chapter, is to review the effectiveness of decision support systems for increasing farm profit, and the potential for reducing nutrient-related environmental problems. Research for improved nutrient use efficiency is not addressed here and we take it for granted that decision support systems must be based on the best available biophysical understanding and should keep up to date with the latest research.

Food production and nutrient use efficiency

World food production has generally kept ahead of population growth during the second half of the 20th Century (Table 1). The proportion of the world population who are chronically malnourished decreased during this time, even though the number of hungry people, 800 million in 2004, is still outrageously large. The delivery of agricultural science to farmers has been crucial in overcoming hunger. There are grounds for optimism that future incremental changes through the continued application of science can continue to keep the supply of food in line with human needs (Evans, 1998).

Improved crop nutrition has been a clear contributor to food security (Table 1). For much of the second half of the twentieth century fertilizer nitrogen (N) consumption increased at the spectacular annual rate of 7.1 percent, about four times the rate of population growth. World N-fertilizer consumption peaked in the late 1980s, after which consumption in Eastern Europe collapsed and economic problems in other parts of the world led to large reductions (Smil, 2001). The U.N.'s Food and Agriculture Organization FAOSTAT database shows that, since then, world fertilizer N consumption has resumed its upward course because rapid growth in Asia and recovery in South America has offset reductions in

Table 1. Growth in world population, cereal production, and consumption of nutrients in fertilizer during the second half of the 20th Century.

	Annual growth (%)
Human population[*]	1.8
Cereals[*]	
Maize	2.7
Rice	2.4
Wheat	2.3
Fertilizer[**]	
Nitrogen	7.1
Phosphorus	4.6
Potassium	3.7

[*] **1961 to 2001 (www.fao.org/waicent/portal/statistics_en.asp)**
[**] **1960 to 1988 (Bumb, 1995)**

Western Europe and North America.

The increasing production of N fertilizer has been possible because of cheap energy in the form of natural gas and steady improvements in the efficiency with which ammonia and urea are synthesized (Smil, 1991). Manufacture of N fertilizer uses about one percent of world fossil fuel consumption. While there is growing concern about future world supplies of fossil fuel, it is not likely that continued use of N fertilizer is especially vulnerable to energy shortages. The real price of N fertilizer, expressed as the ratio of the price of grain to N fertilizer, has not increased during the second half of the twentieth century (Angus, 2001). The common forms of N fertilizer: urea, anhydrous ammonia, ammonium phosphates, and ammonium nitrates, have become freely traded commodities with relatively low profit margins for producers and resellers. In some countries, the consumer price of N fertilizer is artificially low because the natural gas feedstock has been supplied by governments at unrealistically low or even zero cost, a practice now frowned on by the World Bank. The reason for this is to promote food production through increased use of fertilizer. In the European Union, the United States, and Northeast Asia, subsidized grain prices similarly inflate the fertilizer: grain price ratio and encourage N overuse, but without effective discouragement from international organizations.

Environment

One of the most disturbing developments in nutrient management during the second half of the twentieth century has been the escape of nutrients, particularly N, from farmland to the natural environment. The scale of the environmental damage varies from the local, such as acidification of topsoil, to the global, such as the contribution to the greenhouse effect by N_2O emitted during denitrification. At an intermediate scale, nitrate escapes into groundwater and local streams but the problem increases as nutrients continue to move down water bodies so that near-coastal oceans are becoming hypoxic. For example, at the end of the twentieth century there were three water bodies that each released about one million tons of reactive N into oceans each year: from the Baltic Sea into the North Sea (Wulff et al., 2001), from the Mississippi River into the Gulf of Mexico (Goolsby et al., 1999) and from the Jiangsiang (Yangtse River) into the Yellow Sea (Duan et al., 2000). In each case the N flux is increasing, and significant areas of ocean become hypoxic for parts of the summer. Common ecological features of the cropping regions that feed these hotspots are positive water balance and N balance for much of the year. A common economic feature of the three regions is government intervention that influences farmers' decisions about N, either through price subsidies for grain or the directions from command economies. The increasing uses of N fertilizer elsewhere, particularly in Asia and South America, leads to concerns that the similar environmental problems will emerge in regions that are currently unaffected.

The source, pathway and time course of N released into the environment. Because the development of environmental problems involving nutrients coincided with a period of rapidly increasing fertilizer use, it has been widely assumed that the problems are due directly to fertilizer. Several strands of evidence suggest that the direct source of environmental N is not always fertilizer itself and that the pathway from fertilizer to the environment is slow and tortuous. In the UK, Addiscott et al. (1991) reported the use of ^{15}N label to show that recently applied fertilizer was not the source of N in groundwater. They concluded that the main source was mineralization of organic matter that had accumulated under pastures in previous centuries and which decomposed under the increased cropping systems in the second half of the 20th Century. An alternative explanation of the UK case and for European groundwater pollution generally, is that N fertilizer applied to crops contributed to increased soil organic matter or at least to a reduced net decomposition rate of organic matter. If the latter interpretation is justified, the enhanced mineralization and leaching is indirectly due to fertilizer N applied over many years.

The nitrate level in streams in the eastern Baltic countries during the 1990s provides rare information about the path-length and time delays of N in a large system. Wulff (2001) reported that N-fertilizer application stopped in these countries when the Soviet bloc broke up, but there was no change in the nitrate level in streams for the following seven years. His interpretation of this delay is that there is a long and/or slow-moving path of N between the surface of fertilized fields and the streams. The path includes subsoil inorganic and organic N as well as groundwater nitrate.

Longer-term studies of smaller systems have been made in southern and central Sweden, where nitrate concentration of groundwater has been monitored under farmland since the mid 1970s. Johansson and Gustafson (2004) reported data for ten fields monitored over this period. In four of them the levels of nitrate (NO_3) in groundwater was negligible while in the six others the concentration of NO_3-N in groundwater ranged from 0 to 34 mg l^{-1}. For these six fields, the NO_3 concentration decreased over periods of up to 30 years. An example of the decreasing groundwater nitrate concentration under an arable field in southern Sweden is shown in Figure 1. The N management of the particular field was not reported but during the 27-year period, total usage of N fertilizer in Sweden decreased but the average application rate to annual crops remained at about 100 kg N ha^{-1}. The discrepancy between total and average fertilizer use is explained by a set-aside program, which led to reduced area of arable crops. It is likely that set-aside land was less productive than average and also was responsible for a disproportionately large amount of leaching. This interpretation is consistent with conclusions about leaching from organic farms by Kirchmann and Bergström (2001). Their review concluded that organically grown crops produced lower yields and contributed to more nitrate leaching than

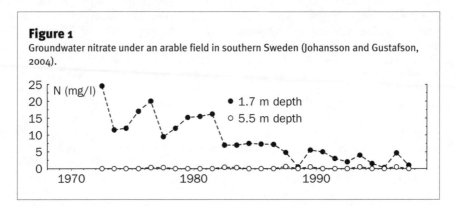

Figure 1
Groundwater nitrate under an arable field in southern Sweden (Johansson and Gustafson, 2004).

equivalent conventionally grown crops.

The largest catchment in which N flows have been monitored is the Mississippi basin.

The study by Mitsch et al. (1999) shows that the large increase in nitrate outflow in the Mississippi River followed 10 to 15 years after a surge in N-fertilizer input (Figure 2). The reasons for the delay between management changes at the farm scale and response at the catchment scale

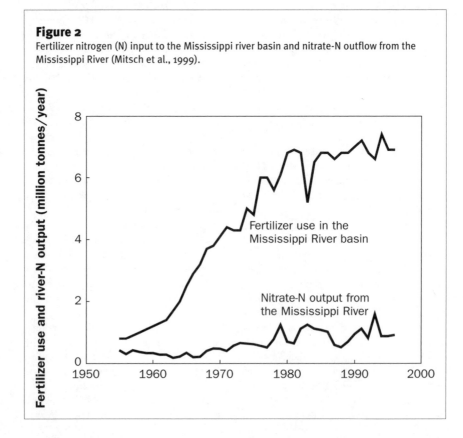

Figure 2
Fertilizer nitrogen (N) input to the Mississippi river basin and nitrate-N outflow from the Mississippi River (Mitsch et al., 1999).

are poorly understood and should be the subject of more research (Hatfield and Angus, 2005, in prep). Meanwhile policymakers should be aware of these delays and that management changes may not affect the environment for decades in the future.

Why is N used inefficiently?

If the environmental consequences of fertilizer are to be overcome it is important to know why farmers apply more fertilizer than is needed for optimum yields. Krupnik et al. (2004) reviewed over 1500 studies with maize, rice, and wheat and reported that the mean recovery was 47 percent of fertilizer N applied, with little difference between estimates based on mass balance and ^{15}N-recovery methods. Some of the remaining amount is recovered by subsequent crops, but most is lost to the environment. Krupnik et al. (2004) reported maximum N recoveries of greater than 75 percent.

One of the reasons for inefficient nutrient use is the high level of application. The diminishing returns of grain to increasing inputs of fertilizer inevitably leads to low efficiency when inputs are high. However, different forms of N and times and methods of application can greatly alter efficiency. There are possibilities to more closely match nutrient supply with crop demand using innovative approaches (Hatfield and Angus, 2005 in prep).

To what extent is N inefficiency due to economics? To evaluate the economics of N efficiency, first consider a situation in which all added N contributes to additional grain, which for the sake of simplicity does not increase in grain N percentage (GNP). In that case the agronomic efficiency is 1/GNP. When we consider the N contained in straw, a more realistic agronomic efficiency is HIN/GNP, where HIN is the harvest index for N, expressed as a percentage. This value represents the maximum value of agronomic efficiency, when there is no loss of N from the crop. In that case,

the added N would just be profitable if the ratio of fertilizer cost to grain price was the same value. For different ratios of fertilizer cost to grain price, the required percentage of N recovered for fertilizer application to just cover costs is given by

(1)

$$\text{Required \%} = \frac{100 \ \text{GNP}}{\text{N recovery} \quad \text{HIN}} \times \frac{\text{Fertilizer N cost}}{\text{Grain price}}$$

where a typical value of a grain N percentage is two percent and the harvest index for N is 75 percent. Where free-market prices give a fertilizer to grain price ratio of six, the required N fertilizer recovery is 16 percent. For subsidized farming systems where the fertilizer to grain price ratio is three, the required N recovery is eight percent. Nitrogen fertilizer use therefore just covers costs when the percentage recovery is at these very low values. Farmers normally expect to obtain a gross return of twice the cost of fertilizer applied, so in practice the required N recovery is double the above estimates, 32 percent for unsubsidized systems and 16 percent for subsidized systems. In the latter case, farmers can make an acceptable profit from N fertilizer even when 84 percent is lost to the environment.

Another example of the consequence of price subsidies is shown in Figure 3. This example is drawn from yield responses of irrigated rice on farms in the Australian Riverina, where yields are similar to wheat in Northwestern Europe and corn in the Midwest of the United States. The curves represent the yield responses to applied N and the vertical lines represent the economically optimum N rate calculated from the slope of the curve, the cost of fertilizer and the price of grain. The economics are best summarized using the ratio of the cost of fertilizer to the price of grain (the 'price ratio'). A value of six is typical for grain producers who receive no price subsidies while a value of three is typical for those

Figure 3

Nitrogen (N) response for average and top-decile irrigated rice crops in the Australian Riverina. The vertical lines show economically optimum rates of N fertilizer calculated for a fertilizer cost:grain price ratios of six, representing world prices, and a ratio of three representing a grain-price subsidy.

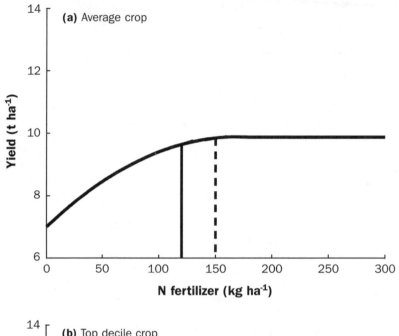

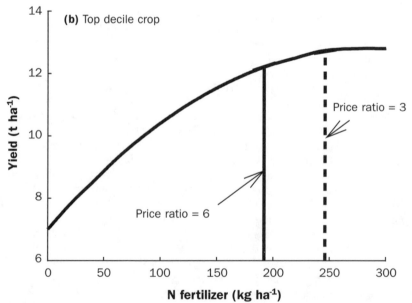

who receive price subsidies. Figure 3 shows that the economically optimum rate of N fertilizer is about 25 percent higher for the subsidized price ratio than for unsubsidized price ratio. The higher optimum N applies at yields of both average crops and those in the top decile, representing close to potential yield in this environment. The optimum fertilizer N rate is 30 kg ha^{-1} greater for average crops and 54 kg ha^{-1} greater for top-decile crops.

Nitrogen fertilizer provides its own self-advertising in the form of rapid responses in crop color and vigor. In some cases, the advertising is deceptive because of subsequent lodging, disease, or the pinched grain associated with 'haying-off' (van Herwaarden et al., 1998). There is a powerful incentive for farmers to identify the optimum level of N when there is a risk of these yield losses. Where these risks are a minimum, the only on-farm consequence of excess N is the cost of additional fertilizer. In such circumstances it is not surprising that many farmers apply more N fertilizer than is needed by average crops. 'Insurance nitrogen' is the amount required by the highest yielding crops (Mitsch et al., 1999). Application of insurance N could be considered as a form of gambling on the weather and crop conditions. Perhaps the study of compulsive gamblers could contribute to understanding excess N application by farmers.

Another driver for excess N is marketing by sales agronomists, whose income partly depends on the volume of fertilizer sold. Fertilizer vendors generally prefer to make sales at or before the time of sowing. This timing ensures a regular ordering and inventory system that minimizes fluctuations in sales due to seasonal or crop conditions. Vendors also rent out specialized equipment such as anhydrous ammonia rigs and provide discounts for early application. The earliest applied N is at greater risk of loss than N applied at or after sowing (Chen et al., 1994). The falling

margins for fertilizer since the late 1990s may reduce the incentive for retailers to promote excessive N.

An interesting way to consider over fertilization is by the 'farming styles' of van der Ploeg (1994). This approach identifies a series of styles which reflect the goals of the farmer. A 'heavy input' style places great emphasis on maximizing yield, with less regard for input costs or net profit. The highly competitive individuals who adopt such a style may be uninterested in the common paradigm of agricultural science, which assumes that farmers are primarily concerned with maximizing profit. New approaches may be needed to redirect the competitive urges of these individuals, for example by encouraging competition for highest fertilizer use efficiency.

Methods to discourage nutrient losses

The aim of nutrient management should be to match the crop demand with the supply from the soil and fertilizer. Nutrients are lost when the supply exceeds the demand. The balance can be restored by increasing crop demand and/or decreasing nutrient supply. Improved crop management practices that increase yield, such as optimum sowing date, disease control and reduced soil compaction also increase nutrient demand. Provided that increased nutrient demand is greater than any increase in nutrient supply, it is possible to increase yield and decrease nutrient loss. In principle, the goals of increasing profit and reducing nutrient loss should be in harmony. In practice, responsibilities for increasing profit and promoting reduced leakage are mostly handled in different ways and by different agencies. Proposed methods to discourage nutrient loss are as follows:

Fertilizer taxes. Several European countries and U.S. states impose tax on N fertilizer to encourage lower application rates. Sweden was one of the first when it introduced a tax of about 15 percent of the cost of N. Since then the national consumption of N fertilizer has decreased by about 12 percent, but the rate per arable hectare has decreased by only five percent (SCB, 2004). The reason for the larger fall in aggregate consumption is the increased area of set-aside land.

In view of the economics of N fertilizer use summarized in Equation 1, it is not surprising that a relatively small increase in cost has led to a small change in fertilizer use. For most of its existence the N tax was small relative to the size of the price subsidy on grain. Effectively the government was encouraging high inputs generally with a subsidy on grain, and discouraging high N input with a fertilizer tax. It is difficult to understand the reason for interfering in the market with opposing price signals. Doering et al. (1999) concluded that taxes on N fertilizer were likely to be ineffective in reducing the nutrient load in the Mississippi River but that regulation to restrict use would be more effective.

Nutrient accounting. The Mineral Accounting System (MINAS) in the Netherlands requires farmers to calculate inputs and outputs of N and phosphorus (P), and imposes a tax on the surplus. This accounting method requires farms to record N inputs such as manure, feed concentrate, and fertilizer as well as N outputs contained in products in order to calculate the net N balance. There is an allowed nutrient surplus, which for example for N on grassland was 300 kg N ha^{-1} in 1998, falling to 180 kg N ha^{-1} in 2003 (Ondersteijn et al., 2002). At the same time the taxation rate increased from € 0.7/kgN to €2.4/kgN (Wright and Mallia, 2003). In a survey of farms in the Netherlands, Ondersteijn et al., (2002) showed that the average grassland farm had a N surplus of 344 kg ha^{-1}. Farms with this surplus would incur a N tax of €31 ha^{-1} for the 1998 rules and € 394 ha^{-1} for the 2003 rules. Despite these ambitious measures to discourage overuse, the Netherlands government faced litigation in the European Court because the level of nitrate in the environment still exceeds the prescribed limits for the European Union. It is too early to conclude whether these high taxes will have a significant effect on the net N balance of Dutch farms or the effect on the level of nitrate in ground and surface water.

Sensitive zones. Some regions and soil types are more likely than others to contribute to nutrient loss. For example, the Netherland's Mineral Accounting System recognizes the greater loss of nutrients from sandy soils by imposing taxes when the nutrient surplus exceeded a relatively low threshold (Wright and Mallia, 2003). Nutrient escape is likely to be greatest from riparian zones where replacement of agriculture with perennial pastures has been proposed (Mitsch et al., 1999).

Better definition of the economic optimum. Many farmers apply a standard rate of nutrients irrespective of soil, crop, or economic conditions. Often the reason is simply that a standard amount is included in their annual budgets. The simplest test of nutrient response is a test strip—a small part of a field where no nutrients are applied, so that a comparison with the adjacent area can show the crop response. The test-strip system was promoted for in Australia 50 years ago (Anderson, 1952). For many years it was popular for detecting micronutrient deficiency in pastures, but has fallen into disuse except where advisers strongly promote it.

Soil tests of mineral N or mineralizable N provide useful information for fertilizer applications at sowing. Plant tests such as total N, nitrate concentration, chlorophyll concentration, and shoot density (for small grains) often provide more reliable indicators of N status than soil tests. They are effective when the efficiency of N applied during crop growth is as efficient as N applied at or before sowing. The value of soil and plant tests can often be increased by combining the data with other data in a decision support system (see below).

New application methods. Agronomic research has given a more prominence on the rate of application, than the form of N, and the method and timing of application. Experiments on rate of application have tended to use the current local timing, N-form and method of application(Hatfield and Angus, 2005) In many cases there has not been enough research conducted to provide decision support on all aspects of N application.

Insurance against yield loss. Where farmers are accustomed to applying excessive N fertilizer they may be reluctant to cut back on rates. To encourage lower application rates a system could be set up to insure against the lower N leading to lower yield (Hatfield, 2004; personal communication). Evidence of the yield loss could be provided using a test strip.

Variable zone management. Soil variation within a field can lead to variable responses to nutrients. The consequence of applying a constant amount of fertilizer to zones with different yield potential may be nutrient deficiency in high-yielding zones and surplus in low-yielding zones. Early approaches to precision agriculture assumed that yields of the poorer zones of a field could be increased with more nutrients, particularly N, a policy that only worsens the problem of surplus nutrients. More recent studies have shown many examples where reducing nutrient input to unresponsive zones leads to higher profit and less residual fertilizer in the soil. Examples of soil conditions that limit yield and nutrient response are low water-holding capacity, soil salinity, and soil acidity. The decision of whether more or less nutrient should be applied to a low-yielding zone has to be based on an understanding of regional soil limitations. Whether the time and cost of variable zone management justifies the additional production is not clear.

From extension to decision support

Taxpayers, through their governments, have long supported farmers to develop more efficient production though research and extension programs. In recent years, the use of 'extension' has been partly substituted by 'technology transfer,' 'decision support,' and 'participatory co-learning.' The changes are not simply due to fashion but reflect a growing understanding of why farmers do or do not adopt practices, which appears to scientists to be more efficient than current systems.

The reason that taxpayers support agricultural industries through research and extension programs is because increased farm efficiency is seen to be a public good. Increased efficiency leads to additional food production, which in turn leads to lower prices for the consumer. This argument is still compelling for developing countries where investment in research and development leads to high returns. The information was usually provided by extension services in the form of blanket recommendations for a region, modified by the experience and commonsense of advisers in relation to the circumstances of individual farmers. The basis for the blanket recommendations was typically experiments conducted on research stations, usually confirmed with on-farm adaptive research.

It is difficult to estimate the number of farmers influenced by this system. At the peak of the advisory service system in the 1960s through the 1980s, there were typically 500 to 1000 farms per government adviser, but it is unlikely that advisers influenced the whole population. Many advisers report that only a small proportion of farmers seek their advice. The effectiveness of public extension programs has therefore been questioned and there has been long-standing dissatisfaction with the rate of adoption, reflected in the lamentation of Heady (1952): "Extension specialists in the technical fields of agriculture often view the apparent tardy rate at which farmers adopt new technologies with despondency." Many governments have cut back or privatized extension programs.

Despite the criticisms, the research and extension system led to the production growth shown in Table 1. In Western Northeast Europe, the United States, and northeast Asia, the production surpluses were so great and the prices to the producer were so low that producers demanded and received subsidies from governments. Faced with paying for both farm products and for research and extension that leads to even more production, many governments started to withdraw resources from agricultural science. At about the same time environmental problems were increasingly recognized and the former advisory services have increasingly taken on the tasks of environmental regulation and administration of subsidies. Advisory services that were previously free are being replaced by consultants who charge a fee-for-service on a time or hectare basis and by sales agronomists employed by agribusiness. Consultants operate in a variety of business models including single operators, partnerships, companies, and as employees of cooperatives. They typically provide advice to 50 to 100 clients each year. In the past, agribusiness advisers were paid from the profits of additional sales that they generated, but this source is being squeezed by the low margins of fertilizers and out-of-patent agrichemicals.

Decision support increasingly describes the activities of modern advisers. Defined broadly, decision support is based on recognition that farmers make decisions on factors in addition to short-term economic efficiency. Examples are debt levels, risk aversion, and the competing requirements of time for different enterprises. The most effective approach is to estimate the profit and risk for different options and leave it to the farmer to integrate this information with the rest of the farm and family activities.

Decision Support Systems

The phrase decision support system was first used in the literature of management science in the late 1970s. Finlay (1994) summarized features of a decision support system, commonly referred to as DSS. It is typically based in a computer and is sufficiently user friendly to be used by decision makers in person. It displays information in a format and terminology that is familiar to users and is selective in its provision of information and protects users from information overload. A decision support sytem should address decisions for which there is sufficient structure for analytical methods to be of value where managers' judgment is essential, but it should not attempt to predefine objectives or impose a solution. It should be sufficiently flexible to accommodate changes in the environment and the decision-maker's approach and objectives.

Agricultural decision support sytems have the potential to provide information about a particular field in a particular season. They have the potential to provide cost-effective advice because of the economies of scale with electronic transfer of information. For example CDs containing the Crop Sequence Calculator are distributed by the U.S. Department of Agriculture to 10,000 farmers in the Northern Great Plains (www.ars.usda. gov/main/docs/.htm?docid=4987). In north-western Europe soil tests for N supply to are provided with the results of a decision support system for half the cereal crops (Lemaire et al., 2004). In Denmark, the Bedriftsløsning system is used by most farmers in estimating optimum N rate (Oleson, 2004). A decision support system can also operate at the regional or national level to provide government decision makers with information about the environmental consequences of policy. For example, the STONE model presents spatially distributed data showing the consequences of different policies on groundwater nitrate in the Netherlands (Wolf, 2003). Decision support tools are of increasing importance in other fields such as medicine, where they are available to patients and medical practitioners (www.nomograms.org).

CSIRO Plant Industry has developed nine decision support systems for Australian crop (cotton, rice, and wheat) and grazing industries since the 1970s (Table 2). Each contains simulation models which are developed using the normal method of calibration followed by validation using independent data. The systems primarily address production topics and also contain simple estimates of costs and returns that assist the user in making decisions about profitability. A common

thread is that they have a strong emphasis on weather and climate to assist decision-making in the highly variable climate in most regions of Australia. The other common thread is that they provide options to users, and strictly avoid making recommendations. Their place is to provide a second opinion to decision-makers. The experience in developing and releasing decision support systems from CSIRO Plant Industry, is the basis for this discussion. Moore et al. (2004) reported independent economic analyses of three of these packages that estimated benefit to costs ratios greater than 10.

Requirements of decision support systems. Farmers in the developed world face a blizzard of information about their

Table 2. Decision support systems released by CSIRO Plant Industry (Moore et al., 2004).

	Purpose	Planning horizon	Intended Users	Year of release
GrazFeed	Nutritional responses of sheep and cattle at pasture	Days	Advisers-producers	1990
CottonLOGIC	Irrigation scheduling, pesticide timing and nitrogen fertilizer rate decisions for cotton	Days-months	Producers	1996
MetAccess	Analysis of weather and climate data	Days-decades	Producers-scientists	1993
MANAGE RICE*	Nitrogen fertilizer rate decisions for rice	Months	Producers	1994
MANAGE WHEAT	Nitrogen fertilizer rate decisions for wheat	Months	Producers	2003
GrassGro	Sheep and cattle grazing enterprises	Months-decades	Advisers	1997
Lime & nutrient balance*	Budgets for multiple nutrients and protons in mixed farming systems	Years-decades	Producers	2003
FarmWi$e	Systems analysis of mixed farming systems	Years-decades	Advisory service	2004

* Developed in collaboration with NSW Department of Primary Industries.

operations from public extension, environmental and regulatory agencies, agribusiness suppliers, and farmer groups. For a decision support system to be accepted by farmers it should deliver more relevant and trustworthy information than these other sources. There is no point in producing a decision support system to provide information that can be adequately conveyed by word of mouth or in a written report.

Not only must the content be useful but its presentation must be acceptable. Many early decision support systems were afterthoughts to modeling projects to make them attractive to funding bodies, and were not designed from the start with a decision maker in mind. The following suggestions for decision support system development are based on the experience in CSIRO Plant Industry.

Model accuracy. A decision support system should first of all accurately represent observations. A typical decision support system contains a model, which may be as simple as a linear regression, or as complex as a large dynamic simulator with daily time steps. The process of model development is generally considered to be calibration with one data set and validation with a separate data. There is general agreement that an appropriate way to assess model accuracy is the root mean square error, (RMSE = $[\Sigma(\text{obs}_i - \text{sim}_i)^2]^{0.5}$). See Kobayashi (2004) for an entry into discussion of model testing. The point that has not been made in the discussion of model accuracy is that the error of prediction is normally inferior to the error of calibration.

An example of the problem of calibration and validation is discussed for the decision support system MANAGE RICE. This system applies to N-fertilizer management of irrigated rice in the Australian Riverina, where the mean yield is 9 t ha^{-1} and the mean N fertilizer rate is 150 kg N ha^{-1}. The high yields are due to high radiation, full irrigation, and low pest pressure. The rice industry is highly regulated and monitored because of the scarce irrigation water.

The environmental limitation to rice yield is low temperature at the microspore stage, which occurs about two weeks before flowering. The damage caused by low temperatures is increased by high crop-N status. The aim of developing MANAGE RICE is to optimize N management by taking account of the risk of low-temperature damage (Williams and Angus, 1994).

The process of developing MANAGE RICE consisted of calibrating a simulation model using a diverse set of crop data (Figure 4a). The root mean square error for the fit of the model to the calibration data was 0.6 t ha^{-1}. However when the model was then validated against an extensive set of experimental data collected in on farms for the past ten years, the root mean square error was 1.2 t ha^{-1} (Figure 4b). How should we judge the accuracy of simulation models and decision support systems? One way is to compare it with the errors in field experiments. In the case of agronomic experiments with rice in the Riverina the least significant difference is typically 1.0 t ha^{-1}. By this criterion, the decision support system accuracy is acceptable. Another evaluation is to the divide the root mean square error into the range of data. In this case, the root mean square error of 1.2 t ha^{-1} and the range of farm yields from 7 to 14 t ha^{-1}. The range error ratio is then (14 to 7)/1.2 = 5.8, implying that MANAGE RICE can distinguish yields into 5.8 classes.

Another way is to evaluate model predictions against farmers' ability to decide for themselves. An attempt was made to evaluate the ability of Australian rice growers to decide on optimum rate of N-fertilizer application before flooding (Angus and Russell, 2004). This evaluation was conducted on 63 farm fields during a project to develop a N-mineralization test (Figure 5). One conclusion from this comparison is that the test is probably not accurate enough to be used commercially, as shown by its large standard errors. Some predictions made with the test could lead to over-fertilization, lodging, or cold damage. Another conclusion is that the decisions by about half the farmers were as accurate as the test, as shown by the data points between the error lines. Finally, the distribution of the data suggests that farmers tended to over-fertilize crops that are naturally high yielding but under-fertilize naturally low-yielding crops.

Here lies a dilemma when agricultural science attempts to predict optimum management for a particular field in a particular season. While it may be possible to improve on the existing performance of many or perhaps most farmers, there will inevitably be examples where a model prediction will be wrong or a farmer's decision will be better than the model prediction. The risk of error for a particular field is loss to the farmer and litigation to the adviser and/or decision support system developer. A small number of farmers are prepared to sue advisers for possible errors in general advice. Errors in the more specific predictions of decision support systems are at more of a risk of litigation unless outputs are hedged with probabilities and the software is protected with disclaimers. The inherent errors in decision support systems mean that they could be subject to litigation if used as part of an environmental regulation or taxation system. Decision support system developers should report the likely prediction error of their models, not only for simulated yield but also for simulations of environmental data such as water and nutrient loss.

Recognizing advisers. The earliest lesson to include advisers as part of decision support systems came from the SIRATAC, developed by CSIRO for tactical pest management of irrigated cotton in the 1970s (Hearn and Bange, 2002). It was a mainframe-based system that required dial-in access. It was marketed directly to growers and partly bypassed the consultants who provided a competing service. Criticism of the system by consultants was partly responsible for the withdrawal of the system in the 1980s. The lessons were learned in the development of CottonLogic, which is provided free to all Australian cotton growers and advisers since the early 1990s. This system is provided on CD for use on PC and hand-held computers. It is still used directly by many growers but the main use is probably by consultants who run them on behalf of growers. From the SIRATAC experience, we conclude that decision support system should not bypass existing advisers, but should provide information that they can use in their business.

Focus on tactics. The SIRATAC system and its descendent, CottonLogic, provide information about optimum pest management which takes account of crop development, counts of pest and natural enemies, and the subsequent weather. Development of SIRATAC was in response to the heavy pesticide applications at the time and growing pesticide resistance in the major cotton pests. It delivered options of 'spray', 'don't spray' and 'count again', which applied for a period of days. Other examples of tactical decision support systems are MANAGE RICE and Grazfeed, both developed by CSIRO and related agencies. The original and still major use of MANAGE RICE is to report the expected response of irrigated rice to top dressed N. This decision must be made in a period of a few weeks at the time of panicle initiation. Like CottonLogic, MANAGE RICE is distributed to all growers and advisers in the industry and is supported by funding from growers. The Grazfeed system reports the optimum supplementary feed for grazing animals. Its major use is by grazers and advisers in southern Australia during drought when supplementary feed is essential. This package is

Figure 4

Calibration and validation of MANAGE rice, a decision support system for N management of irrigated rice in Australia (a) calibration of simulated yields against experimental data (b) validation of predicted yields against field experiments.

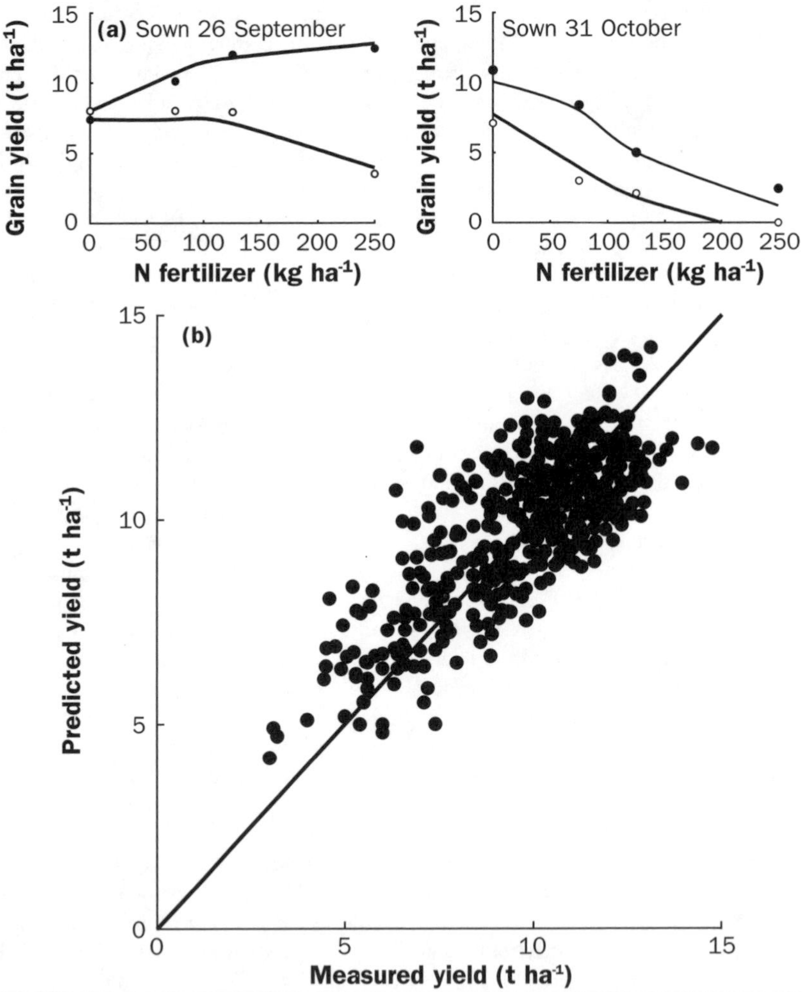

marketed commercially (www.hzn.com.au).

CottonLogic, MANAGE RICE, and Grazfeed are the most widely adopted decision support systems in Australia and all three deliver tactical rather than strategic information. They address problems that arise during a season. Each response to information provided by the user about the state of the system with options for optimum management for the particular field and season.

Decision support systems as educational

tools. Many users of decision support systems, report that they run them to understand their systems better, as well as to assist in making tactical or strategic decisions. Agricultural science students now learn about simulation models and decision support systems during their training. Future farmers and advisers are more likely to be receptive to the information from and decision support systems than the current generation. The University of New England operates a specialized web-based center for educational applications of and decision support systems (http://ed-serve.une.edu.au).

Preserving interest. Once users become familiar with the output of a decision support system, they do not need to use it. To that extent it has done its job. However continued improvement of a decision support system will tend to be ignored if its presentation remains unchanged. The revival of a cotton decision support system in Australia after SIRATAC was discontinued was based on additional features of nutrient and water management as well as improvements to the pest management module.

Our approach to preserving interest in MANAGE RICE has been to add new and useful features. After developing the module for N-fertilizer management we provided annual updates which added internet downloads of current weather, calculation of irrigation water requirement based on current and extrapolated evapotranspiration, estimation of optimum harvest date based on calculated crop development and evapotranspiration, zone management for N fertilizer, and a photographic gallery of current and exotic rice diseases. The new features build on previous features and are generally developed in response to user's interest.

Introducing new features to a decision support system also provides the opportunity for unexpected successes. Stone and Hochman (2004) reported that modules about fertilizer application, sowing time and hybrid selection did little to change New Zealand maize growers' practices, but a sowing density module was intensely interesting to users and assisted in a major industry change. Clearly there is still a lot to learn about why farmers do or do not respond to general or specific advice.

Interactions with users. Part of the success of the CottonLogic and MANAGE RICE packages is because the users are concentrated in relatively small regions and the packages are promoted through existing agencies. Users are in a better position to react to the approach and contents of a decision support system if they can first discuss it among themselves. Reactions are harder to get from a widely dispersed industry such as broadacre cropping or grazing. Nevertheless a marketing strategy of releasing a product such as Grazfeed and standing in the market has worked well. Selection of an energetic marketer with an appreciation of commercial risk, and with no conflicts of interest in the output of the decision support system is also important.

Simplicity. Our experience is that farmers want to understand details of a model that underlies a decision support system so a ready reckoner or calculator is more readily adopted than a more complex system. One non-computer system is the N wheel developed by in Western Australia (J.W. Bowden, 1993; personal communication) This is a circular slide rule that estimates optimum N fertilizer on the basis of previous crops.

Another example of simple system is an N-budget for dryland wheat in Australia, where the average use of fertilizer N was about 5 kg ha^{-1} until the late 1980s, but rose rapidly to about 30 kg N ha^{-1} by 2000. The main reason that fertilizer use had been so low was that crop response to N was unreliable because of widespread root disease. As these diseases were overcome with the adoption of break crops the responses to N became more reliable

Figure 5

Yield of irrigated rice in nitrogen (N)-deletion strips on farm crops in the Australian riverina (a) comparison with yields of the field with fertilizer managed by the farmer (b) comparison of N supplied by the farmer with yield of the zero-N strip and the 'optimum' pre-flood N estimated from a soil test of N incubation.

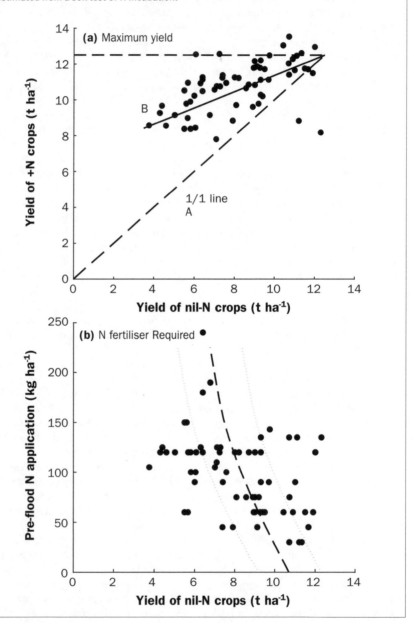

(Angus, 2001). Another reason for the low use of fertilizer N was the justified fear of 'haying off', where excess N leads to decreased yield and pinched grain (van Herwaarden et al., 1998). The most effective tool to balance crop N demand and the supply of N from soil and fertilizer was a simple N budget approach modified from Myers (1985):

$$e_1 (N_{min,0} + N_{min,IC}) + e_2 N_{fert} = (Y_{target} P_{target}) / (0.57 \text{ HIN}) \tag{2}$$

where:

$N_{min,0}$ = soil mineral N before sowing

$N_{min,IC}$ = topsoil mineralization during crop growth

N_{fert} = the amount of N fertilizer required in kg ha^{-1}

e_1 = the efficiency of uptake of soil mineral N by the crop

e_2 = the efficiency of uptake of fertilizer N by the crop

Y_{target} = target yield in t ha^{-1}

P_{target} = target protein %

HIN = harvest index for nitrogen, the proportion of crop N contained in grain

The units of soil and fertilizer N are kg ha^{-1} and the constant 0.57 converts wheat yield and protein to crop-N offtake in this unit. The apparent fertilizer recovery, e_2 varies widely but is commonly estimated as 0.5. The value of e_1 is also estimated to be 0.5 in this environment (Angus et al., 1998). The equation is rearranged to solve for N_{fert}.

The budget was initially presented as a fill-in form (Angus and Pitson, 1994) but was rapidly adapted and modified as spreadsheets by fertilizer companies, advisers, and graingrowers. A significant number of the modifications contained errors, most of which involve interpretation of e_2 and neglect of the N content of straw. An 'official' version was released as a CD and manual to provide a standard (Helyar et al.,

2002). This decision support system contains P and lime budgets presented in similar ways to the N budget.

This simple budget is probably more widely used in Australia than formal decision support systems. Advisers feel ownership of spreadsheets they adapt for themselves and clients feel confident in their output because they understand all the components. Obviously the system has numerous deficiencies. It ignores climatic risk, economics, tissue tests, grain protein and agronomic variables such as time of sowing and fertilizer application. These deficiencies were corrected in a more comprehensive decision support system, MANAGE WHEAT, which was released several years later. Despite its superiority it has not been widely adopted. It was licensed to an agribusiness and released during a prolonged drought so has not been widely adopted. So far its reception and that of the Lime and Nutrient Balance resembles the dismal fate of some other decision support systems (McCown et al., 2002; Hayman, 2004). The developers of these decision support systems plan to learn from successes of the past in further development.

Combining production and environmental objectives in a decision support system. In many circumstances production and environmental goals are in harmony. This is particularly the case where a highly productive crop uses more water and nutrients than a less productive crop, so there is less risk of leakage. A decision support system that helps to manage such a 'win–win' situation is more likely to succeed that one that reports a 'win–lose' (increased profit and damaged environment) or a 'lose–win' (reduced profit and improved environment).

Even when there are environmental costs of nutrients it is important to include them in a decision support system. Where simulation models are used in production decision support system, they can be modified to calculate and report the estimated losses through leaching and other pathways. For example the volume of water and nutrient leached through soil is normally simulated in the models used in decision support systems. The amount and cost of the lost nutrients should be reported to the user, for the particular field and year, with the same prominence as the yield. The prediction error of these simulations should also be reported since they are likely to be less reliable than yield. When the environmental costs are local they can be used in evaluating profitability of the field. For example additional acidification due to N fertilizer can be calculated in relation to additional product removal and NO_3 -leaching from the top-soil (Helyar et al., 2002). The lime required to neutralize this acidification can be reported as an additional cost of applying fertilizer. When the environmental costs are external, for example when leached nutrients leave the field, it is still valuable to report the estimated loss of nutrients and the timing of loss to the farmer. Awareness of the circumstances in which loss occurs is useful information that may assist farmers' future decisions.

Concluding Remarks

Based on experience with existing decision support systems, they are most likely to be effective when: (1) the output is accurate; (2) the use is for tactical rather than strategic applications and they address a problem that cannot be handled easily by word of mouth or paper-based systems; (3) they grow out of an existing institution or extension system and the responsibilities for commercialization, marketing and training are clear; (4) they are developed and continuously improved in collaboration with users and advisers, who have a sense of ownership; (5) the output and calculations are clear to users; and (6) they address a new problem or opportunity.

For use in decisions about nutrients, the effectiveness of decision support systems is likely to be limited when the fertilizer: price ratio favors overuse of fertilizer. If there is a strong economic incentive for high input use it is unlikely that a decision support system will be any more effective than extension programs have been in the past. Reducing the economic incentive to overuse nutrients is a precondition for a decision support system to have an impact. The alternative is to impose more regulations and taxes, although it is not clear how effective these have been.

The achievements of current production-related decision support systems are grounds for optimism that they can contribute to balanced use of nutrients for production and the environment. There is still much to learn about how farmers respond to the impersonal outputs of a decision support system. The experience in decision support system development is a guide to situations where they are most likely to succeed.

References Cited

Addiscott, T.M., A.P. Whitmore, and D.S. Powlson. 1991. Farming fertilizers and the nitrate problem. CAB International, Wallingford, UK. 170 pp.

Anderson, A.J. 1952. Testing pastures for mineral deficiencies. Rural Research in CSIRO 2:9–10.

Angus, J.F. 2001. Nitrogen supply and demand in Australian agriculture. Australian Journal of Experimental Agriculture 41:277–288.

Angus, J. and G. Pitson. 1994. Refining fertilizer strategies. Australian Grain (April–May):6–10.

Angus, J. and C. Russell. 2004. Predrilled nitrogen for rice. Pp. 26–26. In: IREC Farmers' Newsletter. Irrigation Research and Extension Committee, Griffith, Australia.

Angus, J.F., A.F. van Herwaarden, R.A. Fischer, G.N. Howe, and D.P. Heenan. 1998. The source of mineral nitrogen for cereals in southeastern Australia. Australian Journal of Agricultural Research 49:511–522.

Bumb, B.L. 1995. World nitrogen supply and demand: An overview. Pp. 1–40. In: Fertilization and the Nitrogen Environment. P.E. Bacon (ed.) Marcel Dekker, New York, New York.

Chen, D.L., J.R. Freney, A.R. Mosier, and P.M. Chalk. 1994. Reducing denitrification loss with nitrification inhibitors following pre-sowing applications of urea to a cotton field. Australian Journal of Experimental Agriculture 34:75–83.

Doering, O.C., F. Diaz-Hermelo, C. Howard, R. Heimlich, F. Hitzhusen, J.L. Kazmeieraczak, L. Libby, W. Milon, T. Prato, and M. Ribaudo. 1999. Evaluation of economic costs and benefits of methods for reducing nutrient loads to the Gulf of Mexico. Decision Analysis Series No. 20, NOAA Coastal Oceans Program, Silver Spring, Maryland. 115 pp.

Duan, S., S. Zhang, and H. Huang. 2000. Transport of dissolved inorganic nitrogen from the major rivers to estuaries in China. Nutrient Cycling in Agroecosystems 57:13-22.

Evans, L.T. 1998. Feeding the ten billion. Cambridge University Press. 247 pp.

Finlay, P. 1994. Introducing decisions support systems. NCC Blackwell, Oxford. 274 pp.

Goolsby, D.A., W.A. Battaglin, G.B. Lawrence, R.S. Artz, B.T. Aulenbach, R.P. Hooper, D.R. Keeney, and G.J. Stensland. 1999. Flux and sources of nutrients in the Mississippi-Atchafalaya River Basin. NOAA Coastal Ocean Program Decision Analysis Program, Decision Analysis Series No. 17, NOAA Coastal Oceans Program, Silver Spring, Maryland. 130 pp.

Hatfield, J.L. and J.F. Angus. 2005. The need to couple environmental and production research on nitrogen in agricultural systems. (In press)

Hayman, P. 2004. Decision support systems in Australian dryland farming: A promising past, a disappointing present and uncertain future. *In:* Proceedings for the 4th International Crop Science Congress. R.A. Fischer et al. (eds.) Brisbane, Australia, 26 Sept-1 Oct. http://www.cropscience.org.au/icsc2004/symposia/4/1/1778_haymanp.htm

Heady, E.O. 1952. Economics of agricultural production and resource use. Prentice-Hall, Englewood Cliffs, New Jersey. 850 pp.

Hearn, A.B. and M.P. Bange. 2002. SIRATAC and *CottonLogic*: Persevering with DSSs in the Australian cotton industry. Agricultural Systems 74:27-56.

Helyar, K., J. Angus, D. Liu, and H. Ottey. 2002. Lime and nutrient balance. GRDC, Canberra, 40pp + CD (www.grdc.com.au/lnb).

Johansson, G. and A. Gustafson. 2004. Discharge and nutrient losses for the agrohydrological year 2002/03 and a long-term review. Teknisk Rapport No. 83. Division of Water Quality Management, Swedish University of Agricultural Sciences, Uppsala. 38pp.

Kirchmann, H. and L. Bergström. 2001. Do organic farming practices reduce nitrate leaching? Communications in Soil Science and Plant Analysis 32:997-1028.

Kobayashi, K. 2004. Comments on another way of partitioning mean squared deviation proposed by Gauch et al. Agronomy Journal 96:1206-1208.

Krupnik, T.J., J. Six, J.K. Ladha, M.J. Paine, and C. van Kessel. 2004. An assessment of fertilizer nitrogen recovery efficiency by grain crops. Pp. 193-208. *In:* Agriculture and the Nitrogen Cycle. A.R. Mosier, J. K.Syers, and J.R. Freney (eds.) Island Press, Washington, D.C.

Lemaire, G., S. Recous, and B. Mary. 2004. Managing residues and nitrogen in intensive cropping systems. New understanding for efficient recovery by crops. *In:* Proceedings for the 4th International Crop Science Congress. R.A. Fischer et al. (eds.) Brisbane, Australia, 26 Sept-1 Oct. (www.cropscience.org.au/icsc2004/symposia/2/6/index.htm)

McCown, R.L. 2002. Probing the enigma of the decision support system to farmers: Learning from experience and from theory. Agricultural Systems 74:1-10.

Mitsch, W.J., J.W. Day, Jr., J.W. Gilliam, P.M. Groffman, D.L. Hey, G.W. Randall, and N. Wang. 1999. Reducing nutrient loads, especially nitrate-nitrogen, to surface water, groundwater and the Gulf of Mexico. NOAA Coastal Ocean Program Decision Analysis Program, Decision Analysis Series No. 19, NOAA Coastal Oceans Program, Silver Spring, Maryland. 111pp.

Moore, A.D., J.F. Angus, M. Bange, C.J. Crispin, J.R. Donnelly, M. Freer, N.I. Herrmann, H.E. Ottey, D. Richards, L. Salmon, M. Stapper, and A. Suladze. 2004. Computer-based decision support tools for Australian farmers. *In:* Proceedings for the 4th International Crop Science Congress. R.A. Fischer et al. (eds.) Brisbane, Australia, 26 Sept - 1 Oct. (www.cropscience.org.au/icsc2004/poster/4/1/1/index.htm).

Myers, R.J.K. 1985. A simple model for estimating the nitrogen fertilizer requirement for a cereal crop. Fertilizer Research 5:95-108.

Ondersteijn, C.J.M., A.C.G. Beldman, C.H.G. Daatselaar, G.W.J. Giesen, and R.B.M. Huirne. 2002. The Dutch mineral accounting system and the European nitrate directive: Implocations of N and P management and farm performance. Agriculture, Ecosystems, and Environment 92:283-296.

Oleson, J.E., P. Sørensen, I.K. Thomsen, J. Eriksen, A.G. Thomsen, and J. Berntsen. 2004. Integrated nitrogen input systems in Denmark. Pp. 129-140. *In:* Agriculture and the Nitrogen Cycle. A.R. Mosier, J.K. Syers, and J.R. Freney (eds.) Island Press, Washington, D.C.

SCB. 2004. www.scb.se/templates/tableOrChart___32828.asp; www.scb.se/templates/Publikaion___79569.asp

Smil, V. 2001. Enriching the earth. Fritz Haber, Carl Bosch, and the transformation of world food production. The MIT Press, Cambridge, Massachusetts. 338 pp.

Stone, P. and Z. Hochman. 2004. If interactive decision support systems are the answer, have we been asking the right questions? *In:* Proceedings for the 4th International Crop Science Congress. R.A. Fischer et al. (eds.) Brisbane, Australia, 26 Sept - 1 Oct. http://www.cropscience.org.au/icsc2004/ symposia/4/3/1680_stonepj.htm#TopOfPage

van der Ploeg, J.D. 1994. Styles of farming: An introductory note on concepts and methodology. Pp. 7-30. *In:* Born from within: Practice and perspectives of endogenous rural development. J.D. van der Ploeg and A. Long (eds.) Assen, Van Gorcum.

van Herwaarden, A.F., J.F. Angus, G.D. Farquhar, G.N. Howe, and R.A. Richards. 1998. 'Haying-off', the negative grain yield response of dryland wheat to nitrogen fertiliser. I Biomass, grain yield and water use. Australian Journal of Agricultural Research 49:1067-1081.

Williams, R.L. and J.F. Angus. 1994. Deep water protects high-nitrogen rice crops from low-temperature damage. Australian Journal of Experimental Agriculture 34:927-32.

Wright, S and C. Mallia. 2003. The potential for eco-taxes as instruments for sustainability. The Journal of Transdisciplinary Environmental Studies 2:1-14. (www.journal-tes.dk)

Wolf, J., A.H.W. Beusen, P. Groenendijk, T. Kroon, R. Rötter, and H. van Zeijts. 2003. The integrated modeling system STONE for calculating nutrient emissions from agriculture in the Netherlands. Environmental Modeling and Software 18:597-617.

Wulff, F.V., L.A. Rahm, and P. Larsson. 2001. A systems analysis of the Baltic Sea. Springer-Verlag, Berlin. 455 pp.

Integrating Hydrology into Farmer's Decisions

CHAPTER 9

P.F. Quinn, C.J.M. Hewett, and A. Doyle

Recognizing the profound changes that have taken place in the "relationship between the human world and the planet that sustains it," in 1983 the United Nations proposed strategies for sustainable development. This involved examining ways of improving human well being without threatening the environment and addressing potential conflicts between the interests of the environment and economic development. In 1987 this resulted in the publication by The United Nations Commission of 'Our Common Future' (Brundtland, 1987) which was followed by the Earth 'Summits' of 1992 and 2002, and in turn, a comprehensive program of citizen participation through Agenda 21. The fundamental principle of sustainable development is to improve human and environmental well being, 'without compromising the needs of future generations.' While focusing on finding the balance among corporations, states, and communities and between rich and poor, the concept attempts to incorporate environmental considerations with the need for social and economic development, joining economic development with environmental concerns. Promotion of sustainable development is intended to engage with principles of citizenship and environmental justice.

In parallel with these developments, there has been increasing awareness of the need for an integrated approach to the management of water resources and the land, largely driven by the world-wide trend in the deterioration of water quantity and quality standards and in increasingly limited access to water. As Falkenmark (1999) points out, everything done on the land influences the water cycle, "A land use decision is also a water decision."

This recognition has given rise to the concept of integrated water resource management. Integrated water resource management involves the coordinated planning and management of land, water, and other environmental resources for their equitable, efficient, and sustainable use (Calder, 1999). Following the philosophy of integrated water resource management, the Water Framework Directive (WFD) will require all member states of the European Union (EU) to divide their land area into river basin districts and to prepare management plans for these river basins, enshrining in European legislation the principle of integrated river basin management, including a statutory requirement for public participation. This is intended to encourage a holistic approach to the management of river basins, taking account of the interdependence of human and natural factors within the basin. Decisions related to one part of a basin or catchment thus should be informed by knowledge of the consequences for the whole system.

A river basin is defined to be the area of land drained by a river and its tributaries. All of the water falling on the land surrounding a basin is channelled into its central river and out to an estuary or sea. A catchment is an area where the land drains to a common stream or river, usually bound by ridges. River basins and catchments are dynamic living areas that can include human habitation (cities, towns, villages, and individual homesteads) and infrastructure such as roads and railways as well as forests, agriculture, grassland, and wildlife.

This paper outlines the principles behind a water management framework to underpin integrated river basin management and the contribution that research can make to successful implementation. In particular, the role that hydrology could play in bringing together the variety of disciplines essential to effective water management is examined. The importance of public engagement and the range of modelling, data and policy support tools that are needed are discussed and some examples of tools appropriate to different scales are presented.

Our proposed framework consists of first using physically-based models and measurement to generate data on a research catchment, which is usually of a small scale of $1m^2$ - 1 ha (The scale of a catchment can vary from several hectares to thousands of square kilometres, from the size of a local stream to that of a river the size of the Danube). This research scale knowledge is used to get an indication of the likely hydrology at the larger catchment scale. Simple meta models are then used to mimic the dynamics of the physically-based models at this larger scale and the output of these models is translated into risk indicators which are input to a catchment Geographical information system (GIS). Here the researcher has to rely on observation, experience and judgement as the scaling up procedure inevitably introduces a degree of uncertainty that is hard to quantify.

In order to bridge the gap between the information generated and policymakers decision support tools such as the decision support matrices presented in this paper are created. Such tools aim to allow for strategic planning at the catchment scale. Risk indicators generated by the meta

models coupled to a GIS can be used at this stage to target priority areas. In order that the policies developed are implemented, these tools need to assist in persuading land managers and farmers to improve farming practice. One aspect of this is to show them that small changes in practice can have a large impact on the water environment and need not have an adverse affect on their income. Stake-holder workshops and discussion can be used to provide feedback into education and decision support tools and to encourage a sense of ownership of ideas amongst rural communities and institutions. Ultimately any change in land use feeds back into what is done on the research catchment which is then simulated using the physically-based models, closing the loop.

Integrated river basin management and the Water Framework Directive. Up to now the principle of integrated river basin management has remained a topic for research rather than day to day practice primarily because of its complexity, crossing disciplines and scales, and the shortage of the hard evidence needed to underpin decision-making. Integrated catchment management is a planning and implementation process that should allow for good coordination between management authorities and stakeholders such as land owners and farmers. However, in practice, the stakeholders who can most influence land use change within a basin are often far removed from the decision-making, which creates major problems with implementing decisions. While planning at the catchment scale makes the most sense and is in keeping with the philosophy of integrated river basin management, in reality this scale can be huge and thus greatly separated from the field scale, which is often the scale where the greatest effect can be achieved.

The Water Framework Directive is one of the most significant reforms ever undertaken in relation to water quality management legislation. Its overarching theme is integrated water management at the level of the river basin and its principal objectives are to prevent deterioration and to restore and enhance bodies of surface water to achieve and maintain 'good ecological status'; reduce pollution in these water courses; and preserve protected areas. The Water Framework Directive is based on the principles of sustainable development and as such relies on the need for an understanding of management of the catchment hydrological cycle alongside effective public participation and consultation. The Water Framework Directive is a key piece of European legislation, intended to deliver long-term protection of the water environment and improve the quality of all water bodies-groundwater and surface waters, rivers, coasts, estuaries, lakes, man-made structures and wetlands. It is the most substantial piece of water legislation to emanate from the European Commission (EC). New objectives are being set to promote the sustainable use of water. The Water Framework Directive requires all waters, inland and coastal, to reach good status at least by the year 2015. This will be affected through the establishment of structures which set environmental objectives. Water status will be defined and assessed using chemical, biological and physical measures. Negative human impacts on the water environment from specific places, such as farms, mines or factories, and sources such as road networks, must be identified and a program of measures established to address all types of impact. The Water Framework Directive presents an opportunity to develop substantial benefits for the long-term sustainable management of water. As well as ecological benefits the Water Framework Directive will safeguard and improve water quality for present and future generations for their economic, recreational and general amenity use. This legislation is intended to promote healthy rivers and lakes but also attempts to balance the water environment with economic and social considerations.

The Water Framework Directive deals with management of water bodies on a river basin basis. As competent authority for the Water Framework Directive in the UK, the Environment Agency will be responsible for the production of River Basin Management Plans every six years and for the co-ordination of the programme of measures required to meet objectives. Through the River Basin Management Plans decisions will be made at basin level about measures to tackle pollution of water courses.

The need for public involvement in the development of River Basin Management Plans is an important feature of the Water Framework Directive. This involvement is statutory. However, the term public participation covers a wider range of stakeholder engagement approaches than is required by the directive. Only three forms of stakeholder engagement are referred to in Water Framework Directive: 1) Access to background information; 2) Consultation in the planning process; and 3) Active involvement of interested parties in all aspects of the implementation of the Water Framework Directive.

The UK Environment Agency is developing an approach to consultation and involvement through a social policy framework and a communication strategy on how to engage the public, devising approaches to public participation that has *consultation* and *access to information* at its core, and includes wider *active involvement* where this meets the requirements of the Water Framework Directive (http://www.environment-agency.gov.uk/). This is an ambitious program and will require a great deal of thought and hard work if it is to be effective.

When environmental concerns or potential hazards are perceived by resident communities the procedure for getting these issues acted upon is often unclear. Time and financial resources are needed for actions. Participatory environmental initiatives rely on individual citizens committing time and energy to projects, often with no clear outcomes. The Water Framework Directive is a significant opportunity to engage communities in the process of making plans for river basin management and giving fuller consideration to community concerns and local environmental perceptions. It may provide a key to stakeholder participation in environmental actions dealing with issues that concern resident communities, noting scientific, technical, planning, administrative, and economic implications. Opportunities exist through engaging the public in the river basin plan making process to address concerns of 'democratic deficit' in the environmental decision making process. Full participatory programmes offer the opportunity to promote environmental awareness and scientific understanding and to develop mutual understanding through discussion and experiment. Participation can contribute to building and reinforcing a sense of community. Partnership between local

people and statutory authorities can build trust through open and transparent plan making process. Public confidence can be enhanced through a wider awareness of the issues and processes involved. However, it should be noted that so far there are no examples of this being implemented which raises the question of how to transform the ideas from theory into practice.

With this backdrop in mind the key questions arise: How can the necessary partnerships be developed? What is the role of research in this process? How can the problem of disparate scales implicit in integrated river basin management be dealt with?

Figure 1 illustrates our vision of a balanced approach to integrated river basin management involving partnerships between researchers in water and environment, sociology, and agri-economics and stakeholders. The 'cooking pot' in the center of the figure is intended to reflect the importance of discussion across disciplines and with end users such as farmers, residents, local traders, and tourists in the process of arriving at a local catchment plan.

Partnerships. It is clear that periods of

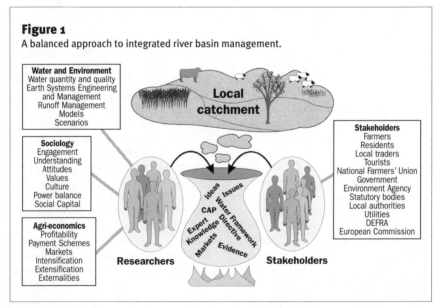

Figure 1
A balanced approach to integrated river basin management.

public engagement must be accepted as an integral part of developing integrated river basin management from the outset. Thus it is necessary to bring together the many research disciplines required at the catchment scale with local and national stakeholders. Meetings of hydrologists, economists, sociologists, agronomists with farmers, local traders, local councils and national bodies such as the National Farmers' Union and the Environment Agency have to be part of the process. The UN Economic Commission for Europe (UNECE) Convention on Access to Information, Public Participation in Decision-Making, and Access to Justice in Environmental Matters, *The Aarhus Convention*, was presented in 1998. It is an international agreement which outlines principles to engender citizens' participation in environmental matters and thus improve the enactment of environmental laws. It grants the public access to environmental information; provides for participation in environmental decision-making; and allows the public to seek judicial redress when environmental law is infringed. By signing the Aarhus Convention in 1998, the EU committed itself to adopting it as EU law. Two directives concerning access to environmental information (Directive 2003/4/EC) and public participation in environmental decision-making (Directive 2003/35/EC) in EU member states were adopted in 2003.

"The Aarhus Convention consists of three pillars, each of which grants different rights: the first pillar gives the public the right of access to environmental information; the second pillar gives the public the right to participate in decision-making processes and; the third pillar ensures access to justice for the public" Aarhus convention (//europa.eu.int/comm/environment/aarhus/)

Thus, there is a need for a future vision of collaboration involving a wide variety of skills and knowledge, as shown in Figure 1. In the box entitled 'Water and Environment' it is clear that a partnership of hydrologists, ecologists and engineers must be created to establish the current water quantity and quality regime for an area (which should be fed by an informative GIS). Such a collaboration may not always be present but great strides have been taken in hydro-ecological understanding (Acreman, 2001) and Earth Systems Engineering and Management (Allenby, 1998, 2000; Quinn and Hewett, 2003). There is huge potential for these parties to integrate into a sensible scaling and uncertainty framework guided by an understanding of the hydrological cycle.

In many cases there is still a partition of land and water scientists from the other key discipline required for sound scientific assessment of catchments. It is almost impossible for scientists to become experts in all these disciplines; hence Figure 1 supports the concept of mutual partnerships between the professional and research scientific disciplines. The researchers are forced to work together at the strategic scale of the river catchment, both exchanging concepts and skills while studying the local catchment properties and learning from the end users *directly*. The stakeholders are also tied to the river basin scale as opposed to the regional or national framework alone. While there is clearly an input from regional, national and European drivers, those components must be translated into a local framework first. The key innovation is to place all the research and local end user needs into the 'cooking pot' where all the issues can be simmered for a suitable period of time. This means much more than paying lip service to participation and involves real engagement with the concerns and needs of stakeholders when building a water management framework. The key here is the willingness of all parties to listen to each other; there should be no dominant ingredient within the cooking pot and no matter how long and difficult the process is, any product from the pot will be a jointly owned, viable vision for the local catchment. As such any proposed land use planning and policy can be created and enforced by the local community.

Earth systems engineering and management. Earth systems engineering and management is the study and practice of engineering systems to facilitate the active management of the dynamics of coupled human and natural systems (Allenby, 2000). The adoption of this management philosophy focuses on the need to understand the complex interaction between anthropogenic and natural influences. It recognises that there is no such thing as the 'natural environment' as all of the Earth's systems have been altered by human activity in the past and will continue to be so in the future. Earth systems engineering and management represents an opportunity to improve the environment and to actively manage the global systems that human activity impacts on in a rational manner. For example, rather than simply aiming to reduce global carbon dioxide emissions, an earth systems engineering and management approach would involve developing 'an institutional ability to deliberately modulate the carbon cycle within specified and desirable domains' (Allenby, 2000).

We propose that applying the earth systems engineering and management philosophy to the river basin is a necessary requirement for successful integrated river basin management. This is complicated by the need to resolve problems at many scales relying on knowledge of a number of disciplines including Earth systems science, engineering, economics and sociology. What is more, the knowledge that can help decision-making must be at a scale relevant to a particular problem.

Water quantity and quality. The quantity and quality of water in the landscape is generated by a variety of interacting processes which must be traced from the

area where water flow begins to the places, either locally or downstream, where problems arise or where the water is required for consumption. This is generally influenced by both human activities and natural processes. Some influences may be traced to a certain point in the landscape, whereas other influences are diffuse across the landscape. Although most problems arise locally, the effects are often apparent at a much larger scale at lower points in the river basin.

The integrated effects of hydrological processes are best viewed in the river, as the water has a trace memory of its contact with the land. Despite the complexity of a catchment, the quality and quantity of water in a river represent the integrated response of all actions taking place in the catchment. Measurements taken in the river provide clues to the health of the whole system. Human activities on land can, and do, change the fundamental driving variables of the hydrological cycle. As Andersson and Quinn (1999) put it, "If there is an ailing river, a sick landscape may be the cause."

In the management of the water environment, the component landscape processes cannot be treated separately and individual locations cannot be treated in isolation. Any change in one component of a land and river system will influence other components in the system, both locally and downstream.

Assessing the water flows through the landscape enables us to understand these influences and thus should be considered a prerequisite to a good river basin management plan.

In Figure 2, an overall conceptual framework is presented, where the balance of input flow paths and the dependency of resources and consumers can be shown. The river basin in the figure is divided into three administrative regions. The water flow that is produced in each region is a combination of three things:

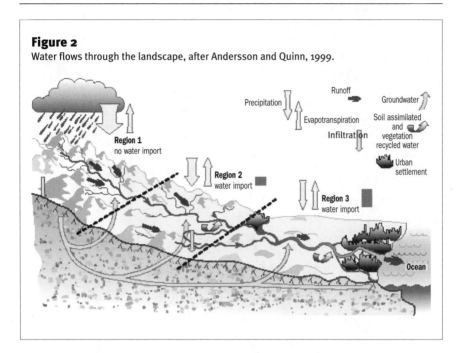

Figure 2
Water flows through the landscape, after Andersson and Quinn, 1999.

1) Rainfall on that area; 2) Water lost by evapotranspiration (the return of water to the atmosphere as vapour, by evaporation from soil, water bodies, etc. and emissions or transpiration from plants); and 3) Water extracted for human use or consumption or for the consumption of livestock. Water that is not evapotranspired or extracted finds its ways into the river channels as surface runoff and sub-surface flow. In some cases there is also an import of groundwater and river flow from higher situated regions.

The land surface itself is the most vulnerable component of the river basin. Sound management of resources in relation to land use practice has a direct impact on the quality of water in receiving watercourses. Thus the management of runoff water quantity and quality from farmland has huge implications for the entire river basin.

In Figure 3, the amounts of locally produced river discharge and the amounts of imported water to the three administrative regions of Figure 2 are shown. The schematic diagram demonstrates that, in addition to the potential water need of each region, the potential for water pollution also increases downstream due to population density, agriculture and industrial activities. The figure is intended to illustrate the dependence of the downstream population on upstream water quantity and quality.

Region 1 has high precipitation and low atmospheric demand for evapotranspiration. The soils are constantly wet, agricultural and industrial activities are limited, thus water is exported from this region to lower regions with a low degree of pollution. This region is the natural reservoir of the basin and released water can maintain channel flow during long periods of downstream drought.

Region 2 has lower precipitation than Region 1 and higher atmospheric demand for evapotranspiration thus less runoff is produced. However, water is imported into this region from Region 1. Besides the surface water, the groundwater may

Figure 3

Water balance for the three regions, showing import and export of flow and groundwater, and summarizing the different land use pressures in each region.

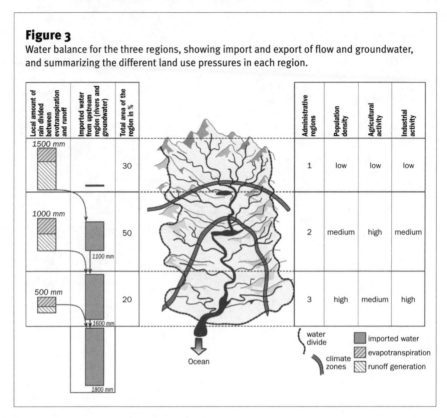

Administrative regions	Population density	Agricultural activity	Industrial activity
1	low	low	low
2	medium	high	medium
3	high	medium	high

also be used as a resource by the human population. Agricultural production in this region is high, making it likely that there will be high demand for water for irrigation. There is also a medium population density impacting on demand for water for consumption and potentially generating pollution from waste water. Thus human activity will alter not only the water quantity but also the quality of the water. The extraction of groundwater over an extended time interval may exceed the rate at which groundwater recharges and this may lead to the drying of streams.

Region 3 has the lowest precipitation and the highest atmospheric evapotranspiration demand. In this region only very high rainfall events can generate significant runoff. This region, with its dense population, is dependent on imported water.

The quantity and quality of that water are strongly influenced by human activity in Region 2. The region may also depend on agricultural products from Region 2.

The dependency of one region on another is clear as water cascades through the landscape. However the politics of water related decision-making may be made in the lower, populated region where demand and dependency are at their highest. This illustrates that, while the hydrological cycle follows the natural gradients of the landscape, the *politics* of water often moves in the opposite direction.

In addition to the need to assess the water flows through the landscape as part of integrated river basin management we consider that there is a need for:

■ continuous assessment of the water quality in the rivers and aquifers for the whole basin;

■ a statement of the basic ecological status of the land and the rivers, in terms of biological and chemical water quality and aesthetics; and

■ an assessment of the present and future water requirements for human consumption, food production and industrial use to be established.

In many cases the size of the basin may be too large for integrated river basin management to be implemented in a full and co-operative manner. The nature of multi-nation and multi-region water transfers may be at the level of international politics and perhaps can only be addressed at that level. However, if there is a commitment to integrated river basin management, then smaller river catchments can still be chosen for planning purposes (perhaps 1,000 km^2 to 10,000 km^2). These catchments should fall within a smaller region and have a similar climate zone where some kind of river basin authority is in operation. Thus, the land unit for assessment is still a catchment (with water imports and exports) but has the potential for regional regulation and stakeholder partnerships. Each catchment must commit to specific goals regarding water quantity and quality so that the environment downstream is not impacted upon adversely by the sub catchments. In conclusion, the first scale issue for integrated river basin management is to create local river basin plans that can take place as part of the regional planning activity. Thus, in contrast to the popular mantra "Think globally, act locally" (coined by Rene Dubos in 1972 during the UN Conference on the Human Environment in Stockholm) we would argue that, for the purposes of integrated river basin management, we should: *Think regionally; act regionally.*

Hydrology and scale. The range of processes and activities that take place at different scales have huge implications for effective integrated river basin management. First, the interests of an individual farmer, a community, a region or a nation differ significantly and are often in opposition and thus dealing with the human dimension at all scales is essential. Second, the hydrological processes at play at the local (point) scale impact on the river basin scale and thus an understanding of upscaling issues is equally important (Beven, 1993; Blöchle, 1997). Here we argue that understanding links between local agricultural activity (the cause) and the impact of that activity downstream (the effect) will provide essential input to a water management framework (which, although implicit in the Water Framework Directive, is not actually described in any detail). The issue is one of where, when and how human activities interact with hydrological processes and the impacts they have on water quantity and quality needs within a catchment.

The hydrological community has already expended great effort in understanding both measurement and modelling across scale and in understanding quantitative uncertainty. Thus there are some key skills that hydrologists can contribute to integrated river basin management including:

■ understanding of scaling issues (aggregation, routing, mixing effects);

■ understanding of plot, hillslope, small catchment and basin scale process; and

■ good practice in terms of modelling skills, especially related to scaling and uncertainty concepts.

However, the hydrological community has not engaged fully with management issues which leads to the danger first that hydrologists may be regarded as 'pure' scientists and not 'applied' scientists and will thus be sidelined in the future and second, that good practice in modelling and dealing with different scales may be missed by relevant land use planners.

We will address first the hydrological scaling issues. Farmers have preferential access to rainfall and they also control the top 1m of the soil, thus their decisions are pivotal to the success and failure of land management. Farmers are the 'applied' hydrologists; they understand water and how to farm water, but often fail to appreciate the wider implications of their actions. Local impacts in local streams and aquifers are generated from local hillslope runoff processes. Downstream impacts are cascaded down through the hydrological cycle with both the water quantity and quality changing radically dependent on management, soils, geology and climate. Thus a scale appropriate set of modelling and management tools are needed for each catchment.

In Figure 4, an attempt is made to summarize the basis of the scaling up and process representation problem. Figure 4a shows a typical 1 m² soil column where runoff is dominated by soil conductivity, roots and macroporosity. This point scale is clearly vulnerable to management activity as the farmer controls the crop cover and the input to the land. Figures 4b and 4c utilize the notion of variable source area and critical source area. A variable source area is a small zone of land that is prone to saturation and runoff production (Dunne and Black, 1970). Its size is dynamic and depends on the rate of subsurface recharge.

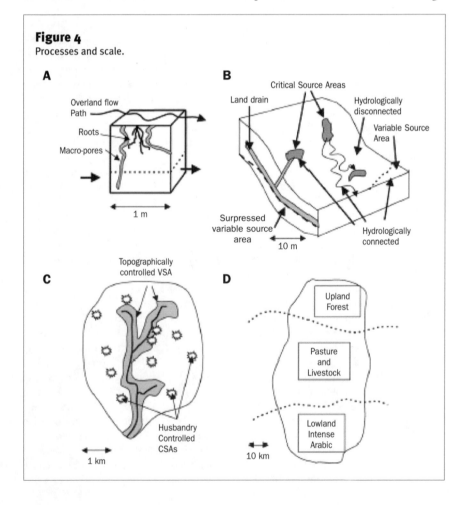

Figure 4
Processes and scale.

A
Overland flow Path
Roots
Macro-pores
1 m

B
Critical Source Areas
Land drain
Hydrologically disconnected
Variable Source Area
Surpressed variable source area
Hydrologically connected
10 m

C
Topographically controlled VSA
Husbandry Controlled CSAs
1 km

D
Upland Forest
Pasture and Livestock
Lowland Intense Arabic
10 km

Variable source areas often act like natural wetlands with large buffering capacity. However, such zones are usually the first to be underdrained, which removes their natural buffering capacity causing any nutrient applied to be flushed away quickly through the land drains (Gburek et al., 2000). A critical source area is any zone where there is a significant source of nutrient input from that area to the receiving waters (Heathwaite et al., 2004). Critical source areas can be local zones of degraded land, farm buildings or even whole fields if underdrained.

Figure 4b shows a typical hillslope section where flow connectivity and the effects of flow integration are observed. Figure 4c shows a small catchment where a distribution of critical source areas and a variable source area dominate runoff production. Recognition of this pattern of runoff and of the potential polluting zones allows 'hotspots' of pollutant to be targeted, for example by introducing buffer zones. Finally, Figure 4d shows a large catchment where dominant land use, topography and rainfall gradients dominate runoff patterns. Here the knowledge of local detail is lost and runs the risk of being ignored and thus a chasm opens up between cause and effect.

The issues, processes and physical properties that are seen at the plot scale are very different from those observed at the catchment and large basin scale. This prompts the debate about the type of data needed at each scale and the type of model most appropriate at each scale. Equally the goals of the experimentation at one scale may be different to the needs of the policy maker at the regional scale. Thus the direct upscaling of findings made at one scale may be inappropriate to another. It is the breaking of these implicit scaling rules that can cause the greatest problems (Beven, 1989). Therefore there are new modelling approaches that pay respect to our current level of knowledge, reflect the levels of uncertainty but moreover are capable of using the evidence we do have,

to inform decision making (Quinn, 2004).

There are many cases where anxiety over levels of uncertainty can lead to policy paralysis, i.e. policy cannot be set until we know the exact answer. However, in reality the exact answer will never be known and policymakers have to accept this fact. Sensible policy can be set even if there is lack of hard evidence or the predictive uncertainty remains high. The sound expertise relating to good and bad land use practice does exist and should be made use of.

Developing effective land use and water policy. Scientists and social scientists need to work in partnership with land use planners at all stages of the decision-making process if land use policy is to be effective. This will only be possible if all parties are trained with greater breadth of vision. While specialisation of, for example, the scientist and the economist, will remain necessary, communication across disciplines and a willingness to listen will be equally, if not more, important. Only if all of the ingredients go into the cooking pot will the best land use plan result.

At the moment, the main problem with land use and water policy is the lack of communication common between those involved in planning and the scientific community. This is largely due to the very different type of training given to decision-makers and scientists. Since we are discussing water management specifically, let us take the example of the land use planner and the hydrologist. The land use planner has usually received general training aimed at building skills in problem solving, but with little scientific expertise. The hydrologist, on the other hand, is trained in a range of technical skills such as modelling, GIS and field experimentation and tends to specialise early. This is not conducive to developing the breadth required for an integrated approach to water management and fails to develop the problem solving skills needed for policy-making, see Figure 5.

Figure 5
The communication problem.

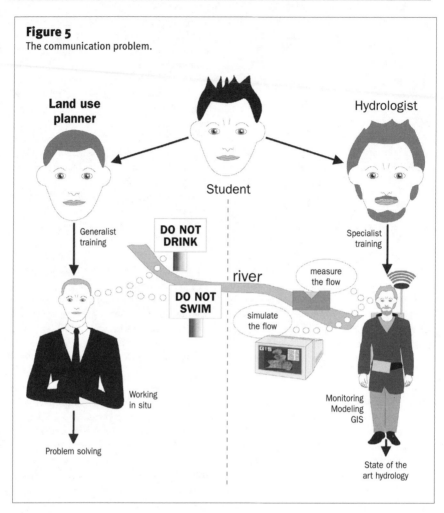

Figure 6
Sustainable livelihoods framework (DfID, 1999).

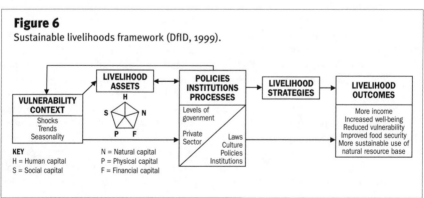

Educating scientists in the true needs of the policymaker will be essential if integrated thinking is to be achieved. As a result policymakers would be fed with the type of information and models that most improve their decision-making (including scaling and uncertainty factors). Policymakers must know many key factors about river basin processes, stakeholders' and policy requirements but their decisions also need to be rooted in a systematic, rigorous, problem solving environmental topic such as hydrology. It is up to scientists to communicate this to the generalists making policy.

Frameworks for analysis and decision support. 'Sustainable livelihoods' approach has become widely used in development planning and interventions. The sustainable livelihood approach promotes poverty eradication, protection and better management of the environment, and places emphasis on people as opposed to resources (Carney, 1998). The UK Department for International Development (DfID) have developed the sustainable livelihood framework, which conceptualizes economic, environmental, and social interactions and influences (DfID, 1999), see Figure 6. However, while this framework can be of value as a "thinking tool" it does not provide any of the tools required to analyse the interactions it is intended to capture. This is all too common with these types of framework.

It is all too easy to be glib with such approaches. Conceptualizing the links between things using a series of boxes with arrows joining them is easily done. Turning this into some useful analysis is not. The problem is, as soon as there are more than two or three factors to consider the number of potential links becomes very large and even drawing all the possible connections between different factors becomes overly complicated, let alone analysing them all, see Figure 7. The real challenge is in moving from a "thinking tool" to a set of appropriate analysis tools or models.

Hydrological multi-scale framework. There is currently still great debate about the type of models, data sets and tools that should be used to support decision making. However, this debate is set largely within an informatics world where the abundance, frequency and resolution of data are constantly increasing. Obviously, many of these technical factors will play a strong role in the future of integrated river basin management and their research should be encouraged. However a clear, multi-scale hydrological framework is needed now to inform policy.

Here a scaling and management framework is proposed as one possible mode to drive the IRBM process forward based on current expertise, taking on board the ESEM philosophy, see Figure 8. It is clearly not the only possibility, but is an approach that can commence now as all of the tools within the framework already exist. The framework reflects scaling and uncertainty issues and includes a range of modelling tools. The example shown is

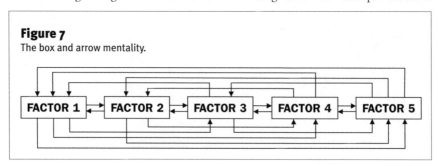

Figure 7
The box and arrow mentality.

based primarily on a nutrient pollution project but has many generic aspects common to other integrated river basin management issues.

To provide the overall framework there are a series of data issues, modelling tools and assumptions to be outlined. With regard to data, we need to know what should be measured, how it should be measured and what the issue is. Here an example of a multi-scale instrumentation programme is suggested which is based on the UK Catchment Hydrology and Sustainable Management project, (Quinn et al., 2003), Figure 9.

It is widely recognised that environmental measurements cannot be scaled-up directly (Beven, 1989). The types of measurements taken at a point ($1m^2$), may differ radically from measurements made at the hillslope scale (1 ha), in small catchments (1 km^2) or in large catchments (1,000 km^2). However, some environmental measurements can be made accurately at all scales, for instance the water balance and nitrate balance, and these can

form the basis of a combined monitoring and modelling strategy for addressing scale issues. In principle, synchronous determinations of the water and nitrate fluxes made at the point, plot, hillslope, catchment and basin scales, offers the best hope of understanding scale dependent effects and determining modelling strategies appropriate to specific scales of application. The Catchment Hydrology and Sustainable Management project, through multi-scale sampling at all scales, offers insight into the causes and effects of land use change. Equally, modelling studies using existing GIS data and multiple time series data is giving excellent insights into multi-scale modeling approaches to suit many ecological and environmental issues. The global hydrological community is awakening to the needs of humans and the environment (and not just reservoirs provision and irrigation schemes). The International Hydrology Program will in the future seek to blend hydrological research with management as reflected in the new UNESCO HELP (Hydrology,

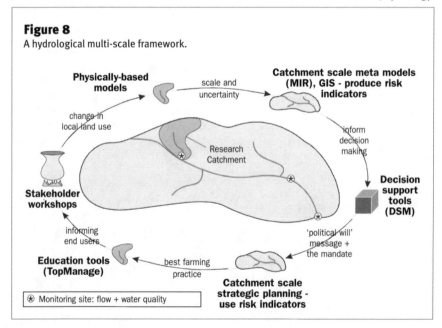

Figure 8
A hydrological multi-scale framework.

Physically-based models

scale and uncertainty

Catchment scale meta models (MIR), GIS - produce risk indicators

change in local land use

inform decision making

Research Catchment

Stakeholder workshops

Decision support tools (DSM)

informing end users

'political will' message + the mandate

Education tools (TopManage)

best farming practice

⊛ Monitoring site: flow + water quality

Catchment scale strategic planning - use risk indicators

Figure 9

An ideal experimental design to address flow and nitrate pollution needs, including the spatial distribution of multi-scale experiments and a recommendation of the type of model suitable for application at each scale.

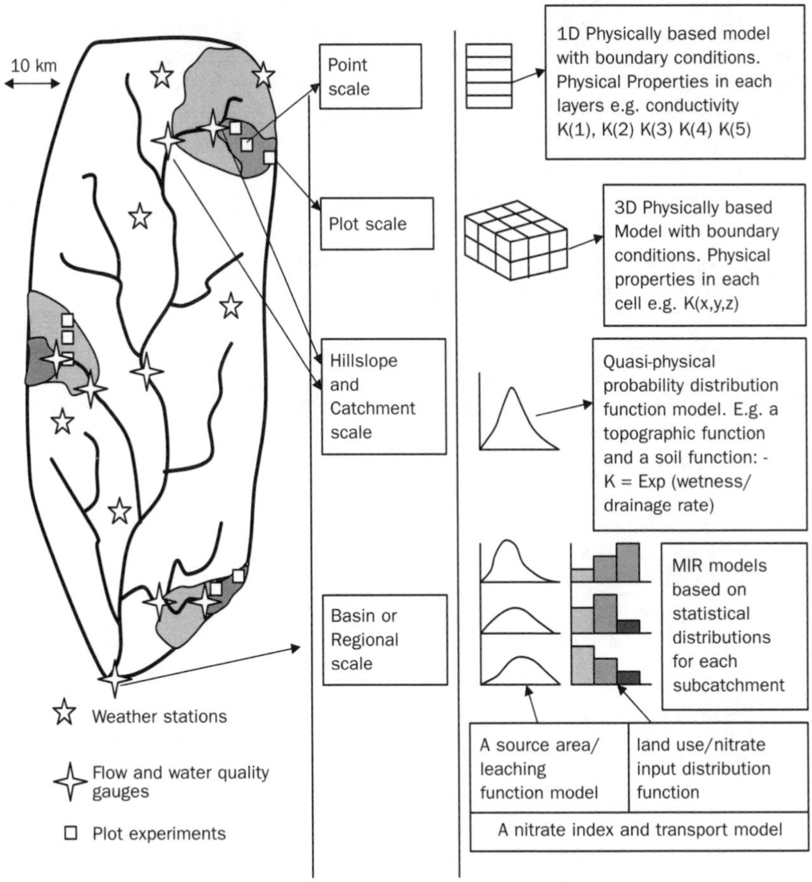

Environment, Life, and Policy) program which is seeking to address sustainability issues through catchment studies.

The choice of model and its parameterisation is now required. Here it is proposed that a range of scale appropriate tools are used. In Table 1, a list of tools as used in the nutrient pollution project are presented. First, physically-based models are run at the 'research scale'. These mod-els are scaled up minimum information requirement models that can mimic the output of the physically-based models. A minimum information requirement model is defined as the simplest, meta–model structure required to satisfy the modeling needs of the policymaker, while still ensuring that the model parameters retain physical significance (Quinn et al., 1999; Quinn, 2004). These simple models can be coupled to a GIS which uses an appropriate land classification scheme (Quinn et al., 1999). Figure 10 shows an example of such a scheme in the UK in which a combination of environmental and land management factors were ranked and presented in a simple manner within a GIS in the form of a 1km risk indicator map (Quinn, 2004).

At the broader policy scale and the catchment, region and national scale, direct engagement is made with policymakers to establish their understanding of the

problems (uncertainty and all). During the engagement stage a new type of tool referred to as the decision support matrix is used to show the nature of the specific problem and the uncertainty associated with it, and crucially also suggest management strategies that will start to resolve the environmental problems. The decision support matrices allows certain land units and land management practices to be investigated in terms of runoff and pollution risk and obvious problems of nutrient loading on vulnerable runoff systems can

Table 1. Scale appropriate modeling and decision-making.

	Model/tool	Method	Input	Output	Scale
Scale up	EPIC/SWAT/ MACRO/DAISY N, P and local runoff models	Physically based 1D soil/crop/ water nutrient models	Soil type, soil structure, crop type nutrient inputs and uptake, validated at the plot scale	Long time series of flow and nutrients losses	$1m^2$ -$100m^2$ or the 'research scale'
	TOPCAT - N&P Catchment nutrient and flow path mixing mode	N-MIR, P-MIR Q - scaled flow and mixing MIR	2N, 2P and 3 Q effective parameters, calibrated to mimic the above model	Long time series of flow and nutrients losses	$1km^2$ - $1000km^2$ IRBM scale
	P indicator & N indicator tools	Risk indicator maps	Quasi-physical models	Relative risk	Basin - national
	N export risk matrix and P export risk matrix	Decision support matrix	Empirical basis, or consensus of expertise	Likely positive or negative impact of a land use change	Policy scale - national or regional
Scale down	River management plans	Prioritized actions	Prioritised map	Action Plan	Region or basin
	TopManage	Flow visualization and runoff management tool	High resolution digital elevation model Simple site assessment or farmer interview	Likely flow paths and the impact of flow controls	Field scale
	Public education tool	Public engagement	Public, presenters, beer and sandwiches	Mutual understanding of IRBM needs	Individual or group of individuals

be highlighted. The mantra of the decision support matrices is then:

> 'Wherever you are in the risk matrix now, you can always move to a lower risk by changing current land use practice without lowering your economic income'
>
> 'It is more important to commence change towards good environmental practices at all possible locations now, even if the catchment scale impact of those changes are impossible to quantify. Direction of change is more important than quantifying the magnitude of the change.'

If carried out correctly, the policymakers using the decision support matrices will establish policy that encourages best management practice (within agri-environment schemes, new regulation and legislation). At the European and national scale, the simple messages and the mandate for change are passed on to the local land use planners.

Land use planners working at the river basin scale are now ready to implement change for their basin. First the GIS and minimum information requirement models should give good indications of where to target first so that strategic plans can be formulated. Thus as we downscale from the political scale, a series of land use management options can be considered and prioritised in space and time and these in turn feed into a river basin action plan. Key environmental strategies such as tackling hot spots of pollution and the creation of riparian management schemes (buffer strips, wetlands and exclusion of animals) can start at once. This can give significant benefit quickly and can demonstrate to the end users that policy is benefiting their own environment.

As stated above there is both a need to communicate the message to the end users and allow the stakeholders (farmers, industry and local government) to take ownership of the problem. Thus we propose using a set of tools that demonstrate the

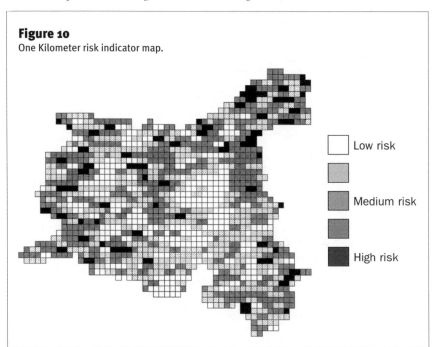

Figure 10
One Kilometer risk indicator map.

Low risk

Medium risk

High risk

key land use changes and reassure the end user that it will not have any adverse effects on their income.

The examples shown here involve three strategies making use of: 1) demonstration farms that exhibit both the problems and the possible solutions to those problems; 2) minimum information requirement models and GIS-based flow visualization tools to assess runoff and potential pollution (up and down scaling); and 3) decision support matrices s that reflect both expert and local knowledge to communicate improvements on current practice that can be made.

Whenever the tools are used, a high level of uncertainty is accepted at all scales of application. However, local experiments, physically-based models, minimum information requirement models, indicator risks map and decision support tools allow us to translate information and inform the decision making process. This is despite the inherent uncertainty and inclusiveness of scaling issues. Good practice in modelling must be to create suitable modelling tools that underpin decision making and that suggest realistic integrated river basin management strategies which take account of uncertainty.

Finally, the public engagement exercises are carried out to a point where the demonstration farms and education tools help the end user to both implement and benefit from the proposed land management changes. Often it is the hydrologist who learns more about integrated river basin management than the farmer does about hydrology and this crucial education can then be fed back into the catchment models and decision support tools.

The models and decision support tools. Now we shall introduce some existing tools to show how they can be used within our multi-scale framework. It should be noted that there are alternative models that could be used within such a framework, but we have deliberately chosen simple models as

this underpins the philosophy of communicating simple messages wherever possible.

Physically-based models can be used effectively at the plot scale (which could be referred to as the research scale) and within-field-scale experiments where the acquisition of data is appropriate to the structure of the model. Problems of parameterizing physical models at the catchment scale, due to heterogeneity and uncertainty, are reported elsewhere (Franks *et al.*, 1997; Beven, 1993). At the hillslope or small catchment scale, many modellers may decide that quasi-physical, semi-distributed models are more appropriate (Beven *et al.*, 1995), but even quasi-physical models may not be applicable at the larger catchment scale. In the minimum information requirement approach the simplest model structure is sought which satisfies the condition that the chosen minimum information requirement must first be able to mimic the output of whichever physical or quasi-physical models have been used at the plot/field scale or hillslope scale and route this flow to the catchment scale. Thus, suitable respect has been paid to the physical factors that influence nutrient pollution, but only the minimum information requirement models are used for policy making and communicating key catchment scale effects.

We propose that the scaling up of cause-and-effect relationships can be achieved by combining the use of the outputs from physically-based models applied at the 'local' scale (i.e. the plot and field scales) and a simple minimum information requirement model that routes and mixes flow downstream so that simulations can be made at any catchment scale. The sources of data needed for the minimum information requirement model should be readily available, for example from a GIS of land use and soil and a range of crucial field measurements (such as rainfall and flow). In this study three minimum information requirement models work together to provide the catchment modelling tool, the first two are a nitrate N-MIR (minimum information requirement) model and a phosphorus P-MIR which emulate output of the physically-based model EPIC (Williams et al., 1990). The physically-based models are first used to produce a number of time series of flow, nitrate and phosphorus at the plot scale. A simple mathematical function is then determined that mimics the output of the model for the majority of the simulations, providing the N-MIR and the P-MIR. The physically-based models can be set up for many agricultural and meteorological scenarios. This includes a long time series (eight years of daily data), differing crops and soil types plus, different application rates and fertilizer timings. In all the cases simulated (Quinn et al., 1999; Quinn, 2004) it is possible to emulate the N and P losses by using simple effective modelling parameters. These factors relate mainly to the volume and type of nutrient added and the propensity of the nutrient to leaching

and, for the case of the P-MIR, the entrainment of nutrient into the overland flow. Both leaching rate and the overland flow rate are generated by the catchment scale hydrological flow path model TOP-CAT (Quinn, 2004).

TOPCAT is a minimum information requirement version of the model TOP-MODEL (Quinn and Beven, 1993). A conceptual picture of the flow model is shown in Figure 11. TOPCAT-NP allows the N and P losses to be tied directly to the hydrological flow paths represented in Figure 11. Flow mixing will give rise to the final N and P concentrations. Careful use of the recession rate and the background flow rate allows the scaling of the flow to the catchment scale. However, it is strongly advised, as a prerequisite of integrated river basin management management, that recession rate, background flow rates and background concentration of N and P be measured at the catchment scale (and at more locations if possible).

Minimum information requirement

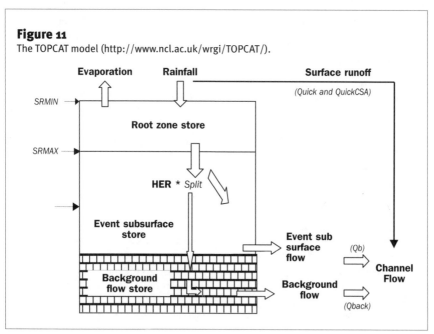

Figure 11
The TOPCAT model (http://www.ncl.ac.uk/wrgi/TOPCAT/).

models work well with catchment scale GIS data. In essence, the GIS data correlates with higher and lower risk land uses and runoff zones. These maps of likely pollution and runoff risk are often called 'indicator' maps and are a vital tool in the integrated river basin management process, where prioritisation of problem areas and strategic planning is needed.

The flow visualization tool presented here, TopManage, is based on simple hydrological flow path concepts and high resolution GIS-based terrain analysis toolkit (Hewett and Quinn, 2003, 2004; Heathwaite et al., 2004; Hewett and Quinn, 2004). High resolution data can be easily acquired for single fields (using GPS or LIDAR data). The resulting digital terrain map provides a close representation of the farmer's field which is input into a digital elevation model. TopManage allows man-made features to be added to the digital elevation model and the impact on flow accumulation software can be approximated and visualised. This allows any overland flow known to occur or any man-made features controlling runoff to be presented visually to the farmer or land use planner. In many instances farmers will back up the evidence presented with their own local knowledge, for example knowing the location of a hidden land drain. TopManage is intended to be a key educational tool to go along with demonstration sites.

The terrain analysis theory used in TopManage is based on the multiple flow direction theory of Quinn et al. (1991). This method differs from the single flow direction option available in the ArcView tools. The software is available for downloading from the TopManage website (http://www.ncl.ac.uk/wrgi/TOP-CAT/TopMan.html).

The key terrain attribute calculated in TopManage is the upslope accumulated area A, calculated in m^2. As flow concentrates, the value of A increases. Thus areas receiving large amounts of overland flow can be visualised clearly. If a design storm is used to give the likely flow depth, for example 10mm of overland flow, then A can be converted to a volume, allowing the capacity of a design feature such as a storage pond to be estimated. In ditch networks the design storm runoff multiplied by A can give an estimate of the total flow in the ditch.

There are two modes for the TopManage toolkit, the first represents the 'effect' of a man-made feature and the second maps the exact hydraulic measurements of a ditch or river (or levee). Features such as the small channels left by cultivation (described as 'tramlines') and land drains are only a few centimetres wide and are still sub-grid scale even at 2m grid resolution. However, it is more important to capture the net effect of the feature and not its actual size and depth. Thus a vector overlay of tramline direction or drain position can be used to manipulate the existing elevation values. For example, in the case of tramlines a sufficient number of lines with a decreased elevation are added to capture the *effect* (perhaps every 10m) of cultivation. This is achieved by dropping the elevation by 1m at the location where the vector crosses a grid cell. It should be clear that one is only capturing the location and the effect of the feature, not its actual flow capacity. Similarly, in the case of hedgerows or barriers the elevation is raised either by the desired height or by some nominal value. Adding such man-made features allows the potential impact on the flow to be depicted. Hence TopManage can be used as part of a runoff management plan (Hewett and Quinn, 2003; Heathwaite et al., 2004).

The maps generated by TopManage show how flow is entering the channel and what pollution it might be carrying. Equally, a series of local interventions that alter flow paths can be proposed and simulated. These interventions can help disconnect flow from ditches, and redirect flow to storage ponds or wetlands. Perhaps a series of strategically based buffer zones and ponds can be recommended. The area occupied by these features should be small and the financial viability of the food production system should not be compromised. Further to this, it is possible, given current technologies, to trap nutrients and sediments and recycle them to the land.

In all cases, the uncertainty of the predictions is very high and is explained in full. Therefore a series of shrewd assumptions are made. For example, for the case of an arable farmer in the UK we assume that it will rain heavily during the winter period on bare soil that has received fresh nutrient loading. Therefore the principal design component is management of the worst case scenario since our aim is to design a robust landscape. Thus pollutant load reduction, good soil management and practical interventions to show how flow is be altered, stored and buffered can all be proposed. Any smaller events should take care of themselves, as the system of protec-

tion is over designed deliberately due to uncertainty concerns.

Figure 12 shows a 3D view of a 2m digital elevation model and for a real case study site in the UK we will refer to as Field A. The field has steep slopes and silty soils on which cereal crops are grown. Fields of this type are known to give large amounts of overland flow when the soil is bare. Winter wheat is grown on this field and it has received bag fertiliser and, more recently, bio-solids and the P index of the field varies between three and five. Tramlines run directly down the steepest slope delivering water across a small floodplain into the river. A track with deep tyre tracks (which operates as a channel during storm events) has been added to the digital elevation model using ArcView. Figure 13 shows the resulting upslope flow accumulation map for Field A obtained using TopManage. The importance of the track and two zones of flow concentration can be clearly seen in the figure. However, it is also known that the farmer cultivates the field along the line of the steepest gradient.

Figure 12
Two meter digital elevation model for Field A.

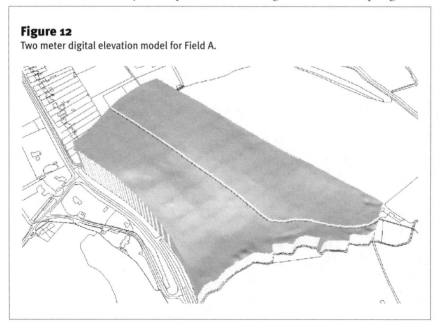

Figure 13

Field A with track (a) 2m digital elevation model (b) Flow accumulation, *A*.

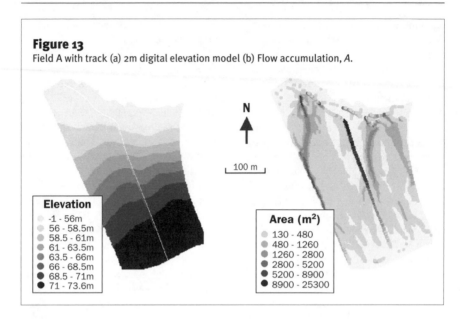

Figure 14 shows the impact of the result-ing 'tramlines' on the overland flow when they follow the topographic slope. Figure 14(a) shows the 2m digital elevation model highlighting the existing tramline vectors to show where the smart pixels will be lowered in elevation to generate map and Figure 14(b) shows the flow accumulation, *A*.

Figure 14

Field A with track and 'tramlines' following topographic slope: (a) 2m digital elevation model (b) Flow accumulation, *A*.

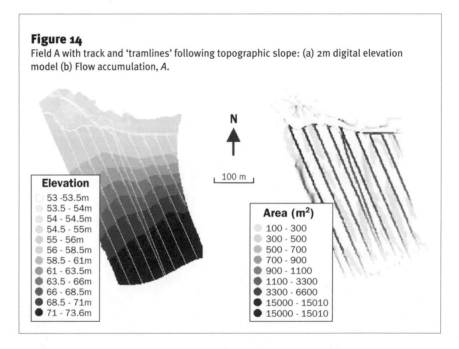

The catchment and farm scale GIS and models discussed above are relatively simple and are designed to provide workable support tools. However, they may still be inappropriate to regional or national decision-makers. Therefore decision support matrices are developed for this specific role. To date there are three decision support matrices s relevant to this paper; a nitrate tool called the Nitrate Export Risk Matrix (Quinn, 2004), the Phosphorus Export Risk Matrix, (http://www.ncl.ac.uk/wrgi/TOPCAT/NERMPWelcome.html) and the Flood Risk and Management Matrix (this work is ongoing). As an example, the Phosphorus Export Risk Matrix is presented.

The Phosphorus Export Risk Matrix is designed to enable farmers and land use planners to assess the risk of P loss from their land and to explore options to reduce P loss while maintaining farmer income. The aim is to integrate and prioritise the key factors controlling P pollution (Quinn and Hewett, 2003). The Phosphorus Export Risk Matrix has been developed in collaboration with stakeholders, including farmers and policymakers, as part of the SEAL project, a multi-disciplinary research project involving field experiments and predictive modelling at a variety of scales to meet the pressures on land and water resources linked to sewage sludge recycling to land (www.sheffield.ac.uk/seal). The Phosphorus Export Risk Matrix described here is designed for arable farming and targets the farm scale as the key scale where the greatest impact on P loss can be achieved. It is assumed that farms and catchments can be treated in the same way, i.e. hillslopes feeding channel networks.

It becomes clear that many farming practices are targeted towards crop and soil management that give high yields with the lowest soil nutrient surplus. The secondary and less understood factor is how nutrient pollution reaches the larger receiving channels. In the ongoing rural management projects, despite the complexities of the farming activities and runoff variability, it is possible to communicate both how runoff mobilises available nutrients and how it moves them on and through the fields to the ditches and hence to the larger receiving waters. Pollution risk can often be assessed just by asking informed questions relating to farming intensity and practice. This information, combined with the concept of runoff management, points towards straightforward

Table 2. Innovation in watershed management practices as opposed to traditional approaches (Schreier and Brown, 2004).

Traditional approaches	Innovative approaches
Creating impervious surfaces	Minimising imperviousness
Minimising vegetated buffer zones	Maximising vegetated buffer zones
Draining wetlands	Creating wetlands
Piping stormwater into streams and channels	Detaining stormwater in ponds and encouraging infiltration with infiltration galleries
Channelizing streams	Turning streams back into natural channels
Focus on point sources of pollution	Focus on nonpoint sources of pollution
End of pipe treatment	Source control
Focus on single pollutants	Focus on cumulative effects
Expanding water supplies	Controlling demand
Creating dams	Removing dams

mitigation strategies. The Phosphorus Export Risk Matrix includes a number of innovative approaches to watershed management, reflecting recent changes in practice that are a complete reversal of what was done traditionally (Schreier and Brown, 2004). Table 2 shows some of these reversals.

Figure 15 shows the three dimensional Phosphorus Export Risk Matrix which takes account of fertiliser application and soil management, flow connectivity and soil type (Hewett et al., 2004). Assuming that the soil type within a specific field does not vary then we need only to use a two dimensional matrix which can be visualised as the front face of the cube shown in Figure 15. This assumption is a pragmatic response to dealing with soil spatial heterogeneity, allowing the approach to be developed in this instance. The aim is to allow farmers to assess their current land use practice and compare it to alternative

land management options.

The Phosphorus Export Risk Matrix reflects both the P available to the transport processes and the mechanisms by which the flow propagates through and off the farm. Hence, the Phosphorus Export Risk Matrix identifies a range of viable mitigation strategies to control, intercept, buffer and remediate polluting runoff. The management of P losses is depicted in a simple form despite the complexity of the P problem.

The vertical axis of the matrix and its five corresponding questions relate to the relative risk of mobilising the P available in the soil; fertiliser application and soil management. These involve the P loading, the type of P and type of fertiliser applied, the crop and tillage regime and the soil P index. The first row of Table 3 provides the questions and the subsequent rows the available options. The higher the answer (2nd row = highest value, 7th row = lowest

Figure 15
The Phosphorus Export Risk Matrix (PERM).

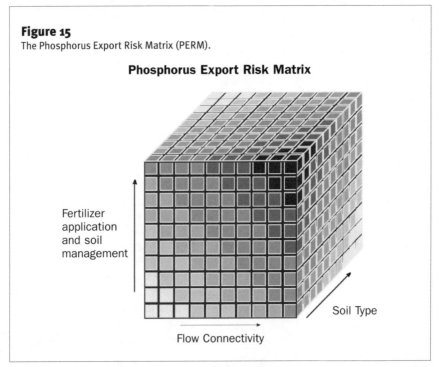

Phosphorus Export Risk Matrix

Fertilizer application and soil management

Soil Type

Flow Connectivity

Table 3. Questions related to phosphorus (P) loading and soil management.

Q1 Total P loading: How much P do you intend to apply?	Q2 Type of P applied	Q3 Sludge farmyard manure and fertilizer	Q4 Crop and tillage regime	Q5 Current soil P index
More than 20 kg/ha	Fresh slurry	Thick surface application in wet conditions, no incorporation	Bare soil, ridges and furrows, tramlines, connected to ditch. Low P consumption crop	5
Between 15 and 20 kg/ha	Bag fertilizer	Surface application, no incorporation, on bare soil	Bare soil, ridges and furrows, tramlines with small buffer strips or headlands	4
Between 10 and 15 kg/ha	Composted manure	Shallow and delayed incorporation	Bare soil or young crops with tramlines but using buffer zones and large headlands	3
Between 5 and 10 kg/ha	Sludge	Deep and delayed incorporation	Medium P consumption and 50 percent crop cover	2
Between 0 and 5 kg/ha	Very low application rate	Immediate deep incorporation in dry conditions	High P consumption in crop and 100% crop cover in early winter	1
None	No application	No application	Natural grass or forest	0

value) the further the risk marker moves up the vertical axis on the Phosphorus Export Risk Matrix.

The horizontal axis and its ten corresponding questions relate to natural and man-made features that control the runoff and buffering processes in the field. The first five questions, given in full in Table 4, are related to factors which *increase* risk of P loss; crop cover, land drains, critical source areas, tramlines, tyre tracks and roads. The higher the answer (row) the further the risk marker moves to the right.

Questions 6 to 10, given in Table 5, relate to remediation measures which can result in *reducing* P loss; hedgerows, buffer zones, wetlands and ponds and thus move the risk marker to the left on the matrix.

To help the user of the Phosphorus Export Risk Matrix (the farmer or land use planner) to visualise different levels of risk, two example fields are presented: 1) The field shown in Figure 16a (on the left) is characterised as having low flow-connectivity and low risk due to fertiliser application. This corresponds to a low-medium risk area of the matrix, adhering to best farming practice (Environment Agency, 2001). It is worth noting that only five to 10 percent of the field is lost to production and that 90 to 95 percent is under typical intense farming; and 2) The field shown in Figure 16b (on the right) is characterized as having high flow-connectivity and high risk due to fertiliser application, corresponding to a high risk area of the matrix.

The Phosphorus Export Risk Matrix is used in the following ways: 1) The farmer or land use planner answers both sets of questions according to the current land use for a particular field or set of fields. This provides a plot of the current risk level; and 2) The user can then change the answers to some (or all) of the questions enabling the user to assess how changes in practice may increase or decrease the risk of P loss from the field.

The philosophy behind the Phosphorus Export Risk Matrix is to give a *qualitative* rather than a quantitative result. What is important is whether a change in land use increases or decreases the risk, not the absolute level of risk. The principal mes-

Table 4. Flow connectivity related to increasing risk.

Q1 Crop cover	Q2 Land drains	Q3 Critical source areas (CSAs)	Q4 Tramlines	Q5 Tire tracks and roads
Bare soil September February, e.g. winter wheat	Full land drains in full working order	Bare/compacted /de-graded soil prone to capping and wash-off (100% CSA)	Dense tramlines in direction of slope. Connected directly to ditches.	High density with clear evidence of surface flow reaching the ditch.
Small amount of crop cover	Full land drains in reasonable condition	Large areas prone to surface runoff (75%) e.g. hardstandings, bare/compacted soil adjacent to ditches	Dense tramlines in direction of slope. Partially connected to ditches.	Medium to high density with evidence of surface flow.
Stubble or fast growing cover crop	Full land drains in poor condition	25 - 50% of field prone to surface runoff	Dense tramlines in direction of slope but large distance from ditches.	Medium density but with evidence of surface flow.
50 - 75% protection from crop cover	Partially operating land drains	5 - 25% of field prone to surface runoff	Medium density tramlines across hillslope, large distance from ditches.	Low - medium density
100% crop cover in early winter	A few old land drains	Up to 5% of field prone to surface runoff	Low density tramlines across hillslope, large distance from ditches.	Low density
Natural grassland or forest	No land drains	No CSAs	No tramlines	No tire tracks or roads

Table 5. Flow connectivity questions related to decreasing risk.

Q6 Hedgerows	Q7 Buffer zones	Q8 Wetlands	Q9 Ponds	Q10 Remediation options
No hedgerows	No buffer zones	No wetlands or water-logging zones	No ponds	No remediation
Low density of hedgerows	Very small riparian zone	Small wetlands and water-logging zones	Some temporary ponds seen during storms	Attempts to bind P into the soil or in ditches
Medium density of hedgerows	Some buffer zones e.g. 1-2m riparian strips	Medium wetlands and water-logging zones	Some existing ponds, some temporary ponds seen during storms	Attempts to bind P into the soil or in vegetated ditches with good sedimentation
Medium - high density	Some buffer zones e.g. 2-10m riparian strips	Large wetlands and water-logging zones	Small designed and constructed ponds to trap/filter sediment	Small specifically designed ponds/wetlands/filters designed to strip
High density, no evidence of ponding	Large buffer zones e.g. >10m riparian strips	A small designed constructed wetland processing all the runoff from field	Medium designed and constructed ponds to trap/filter sediment	Medium specifically designed ponds/wetlands/filters designed to strip P
High density of hedgerows acting as barriers to flow e.g. ponding	Large buffer zones especially in zones of flow concentration e.g. hollows	A large designed constructed wetland processing all the runoff from field	Large designed and constructed ponds to trap/filter sediment	Large specifically designed ponds/wetlands/filters designed to strip P

sage is that if you are farming there are ways of reducing nutrient loss, or "no matter where you are on the matrix, you can always improve." However, for the sake of example a nominal scoring system is assigned to the questions—in this case going from three (top row) down to zero (bottom row) with an equal weighting. The nearest integer to the total score due to answering all five questions results in a shift by that number of squares on the matrix. It is, of course, possible to assign different weights to different questions, but there was a conscious decision not to do so

in this case. In our view the way to improve farming practice is to move forwards on all fronts and we decided that weighting the questions clouds the issue and complicates the message.

In many cases of intense arable farming an honest answer to the questions in the Phosphorus Export Risk Matrix will give rise to high risk of P loss unless significant changes to P application, flow connectivity or soil management are implemented. This should focus the emphasis of change onto runoff management where more mitigation options are available. In cases

Figure 16

(a) Low flow-connectivity and low risk due to fertiliser application; (b) High flow-connectivity and high risk due to fertilizer application.

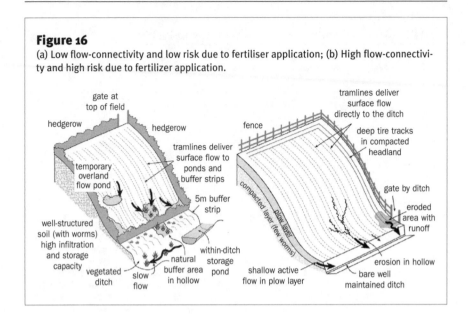

where there is low risk of P loss, such as land with low slopes and low rainfall, this should be picked up by the Phosphorus Export Risk Matrix. Ideally the Phosphorus Export Risk Matrix would allow intense profitable farming to occur over most of the land while carefully designed ponds, buffers and wetlands counteract and trap P and sediment. Ultimately a well-designed remediation strategy would recycle P back to the land or remove it from the system.

Figure 17

The effect of cross-slope cultivation on the overland flow.

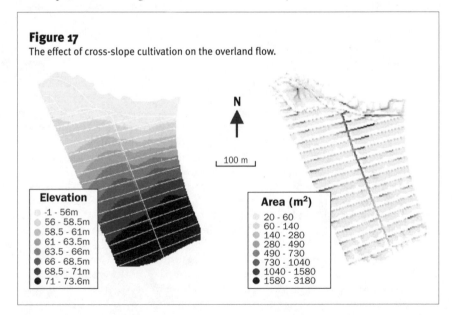

N

100 m

Elevation
-1 - 56m
56 - 58.5m
58.5 - 61m
61 - 63.5m
63.5 - 66m
66 - 68.5m
68.5 - 71m
71 - 73.6m

Area (m^2)
20 - 60
60 - 140
140 - 280
280 - 490
490 - 730
730 - 1040
1040 - 1580
1580 - 3180

There may be concerns that specific P management options may increase nitrate loss. For example, there is evidence to suggest that artificial drainage in catchments decreases P loss by reducing surface runoff, but N leaching may be enhanced (Turtola and Paajanen, 1995). The Phosphorus Export Risk Matrix presented here does not deal with management options that might conflict explicitly as it takes no account of nitrate. However, astute choices of land management options should provide a good combination of options for reducing both P and N loss from farmland.

Field A provides an illustration of how TopManage can be used to visualise management options and how the Phosphorus Export Risk Matrix is applied to a case study site. Figures 13 and 14 showed flow accumulation maps for Field A with the effect of the track and 'tramlines' included in the analysis. Figure 17 shows the impact of changing the cultivation direction. For Figure 17 it is likely that the tramlines will spill at the locations of high flow accumulation, which appear as dark areas along the tramlines on the flow accumulation map in Figure 17.

However, in fields such as this where the hillslope is steep, cultivation across the slope is not a practical option for safety reasons. Thus, in order to control the overland flow from this site it is proposed to create two diffuse storage ponds positioned in the natural topographic hollows of the field, see Figure 18. The ponds are designed to accept 10mm of overland flow. These storage ponds should only fill for a few hours or days and they are designed to allow flow to either infiltrate or percolate through the barrier itself. These features also give an opportunity to sediment out material, to strip phosphate and buffer nitrate.

Figure 19 shows the two dimensional Phosphorus Export Risk Matrix resulting from current practice on Field A. The

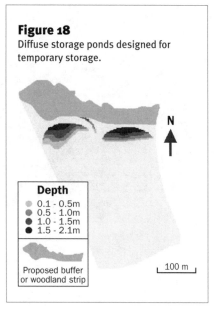

Figure 18
Diffuse storage ponds designed for temporary storage.

Depth
- 0.1 - 0.5m
- 0.5 - 1.0m
- 1.0 - 1.5m
- 1.5 - 2.1m

Proposed buffer or woodland strip

N

100 m

vertical axis of the matrix and its corresponding questions (related to fertiliser application and soil management) give the initial plot position shown on the left of Figure 19. The horizontal axis and its corresponding questions (related to features that control runoff and buffering processes) result in the final plot position on the matrix shown on the right of Figure 19. Changing the answers to some, or all, of the questions enables farmers or policy makers to assess how changes in practice may increase or decrease the risk of P loss from the field. Note that the bottom left hand corner represents the lowest risk and the top right hand corner the highest risk.

Tools like TopManage and decision support matrices s can be used within stakeholder workshops, where the scientists, the professional bodies (councils and water authorities) and the local end users (in this case land owners and farmers) can meet. The tools are based on field studies and hydrological theory but they reflect factors observed by the local stakeholders and in more general terms by the local policy maker and planners. However, just

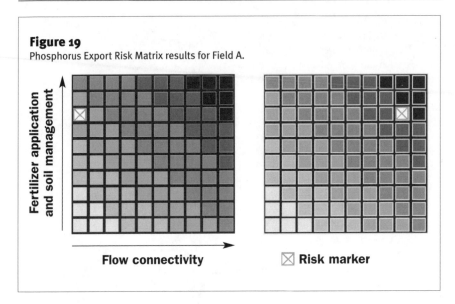

Figure 19
Phosphorus Export Risk Matrix results for Field A.

reflecting the local processes is not enough. The stakeholders must be encouraged to take part in creating the future land use policy that ultimately satisfies their own needs and the policymakers' requirements. Simple viable interventions such as: i) minimizing poor farm practice; ii) moving to best farm practice (maybe with an incentive); and iii) local hydro/engineering interventions such as creating ponds, buffer strips and wetlands can be added to reduce pollution, reduce flood risk and increase biodiversity. None of the above list should impact on farmer incomes but should greatly improve the local environment for all.

Once a future plan is agreed, trial areas of change could be proposed (perhaps within the research catchment). Physically-based models can be built to study the local impacts of changing land use. Meta models and modified risk indicators can reflect this at the catchment scale (uncertainty included). In the long-term, a push for environmental land management is obvious even if the uncertainty of the impacts cannot be quantified in detail. The policy-maker must be given confidence that practical land use change can be created and that the benefits will be positive.

Concluding Remarks

Increasing awareness of the need for an integrated approach to managing water resources has given rise to the concepts of integrated water resource management and integrated river basin management. This underpins recent European legislation such as the Water Framework Directive, which includes a statutory requirement for public participation. The Water Framework Directive represents an opportunity to develop a balanced approach to water management which would involve partnerships between researchers in science, engineering, economics and sociology and stakeholders. Periods of public engagement will be an essential ingredient to building successful partnerships and will need to involve stakeholders tied to all scales of water management, from the individual farmer or local trader through to decision makers at national level.

We argue that knowledge of hydrological processes and how they change with scale is essential to effective land use and water policy. A multi-scale water management framework is proposed that takes on board the ESEM philosophy, capitalising on current hydrological expertise and input from the social sciences and stakeholders. The models and tools within the framework are interchangeable and have been chosen for their simplicity and thus potential to aid communication. Stake-holder involvement is an essential part of the loop for generating robust decisions. The key strength of the framework proposed is that the type of tools presented already exist and are readily useable, meaning that the approach can be implemented immediately.

References Cited

Acreman, M.C. (ed.) 2001. Hydro-ecology: Linking hydrology and aquatic ecology, International Association of Hydrological Sciences.

Allenby, B. 1998. Earth systems engineering: the role of industrial ecology in an engineered world. Journal of Industrial Ecology 2(3):73-93.

Allenby, B. 2000. Earth systems engineering and management. IEEE Technology and Society Magazine 19(4):10-23.

Andersson, L. and P. Quinn. 1999. Natural rules of the game in water: A reflection of land use. Pp. 31-49. Swedish Natural Science Research Council, Stockhom, Sweden.

Beven, K.J. 1989. Changing ideas in hydrology: The case of physically based models. Journal of Hydrology 105:157-172.

Beven, K.J. 1993. Prophecy, reality, and uncertainty in distributed parameter models. Advances in Water Resources 16:41-51.

Beven, K.J., R. Lamb, P.F. Quinn, R. Romanowicz, and J. Freer. 1995. TOPMODEL. Pp. 627-668. *In:* Computer Models of Watershed Hydrology. V.P. Singh (ed.) Water Resources Publications.

Blöschl, G. 1997. Special edition: Scale problems in hydrology. Water Resources Research 33(12).

Brundtland, G.H. 1987. Our common future. The Brundtland Report: World Commission on Environment and Development. Oxford University Press, Oxford, New York.

Calder, I.R. 1999. The Blue Revolution. Earthscan, London, UK

Carney, D. 1998. Implementing the sustainable rural livelihoods approach. *In:* D. Carney (ed.) Sustainable Rural Livelihoods, What contribution can we make? Papers presented at the Department of International Development's Natural Resource Adviser's Conference, London, July, 1998.

DEFRA. 2005. Water Framework Directive," at www.defra.gov.uk/environment/water/wfd/faq.htm#10

DFID. 1999. Livelihoods approaches compared. At http://www.livelihoods.org.

Dunne, T. and R.D. Black. 1970. Partial area contributions to storm runoff in a small New England watershed. Water Resources Research 6:1296-1311.

Environment Agency. 2005. Public Participation under the Water Framework Directive. http://www.environmentagency.gov.uk/business/444217/444663/517208/525194/572350/?lang=_e

Falkenmark, M. 1999. The purpose of this book, in water: A reflection of land use. Pp.10-16. Swedish Natural Science Research Council. Stockholm, Sweden.

Foy, 2003. Personal communication. COST conference 2003. Cambridge, UK.

Franks, S.W., K.J. Beven, P.F. Quinn, and I.R. Wright. 1997. On the sensitivity of soil-vegetation-atmosphere transfer (SVAT) schemes: Equifinality and the problem of robust calibration. Agriculture Meteorology 86:63-75.

Gburek, W.J., A.N. Sharpley, A.L. Heathwaite, and G. Folmar. 2000. Phosphorus management at the watershed scale. Journal of Environmental Quality 29:130-144.

Grayson, R. and A. Western. 2001. Terrain and the distribution of soil moisture. Hydrological Processes 15:2689-2690.

Heathwaite A.L., P. Quinn, and C.J.M. Hewett. 2004. Modeling and managing critical source areas of diffuse pollution from agricultural land by simulating hillslope flow connectivity. Journal of Hydrology 304:446-461.

Hewett, C. and P. Quinn. 2003. TopManage: A high resolution GIS digital terrain analysis tool to study the management of flow on farms. 7th International Specialized Conference on Diffuse Pollution and Basin Management, Dublin, Ireland.

Hewett, C.J.M., P.F. Quinn, P.G. Whitehead, A.L. Heathwaite, and N.J. Flynn. 2004. Towards a nutrient export risk matrix approach to managing agricultural pollution at source. Hydrological Earth System Sciences 8(4):834-845.

Hewett, C.J.M. and P.F. Quinn. 2004. Hydroinformatics tools to aid decision making for nutrient remediation at source. *In:* Liong, Phoon, and Babovic (eds.) Proceedings of 6th International Conference on Hydroinformatics, June 2004, Singapore.

Quinn, P.F., K.J. Beven, P. Chevallcer, and O. Planchon. 1991. The prediction of flow paths using digital terrain analysis. Hydrological Processes 5(1):59-80.

Quinn, P.F. and K.J. Beven. 1993. Spatial and temporal prediction of soil moisture dynamics, runoff, variable source areas and evaporation for Plynlimon Mid Wales. Hydrological Processes 7(4):425-448.

Quinn, P.F., S. Anthony, and E. Lord. 1999. Basin scale nitrate modeling using a minimum information requirement approach. Pp. 101–117. *In:* Water quality: Processes and policy. S. Trudgill, D. Walling, and B. Webb (eds.) Wiley, New York, New York.

Quinn, P. and C. Hewett. 2003. An earth systems engineering approach to the direct management of runoff flow paths and nutrient remediation at source. 7th International Specialized Conference on Diffuse Pollution and Basin Management. Dublin, Ireland.

Quinn, P.F., P.E. O'Connell, C.G. Kilsby, G. Parkin, J.C. Bathurst, P.L. Younger, S.P. Anderton, and M.S. Riley. 2003. Catchment hydrology and sustainable management (CHASM): Generic experimental design. *In:* Monitoring and modeling catchment water quantity and quality 8th Conference of the European Network of Experimental and Represent-ative Basins (ERB), Ghent (Belgium), 27-29 September 2000. N. Verhoest, J. Hudson, R. Hoeben, and F. De Troch (ed.). International Hydrological Programme.

Quinn, P., 2004. Scale appropriate modeling: Representing cause and effect relationships in nitrate pollution at the catchment scale for the purpose of catchment scale planning. Journal of Hydrology (In Press).

Schreier, H and S. Brown. 2004. Multiscale approaches to watershed management: Land-use impacts on nutrient and sediment dynamics. Scales in Hydrology and Water Management 287:61-75.

Turtola, E. and A. Paajanen. 1995. Influence of improved subsurface drainage on phosphorus losses and nitrogen leaching from a heavy clay soil. Agriculture Water Management 28:295-310.

Williams, J.R., C.A. Jones, and P.T. Dyke. 1990. EPIC: Erosion/productivity impact calculator 2. user manual. Pp. 127. *In:* A.N. Sharpley and J.R. Williams (eds.) U.S. Department of Agriculture Technical Bulletin No. 1768.

Spreading Precision Farming to the Unbelievers

CHAPTER 10

M. Tooze

Geospatial technologies are revolutionizing collection, storage, and distribution of spatially related data (including earth science data). These advances are enhancing the decision making process in a wide variety of research arenas and markets. Geospatial technologies (Geographic Information Systems, Imagery, and Global Positioning Systems) have reached maturity in some vertical markets. In others—such as the agricultural arena—application and use of spatial technologies is seemingly stalled, lagging behind or patchy (in terms of extent of application). Early adopters embraced precision farming technologies, but it seems a critical mass has not been reached. Indeed, early adoption of these technologies led to a backlash as the promised capabilities were not delivered in some application areas.

Promises of increased production and decreased costs through the use of geospatial technologies have not been realized. Application of geospatial technologies seems stalled at the field level of precision agriculture. For example, although producers are installing yield monitors on their combines, the majority of them just watch the yield numbers on the in-cab display. Very few are using technology to its fullest extent.

Compounding this is the very broad user base that is the basis of agriculture is in most first world countries. There were approximately two million farming operations in the United States in 1996, producing everything from turkeys to potatoes (USDA, 1996). Diverse applications, combined with few effective ways to group together to utilize advanced technologies, spread the cost and difficulties associated with using spatial technologies, has meant slow adoption of these technologies. In the corporate and municipal world, there are no companies or government departments with that many users with such diverse needs. Advanced technologies are better suited to tailored specific applications. The U.S. government, through the various branches of the U.S. Department of Agriculture (USDA), tried to encourage adoption on these technologies through scientific research participation and workshops, and by building the required data infrastructure, with varying success. However, geospatial technologies are relatively expensive, and accessibility to geospatial technology is limited due to cost.

Geospatial technology has matured at different rates within different vertical markets. Geospatial technology adoption has been driven in the United States by a combination of federal investment through legislation and return on investment sought by corporations leveraging the initial government investments in geospatial data infrastructure. For example, GPS technology has reached maturity as measured by the high level of market acceptance ["Wal-mart" grade Global Positioning Systems (GPS)] for recreation applications; level of integration and embedded nature of technology in everyday use (e.g., On Star Navigation and motorist aid system) and upcoming embedded GPS cell phone technology. GPS in this case has been aided by initial government infrastructure investment

Figure 1
Geospatial application areas in agriculture (ESRI, 2004).

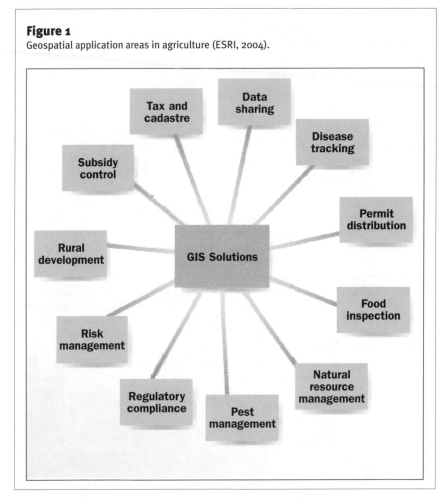

(Navistar satellite system), combined with the rapid drop in price point for GPS chip technology and reduction in size/power requirements.

Trends in information technology and geospatial technologies

Three major market directions have appeared in recent years in the geospatial or information technology (IT) world:

1. Internet connectivity is becoming increasingly common throughout the world. Internet connectivity, especially high bandwidth (non–dial up) connectivity is widespread. For example, in Nebraska, US, the majority of small town (less than 5000 people) and environs have broadband capability, thanks in part to government initiatives to brings connectivity to schools in rural areas and benefiting the rest of the community.

2. Broadband connectivity is rapidly being deployed, enabling very fast upload and download of large amounts of data. Internet based geospatial technologies Internet mapping services demand broadband connections because of the bandwidth demands of a highly visually oriented

technology. As broadband connectivity has become widespread, we have seen Internet mapping services applications begin to make up a larger proportion of the GIS market as opposed to traditional desktop mapping. Broadband connectivity means feature rich content may be delivered to users.

3. Movement from mainframe to personal computers (PC) to appliance. The early growth in IT was fueled by the massive growth in PC usage. Appliance based technologies are hardware/software combinations with limited application and scalability. They are built for a specific purpose…the necessary geospatial technologies are embedded into them. For example, yield monitor/hardware/software units in combine harvester cabs that perform yield monitoring. The appliance unit performs all the collection analysis and display of results, negating the need for a computer at the home office. By distributing computing power out onto the desktop via PCs gave users autonomy and reduced reliance on sometimes unreliable centrally served data processing and analysis capabilities. What this shift really did was simply spread the computing problems amongst all machines and users, rather than keep it to the mainframe administrator. Distributed computing has made the IT administrator's job more complex and IT in general more prone to problems. The latest move from PC based systems (comprised of a multi-task oriented CPU/ancillary hardware, with multi-task capable operating system, and task specific software) to appliances that are completely single task oriented. The hardware, O/S and task software are melded into one unit, reducing costs, and increasing simplicity both from a user and administrative standpoint (for example, rather than using a laptop, with a full featured, multi application O/S such as Windows XP and an email application, you can utilize one of the new wireless email communication devices

such as the BlackBerry—a task oriented appliance level device that performs one function simply and easily (email). Movement from server to workstation to PC to appliance. The transfer of technology from workstation based technology to cheaper, more accessible PC based technologies is complete. In fact, we sit on the verge of a major second wave as we move from PC based technologies, where multiple programs/application resides on an expensive, difficult to maintain PC to appliance-based technology.

The maturity of the geospatial market in general is difficult to pinpoint. Depending on the vertical market and application, the relative maturity levels of these technologies is widely varied. Using the following definition in agriculture GIS, the majority of agricultural geospatial applications are not at all mature:

1. Purely technical characteristics, such as reliability and ease of use. If the technology is not easy to use, it will not be adopted.

2. The convergence and stability of successive versions. If the technology is rapidly changing, it will not be adopted.

3. In terms of elapsed time since launch or critical mass of users. Attainment of a critical mass of users for a technology increases the value of that technology to all users.

4. The relative invisibility of the technology.

In general, acceptance of GIS technologies has occurred rapidly in the last fiver years. Beginning with the advent "desktop" GIS with ESRI ArcView the early 90's accelerated the G⁻ tion trend through the 90's. point, GIS remained a c⁻ frame based technol⁻ by government institutions. T⁻ to Micros⁻ the late 1⁹. the available the relationship of geospatial technologies with cheap and readily available PC based hardware. There has been a minor backlash by non-Microsoft vendors that have pushed back with Java based technologies, but by far ESRI based technology is the predominant geospatial technology. ESRI hold has been consolidated by the recent move of the U.S. federal government to select ESRI technology as the federal "standard" government wide, as opposed to negotiating with the each branch. This has been reflected in the agricultural geospatial application world, with agriculture specific products being built on ESRI technology.

Barriers to GIS proliferation in agriculture

What are some of the potential reasons for the lack of progress on geospatial technologies in agriculture? The make-up of the potential user community is very different in comparison to the corporate and municipal user base. Geographically separated single users, with little or no user community structure, define the agriculture user population. Compared to the usual corporate or municipal structure, agricultural users are left out and alone! Some producers may benefit from some vendor provided support from seed companies, co-ops and crop scouts, but usually these vendors' capabilities are minimal.

Perhaps the agricultural user should continue to rely on the academic and government programs that continue to push geospatial decision support systems? The majority of these programs have not been the huge successes predicted. There seems to be an ongoing issue with bringing new technology to market because of lack of operationalization ability at the research level. Experience has shown that a wealth of useful, but incredibly complex research available in academic and government research institutions, but the technology mechanisms are still weak, espe-

cially in the agronomy arena. There are efforts by research institutions to transfer this technology to market; however, the necessary jump from the research frame of mind to business is difficult. Some successes have been seen though the pairing of businesses with academic institutions to enable these technologies.

The agricultural geospatial arena is littered with application failures. In that regard, both researchers and corporations pushed the capabilities of geospatial technologies too hard by over promising and under delivering. Particularly, there was a bubble in imagery based application service providers in the late 90s. These companies offered field scale management tools, and made satellite imagery derived products the basis of management decisions. The applications were complex; heavily weighted towards imagery-based analyses, with few other conflationary data sources, and perhaps, did not really enhance what the farmer already knew about his field performance. Combined with the cost, the producer's return on investment just didn't exist. Using imagery based geospatial applications for broad temporal/spatial scales have proven valuable to long-term decision-making.

As the temporal and spatial scale tightens, the applicability of satellite imagery based technologies drops off dramatically in terms of return on investment, primarily because the cost of the source data increased exponentially. Throughout recent history, the application of imagery to farm level research has pushed past the limits of what imagery-based information can truly deliver causing skepticism about these technologies in the future. A myriad of researchers have tried to link, and continue to try and link reflectance values to a myriad of field based values (yield, photosynthetic capability, nitrogen levels, moisture content, etc), with only a modicum of success, and not any level of success that would encourage widespread utilization of these technologies at the current point in time.

Geospatial technologies in their current form are simply too complex for the average producer to gain maximum benefit in their operations. A brief survey of the online discussion forums reveals the typical issues that producers are encountering on a daily basis when trying to utilize this technology.

In the United States, the U.S. government is the largest data infrastructure provider. This is unlikely to change, given the costs associated with collecting and maintaining these data. The United States remains one of the most GIS data rich countries in the world, especially in relation to agriculture. Over the last decade, the U.S. government invested millions of dollars in building geospatial data infrastructure. Data infrastructure such as:

- Digital soil survey (USDA, Natural Resources Conservation Service (NRCS), Soil Survey Geographic (SSURGO) database, and Soil State Soil Geographic (SSURGO) database).

- Aerial imagery (U.S. Geological Survey (USGS), National Aerial Photography (NAPP), Digital Ortho-Quarter-Quad (DOQQ) program, USDA Farm Service Agency (FSA), and Aerial Photography Field Office (AFPO) DOQQ program.

- Terrain Elevation (USGS digital elevation model (DEM) 10 meter and 30 meter programs).

- Census data (US Bureau of the Census Topologically Integrated Geographic Encoding and Referencing (TIGER) data.

Figure 2

FarmWorks, Inc. public discussion forum from November 3, 2004. The FarmWorks user demonstrates the typical issues associated with trying to utilize a complex technology for his farming operation.

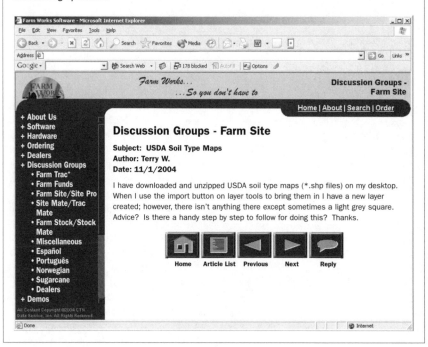

Figure 3

From the SSToolbox, Inc. public website, showing the many hundreds of data formats supported by this particular agro-GIS package. Unfortunately for every one format supported, there are ten others that aren't.

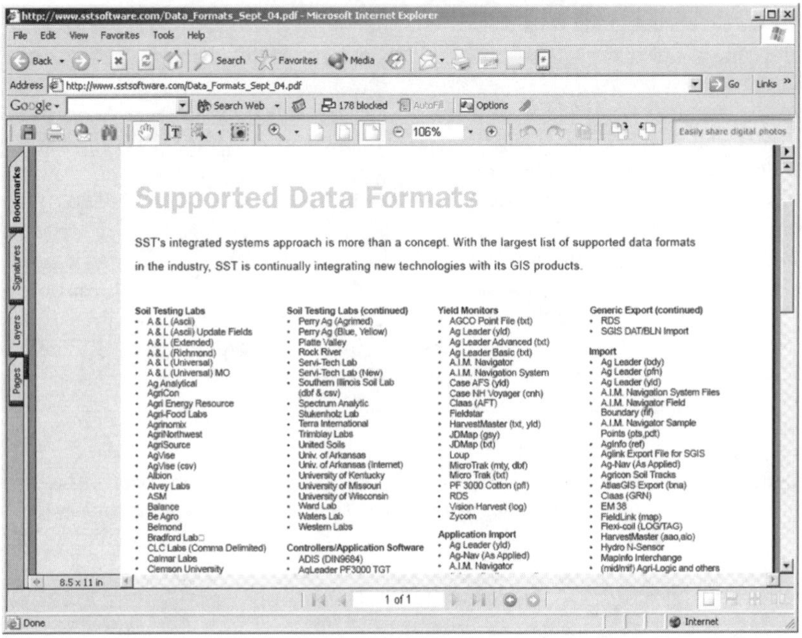

■ Reference grids (Public Land Survey System (PLSS), National Oceanic and Atmospheric Administration (NOAA), National Geodetic Survey (NGS) High Accuracy Reference Network (HARN)).

■ Hydrography (USGS National Hydrography Dataset (NHD).

These data are not simple to access. Complex websites designed for access by GIS professionals and academics for professional GIS users and academics. Data are provided in raw formats that require special processing capabilities (e.g., ESRI E00 format) using high end, expensive GIS software (e.g., ESRI ArcInfo). Data are generally not kept in typical geographic tiles that the layperson may recognize (e.g., by county boundary), but by USGS topographic quad, quarter quad, one-degree

blocks, or other divisions that may not be recognizable or translatable by the average producer/user. Despite the U.S. government's best efforts to implement a metadata program, through the Federal Geographic Data Standards Committee (FGDC), many public and for profit GIS users avoid the creation and maintenance of metadata because of the time and trouble involved in the federally imposed requirements. Thus, undocumented geospatial data is the norm, making it difficult for all users to identify the quality, accuracy and source of data.

Weather and climatic data are in worse shape in the United States. With weather and climate being the prime factor in any farming system, how can these data have been absolutely ignored in agricultural geospatial applications? The link between potential user (producer) and the data gath-erer (U.S. government, but increas-ingly, private enterprise, e.g., Meteorlogix Corporation) does not exist. About the only way a producer can get to weather and climatic analysis is through the cable TV weather channel, and www.weather.com. There has been no wholesale effort to make these data available in any kind of easy to use format. Some entities (e.g., the High Plains Regional Climatic Center) have made some progress by making ready-made climatic condition maps available to the general public (e.g., publication of the weekly U.S. drought map in local newspapers).

Embedding geospatial technology and making it disappear

"To be truly successful, a complex technology needs to "disappear" (The Economist, 2004). The electricity generation and transmission business provides an excellent conceptual technology path to invisibility. Initially, electricity was expensive and unreliable. Well to do households had their own generators, for when grid power failed. Within a short time electricity has been reduced to a simple proposition… you plug in and its there and available. No attention is paid to how that electricity was transmitted or routed, the complexities for supply/demand and the stresses placed on the transmission system. When was the last time you failed to receive power at an

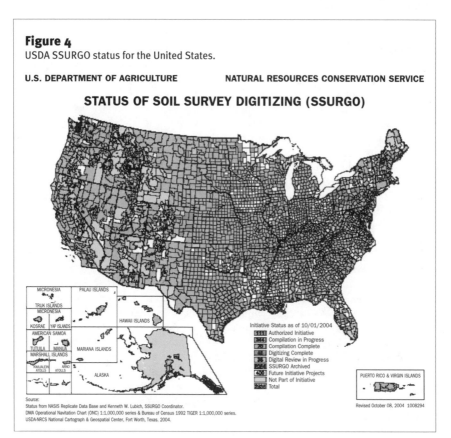

Figure 4
USDA SSURGO status for the United States.

U.S. DEPARTMENT OF AGRICULTURE   NATURAL RESOURCES CONSERVATION SERVICE

STATUS OF SOIL SURVEY DIGITIZING (SSURGO)

Initiative Status as of 10/01/2004
- Authorized Initiative
- Compilation in Progress
- Compilation Complete
- Digitizing Complete
- Digital Review in Progress
- SSURGO Archived
- Future Initiative Projects
- Not Part of Initiative
- Total

Source:
Status from NASIS Replicate Data Base and Kenneth W. Lubich, SSURGO Coordinator.
DMA Operational Navitation Chart (ONC) 1:1,000,000 series & Bureau of Census 1992 TIGER 1:1,000,000 series.
USDA-NRCS National Cartograph & Geospatial Center, Fort Worth, Texas. 2004.

Revised October 08, 2004 1008294

outlet because you failed to upgrade the power outlet software or make sure your power source was the right "format" for your application?

As geospatial technology becomes entrenched, we are witnessing an increasing level of invisibility in application of the geospatial technology in some markets. In fact, one might argue that the level of success enjoyed by technologies employing any kind of geospatial technologies is directly related to the level of invisibility the geospatial portion of the application. In other words, the user doesn't need to know the application is using GIS or GPS technologies, and perhaps doesn't even care that geospatial technologies are being employed, but is directly benefited through delivery of precise and correct information due to it. In many cases, it seems users manage to gain information from geospatially-enabled data in spite off, not because of the application of the technology!

Transparency of the geospatial technology may be exemplified in emergency 911 services in the United States. Government regulators predicted the explosion of wireless (cellular phone) 911 calls a number of years ago. Sending emergency responders to the correct location when calls are made from cellular phone was problematic. There are many examples of callers requesting help, but could not communicate their location effectively because they did not know where they were located. The federal government legislated new standards for wireless carrier's abilities to transmit location information, and route wireless 911 calls. In addition, the federal government enabled local government to add a surcharge to wireless 911 bills (collected and passed on by the wireless companies) to pay for upgrading dispatch systems with GIS technology to enable mapping of 911 calls. Of course, when the average person dials 911 from their cell phone, they have little idea that their call is being routed and managed by a spatially

based decision support system. They only care that emergency service is provided quickly and accurately.

Conceptually, a similar case for geospatial technologies may be made in agriculture. Research institutions are doing an excellent job of examining spatially related agronomic data, using ever more advanced models and larger and larger data sets and multiple scales. We are still not making near enough effort to transfer this research to the producer/user in a meaningful manner.

There are numerous examples of GIS technology making certain kinds of analyses and reporting possible in municipal government. The use of GIS technology is not readily apparent and users may not even be aware that the information is producing by a spatially enabled analysis methodology. A new application area for municipal government that exemplifies the movement towards embedded geospatial technology is in the economic development arena.

Local governments are employing increasingly technically oriented means to attract new business and investment to their towns and cities. A site selection industry that revolves around finding the most suitable location for business investment has sprung up in recent years, and local government is keen to cooperate with site selectors in the hope of enticing them to point new businesses and relocating businesses to their location. A lot of the information that the site selector wants to know about a particular city, and location within a city, is spatially related. For example, a manufacturing company may be looking for a ~10,000 square foot facility, within two minutes drive time of an interstate interchange, and located in land use zone designated industrial.

Moreover, they require a certain demographic labor supply to fill their employment needs. Fort the local economic development agency to search for sites and locations meeting these requirements made for several weeks of calling contacts in the real estate market, hunting down demographic and labor supply reports they may have purchased several years ago, and then compiling this into a suitable report.

The majority of the work performed to locate suitable properties and other information is inherently spatially based analyses. Analyses that a geospatially enabled application could very quickly answer.

The "LocateLincoln.com" application combines together a number of spatially related data elements, and allows the analysis of these spatially related data without the user having any GIS training or GIS knowledge. Initial location information about site locations is provided simply through the location address. This address is "geocoded" (a process that assigns an X, Y location to the feature). Other geospatial information, such as the location of interstate interchange locations may now be related to the XY location of a single

location, or all site locations in the database. Multiple spatial analyses may be combined through selection of queries involving proximity to utilities and services. These data are NOT maintained in the real estate database. This is a benefit because, for example, if a zoning ordinance action occurs changing the zoning in a particular area, there is no longer a requirement to update individually affected properties in the real estate database with updated zoning information. The spatial information and proximity analysis is performed on-the-fly by intersecting the property location with the zoning layer.

Results from the search are listed and made available to the user. The final result of the analysis is the same as if made through a tabular search, but the embedded GIS analysis technology reduces database maintenance while making searches much more accurate. Geospatial enabling applications does not necessarily entail training users on how to use complex technologies.

Figure 5

Example of an economic development site selection website (http://www.locatelincoln.com) exemplifying embedded, invisible GIS analysis technology.

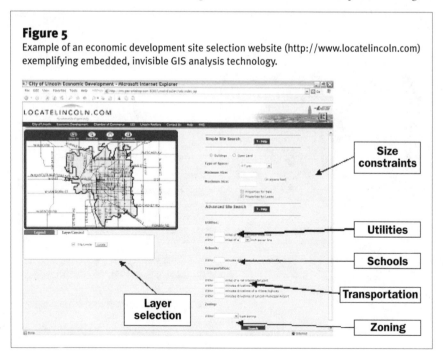

The second example shows how GIS technology can enable new, powerful geospatial analyses not previously possible without a tremendous amount of effort and understanding of soils physics and GIS analysis tools. As part of a pilot project for the University of Nebraska-Lincoln National Agricultural Decision Support System (NADDS) under guidance from the USDA- Risk Management Agency (RMA), this application was built to demonstrate a how one could translate a powerful soil analysis tool into a simple to use application driven by geospatial technology for crop risk assessment.

The application allows the user to simply delineate a field boundary for the target field, and then delineate a field boundary for the field addition.

The application takes the field boundaries and intersects them with the USDA-NRCS SSURGO dataset and calculates the individual soil rating for plant growths for each field, and changes in soil rating for plant growth to indicate potential increase or decrease in risk associated with farming those fields. Comparing these values is a powerful capability, operationalized by the simple application of geospatial tools.

Concluding remarks

Producers are increasingly becoming confused and disenchanted by these technologies. Concerns about complexity are warranted. These technologies are expensive, difficult to use, and not apt to make great changes in economic gains. Granted, there may be additional environmental benefits by choices made as a result of using these technologies, but the bottom

Figure 6
Results from geospatial site search.

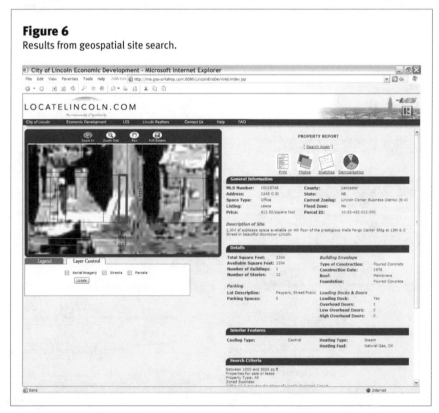

Figure 7

NADDS Field Analyst web tool. This tool allows RMA staff to quickly calculate the relative risk associated with farming at a particular location at the field scale by delineating a field boundary. The application calculates the average soil rating for plant growth (SRPG) (Sinclair and Terpstra, 1995).

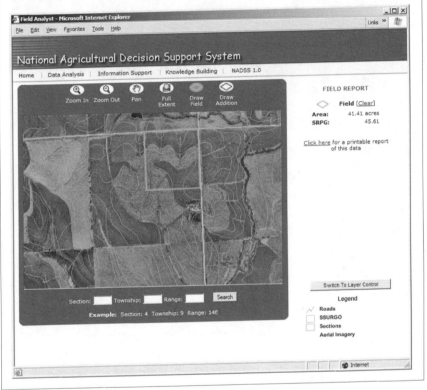

line really does matter the most! At the stage agricultural geospatial technologies are at today in the maturity cycle, there may be light at the end of the tunnel. As tool development gets increasingly complex, the agricultural scientists are seceding from the implementation side of decision support system and bringing in trained software professionals. As web-based technologies gain pace, the movement towards "Light Switch Geospatial Technology" is occurring. By adding "invisibility" to geospatial applications at the producer level—producers are more apt to utilize an application if it is simple to use and pro-

duces meaningful, trustworthy results. The former point is a better issue for the software developers to tackle. The latter is for the scientists to ensure through normal scientific discourse.

A number of other items must be successfully tackled to help this movement. Simplification of the core agricultural data structure (soils, climatic, imagery, and weather data) must happen to ensure the successful growth of GIS in agriculture. The standard method of distributing geospatial data—by putting up thousands of large flat files on a standard FTP server must give way to more seamless distribu-

Figure 8
Field addition digitized and risk factor change (soil rating for plant growth change).

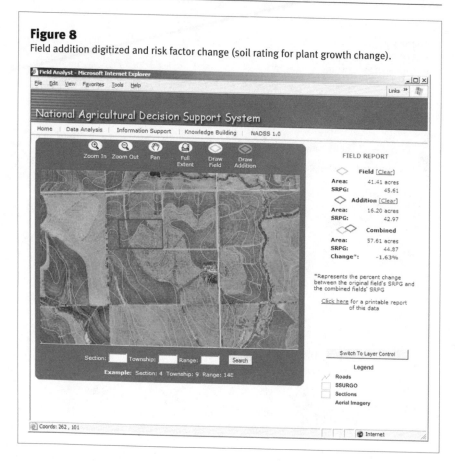

tion methods. A number of false starts (e.g., U.S. government STDS format) have hindered progress, but we are starting to see private enterprise step up to take over the collection and distribution of these data though communal efforts such as the ESRI geography network.

By removing the data layer, information layer and presentation layer from the client, the complexities of getting the technology to work is removed from the potential user, and placed squarely where is should be—in the realm of the system administrator. As Sun's Mr. Papadopoulos says, "You shouldn't build your own aircraft, shouldn't own them, and shouldn't rent them. Just rent a seat on one." This is not to suggest

that producers are competent with computers, or belittle their capability to learn...but surely their efforts are best spent farming, not figuring out the tools that are meant to help them farm. These efforts would eased along by accepting new commercial, off-the-shelf technologies, specifically web based GIS technologies that are now available for analysis and presentation. One might even argue we have come full circle from green screen WYSE terminals connected to a central mainframe, moved through the distributed computing era, with a PC on every desk, to once again, a centralized computing environment aided by internet connectivity. Finally, consider the operational aspect of your research. More often that not, funding agencies are being asked to account for usefulness and impact of research. How do you plan to operationalize your theory(s) and push them out to the producer or user?

References Cited

ESRI. 2004. Marketing flyer: GIS Solutions in Agricultural Government. www.esri.com

Sinclair, H.R. and H.P. Terpstra. 1995. Soil ratings for plant growth. Iowa State University Statistical Laboratory, Ames, Iowa.

The Economist. 2004. A survey of information technology: Now you see it, now you don't.

U.S. Department of Agriculture (USDA). 1996. National Agricultural Statistics Service's statistics retrieved December 1, 2004. http://www.nass.usda.gov:81/ipedb/farmnum.htm

Supporting Commercial Agriculture with "Action Research"

CHAPTER 11

P.S. Carberry, Z. Hochman, and R.L. McCown

Has our science matured as a source of innovation in farming practices? An impression is of a declining rate of emergence of new knowledge and technology options in these research fields. A quick review of papers at the recent 4th International Crops Science Congress (www.cropscience.org.au/) supports this view, despite discussion of technologies such as precision agriculture, decision support systems and seasonal climate forecasts. Anecdotally, this view was supported by comments of farmers met at the conference. If this hypothesis holds some truth, then where do we go now for those of us with these disciplinary skills?

Three pathways are identifiable; two are already well recognized by researchers who have moved into these fields of application and the third is emerging but may be a less popular option. Many research agronomists are now applying their science to addressing the environmental challenges caused or exacerbated by modern agriculture. In many regions supporting commercial agriculture, agronomic research has moved from a production focus to addressing issues such as environmental pollution from agricultural chemicals or land degradation from erosion, salinisation, or nutrient rundown. The key client for such research appears to have also shifted from farmers to policy-makers, defined broadly to include those setting research directions through to those with input into industry or governmental regulations. The fact that the so-named *First* Inter-national Nitrogen Conference occurred as late as in 1998 (Erisman et al., 1998) and addressed nitrogen solely as a pollutant is an indicator of the shifting emphasis in our profession. This research pathway is distinguished by a focus not only on the environment but also by seeing policy research as its delivery pathway.

Others have placed new hope for crop physiology in moving up-stream towards more basic research by seeking a stronger role in plant breeding, especially with the emergence of biotechnology and genetically-engineered crops. Even crop modellers have recognized a potential role through identifying and assessing plant traits via gene-to-phenotype modelling (Hammer et al., 2002). The increasing interest in basic plant science as input into biotechnology is understandable given the attraction of high-level, well-funded science, which has ready clients, particularly in the commercial agribusiness world. Here, the delivery pathway is relatively easy, via commercially-sold seed, assuming of course the ethical and political issues can be overcome (Frewer, 2003).

The third pathway is one that this paper addresses, one which does represent an alternative approach for how our science can contribute to better farming practices. The key distinctions from our traditional research, development, and extension approach are in the changed role scientists play in the research process, in the increased level of farmer participation and leadership in the design, conduct, interpretation, and communication of research projects and in the conduct of research within the context of real-life farms. This "action research" approach is distinguished by how control of the research is shared between the research experts and farmer practitioners, where the researcher is not an outside expert but rather a co-worker with other stakeholders in researching practical problems and exploring real-world opportunities (Zuber-Skerritt, 1993). This third way maintains farmers as the preferred pathway for achieving benefits from research.

In recent years there has been an increased call for researchers to become more participative in their research approach and, in doing so, to concede some trade-off in traditional science rigour in order to achieve greater relevance (Carberry, 2001; 2004). However, while keen to promote participatory action research as a pathway for the application of our traditional disciplinary skills (Carberry et al., 2002), the limited on-ground evidence for justifying such reorientation is a concern (Carberry, 2004). How a change in research paradigm will address the opening challenge to this paper, of whether science can continue to be a source of innovation in farming practice, is not immediately apparent.

The objective of this paper is to examine the possible future roles for both researchers and farmers in addressing the challenge of achieving innovation in farming practice through an action research approach. In doing so, we intend to first reflect on the experience of the research team of which we are members. Over the past 13 years, the FARMSCAPE[i] team has been successful in applying an action research approach to exploring agronomic management of dry-land farming systems in Australia (Hochman et al., 2000; 2002; Carberry et al., 2002). Its focus has been on exploring how better monitoring of system resources and consequent simulation of management options

may assist farmers in their management decisions. However, we are now asking where to next for our research and this paper will attempt to elicit learning from this reflection.

The second dimension to the paper's objective is to explore the role of farmers in research. In Australia, an increasing number of farmers are joining pro-active, organized farmer groups, which have explicit goals of leading and conducting their own research (McCelland et al., 2004). Examining this farmer-led movement and its relationship to traditional public research organizations is also a source of reflection.

We have thus interpreted the given title of, "Supporting Commercial Agriculture with 'Action Research'" as a request to explore ways of achieving greater involvement of farmers and other stakeholders in the research process. Two ways will be explored, first, how our own research team has adopted a participatory action research approach and second, how farmers themselves have taken on a research agenda.

System of system methodologies

As crop physiologists/agronomists consider the place of research in systems thinking and systems practice, two conceptual models have been helpful. The first is Oquist's (1978) typology of research (Table 1), where one's approach to research can be classified into four broad categories. These categories are well explained by McCown (2001a):

"(The first) three paradigms of research, i.e. (1) documenting contrived experiences (experiments), (2) figuring out underlying mechanisms in the production system, and (3) using theory to design best practice correspond to descriptive, nomothetic, and policy research in the typology of Oquist (1978). The output of descriptive and nomothetic research is knowledge concerning 'what is the case' in the world; the output of policy research is knowledge concerning best practice, with reference to theoretical possibilities and limitations. This dichotomy is often abbreviated (as) 'knowing that…' and knowing how'. The fourth research type of Oquist, Action Research also concerns 'knowing how' in practice. But instead of reference to *theory*, the referent for Action Research is the *experience in the practice situation*. Practitioners and professional researchers together conduct research, taking advantage of the so-called action learning cycle: Act → Observe → Reflect → Plan → Modified act…. Oquist (1978) claims for his typology that each type assumes and builds on the prior type, i.e. *Nomothetic* 'standing on the shoulders' of *Descriptive* research and underpinning *Policy* research."

Table 1 is helpful because it applies both context and legitimacy for the contribution of different research paradigms. Crop physiology, for example, incorporates both descriptive and nomothetic research as physiological processes such as leaf appearance, expansion, and senescence are closely studied, providing the insight required to develop predictive relationships for crop canopy development in response to genetic and environmental stimuli. Likewise, much agronomic research can be classified as policy research, where the initial agronomic knowledge on many technologies, such as fertilizer or tillage operations, was gained in small-plot experiments conducted by researchers with the resultant findings extended to farmers. Most modelling applications, whether addressing crop agronomy or landscape-scale processes, fall within a policy research paradigm. These first three research types are often termed 'hard systems' science because it concerns scientists creating knowledge through creating and manipulating objective representations of the world, e.g. quantitative descriptions, models, analyses, simulations, etc.

An important distinction here is between 'policy research' and 'government policy', with the latter a higher-order subset of the former. Most people think of government regulation when concerned with the term 'policy.' Policy research can be much broader than referring to decisions of government and it can incorporate how we as individuals make decisions—we have our own policies, which "regulate desires, will, intent etc., resulting in the consistency of action that characterises 'practice'" (McCown, 2001b). Whenever research is conducted to generate recommendations for 'best practice' it is policy research.

The fourth research paradigm of action research is distinguished by scientists creating knowledge through 'trying' to improve practice. This is 'soft systems' knowledge

Table 1. Oquist's (1978) typology of research, as described by McCown (2001a).	
Typology	**Description**
Descriptive research	Delimits phenomena within typologies of facts and events.
Nomothetic research	Attempts to explain and/or predict phenomena with regard to the external relations between a given phenomenon and one or several variables and constants. [Model-making research]
Policy research	The production of knowledge that guides practice, with the modification [in practice] of a given reality occurring *subsequent* to the research process.
Action research	The production of knowledge that guides practice, with the modification [in practice] of a given reality occurring *as part of* the research process.

because it is grounded in subjective perceptions and experiences of participants, which are then objectified through critical discussion and negotiation among co-participants. As stated earlier, action research can build on and utilise hard science tools and approaches.

A complementary conceptual model (Figure 1) is that of Jackson (2000) which describes a 'system of system methodologies'. Figure 1 provides a framework defined by, on the horizontal axis, increasing divergence of values and goals of participants concerned by the issue being researched and, on the vertical axis, by the complexity of the system being studied—simple characterised as having few elements and interactions, complex as having

many elements and stochastic interrelationships (Jackson, 2000). It's helpful because this matrix provides a context, which helps guide thinking about choice among alternative research approaches.

According to Jackson (2000), hard systems sciences are best suited to simple, unitary systems as problems are readily negotiated and research findings can be broadly extended. Organisational cybernetics, or complex systems sciences, address "elements in close interrelationship, probabilistic, open to the environment, evolving over time, subject to human influence and having purposeful parts... (but) are weak on procedures for resolving differences of value and opinion and conflict." (Jackson, 2000) Soft and emancipatory systems

Figure 1

Jackson's (2000) classification of systems approaches according to the assumptions they make about problem contexts.

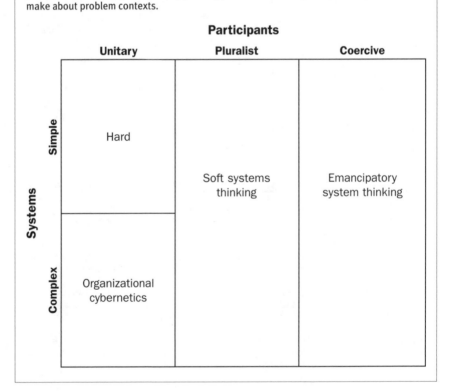

thinking represent approaches to addressing increasing participant views on the research problem, with a distinguishing feature being the issue of power of control over the problem situation.

When first exposed to the thinking captured in Figure 1, one is challenged by narrow scope of the simple, unitary domain that contains our traditional applied science disciplines. The FARMSCAPE experience (Carberry et al., 2002) edged our team over into the simple, pluralist systems through the application of participatory action research in collaborating with farmers and their advisers in addressing problem issues such as dealing with climatic risk. The question now is whether our tools and methodology can be effective in dealing with systems issues that are more complex and dis-harmonious.

The FARMSCAPE experience. Agricultural systems better equipped to deal with climate variability and risk, have been a sought-after research goal for many decades. Any success on this issue would certainly offset the opening concern of this paper of declining innovation in farming practices. While computer-based decision support systems were seen by researchers for many years as a technology-answer, their level of adoption by farmers has been disappointing (McCown et al., 2002). Thirteen years ago in Australia, this challenge resulted in the formation of the Agricultural Production Systems Research Unit (APSRU) (www.apsru.gov.au), the development of the Agricultural Production Systems Simulator (APSIM) (Keating et al., 2002) and the instigation of the FARMSCAPE research program (www.farmscape.cse.csiro.au). It is worthwhile today to evaluate progress against this challenge and ask where to next.

The FARMSCAPE research program worked with farming communities around Australia to explore whether farmers and their advisers could gain benefit from tools such as soil characterization and sampling,

climate forecast systems and simulation modelling. The FARMSCAPE experience, including its impacts and learning to date, is well covered elsewhere (McCown et al., 1998; Hochman et al., 2002; Carberry et al., 2002; Carberry, 2004). In summary, significant progress has been achieved in facilitating Australian farmers to use resource-monitoring technologies, seasonal climate forecasting systems, and simulation modelling to better manage their paddock-based crop agronomy.

In studying the FARMSCAPE experience, along with other related examples as well as the broader systems literature, McCown (2002) concluded that there are four potential paths for model-based information systems aimed at assisting farmers make management decisions under climate risk:

1. Use of a decision support system as a tool in farm decision-making for highly structured tasks—characterized by either providing novel information (eg. plant mapping) or useful calculation (eg. yield targets) on technical issues comfortably delegated to a computer or consultant;

2. Use of a versatile simulator in farm consulting—characterized by use of a flexible simulator (computer model) which can be contextualized for a farmer's specific issue and used to explore the consequences of his/her tactical and strategic management decisions;

3. Use of a versatile simulator in facilitation of farmer learning and development—characterized by the creation of insights into farming systems and their management by using the flexible simulator to achieve mutual understanding between researchers and farmers; and

4. Use of a decision support system in meeting external regulatory demands—characterized by using the decision support system to justify external requirements for management (eg. industry regulations).

By 2004, our accumulated experience, including formal evaluation studies, supports farmer benefits accruing from the first three applications. However, the notable deficiency in much of this experience has been its continued reliance on public research funding. Sustained success means that farmers gain real benefit from access to these technologies and so are willing to pay for such a service, likely supplied from the private commercial sector. Accordingly, our current focus is supporting the implementation of commercial delivery systems with industry partners, especially in the first two categories above. Such support largely encompasses determining parameters for Agricultural Production Systems Simulator application in new regions and validating its performance over an increasing area of application.

The first decade of FARMSCAPE was truly exciting for the research team implementing the twenty or more associated research projects which were all targeted at this central issue of whether farmers could benefit from access to systems simulation. It was exciting because of our discovery and adoption of the action research paradigm, which placed us into the problem domain with farmers and their communities. It was rewarding because of the progress made in gaining credibility and enthusiasm for our tools and approaches. And we were stimulated by the broader systems thinking and methodologies to which we were exposed and challenged.

Our team remains committed to following through with our efforts to discover whether sustainable delivery of systems simulation can be integrated into routine commercial services. However, the immediate task is largely a combination of technical support and market research and evaluation. Therefore, it is important that the next dimension of FARMSCAPE is elicited as a research question capable of attracting the interest and commitment of our broad research team.

The next dimension of FARMSCAPE. In thinking of the next steps for our team,

a starting point might be to populate the systems framework of Jackson (2000) with issues important to agriculture in Australia and elsewhere. Figure 2 attempts this and, in doing so, suggests that basic crop agronomy is a relatively simple systems problem being addressed by participants who are unitary as to the purpose of their research outcomes. In contrast, rural poverty in developing countries is extremely complex and conflictual due to the social and political influences involved.

The second modification in Figure 2 has been to superimpose a solid contour (-) to signify where the FARMSCAPE research program has largely operated over the past 13 years. Improved agronomic management targeted at dealing with high climate variability and risk has been our research domain. While we employed hard systems science (descriptive and nomothetic research) in developing and adapting Agricultural Production Systems Simulator to regionally-different cropping systems around Australia, participatory action research proved to be an effective approach in working with farmers on the dominant issue of climate risk, and has become our trademark.

In regard to the next challenge for FARMSCAPE, a second frontier (- - -) is suggested as a possible new boundary to our research portfolio (Figure 2). This boundary proposes a research program which incorporates more pluralism amongst research participants, notably by encompassing issues which address natural resource management and the trade-off between agricultural production and environmental degradation—examples include soil health, dryland salinity and biodiversity. Such issues are pluralistic, and not conflictual, if one accepts the assumption that most farmers agree with the environmental sustainability goal but they struggle on how it can be achieved under their economic constraints. This is a worthy next big challenge.

Figure 2
Modification of Jackson's (2000) systems classification to include important issues for agriculture.

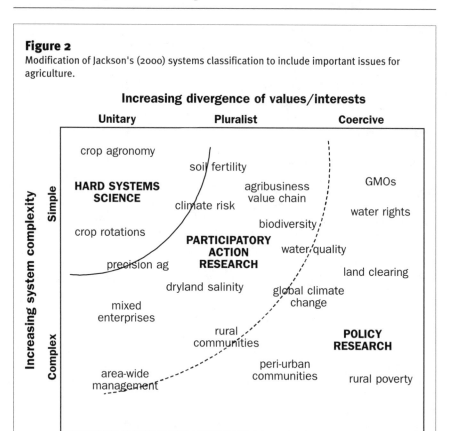

If most research effort on natural resource management seeks input into industry or government policies and regulations, then the distinguishing feature of this next phase of FARMSCAPE will be in adopting an action research approach to addressing such issues. The task will be to join farmers in their inquiry as to how to achieve multiple sustainability goals. Our comparative advantage in this research is the use of a versatile simulator, which can facilitate farmers learning about the consequence of management decisions on production and environment. This approach is well aligned with the third path for successful model-based information systems aimed at assisting farmers make management decision as identified by McCown (2002).

Over recent years, we have been engaging farmers on their natural resource management and strongly believe that a FARMSCAPE approach has promise. This is notwithstanding early experiences, which demonstrated the challenges. In response to Agricultural Production Systems Simulator simulations indicating significant deep drainage under current crop rotations for a particular farm, the collaborating farmer responded with *"this is only a model, so how do we know if it is telling the truth on this."* This response occurred despite this farmer and his neighbours having engaged enthusiastically with APSIM on agronomic management decisions over several years. Clearly, the APSIM was seen as credible and useful

for improving their agronomic management and economic viability, but this credibility did not transfer unchallenged to
issues of environmental consequence. Our
response has been to join these farmers in
testing the APSIM on their farms not only
against yield production criteria but also
against sustainability indicators such as
deep drainage.

The re-drawn FARMSCAPE contour
also encapsulates a wider clientele than
farmers by including the agribusiness value
chain and it touches on issues relevant to
rural communities (Figure 2). The relatively simple but pluralistic research issues
of interest within the value chain include
exploring the use of our systems tools in
the agribusiness service sectors of insurance and finance. Opportunities in this
area are emerging from our participation
in the current commercialization process.
Research issues relevant to rural communities, in contrast, are far more complex.
While not believing that we can cover
many of their issues, some are of interest.
These include better quantifying the interrelationships between rural towns and their
surrounding farms in terms of economic,
environmental and social indicators (eg.
Ridley, 2003; McCelland et al., 2004). It is
important that our research team is con-
versant in contributing research outcomes
with triple-bottom-line benefits.

The overarching research question for
the next dimension to FARMSCAPE is
really to work at the interface between
science and practice to learn how we as
researchers can intervene effectively with
economic, environmental, and social benefits. Our past research approach and tools
remain highly relevant, but the issues
become more complex and pluralistic. In
response to this challenge, our research
team is being broadened to include ecological (biodiversity) disciplinary skills and
researchers with social science training.

In defining our research domain, it
can be useful to be clear about what

we exclude. At this point in time, the
FARMSCAPE team is not concerned
with issues dominated by conflictual views
(Figure 2). In Australia, such issues include
adoption of genetically modified organisms (GMOs), access to irrigation water or
land clearing rights, all of which are currently dealt with by policy regulation
where research is but one viewpoint. We
acknowledge the important role research
can play in helping to form such policies,
but this role is for other research teams to
lead. Our comparative advantage is in our
implementation of participatory action
research with farmers and their communities who have agency to act and to change
their own practices. We will thus continue to build on our excellent relationships
with many small and large farmer groups
around Australia.

Farmer-driven research. Farmers conducting trials on their own farms are not a
new phenomenon, whether they are using
simple fertilizer strips or exploring more
complex issues. However, over the past
ten years in the Australian dryland farming
areas, there has been an emergence of
pro-active, coordinated farmer groups with
explicit aims of undertaking organized
research into their farming systems—the
Birchip Cropping Group is a well-known
example (www.bcg.org.au; McCelland et
al., 2004). In fact the traditional research,
development, and extension funding
organizations in Australia have not only
recognized the emergence of farmer
groups undertaking organized research but
are directly funding such groups to deliver
research outcomes.

A common rationale for initiating
research-focused farmer groups is both the
desire to have locally-relevant research
activities as well as some sentiment that
such localities were *"in a bit of a no-man's-
land"* for publicly-funded research, development, and extension effort. After early
successes, such groups have sought more
ambitious goals with a stated belief that

"leading edge growers will become the deliverers of research information and the marketers of regional innovation." Such groups are now employing agricultural graduates, developing research infrastructure such as long-term trial sites and laboratories, gaining sponsorship from agribusiness and industry funders and are producing their own trial result and extension publications.

Any review of these grower groups must start with the observation that such organizations have often created new businesses that attract and keep talented staff in rural towns. The existence of such organizations in rural Australia can have significant impacts on the sustainability of rural towns and on the social fabric of the surrounding farming community and on their membership (some groups have up to 500 farming businesses). The capacity to keep staff motivated and to keep an agricultural research- and extension-based business growing, when many public agencies and private agribusiness firms have reducing their on-ground research, development, and extension investment, is a testament to the achievements of the leadership and management of many of these groups.

It is difficult to critique the growing efforts of "farmer-driven research" in the Australian dryland farming systems given a lack of formal documentation. What is clear is that their research portfolio is dominated by simple agronomic trials addressing practical issues of interest to farmers in the immediate term. Much of this trial research appears simply a substitute for the research efforts that in the past were conducted by public agencies ('rates and dates') or private chemical companies ('spray and weigh'). The public agencies have withdrawn from such work as the environment has become a greater imperative and agribusiness has reduced their efforts to save costs. Under such circumstances, farmer groups appear to be filling a valuable niche vacated by others.

In reviewing a 1999-2000 report from four farmer groups, Carberry (2001) made a number of observations regarding their reported activities:

1. Many of the trials appeared little different from traditional research trials, employing small replicated plots suited to using Analysis of Variance to determine treatment differences.

2. A high proportion of trials addressed simple technologies, such as herbicide application strategies at rates different to those recommended by agri-chemical companies.

3. There was generally little attempt to interpret results beyond the site and season experienced in the trial under study. A number of trials were repeated over several sites and seasons, yet interpretation of results in this context was limited both by the trial designs and analysis tools.

4. Unexpected results from trials were found difficult to interpret. Such difficulties were compounded by limitations in data collection methodologies and design.

5. Speculation about results and their consequence was common, with many conclusions made on results from single trials influenced by the site and season experienced.

6. What quality checking was undertaken of the published results and interpretations is unknown.

While such a critique was cursory, without substantial review of procedures and results beyond that reported in the reviewed manual, it is based on the information, recommendations and conclusions as were distributed to 14,000 grain growers in Australia.

A more recent review of grower groups in Australia identified over 20 such groups supported by the GRDC[ii] alone (www.grdc.com.au/growers/res_summ/HAS00002/contents.htm). This report confirmed economic, environmental, and social benefits, which have accrued from the research, development, and extension activities undertaken by these groups and provided strong recommendation for continued investment in this approach. However, such recommendations also included an imperative that these farmer groups address issues of environmental sustainability in more meaningful ways than previously attempted.

The research-focused farmer groups in Australia were initiated with a strong focus on hard science approaches to simple, common issues relevant to their own region—they were comfortable in the top left corner of Figure 2. They created space for themselves in the research in Australia by attracting sponsorship and employing their own staff. As their research, development, and extension legitimacy and capacity has grown, their desire has been to expand their systems research boundary to approach the second contour (- - -) in Figure 2. To do so, they require partnerships with other research agencies with relevant disciplinary skills. The opportunity for action research with farmers and researchers joining as co-workers researching the key production and environmental trade-off issues can be clearly enhanced through the efforts of farmer groups.

Concluding remarks

Even if our science has matured as a source of agronomic innovation in farming practices, there remains a challenge for science to contribute to the environmental stewardship of agriculture. Many see a policy research approach as the means of contributing to this challenge. Alternatively, there are two modes of operation where farmers, and others in their community of practice, can provide significant input into agricultural research programs. Neither asks the farmers to become trained as professional researchers. One approach is for research teams to adopt a participatory action research process whereby farmers become co-researchers alongside professional research teams. This has been the FARMSCAPE model. A second approach is for farmers to self-organize into groups, which employ or contract research professionals to implement research programs prioritized and managed by the group. This second model is gaining strong momentum in Australia.

The strong commitment to participatory action research running throughout this paper, whether controlled by researchers or grower groups, is somewhat in tension with limited on-ground evidence for justifying such a reorientation as a pathway for addressing environmental issues. However, this reorientation is posed as a hypothesis and thus a challenge to both researchers and farmers. The high time-cost of action research, and its' reach beyond immediate participants are concerns which require attention.

We propose that participatory action research has potential to contribute to improving the balance between agricultural production and environmental quality through enhanced decision-making. While our experience in addressing such balance is limited at this stage, we see this issue and an action research approach as forming our research agenda over the coming years.

Endnotes

[i]'Farmers', Advisers', Researchers' Monitoring, Simulation, Communication And Performance Evaluation

[ii]Grains Research and Development Corporation (www.grdc.com.au)

References Cited

Carberry, P.S. 2001. Are science rigour and industry relevance both achievable in participatory action research? Agricultural Science 14:22-28.

Carberry, P.S. 2004. Crop scientists as change agents. *In:* New directions for a diverse planet. Proceedings of the 4th International Crop Science Congress, 26 Sep - 1 Oct 2004, Brisbane, Australia. Published on CDROM. Website www.regional.org.au/au/cs.

Carberry, P.S., Z. Hochman, R.L. McCown, N.P. Dalgliesh, M.A. Foale, P.L. Poulton, J.N.G. Hargreaves, D.M.G. Hargreaves, S. Cawthray, N. Hillcoat, and M.J. Robertson. 2002. The FARM-SCAPE approach to decision support: Farmers', advisers', researchers' monitoring, simulation, communication, and performance evaluation. Agricultural Systems 74:179-220.

Erisman, J.W., T. Brydges, K. Bull, E. Cowling, P. Grennfelt, and L. Nordberg.1998. Summary statement. Environmental Pollution 102:3-12.

Frewer, L. 2003. Societal issues and public attitudes towards genetically modified foods. Trends in Food Science and Technology 14:319-332.

Hammer, G.L., M.J. Kropff, T.R. Sinclair, and J.R. Porter. 2002. Future contributions of crop modeling—from heuristics and supporting decision-making to understanding genetic regulation and aiding crop improvement. European Journal of Agronomy 18:15-31.

Hochman, Z., J. Coutts, P.S. Carberry, and R.L. McCown. 2000. The FARMSCAPE experience. Pp. 175-188. *In:* Simulations Aid Participative Learning in Risky Farming Systems in Australia. M. Cerf, D. Gibbon, B. Hubert, R. Ison, J. Jiggins, M. Paine, J. Proost, and N. Röling (eds.) Cow up a Tree: Knowing and Learning for Change in Agriculture. Case Studies from Industrialised Countries. College Science Update, INRA Editions, Paris.

Hochman, Z., P.S. Carberry, R.L. McCown, N.P. Dalgliesh, M.A. Foale, and L.E. Brennan. 2002. APSIM in the marketplace: A tale of kitchen tables, boardrooms, and courtrooms. Acta Horticulturae 566:21-33.

Jackson, M. 2000. Systems approaches to management. Kluwer Academic Publishers, New York, New York.

Keating, B.A., P.S. Carberry, G.L. Hammer, M.E. Probert, M.J. Robertson, D. Holzworth, N.I. Huth, J.N.G. Hargreaves, H. Meinke, Z. Hochman, G. McLean, K. Verburg, V. Snow, J.P. Dimes, M. Silburn, E. Wang, S. Brown, K.L. Bristow, S. Asseng, S. Chapman, R.L. McCown, D.M. Freebairn, and C.J. Smith. 2002. The Agricultural Production Systems Simulator (APSIM): Its history and current capability. European Journal of Agronomy 18:267 - 288.

McClelland, I., A. Gartmann, and H. van Rees. 2004. The power of the group. *In:* New directions for a diverse planet. Proceedings of the 4th International Crop Science Congress, 26 September - 1 October 2004, Brisbane, Australia. Published on CD-ROM. Website www.regional.org.au/au/cs.

McCown, R.L. 2001a. Farming systems research and farming practice. Proceedings of the 10th Australian Agronomy Conference (Australian Society of Agronomy: Hobart, Tasmania) www.regional.org. au/au/asa/2001/.

McCown, R.L. 2001b. Learning to bridge the gap between scientific decision support and the practice of farming: Evolution in paradigms of model-based research and intervention from design to dialogue. Australian Journal of Agriculture Research 52:549-571.

McCown, R.L. 2002. Changing systems for supporting farmers' decisions: Problems, paradigms, and prospects. Agricultural Systems 74:179-220.

McCown, R.L., P.S. Carberry, M.A. Foale, Z. Hochman, J.A. Coutts, and N.P. Dalgliesh. 1998. The FARMSCAPE approach to farming systems research. Proceedings of the 9th Australian Society of Agronomy Conference, Pp. 633-636. Australian Society of Agronomy, Wagga Wagga, NSW.

McCown, R.L., Z. Hochman, and P.S. Carberry (eds.). 2002. Probing the enigma of the decision support system for farmers: Learning from experience and from theory. Agricultural Systems 74:1-220.

Nelson, R.A., D.P. Holzworth, G.L. Hammer, and P.T. Hayman. 2002. Infusing the use of seasonal climate forecasting into crop management practice in North East Australia using discussion support software. Agricultural Systems 74:393-414.

Oquist, P. 1978. The epistemology of action research. Acta Sociologica 21(2):143-163.

Ridley, A.M. 2003. The role of farming systems approaches in achieving sustainability in Australian agriculture. 1st Australian Farming Systems Conference. Published on CD-ROM.

Zuber-Skerritt, O. 1993. Improving learning and teaching through action learning and action research. Higher Education Research and Development 12:45-58.

Managing the Farm from the Producer's View

CHAPTER 12

M. McNeill

Many variables impact production agriculture causing decision making to be very challenging and complex. Agricultural producers are continually searching for tools that will make this job easier while providing more accurate answers. Due to the broad subject range of these variables, the producer wants decision making tools that combine scientific knowledge, historical experiences, social and cultural pressures, and the present situation to make an informed decision. There are several schools of thought on how these tools and systems should function to support decision-making. One school subscribes to the concept of experts formulating a model, system, or tool that the producer can plug in certain situations and an answer or decision will be produced. An emerging school of thought is a model, system, or tool that is more interactive with the agricultural producer. It provides for probabilities of outcomes dependant upon varying circumstances and choices. This type of decision support tool or system is usually most attractive to consultants, farm managers, and relatively large producers. This emerging school of thought is being driven by an increasing desire on the agricultural producers part to have more say and more participation in agriculture research. This is shown by the agricultural producer's increased interest in partnering with the scientific community to develop large plot on-farm trials. These trials are developed and supervised by the research scientist and conducted on the producer's farm. An excellent example of these large-scale trials, are the nitrogen and

tillage trials being conducted in Iowa under the supervision of U.S. Department of Agriculture and Iowa State University scientists. Some of these trials are conducted on one hundred or more farms.

During the past decade we have seen many decision support tools and systems created. Although some have not been widely accepted by the agricultural producer, others are quite popular. Tools such as predictive weather models and commodity-pricing models are frequently used. With the advent of geographic information systems (GIS) and global positioning systems (GPS), producers are using decision management tools such as yield and nutrient mapping to make better decisions about which varieties to plant and how to better meet the nutrient needs of these varieties.

A major question arises as to why many other decision support tools that have been developed have not had wide scale acceptance. In exploring an answer to this question there are three key factors that make a product attractive to the agricultural producer and impact everything from their use of predictive models and decision support tools to crop inputs and machinery purchases. These key factors are fast, easy, and low cost. Successful producers are very cognizant of the economic value of time. Reaction time in the face of weather change, market change, and equipment failure has taught them well. Getting crops planted, weeds and diseases sprayed, and crops harvested on time make up the major part of a producers workload. It is, therefore, very important to the producers that any products or tools that they choose to use, allows them to accomplish their tasks faster. Because the job of production agriculture is so complex and difficult to manage, tools that make the job easier equates quickly to financial gain. It is extremely important for decision support tools to be relatively easy to use in order for wide acceptance on the part of the agriculture producer. Just what makes a tool easy to use is often very difficult for the modeler to understand. It must be very understandable by the producers as to what inputs they must use in the model or decision tool. It must be designed to be easy to enter and retrieve data, as well as, easy to interpret the results. In order for a decision support system to be attractive to the producers, they must perceive it to be of good value. The necessity of being a low cost producer has been deeply engraved in their thought processes. Pricing of decision management tools or decision support systems is very important to their acceptance. If priced too low, they will be perceived to be of low value. If priced too high, the producers will be inclined to think they can get along without using the product. This economic factor makes it necessary to design the tool or model to answer the pertinent questions only. To adequately answer the producers questions, the system should not be so detailed that it gets out of the "good value range" or so general that it becomes only a guideline support tool. Site specific or situation specific support tools are needed to replace the old guideline tools.

In addition to the three trigger factors of fast, easy, and low cost, a decision tool or decision support system must have sustainability factors built in. This provides the tool or model with the environmental protection factors necessary for it to be effective and acceptable to all of society. This simply means that decisions or solutions produced by the decision tool or decision support system will endure for-

ever with no negative impact. This added dimension poses a large challenge for any tool or system that is developed. Training for modelers in this area is often deficient or non-existent.

An important acceptance factor of decision support systems is accountability. A major concern voiced by the agricultural producer is, "Can I trust the results when I use these tools?" This is a serious concern for the tool developer and the modeler. Legal fees and insurance costs, as well as concern over lawsuits, have in some instances, prevented further development of some excellent tools. A better solution to this problem must be developed in order for new products to rapidly develop. An intermediate step emerging appears to be the increased use of the consultant who acts as an interpreter between the system developer and the end-user. This has an advantage in that the consultant takes the time necessary to gain knowledge of complex tools. This occurs because the consultant may use the tool or system on a more frequent basis, where as the agricultural producer may use it infrequently and would be required to relearn many of the aspects of the system. In addition, consultants may have a higher level of training enabling them to more quickly adapt to a complex tool or system and be able to communicate the results to the producer in terms the producer can understand. This buffer not only improves the effectiveness of the tool, but also adds accountability in the eyes of the producer. The producers feel that they have a name and a face for accountability making the information more personal in nature and providing the site specific and situation specific factors that are needed.

From a producer's point of view, there are several elements necessary in creating a useful management decision tool. An example of this would be a short-term weather predictive tool. It must have the elements of fast, easy, and low cost as well as sustainability built in. For example, a visual presentation like a live weather radar map would provide information on the current weather situation plus predict the weather system movement. It must also include factors that might change the predictive model. A visual presentation such as geospatial maps with an attached probability of each scenario occurring would be very helpful. This type of tool will provide both the general and site specific information needed to definitively answer producer's questions. For long-term weather forecasting, predictive models need to be presented in a visual format with the factors affecting the various scenarios and their probability of occurrence included in the tool. For example, models indicating the impact of changing Pacific Ocean temperatures on Midwestern U.S. rainfall patterns would be very useful to the producer in choosing crop varieties to plant for the coming season.

Disease and insect pest forecasting is another area in which decision management tools can play an important role. An effective tool for disease or insect forecasting is a frequently updated map showing the location and intensity or severity of the problem, as well as the direction of movement of the disease or insect infestation over time. In addition to this visual presentation, a database providing detailed control procedures is necessary. A good example of this type of tool is the website developed by a group of independent crop consultants in Iowa in partnership with the Iowa Soybean Association (www.isa-farmnet.com). The crop consultants thoroughly scout and document selected fields across the state throughout the growing season for crop production problems. This information is sent to a collection center where the data is processed and put on to maps. By viewing these maps, the agricultural producers can make decisions as to the appropriate action necessary for them to take. This type of decision-making tool

takes a major coordinated effort on the part of many people across many disciplines. Cooperation across many fields of interest will become extremely important as new decision making tools are developed. In addition to this current situation tool, a long range forecast tool is also extremely useful. A long-range decision tool would include maps showing the potential regions that disease or insect pests may spread to, as well as the probability of severity and rate of spread. A database with information on long-term control measures such as genetic resistance, crop rotations, and tillage practices needs are also helpful.

Nutrient management decision support tools have become popular with the development of the new GIS/GPS technology. They are more widely accepted and more rapidly adopted by the agricultural producer than many of the other decision support tools. This rapid acceptance is partially the result of the GIS/GPS gadgets associated with the use of these tools attracting the producers interest, as well as the broad use by agri-industry as a sales and marketing tool. A good decision support tool for nutrient management needs to have four basic components. A visual presentation of site-specific nutrient availability information with a corresponding site-specific fertilizer spread map is useful. Also helpful are site-specific maps designating environmentally sensitive areas. These maps help alert the producer to special environmental protection actions needed in the specified areas. This is especially useful when nutrient application equipment is programmed to automatically turn off when entering an environmentally sensitive area.

The capability to overlay map data from several sources improves the value of any decision support tool. When determining the appropriate amount of nitrogen to apply, it is helpful to be able to overlay information from soil type maps, late spring nitrate test maps, precipitation maps, historical crop yield, stalk nitrate maps, and predictive climatic maps. This capability improves the agricultural producer's ability to make faster and more accurate decisions. An extensive database which includes information on crop nutrient requirements, nutrient sources, fertilizer application systems, and the environmental impact of these will complete this decision support system.

Marketing decision support tools are plentiful and range from the use of historical charting of market cycles to models using current supply and demand data, which include variables affecting supply and demand. These tools have proven to be challenging for most agricultural producers. Factors and interactions among these factors affecting commodity prices are extremely complex. As a result many producers turn to consulting experts that work solely in the area of commodity marketing for help in making marketing decisions. The decisions produced from this approach are aimed at getting the best possible price of a commodity for the producer. At first glance, this appears to be an appropriate goal. However, a good marketing decision support tool must take into consideration not only the complex market factors but also the goals and financial risk taking ability of the producer. It is also important to consider spot markets that are available to producers, as well as the impact of rapidly changing consumer desires.

A constant challenge for the agricultural producer is selecting the appropriate inputs for optimum production. These inputs involve seed, chemical, fertilizer, fuel, and equipment selections. The producer's choices are affected by numerous factors like cost, climate interactions, social and peer pressure, environmental limitations, and product availability. A decision support tool that encompasses all of these factors and factor interactions would be fantastic. Achieving development of this tool will be an arduous task. This is especially true if it is to be fast and easy to use, as well as low cost. However, development of this type of tool will make the producer's task easier and more accurate, and help build in environmental safeguards to make agricultural production truly sustainable. It will also provide a vehicle for earlier adaptation of improvements in agricultural production by making the producer more readily aware of new technology and farming systems.

In summary, decision support tools and decision support systems for agriculture are becoming more popular with producers. Tools or systems that are more interactive with the producer allowing them to acquire increased site or situation specific information will be in increased demand. Improved acceptance of newly developed tools will come about by making them faster and easier to use, as well as low cost for the producer. Building in concepts that make agricultural production sustainable is very important. For the more complex tool or system, marketing is best directed toward consultants with expertise and experience in agricultural production.

Equipment Achieves Profitability and Environmental Goals

CHAPTER 13

N.C. Wollenhaupt

Farmers around the world continue to make changes in their farming practices in order to remain profitable and sustainable. There has been a growing recognition that some historical food and fiber production practices are not resource sustainable which have resulted in soil and water degradation. Decision support systems created by researchers have played an important role in identifying the processes that lead to resource degradation, and subsequently recommendations for changing farming practices.

Conservation tillage

For example, conservation tillage practices that maintain crop residues on the soil surface have greatly reduced detachment and transport of soil particles (soil erosion). I speculate that very few farmers actually adopted conservation tillage practices because they better understood the "science" of soil erosion. The complex erosion prediction models were summarized into the simplified Revised Universal Soil Loss Equation (RUSLE). This decision support tool was understandable and defendable by most applied science educators. Educational efforts with pictures of raindrops detaching soil particles, rills and gullies, and drainage ditches filled with sediment were effective visual summaries of the problem. While use of the RUSLE model lead to recommendations for keeping crop residues on the soil surface, many farmers learned from experience that farming with tillage and planting equipment that kept crop residues on the soil surface was simply more profitable.

One of the key developments leading to adoption of crop residue management was the modification and/or creation of new tillage and seeding equipment. Without the proper farm equipment, the economic and environmental benefits would not have been achieved.

I believe the conservation tillage example demonstrates that environmental quality benefits can be achieved without sacrificing production profitability. Appropriate equipment is essential for new practice adoption, leading to improvements in environmental quality.

Application equipment and nutrient management

Equipment manufacturers have historically responded with modified or new machines after a new practice is legislated or recommended. An exception has been the integration of a variety of new technologies to enable site-specific application of nutrients. Variable rate application of single and multiple fertilizer products is a common commercially offered practice. Site-specific nutrient application is profit driven and also has potential environmental benefits. Decision support system tools are used to manage large amounts of data and transform the information into site-specific nutrient recommendations that machines can interpret and apply. In turn, the application machines record the actual application rates. In the case where biosolids are applied, the ratio of nutrients applied in the product usually does not match plant requirements. The final nutrient solution may require a second run through the decision support systems to compute the remaining nutrient requirements, which are also machine applied.

Unlike tillage and planting decisions, nutrient management decisions often are not made directly by a farmer. Adoption of new nutrient management practices is strongly influenced by the ability of the private industry consultant, contractor, and/or agriculture retailer to convince the farmer/customer that the practice is in the farmer's best financial interest, and to some extent, lowest risk. Increasingly, these practices require more expense in gathering decision support system data like soil tests and spatial maps (time and supplies), and more sophisticated application machines. Thus adoption may be constrained by the additional cost to implement the practice. While farmers may receive incentive payments to adopt a new practice, the costs for making the practice adoption a reality is taken on by "industry."

Other constraints may also exist including logistics in moving a product like animal waste, small window of application, and placement restrictions like the need to maintain crop residue ground cover after application. Regardless of the decision process that leads to a nutrient management strategy, the "best management practice" decision including what products, how much, where applied, and when applied is implemented through one or more machines in a farm field.

Treating animal biosolids as a nutrient source on a farm

The following example is presented to show how decision support system tools and application technologies can be used in a sustainable nutrient management business. The objective is to improve widely accepted traditional nutrient management practices by using readily available field condition descriptive data, refinements in crop nutrient recommendations, new best management application rules, and new equipment application technologies.

Example scenario. A mixed grain and livestock farm consists of seven farm fields totaling 101 acres and has a livestock facility producing animal biosolids in the form of slurry. Detailed research studies and decision support system tool models lead to the following recommended practices for animal waste:

■ apply N, P, and K according to soil test levels and estimated crop removal

■ inject or incorporate

■ maintain 30 percent crop residues to control nutrient losses from soil erosion

■ do not apply on soils with slopes greater than 8 percent when the ground is frozen

■ do not apply biosolids within 300 feet of a watercourse.

The information available for crop nutrient planning includes:

■ geo-referenced field boundaries (polygon)

■ geo-referenced soil sample data (points)

■ digital soil survey (polygon)

■ digital stream buffer map (line)

■ crop nutrient recommendations from a university extension guide.

Software. In this example, a commercial customized geographic information system for mapping and data management, SGIS, is used to manage the point, line, and polygon data. This application uses ESRI Arc 8 Object GIS technologies, a Microsoft Access database for organization of relational and spatial data, and a custom application called Prox to code the decision support rules. Templates and import wizards are used to facilitate the import and management of data. SGIS is designed for professional Agronomists who need to make nutrient management recommendations using a variety of disparate data sources. Quick and repetitive data processing on many farm fields on a daily basis is a critical requirement for their businesses.

Outputs include a variety of nutrient status maps, maps of managed attributes such as yield data, and product application maps and reports.

Figure 1 shows a map view from SGIS for the geo-referenced field boundaries, digital soil survey, soil sample locations, and a stream overlain on a geo-referenced photo. The layers are classified and themed to show the location of steeply sloping soils, soil test P levels and the location of a 300-foot buffer around a stream. These layers are managed in SGIS to facilitate easy access and quick display and report printing.

Nutrient management recommendations vary from region to region based on field research, local experience, and customer crop production objectives. SGIS includes a software module (Prox) that allows customers to build a decision support tool for nutrient recommendations. The application takes advantage of SGIS managed data as well as external data sources. The equation syntax structure is a logical, "If… (condition)…Then…Apply" (Figure 2). The "If" statements can be nested to create a robust nutrient recommendation, utilizing a variety of data types and conditions.

A common nutrient management objective for non-mobile nutrients is to try and maintain an optimum soil test level (Figure 3). When soil test levels are below optimum, nutrients are added to meet expected crop removals and to build soil test levels over a period of time. In contrast, if the levels are above optimum, it allows crops to drawdown nutrient levels through crop removal.

SGIS computes nutrient requirement maps using the recommendation logic and the appropriate conditional data. The program then computes the amount of one or more nutrient containing products to meet the nutrient requirements. The

Figure 1

Digital soil survey, soil samples, field boundaries and a stream overlain on a geo-referenced photo. Soil test P, steep slopes and the 300 foot stream buffer are classified and themed for quick visual inspection.

Barron County

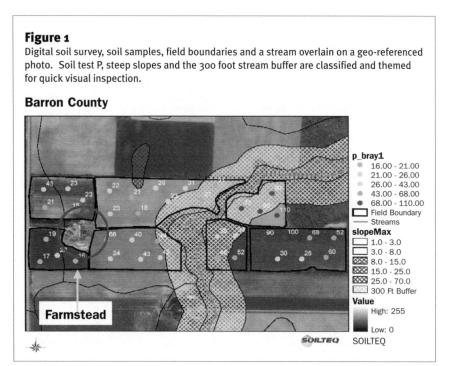

Figure 2

Prox syntax used to allow customers to imbed their decision support logics for nutrient recommendations in SGIS.

```
If (condition...) Then
    Apply (something...)

Elseif (condition...) Then
    Apply (something...)

or

Else
    Apply (something...)

Endif
```

program output is a set of product application maps. In this example, swine slurry is applied at a variable rate to meet the total crop and soil P requirement (Figure 4). No slurry is applied in the P management buffer around the stream. Urea and potash are used to balance the crop nutrient requirements in this example (Figure 5).

Field application equipment. Commercial slurry application equipment was originally designed to apply high rates of product into the soil while minimizing

Figure 3

A generalized equation for managing soil test levels at an optimum level.

Build — Maintenance — Draw Down

For SGIS the generalized equation is:

```
If (SoilTest < CritLevel) then
    Apply ( (CritLevel – SoilTest) * SoilBuf/BuildYear) + (YieldGoal * NutRem))

Elseif (SoilTest < MaintLimit) then
    Apply (YieldGoal * NutRem)

Elseif (YieldGoal * NutRem < = (SoilTest – MaintLimit)  * SoilBuf/DrawDownYear) then
    Apply (0)

Else
    Apply (YieldGoal * NutRem – (SoilTest – MaintLimit)  * SoilBuf/DrawDownYear)
Endif
```

Figure 4
Swine slurry application map where the slurry is applied to meet P nutrient requirements.

Swine slurry manure application map

Demo map

Min. rate: 0.0 (gal/ac)

Max. rate: 4087.5 (gal/ac)

Avg. rate: 1889.4 (gal/ac)

As-intended report

compaction. A typical high flotation machine is shown in Figure 6. The injection devices buried most crop residues. These machines meet the goal of rapid, low cost application.

Regulatory rules now call for leaving the soil surface protected with crop residues and reduced rates of application. The equipment industry has responded with new incorporation devices and

Figure 5
Nitrogen and potassium requirements are balanced using urea for nitrogen and potash for potassium.

Urea application map

Demo map

Min. rate: 54 (lb/ac)

Max. rate: 380 (lb/ac)

Avg. rate: 241 (lb/ac)

As-intended report

Potash application map

Demo map

Min. rate: 51 (lb/ac)

Max. rate: 604 (lb/ac)

Avg. rate: 356 (lb/ac)

As-intended report

Figure 6
Typical biosolids applicator injecting into the soil and leaving the soil surface unprotected.

Figure 7
New TerraGator uses a positive displacement pump to allow low or high rates of application.

metering systems. The TerraGator in Figure 7 uses a positive displacement pump to apply at rates as low as 500 gal/ac. The metering system is controlled by a computer reading pre-planned rates from a digital raster application map (Figure 4).

New incorporation devices can now place slurry below the soil surface and manage crop residues according to customer requirements. The goal in Figure 8 is to inject slurry and prepare a seedbed with 30 percent or more crop residue cover in one pass. In this example, the farmer planted corn after slurry application without additional soil preparation. Other attachments can directly inject into sod (Figure 9) or accomplish primary tillage (Figure 10).

Other innovations increase the efficiency of the application machines and support

Figure 8
New incorporation equipment keeps crop residues on the soil surface while incorporating biosolids in the soil.

staff. The machines only generate income when they are actively applying slurry. The use of portable storage at the edge of a field insures that neither the applicators nor the tankers used to transport the slurry to the field are setting idle. Pictured in Figure 11 is a fractionation tank typically used in the oil and gas drilling industry. It is mounted on wheels for easy transport. Tanker trucks haul to and from livestock facilities and empty into the storage tank independent of the field application equipment. The applicators are equipped with a flexible load tube that can be manipulated by the machine operator from the cab (Figure11). The machines can load 4500

Figure 9
Direct injection of biosolids into a sod forming crop.

gal in less than 3.5 minutes without the operator leaving the comfort of the cab. In this configuration, a single machine can apply 25,000 gal per hour. Two applicators nursing off one storage reservoir have been documented to apply 600,000 gal per day.

Discussion

Farming is a complex business. This example only addresses nutrient management issues associated with the farming operation. However it does demonstrate that potential environmental quality improvements may be achieved with a minimum of risk to the farmer. Decision support tools by themselves will not lead farmers to change their current nutrient management production practices. Several key steps may be drawn from the above example.

First, farmers and the people who advise farmers must have a clear understanding of how farming practices affect the quality of air, soil, and water resources. Perhaps deci-

sion support tools can be used to reinforce that this is not just the "neighbors" problem. Acceptance of this responsibility is a perquisite for justifying changes in farming practices. Ag retailers and consultants should play an import role in educating their customers since they will likely provide the equipment and services to accomplish a practice change. These practice changes must also be profitable for the farmer and business to be sustainable.

Financial risks associated with a practice change may not be a concern for the individual farmer. In this example, the financial risk associated with changes in slurry application was born by the agriculture service provider. Approximately one million U.S. dollars, was invested in specialized transport and application equipment by the service provider. This investment will only be profitable if the farmer customers are willing to pay an appropriate charge for the new services. Perhaps incentives need to be targeted to

Figure 10
Biosolids application with tillage and incorporation accomplished in one pass.

the supplier of environmentally sound services instead of individual farmers.

Ag service providers do not need new decision support system tool software that works independent of their business needs. Instead they need a clear concise set of guidelines or rules to integrate into existing software tools used in their businesses. In this example, inputs include, percent slope, slurry application based on a P standard, and restricted application in proximity to a stream were simply modified to established nutrient management strategies based on soil test levels and crop nutrient removals. This way, risks are kept to a minimum by building on a traditional practice.

The equipment industry has responded with new application machines and by integrating new technologies into nutrient application machines. Variable rate and low rate positive displacement metering, map based application utilizing GPS, and new incorporation attachments that also manage crop residues have been developed and made available in response to the need to change nutrient application practices.

Whether or not the equipment industry continues to build these machines will depend on the purchaser's ability to profitably integrate the investment into their business. This is true for both farmers and agriculture service providers.

Concluding remarks

Achieving a balance between "economic agricultural production" and "environmental quality" is not likely to occur solely through the building of better decision support software. If the outcome of the decision support system tools cannot be implemented as part of a sustainable business, the potential environmental quality benefits will not be realized. Agricultural businesses provide services and equipment that are essential for farmers to adopt new practices. They also play a vital role in education, helping farmer's transition to new practices with a minimum of risk. Future decision support system development might focus on the operational and financial components that must be in place for a successful business implementation.

Figure 11
Applicator filling from a portable storage tank at the edge of a farm field.

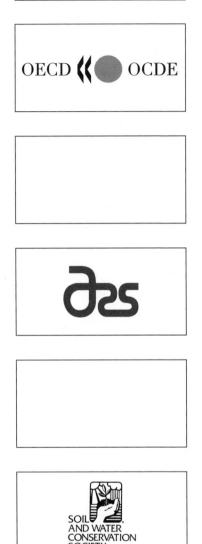

List of Contributors

Jerry L. Hatfield (editor)
USDA/ARS National Soil Tilth Laboratory Director
2150 Pammel Drive
Ames, IA 50011-4420
USA

Will Allen
Landcare Research New Zealand Ltd.
P.O. Box 69
Lincoln, New Zealand

John F. Angus
CSIRO Plant Industry
GPO Box 1600
Canberra ACT 2601
Australia

David W. Archer
USDA-ARS North Central Soil Conservation
  Research Laboratory
803 Iowa Avenue
Morris, Minnesota 56267-1065
USA

Peter S. Carberry
Agricultural Production Systems Research
  Unit (APSRU)
CSIRO Sustainable Ecosystems
203 Tor Street
Toowoomba QLD 4350
Australia

Aidan Doyle
Institute for Research on Environment &
  Sustainability
University of Newcastle Upon Tyne
Newcastle Upon Tyne NE1 7RU
United Kingdom

Gerard W.J. Giesen
Wageningen University
Hollandseweg 1
6706 KN Wageningen
The Netherlands

Caspar J.M. Hewett
Civil Engineering and Geosciences
University of Newcastle Upon Tyne
Newcastle Upon Tyne NE1 7RU
United Kingdom

Zvi Hochman
Agricultural Production Systems Research
Unit (APSRU)
CSIRO Sustainable Ecosystems
203 Tor Street
Toowoomba QLD 4350
Australia

Ruud B.M. Huirne
Wageningen University
Hollandseweg 1
6706 KN Wageningen
The Netherlands

Margaret J. Kilvington
Landcare Research New Zealand Ltd.
P.O. Box 69
Lincoln, New Zealand

Geza J. Kovacs
Research Institute for Soil Science and
Agricultural
  Chem. of Hungarian Academy of Sciences
1022 Budapest Herman
Budapest, Hungary

James M. Lynch
Forest Research
Alice Holt Lodge
Wrecclesham, Farnham
Surrey, GU10 4LH
United Kingdom

Robert L. McCown
Agricultural Production Systems Research
Unit (APSRU)
CSIRO Sustainable Ecosystems
203 Tor Street
Toowoomba QLD 4350
Australia

Michael McNeill
Ag Advisory
P.O. Box 716
222 E. Call Street
Algona, Iowa 50511

Oene Oenema
Wageningen University and Research Center
Alterra
P.O. Box 47
NL-6700 AA Wageningen
The Netherlands

Christien J.M. Ondersteijn
Wageningen University
Hollandseweg 1
6706 KN Wageningen
The Netherlands
Email Oene.Oenema@wur.nl

Alfons G.J.M. Oude Lansink
Wageningen University
Hollandseweg 1
6706 KN Wageningen
The Netherlands

Peter F. Quinn
Civil Engineering and Geosciences
University of Newcastle Upon Tyne
Newcastle Upon Tyne NE1 7RU
United Kingdom

Marcus Tooze
GIS Workshop, Inc.
415 N 66th Street, Suite 7
Lincoln, Nebraska 68505
USA

Robert L. Williams
University of East Timor
Dili, East Timor

Nyle C. Wollenhaupt
Worldwide Agronomy Manager
Global Technologies by AGCO
5850 Opus Parkway, Suite 160
Minnetonka, MN 55343

Index

Pages listed in **bold** include photographs or illustrations.
Pages listed in *italics* include tables.